THL GOLDEN CHAIN

FIFTY YEARS OF
THE JEWISH QUARTERLY

EDITED BY
NATASHA LEHRER

VALLENTINE MITCHELL
LONDON • PORTLAND, OR

First published in 2003 in Great Britain by
VALLENTINE MITCHELL
Crown House, 47 Chase Side, Southgate
London N14 5BP

and in the United States of America by
VALLENTINE MITCHELL
c/o ISBS, 5824 N.E. Hassalo Street
Portland, Oregon, 97213-3644

Website: www.vmbooks.com

British Library Cataloguing in Publication Data

The Golden Chain: Fifty years of the Jewish Quarterly
1. English literature – Jewish authors
I. Lehrer, Natasha
820.8′ 08924′ 09045

ISBN 0-85303-481-8 (cloth)
ISBN 0-85303-480-X(paper)

Library of Congress Cataloging-in-Publication Data

The Golden Chain: Fifty years of the Jewish Quarterly / editor, Natasha Lehrer.
        p. cm.
     "To celebrate the fiftieth anniversary of the Jewish Quarterly, this anthology brings
together the very best writing to have appeared in the magazine since it began."
     ISBN 0-85303-480-X (pbk.) – ISBN 0-85303-481-8 (cloth)
     1. Jews–Intellectual life–20th century. 2. Jews–England–Intellectual life–20th century.
     3. Jews–Intellectual life–History–20th century. 4. Jewish literature–20th century.
     5. Jewish literature–20th century–History and criticism. I. Lehrer, Natasha. II. Jewish
     quarterly.

DS113.F46 2003
909′.049240825–dc21   2002044454

Typeset & designed by Random Design, London
Printed in Great Britain by MPG Books Ltd, Bodmin, Cornwall

CONTENTS

ON WRITERS AND WRITING

LITERATURE

ISRAEL

INTRODUCTION

A magazine 'which would be Yiddish in English' – thus the artist Josef Herman recalled his close friend Jacob Sonntag's plan to launch *The Jewish Quarterly* in 1953. It is a fascinating phrase, at once subtly illuminating and profoundly sad, the simple paradox reminding us that Yiddish was, and is, far more than simply a language. Sonntag, like so many of his generation, was a refugee, exiled from his birthplace, his language, his roots and his culture. The establishment of *The Jewish Quarterly* was his personal contribution to *die goldene keyt*, the golden chain of generations.

At a dinner in 1974 to celebrate the *Quarterly's* 21st anniversary, Sonntag spoke of the conviction which led him to establish *The Jewish Quarterly*:

> If I were asked how I envisaged *The Jewish Quarterly* when I started it more than twenty years ago, I would say that it was to cultivate literary journalism in the best tradition of Central and Eastern Europe and, in particular, in the best tradition of Eastern European Jewish writing . . . I belong to the generation which looked for a synthesis between our Jewishness and our Europeanism, between our nationalism and our socialism, between the particular and the universal . . . Part of our upbringing was to revere the printed word, to adorn it with a power of its own. How could truth and reason not prevail? It was just a question of finding the right word, the right combination of words, and everything else would follow from it. Literature was a living thing for us, and the world of books knew no boundaries. We cherished the illusion that 'you have only to will it and your dreams would cease to be fairy tales' . . . We felt as a collective, we had a sense of community, we felt called upon to add a link to the 'golden chain', handed to us by an earlier generation.

In an era in which a passing interest in kabbalah or klezmer is as much of an element of contemporary Jewish identity as kashrut or kippah-wearing, Sonntag's passionate belief in the transforming power of intellectual Jewish culture, and his mission to transmit it, seem intensely romantic. But it was surely not romance which led Sonntag to establish the *Quarterly*. In 1953, when the first issue of the magazine appeared, the world was no longer the world of Sonntag's youthful idealism. The Holocaust had ruptured the notion of past and present and future. The age-old cycle of rebirth and renewal had been broken. Millions of Jews had, in the most perverse transgression of Jewish tradition, been reduced to ashes. What was the meaning of the *goldene keyt* in a world where only a tiny fraction of those millions of Yiddish-speakers alive before World War II were left who were able to understand the words, let alone the idea?

One may probe for a deeper understanding of Sonntag's missionary conviction in the interstices of his early history, whose dislocated geography maps a typical route of twentieth century Ashkenazi migration. He was born in 1905 in Viznitz, Northern Bukovina (part of the then Austro-Hungarian Empire); as a child he moved with his family to the small town of Kosov in Eastern Galicia. When the First World War broke out the family fled in advance of the Russian invasion and eventually settled in Vienna. As a young man Sonntag spent time in Palestine and Czechoslovakia before coming to Britain in 1938; he was in London during the war which ravaged his homeland and saw the wholesale slaughter of European Jews in the Shoah. He must have felt the conflict inherent in being one of the fortunate few 'who were spared because "we were not there,"' as he himself once put it in an editorial. It is not too far-fetched, I think, to see *The Jewish Quarterly* as, partly, a tribute and an atonement for this survival. The gaze of the *Quarterly* in the first three decades was turned eastwards, towards the ravaged European landscape of Sonntag's past. The magazine focused on three main areas – the legacy of the Holocaust, Israel and Zionism, and the cultural heritage of Eastern Europe – the Jew as victim, survivor and visionary. Its sober, serious concern with this threefold world is a gesture both of reclamation and of restitution.

It was never easy for Sonntag, who was, as many have testified, not at all interested in the kinds of practical issues – like money – which are an inevitable part of the enterprise of magazine publishing. It can with justification be claimed that one of the keys to the success of the magazine is also one of the reasons for its constant struggle for existence – its independence from traditional Jewish institutions. The *Quarterly*, through this autonomy, has been able to maintain an untarnished reputation for editorial integrity and 'the highest standards of intellectual debate'[1]. But as Sonntag discovered, the fact that the magazine was obliged to depend for its existence on sponsorship from those few individuals who shared his serious commitment to literature and the arts meant that it was at times in an extremely precarious position, and this led to a certain amount of bitterness. Rafael Scharf, his colleague on the magazine from the beginning, wrote in a 1993 tribute:

> The community, even the tiny minority which constitutes its reading and articulate part, rarely gave a sign that it understood that Jacob Sonntag was special, that he deserved respect and appreciation, that he was selflessly offering his labours and talent in the service of a good cause. On the contrary, and this has to be said reproachfully, virtually throughout his career, his thirty plus years of editing *The Jewish Quarterly*, the community at large remained indifferent and afforded him no understanding and no recognition, leaving him to plough a lonely furrow (Summer 1993).

This volume is a testimony to the deep esteem in which his memory is held, almost twenty years after his death.

★

The 1950s, the early years of the *Quarterly*'s existence, was a decade which saw an unprecedented flowering of Jewish writing in England. Reading through the *Quarterly* archives, one is struck by the recurring names of contributors, many of whom were then at the beginnings of their careers, who today make up a veritable roll-call of venerable British Jewish writers and intellectuals of the post-war period. Dannie Abse, Alexander Baron, Chaim Bermant, Gerda Charles, Elaine Feinstein, Brian Glanville, Josef Herman, A.C. Jacobs, Louis Jacobs, Bernard Kops, Joseph Leftwich, Barnet Litvinoff, Emanuel Litvinoff, Hyam Maccoby, Wolf Mankowitz, Frederic Raphael, Bernice Rubens, Jon Silkin, George Steiner, Arnold Wesker and Renée Winegarten were all regular contributors to the *Quarterly*, some pretty much from the beginning. Looking back – with requisite hindsight – one can say without exaggeration that there had never been such a good moment to set up a literary magazine devoted to the talents of Jewish writers and artists.

The richness and diversity of the cultural world which the *Quarterly* has explored for fifty years does not lend itself easily to being distilled into a single volume. I have chosen to structure the anthology by theme, rather than any chronology. By selecting a few broad and representative strands, I have tried to include as diverse as possible a selection of poetry and prose, and to reflect the way in which, since Jacob Sonntag's death, each subsequent editor has brought a unique cultural and political sensibility to the role. Tony Lerman (1984-1985), Colin Shindler (1985-1994), Elena Lappin (1994-1997) and the current editor, Matthew Reisz, have each brought to the *Quarterly* during their respective tenures a renewed vision, and it is wealthier – and healthier – for it.

★

Apart from the Summer 1987 issue dedicated to London's East End, there has never been a concerted editorial intention to collect material about London. But it was inevitable that much material about the city would accrue in the *Quarterly*'s pages; so many of its writers were born there, and found inspiration in its extraordinary multiplicity of characters and cultures. Those who were not born there but found refuge amongst its cosmopolitan crowds often paid tribute in their writing to the city which they had made their home.

The East End and Hackney figure particularly vividly as the place from which Bernard Kops, Harold Pinter and Arnold Wesker took inspiration to forge illustrious careers as playwrights. Wesker's poem 'Time parts memory' evokes a potent nostalgia for the place that was a powerful fuel for his writing, wistfully recalling the kind of social radicalism that Joseph Leftwich describes so vividly in his portrait of Rudolf Rocker, the non-Jewish German-born anarchist who did so much for the rights of Jewish workers in the East End. Emanuel Litvinoff's memoir of his youth and early adulthood, *A Jew in England*, is a compelling, bittersweet, personal account of the early twentieth century Jewish journey towards integration. Litvinoff's account of growing up around Bethnal Green is rank and redolent with the smells and sounds of the tenements. Litvinoff ends on a strikingly moving note, describing his contingent sense of belonging: 'England made me . . . [M]y neighbours . . . might not understand why I am sometimes overtaken by desolation watching my small daughter playing in the sunshine, why a child's discarded shoe can germinate terrible images in my dreams. But if they ever guessed these things, I would be confident of their compassion. Most of them, anyway.' Litvinoff, a superb stylist and storyteller, is today recovering his reputation as a significant literary figure of the period. In his autobiography *Goodbye Twentieth Century* (Pimlico, 2001) Dannie Abse records the occasion when Litvinoff read his poem 'To T. S. Eliot' at the ICA with Eliot himself in the audience, to the horror of an irate Stephen Spender. (There is a poignant footnote to *London*: this year, 2003, when *The Jewish Quarterly* is celebrating an almost undreamt-of longevity, is the year when the Whitechapel Library, which nurtured the talents and fed the aspirations of at least two generations of East End writers, including several whose work appears here, will finally close.)

Whitechapel was then, and remains, the locale of many different narratives. It fed the work of several prominent English language writers and poets, but as Litvinoff describes, Yiddish was the lingua franca of the streets in the early decades of the twentieth century, and it remained the literary language of certain post-war writers. Among the Yiddish writers published by Jacob Sonntag – who believed fervently in the mission both to transmit and to revitalize Yiddish, and who published considerable quantities of Yiddish poetry and prose, often in his own translations – was Avrom Nuchem Stencl, the legendary poet who escaped from Nazi Germany in 1936 and found his way to Whitechapel. Stencl published his poetry with some regularity in his own pamphlet, *Loshn un Lebn* (Language and Life) until he died, penniless, in 1983. In the Summer 1967 issue, Sonntag wrote the introduction to an early poem by Stencl, which he himself had translated:

> Undeterred by poverty and the indifference of a dwindling public, [Stencl] carries on the Eastern European cultural tradition, blending deep-seated religiosity with modern thinking, in the only language he knows, loves and likes – Yiddish. When he left his distant shtetl in deepest Poland, as a young man, he took with him on his wanderings across Germany and Holland before he arrived here in the mid-thirties, not only the shadows of the Yeshiva, but also the smell of freshly-ploughed fields and of apple trees in blossoming orchards planted on the foot of black coal mines not far away. They live with him to this day, and follow him to the darkest corners of Whitechapel.

To a whole generation of increasingly acculturated, English-speaking Jews, Stencl personified the romance of the shtetls of Eastern Europe. Today, Stencl's Whitechapel is no more, but it too has become the subject of mythification, as Jane Liddell-King's and Sylvia Paskin's essay on the synagogue at 19 Princelet Street suggests. 19 Princelet Street has, in the last decade, become the site of a fluid, evocative and haunting narrative of the Jewish East End experience. And, as Liddell-King and Paskin describe, it has become a symbol of the knotted experiences of generations of immigrants from different shores, from the seventeenth century Huguenots, one of whom built the house, to the Bangladeshis, who today make up the majority of the population living and working in and around Brick Lane.

Sonja Linden's description of her work as Writer in Residence with the Medical Foundation for the Care of Victims of Torture highlights the distance that London Jews have travelled in little more than a generation. To the refugees and asylum seekers with whom she works to overcome the appalling mental and physical scars left by torture, Linden, the daughter of refugees from Nazi Germany, represents the security of the truly assimilated. Parallel with this successful absorption into English society, the physical move west from the eastern arrival point in London has been a common trajectory for the capital's Jewish community. But Gharda Karmi's description of growing up in Golders Green as a young Palestinian, exiled from her Jerusalem birthplace, is a reminder that it was not only Jews who found their homes in the leafy suburbs – and not only Jews who were driven into the Diaspora from the Promised Land.

★

The identity of what is known as 'Anglo-Jewry' has never been as homogeneous and easily-defined as that phrase suggests. Jews in England were not granted full equality, civic or political, until the latter part of the nineteenth century. Such was the fear of being stigmatized for what were seen as 'typical' Jewish traits and characteristics, that, as David Cesarani describes, the nineteenth-century Jewish advocates of emancipation for Jews 'practised a form of social engineering on the Jewish population in order to eliminate the features which seemed obnoxious to non-Jews and tried to mould Jewish society more closely to the contours of respectable English society.' [2]

Describing his father in his memoir 'The Curiousness of Anglo-Jews', Frederic Raphael pinpoints the classic post-emancipationist vision of the English Jew as a good citizen, embodying 'all the bourgeois ideals of the patriarchal family, entrepreneurship, and religious communalism'[3]. Raphael's description of his father's confidence, when the family moved from New York to London, in the ability of the Jew to assimilate in Britain seems strange to us now, given as we are to wonder at the ease of the American Jew to make it almost as far as Vice-President without his Jewishness being seen as a handicap:

> 'Well, Freddie boy', he said, 'at least you'll now be able to grow up to be an English gentleman and not an American Jew.'

Barnet Litvinoff's lampoon 'Chaim Superman encounters a Jewish Intellectual' is considerably less sympathetic to the 'Englishman of the Mosaic persuasion'. Litvinoff satirizes the 'rich communal life' of the English Jews, their 'Parliament', their parochialism and their snobbery. Litvinoff's 'Jewish intellectual' (typical of those who all this time had steadfastly ignored the efforts of Jacob Sonntag and his colleagues) embodies the stereotypical Anglo-Jewish trajectory from east to west, from Yiddishness to Englishness, with all the concomitant loss of cultural wealth that the determined attainment of material prosperity might suggest.

Michael Rosen, in 'Trying to be Jewish', underlines with his characteristic deadpan lyricism the ambivalence with which liberal Jewish identity is freighted in England: 'a whole mob of us / took part in that traditional Jewish custom, / carol-singing.' Rosen's Jewishness is sited in his family; nothing can compromise the security of his identity, and it needs no embellishment. But Ruth Fainlight's poem 'The English Country Cottage' is less certain; for her, the fusing of cultures which have forged her identity might have come about at a greater cost than even she can imagine: 'Sometimes I wonder if I should have known better: / to sweetly smile and eat the mess / of pottage – but never sell my birthright / for an English country cottage.' Fainlight suggests, deftly and with a subtle sense of mourning, that to be settled, fixed, to belong, has not made her less of an 'alien', and may have cost her something more – her freedom to follow yearnings more ancient still than the yew tree rooted in the village churchyard.

Rare as it is to encounter amongst the Orthodox the idea of pragmatic and humane compromise with the secular world, Alexander Flinder's charming story 'The Yom Kippur Swimming Gala' is a gentle, cheerful counterpoint to Jonathan Freedland's 'Modest Proposal for Democratizing the Jewish People'. The sly allusion to Swift suggests that Freedland knows how outrageous his radical clarion call for an end to the complacency that governs the Jewish communal politics of the Diaspora will appear to many of those whose ideology of stasis he challenges. His target is worldwide Jewish institutions, but his examples are taken from his encounters with Jews in England, whose intellectual laziness and complacency he challenges with devastating logic. In spite of his clear-eyed arguments, one doubts that his call for revolution will have any more immediate effect on Jewish institutions than his call for an end to the monarchy in *Bring Home the Revolution* (Fourth Estate, 1998) is likely to have on the British constitution.

★

For years after the war, with few exceptions, the world which drew the focus of the Jewish historian, and that of many of the *Quarterly's* writers, was the devastated European world that had for hundreds of years been home to the vast proportion of Ashkenazi Jewry. It is only in the last decade or two that there has been a wide and proper recognition of the breadth of Jewish experience, of the cultural treasures to be found in the communities around the globe which remain – and of the losses which other communities have sustained throughout the millennia of Jewish history.

Liz Cashdan's remarkable epistolary poem 'The Tyre-Cairo Letters' evokes with startling immediacy a world so far away, so exotic and thrilling, yet with concerns so mundane and similar to our own, that one can excavate from her beautiful verse a sense of time and place as concrete as from the finest historical writing. No less moving and direct is the lament, in a muscular and scholarly translation, of Yehuda Abravanel, mourning the tragedy of his own family in 1492 Spain. Hyam Maccoby's erudite exploration of the roots of the image of the Wandering Jew takes the reader on a fascinating, disturbing journey through the medieval and pre-modern world. Maccoby asks profound and difficult questions about the relationship between Christians and Jews which, in his thesis, remain unresolved.

The Holocaust is, of course, the emblematic Jewish experience of modern times. It is pertinent to reflect that, although writing about the Holocaust began to appear almost simultaneously with the events themselves, the extraordinary proliferation of all kinds of writing about the Holocaust in every imaginable genre, including personal testimony, history, philosophy, social science, literature and literary criticism, did not begin in earnest until many years after the end of the Second World War. It is astonishing to encounter writing about the Holocaust that is as devastating today in its immediacy as it must have been when it was originally published in the *Quarterly* over thirty years ago. Reading Vera Elyashiv's account, written as an adolescent, of her incarceration in the Kovno ghetto followed by her deportation to a series of concentration camps is almost overwhelming – partly, I think, because of its unsophisticated, eloquent directness, which contrasts starkly with the complex analysis which – necessarily – characterizes much Holocaust scholarship today.

The visceral importance of testimony is underlined by Rafael Scharf who, in his essay on the Warsaw Ghetto, describes the urgent necessity of bearing witness for those who endured life under the Nazis:

> The Jewish people were determined to leave a trace of their fate, at whatever cost. Feeling abandoned by God and man, they were haunted by the thought that the world would not know how they lived and died. Writing made dying easier.

Or, as James E. Young has written, 'when survival and the need to bear witness become one and the same thing, this desperate urge to testify in narrative cannot be underestimated.'[4]

The most famous writer of the Ghetto is Emanuel Ringelblum. In the latter half of 1943, whilst hiding with his family and thirty-five other Jews in the cellar of a Polish worker in Warsaw, he wrote a study in Polish entitled 'Polish-Jewish Relationships during the Second World War'. He also wrote a number of biographical sketches, in Yiddish, of some of the leading Jewish characters of the Warsaw Ghetto. On 6 March 1944, the bunker where Ringelblum was hiding was betrayed to the Gestapo. All of its occupants were arrested and executed. Ringelblum had, through a Polish intermediary, arranged for the transfer of the two manuscripts to Adolph Berman, a colleague of his in the Warsaw Ghetto Underground. Berman, who emigrated to Israel after the war, handed the manuscripts over in 1957 to the Jewish Historical Institute of Warsaw, which became the home of the original Ringelblum Archives. It was there that Yuri Suhl first came across the biography of Janusz Korczak and was given the opportunity to translate it for the first time into English.

Mark Mazower's evocative and authoritative essay on Salonika is part of a general contemporary redressing of the absence of the account of the terrible destiny of the Salonikan Jews – and Sephardi Jews in general – from almost all conventional accounts of the Holocaust. Mazower tells not only of the murder of 90 per cent of the Jewish population of Salonika after the mass deportations of 1943, but also of the complexity of the centuries-long relationship between Salonika and its Jewish populace, of the marvellous vitality of Salonikan Jewish cultural life, and of the scars of Jewish experience that today remain imprinted on the city and its inhabitants.

Frederick Goldman's account of his return to Poland in 1946 superimposes disturbing pre-war childhood memories onto the immediate post-war Polish landscape. His reminiscences provoke a vertiginous sense of dislocation, for the reader no less than for the author of these experiences. His childhood memories of pre-war Poland are vibrant, almost exotic, and yet intensely unsettling; his encounters with representatives of the Catholic Church in Poland verge on the surreal, as priests use language to alienate and destabilize, in the guise of reconciliation.

There is a terrible symmetry about the halfway point of the twentieth century, for the war and Stalin's persecutions mark what was effectively the end of life in the Jewish heartlands of central and Eastern Europe and Russia as Jews had known it for hundreds of years. Shimon Markish's reminiscences of his father recall a golden age of modern Yiddish writing. For Markish, the consolation he draws from his memories of his father is a way to a deeper understanding of the direction that his own life has taken. James E. Young's essay on the use of the Holocaust in one Israeli's art, that of the rock star Yehuda Poliker, is a pointer towards the way in which the memory of the Holocaust has become a conduit for new ways in which we can interpret our own times; modern aesthetic experience after the Holocaust, as Adorno emphatically claimed and as many others have since reiterated, cannot aspire to straightforward lyricism or innocence.

★

In a presentation made at a 1984 colloquium on literature and the contemporary Jewish experience, organised by the *Quarterly* (reprinted in the Autumn/Winter 1984 issue), Aharon Appelfeld looks inside himself to try to explain why he became a writer:

> Why had I turned to literature? Probably to open the darkness and chaos within me. A
> deep desire to break up the old vocabulary, to say something of my experience.

For Appelfeld, who was deported to a concentration camp as an eight-year-old child, and who then escaped and spent the remainder of the war years in hiding, before making his way, via Italy, to Palestine in 1946, writing makes living possible – the mirrored inversion of Rafael Scharf's assertion that 'writing made dying easier' for those trapped in the Warsaw Ghetto, the ante-room to Auschwitz. Self-expression during times of sorrow and destruction is part of the Jewish tradition, as ancient as Judaism itself; Appelfeld's writing is a continuation of that tradition. Here he traces his literary lineage back to Kafka; he finds in Kafka – as Appelfeld reads him, the most Jewish of secularised, non-identifying Jews in modern literary history – a strange consolation, a way into himself and, finally, into writing.

Appelfeld's fiction derives its enormous power from the central ellipsis in its narrative. In each of his works he assumes a context, demands a knowledge of the terrible events which foreground all of his works, which the reader is obliged to bring to the book. Edmond Jabès crafted an elusive, imagist poetics on the subject of the Holocaust by making a similar demand on his readers. An early poem, written some time between 1943 and 1945 whilst he was still living in Egypt, entitled 'Song of the Last Jewish Child' (translated by Anthony Rudolf), suggests the strategy he will employ later when he comes to write *The Book of Questions*:

'My father hangs from a star, / my mother flows with the river, / my mother shines / my father is deaf, / in the night which denies me, / in the day which destroys me. / Stone is not heavy. / Bread is like a bird, / I watch as it flies. / Blood is on my cheeks. / My teeth / seek a less empty mouth / in earth or in water, / in fire. / The world is red. / All the iron bars are spears. / Dead horsemen always gallop / in my sleep and in my eyes. / On the lost garden's ravaged body / flowers a rose, flowers a hand / of rose I shall squeeze no more. / Death's horsemen bear me away. / I am born to love them.' This early rejection of mimetic representation for that which is beyond representation is central to Jabès's entire enterprise.

Jabès, like Appelfeld, like the writers of the Warsaw Ghetto before them, and in common with generations of writers going back through centuries of Jewish suffering and exile, explicitly finds a commonality between written discourse and Jewish experience: 'Judaism and writing are but the same waiting, the same hope, the same wearing out.' Howard Jacobson sees a similar inherent commonality, but in as different a way as one could hope to expect from one of today's most coruscatingly funny writers. Jacobson sites himself – 'a comic Jewish novelist – a doubly marginalized figure in an already marginalized culture' – on a kind of dialectical roller-coaster between Talmudic discourse (vitalized by his time at Cambridge studying under F. R. Leavis) and Freud – the Jewish writer as argumentative, hair-splitting, repressed and (of course, given the weight of history) ironic. It is, suggests Linda Grant, in her essay on American writer Delmore Schwartz (immortalized by Saul Bellow as the eponymous Humboldt in *Humboldt's Gift*), the lack of this last quality that left Schwartz at his death the burnt-out, unfulfilled shell of his early promise. The hugeness of the American cultural landscape and modern American creative sensibility, which, at the height of his writing powers, he in some sense exemplified, ultimately proves too much for Schwartz – 'the suffering heart to whom everything matters too much'.

In conversation with Rachel Spence, Adrienne Rich describes herself, with economy and characteristic ambiguity, as 'a person of the book.' A passionate sense of mission, both as a writer and as a socio-political activist, suffuses her writing. One of the most important contemporary American poets, Rich has for decades been challenging the status quo in her poetry. Rich writes because she must; her passion, her soul, her self seem to the reader to be inscribed upon the page. Her Jewishness is a marginal part of her poetic identity. But it is there, and, champion and voice of the marginalized, she does not seek to repress it: 'Split at the root, neither gentile nor Jew / Yankee nor Rebel, born / In the face of two ancient cults / I'm a good reader of histories.'

David Sylvester is a good reader of histories too. An incisive, brilliant interpreter of modern art, Sylvester's conversation crackles with speculative intensity. He is a man who, even as he nears the end of his life (he died of cancer just a few months after his interview with Michael Kustow took place) is still formulating and reformulating his ideas. Kustow calls him a 'master-steersman,' whose journeys 'give us heart and help us navigate' – a superb description of the rare ability of the truly great critic to go beyond mere critical examination, to spark into life a spiritual bond which unites reader, interpreter and subject in an epiphanic moment of understanding.

★

When the German-born poet Nelly Sachs (who escaped from Berlin to Sweden in 1940, where she spent the rest of her life) was awarded the Nobel Prize for Literature with S. Y. Agnon in 1966, the

Quarterly was the only British magazine to have published translations of her poetry in English (Winter 1965-6) – even the BBC was after a copy. Gertrude Kolmar and Selma Meerbaum-Eisinger both died in the Holocaust before they had become published poets, and remain today barely translated and almost unknown outside their native Germany. Together with Nelly Sachs, they represent here a remarkable triumvirate of German Jewish women poets of the Holocaust. Kolmar, in her poem 'Jewish Woman', seems almost to prefigure her obscurity: 'I am a stranger. / Since no one dares approach me / I would be girded with towers / That wear their steep and stone-grey caps / Aloft in clouds.'

A vast array of writers, both better- and less well-known, writing in English or translated from other languages, have published fiction and poetry in the pages of the *Quarterly*. Every editor has shared Sonntag's serious commitment to literature, and the quality and eclectic variety of so much of what has been published is testimony to this. There is no better way of representing this than with a diverse selection of poetry and prose. Michael Hamburger's dense meditation on Adolf Eichmann, Al Alvarez and Tony Dinner on birth and death and the filigree reflections on family of Anne Atik and Elaine Feinstein, Gabriel Levin's deft and allusive exegesis on translation, are set alongside Bernard Kops' wonderful, rumbustious 'Shalom Bomb', Sholom Aleichem's burlesque story of a military call-up, the tortured angst of Arnold Wesker's frustrated novelist doing battle with a blank sheet of paper, and Bernice Rubens' smart, cynical story of mothers and daughters.

★

T. R. Fyvel's depiction of an extended stay on Kibbutz Mishmar Haemek in 1935-6 describes, from the perspective of fifty years (he is writing in the 1980s), an arc of nostalgia and disillusion. In the early decades of the twentieth century the kibbutz symbolized the progression towards an entirely new formulation of the social order – the necessary break with history – that would enable the Jewish people to re-imagine itself as a sovereign nation for the first time in two millennia. Fyvel's essay suggests that the decline of the socialist kibbutz movement was inevitable because of its failure to grapple with the fundamental question of Arab-Jewish relations. This failure can be read as a synecdoche for the larger failure that all but the most blinkered Zionists today have accepted – the refusal of almost all Zionist leaders to acknowledge that Jewish national claims on Palestine were made at the expense of its existing Arab inhabitants. As Walter Zander states in a pamphlet published in 1948 (an edited version of which appeared in the *Quarterly* of Autumn 2001):

> Never in the thirty years' argument have we admitted that our return, justified as it appears to us, inevitably requires from the Arab a sacrifice of the first magnitude – the sacrifice of giving up his right to rule himself.

In a series of editorials in the late 1980s and early 1990s, Colin Shindler probed the Zionist convictions of the loyal supporters of the State of Israel in Britain. He argued that the admiration for and pride in the existence and achievements of Israel in the early years of statehood had given way to a lack of vision amongst Diaspora leaders, leading to 'a shallow pro-Israelism' which still holds sway amongst many British Jews – an ugly neologism but a fair accusation. As far back as the Suez Crisis of 1956 Jacob Sonntag argued the importance of the right of Diaspora Jews to challenge received wisdom:

> In most cases, those who expressed opposition to the Israeli action did not do so because they questioned Israel's right to defend her freedom and independence. On the contrary, because they cherished her independence and cared for her existence and freedom, they expressed doubts about the wisdom and long-term effects of her action. (Editorial, 1956/7)

Increasing numbers of Diaspora Jews are today expressing their disillusion and anger with Israel's current policies, rejecting the traditional line that those outside Israel must display unequivocal support for its internal policies. Michael Kustow's e-mail debate with Joshua Sobol explores the profound polarization of vision which divides an increasing number of Diaspora Jews today from many Israelis:

> You and I inhabit different places, and our histories overlap but do not coincide. What is certain is that we are both surrounded by loud ignorance, sentimental myth, primitive fundamentalism.

Sobol's passionate response to Kustow describes the profound, existential debate being negotiated within the ranks of the Israeli Left: 'Can we still do anything to stop this useless war from breaking out? . . . It has never been so urgent to go on with an Israeli Arab-Jewish dialogue.' Alongside this correspondence, David Herman's judicious assessment of Edward Said's work is a sympathetic and acute analysis of the political philosophy of one of the most important advocates for Palestinian nationalism.

Israel is not however just a place of political conflict and images of death and horror and military aggression. As David Grossman's grave, loyal and measured meditation on Israel's fiftieth anniversary reminds us, it is a place where millions of people carry on their lives, where 'children play and love and fight in a language that no one spoke for two thousand years'. Zvi Jagendorf wanders the alleyways of Mahane Yehudah, the central market of West Jerusalem, pungent with the smells of herbs and spices and frying food, loud with an impossible Babel of languages. He portrays a world in miniature teeming with the multiplicity of different cultures that exemplifies Jerusalem. Israeli novelist Ronit Matalon, whose family originates from Egypt, excavates her family history as she explores changing notions of identity and immigration in Israel and discovers how this exploration has enriched her own identity as a novelist. Jo Glanville recounts her experience of living amongst Jerusalem's Palestinians in the Old City. In exchange for lessons in Arabic, she agrees to help a young Palestinian girl who is studying Shakespeare's *Merchant of Venice*. The episode has unexpected consequences: '[Nisreen] had the humanity to see both sides of the story and taught me a lesson about my own prejudice.'

This is another Israel, one where chance encounters give us new perspectives on ourselves and on each other. These pieces offer us a chance to visit a place where, for all the heavy weight of history, we may find yet inspiration, humility and, one hopes, wisdom and humanity. Our future depends on it.

★

Simon Louvish declared in a guest editorial of Summer 1990 that the *Quarterly* 'will continue to challenge, awaken, arouse passions, kindle debate and controversy, without which we may all as well be wax figures in the unvisited museum of defunct ideas.' This anthology marks a proud achievement – half a century of the *Quarterly*'s continued existence. The purpose of an anniversary is not only to look back; we have to look *forward* too – to another fifty years of the kind of provocative, stimulating, creative and intelligent writing that is the life-blood not only of *The Jewish Quarterly* but – and perhaps this is more important, for without them there is no magazine – of its readers too.

London, December 2002

---

1 *Post-war Jewish Fiction,* David Brauner (New York: Palgrave, 2001) p19.
2 *The Jewish Chronicle and Anglo-Jewry 1841-1991,* David Cesarani (Cambridge: Cambridge University Press, 1994) p6.
3 *Contemporary Jewish Writing in Britain and Ireland,* edited by Brian Cheyette (London: Peter Halban, 1998) pp xvi-xvii.
4 *Writing and rewriting the Holocaust: narrative and the consequences of interpretation,* James E. Young (Bloomington and Indianapolis: Indiana University Press, 1988) p17.

Itsik Manger in Paradise

Manger sits in *Gan Eden*
Drinking a glass of tea.
The 'Heavenly Literary Supplement'
In Yiddish is on his knee.

He sees a review of his poems.
The finest he's over read:
A *mehayye,* he says, to be written about
This way after I'm dead.

He looks to see who wrote it,
This critical masterpiece.
Aha, it was *Dovid Hamelech* –
Wonders will never cease.

And then he sees a translation
Of a poem written by me.
A. C. Jacobs, he murmurs,
Now who on earth could he be?

He reads it through without stopping,
Oy, is this a poem, says he.
It's the best I've read in ages,
I mean that literally.

Then he turns to Kafka,
Asks, Franz have you seen this?
Tell Heine and Yehuda Halevi
Here's something they shouldn't miss.

We must get his work included
In God's Oxford anthology,
And tell the Angel Gabriel
To send him a generous fee.

A. C. Jacobs
Spring 1979

1

LONDON

London Jewish Bakers' Union banner, (c.1920-1926) paint on silk / *Summer 1987*

TIME PARTS MEMORY
Arnold Wesker

Time parts memory and the mind opens
Old alleys in new lights. I lift the veil and beckon
The green boy back with his laughter,
Laugh with him at his loving days
When wars went past his indolent sense
And halted among shelter smells.

They were the days to dream about:
When the world was wrong and he was right
And no mad mother slapped her laws upon him.
The slum held him, lapped like a loving dog
His tin-can-copper days of lovely dirt
With the playground-boys of bad ways and truant times.

Where are these lovely boys? Age lost them
Down the Lane of stalls and smells
And melted them from sight or blighted them;
Faces pale now on potato pavements
Smashed by smiles and old promises
Which died beneath the marriage masque –
Sweet is the song a synagogue can sing.

Where are those lovely boys? Gone from their mothers
And mourned by masters endlessly teaching,
And toiling rabbis from the Talmud Torahs.
They burn at the stake of their sad ambitions
Having traded 'better times' for youth,
Prepared to barter back again
The games and alleys of deceit.

They say only age dies of nostalgia, yet
Still young, I lift ten years to watch the Lane.
All are lanes, and all the lanes of evening
Open up the screaming lands of their hearts,
And birds come dropping whiteness into the dark streets
Where the boys bounce over the toys and ruins
Left by the wars of their parlour fathers.

Look how Wentworth Street winds back
A bed-plagued booba-mine and the time
Of her farthings from heaven under her pillow
And the little bastard everybody knew I was
Plays marbles in the prison of his aunties' playground,
Where the windows watch their sons and daughters
Dying where the dust is bare and laying.

The Land of the Lanes are stalls manned
By bearded fathers of forgotten times;
The skull cap covers up their shame to God
The crimes of their cries are lost
And taken up by their sons now old as they.
But no man sold his soul, that song
Was banked between the Bibles of his prayers.

The shocks of Sabbath stabbing
At the heretic a background was
Have turned a trail through the pale quarters,
Where God was God and men stood singing
Socialism on the boxes of their dreams.
And May Day called for red banners
In the torrent of so much talking.

When will he hear again the mad marches
That bore him shoulder high
Upon paths of poverty and pride?
These were men taking the boy
Somewhere solid with singing
And strikes and stern orders of unity,
And undying love in the pockets of their humanity.

Where will he find again the ardour
Age wrenched from the playmates of his school?
Their wives have weaned them back to old lines
And banks have brought them stagnant
To a strange disaster that their minds
Undreamed of, never stored against,
A sort of happiness unbargained for.

But one boy burned away and all the seas
Sang foreign hymns to hear his laughter
All the foreign towns of England
Died with hospitality but stared
With strangeness at his alien ways.
One happy boy did burn away
And left a life lived many times
Before his birth bounced in a cot
And caged his curls and mother's eyes.

He bears the print, Jew that he is,
Of all the sands stored in his bones,
Bears with the unforgiving families
Of fear who hound the houses of his hopes.

He bears the stigma of a history
That Christ forgives and Christians
Can't forget, and laughs and loves
And cries alone among pale stones of sighs.

Time parts the memory and prepares new paths.
New years leap up that cannot be lived down.
Hope is ashamed yet cannot help itself
And spring, thank God, turns age into a simple mind.

Winter 1959-60

A JEW IN ENGLAND
Emanuel Litvinoff

Before me as I write is a school photograph: I am the fourth boy on the right. Forty six of the other boys in the photograph are also Jews - Kantorovich, Zelinikoff, Cohen, Dubovsky, Shrebnik, Abramovich, Segal, and others whose names I cannot now recall. The one goy stands forlornly in the back row, and across the fading years I still remember how lonesome he was, the unreflective cruelty of our indifference.

Outside the school yard where we self-consciously pose are the back streets of Whitechapel and Bethnal Green, a hard-working district of sinewy cabinet-makers, round-shouldered tailors, itinerant street-vendors hoarsely praising the goods on their barrows, furriers, button-hole makers, housewives battling the daily grime that seeps in from the littered pavements. Backrooms vibrate to the noise of machines. There are shops heaped with rags, cracked gramophone records, chipped crockery, old iron, ancient magazines. Whatever it is, someone can make a living out of it. The district stinks of too many people occupying too little space, of drains ill-equipped to flush away the waste of so many bodies, and this effluvia of poverty is spiced with the smell of sour pickles, herring, garlic and meat rotting in the open windows of kosher butcher shops. People stand on pavements speaking Yiddish, but they avoid the corners occupied by pubs, which are numerous, and they seldom stand for more than a few moments near the marble crucifix implanted on the grass-bearded forecourt of the Catholic church. East London 1929 . . .

I lived near the school in a street of small two-storey cottages, some with cellars under the pavement in which whole families spent their days in artificial light. My home was in the tallest building of the street, a tenement of sooty brick whose squalor in retrospect seems unbelievable. But conditions were much the same all around us, acreages of slums boiling with humanity, and we were not at all conscious of special hardship. Most of the people in our street were East European immigrants and even if they could afford the luxury of privacy I doubt if they would have thought it worth buying.

Life varied according to light and season. In summer, when it was hot, we were both more languid and more violent, occupying our doorsteps like the sands of a Mediterranean beach; in winter, we hurried indoors to jostle peevishly for a warm place near the fire. Twilight transformed people's faces and voices, enveloping them in a kind of loneliness. The sluggish movement of life at day's end made even us children reflective and philosophical, like old men on park benches; but when street-lamps lit up the night people came out to enjoy themselves, with a feeling that they'd earned it. The fat started to sizzle in fish-and-chips shops, thumping pianos sounded from pubs, brilliantined young fellows in sharp suits stared with insolent lust at the plump buttocks of high-stepping girls, and crowds skirmished around the picture-palaces trailing peanut shells wherever they went.

I have a habit of thinking about that past in collective terms, partly because my memories have become generalized but chiefly because in my childhood we were still members of a tribal community, our neighbourhood a village remote in spirit from the adjacent cosmopolitanism of the great city of London. The way of life was still much like that of the small Jewish towns scattered across the lands of Eastern Europe from Poland in the north to the southern Black Sea town of Odessa, where my own parents had been born. We shared the same Sabbaths and festivals, ate the same food, sang traditional songs in the same minor key, laughed at the same Jewish jokes. We were a foreign colony, like the Italians of Saffron Hill or the Chinese of Pennyfields, but unlike them I do not think that as children we felt at all un-English, or regarded the goyim in the next street as more native than ourselves. If anything, we thought ourselves to be a superior kind of English, because we were also Jewish and, therefore, cleverer, cleaner, more industrious and sober, less a different race than another class, and any hostility we encountered was put down to envy of our superior qualities.

My first serious experience of antisemitism was in my fourteenth year when I won a trade scholarship. Successful candidates were allowed to nominate, in order of preference, the trades they wished to learn. I chose, first, a school of lithography, then one for catering and, finally, a study course in electrical engineering.

The school of lithography rejected me without explanation after an interview, in which I had politely and correctly answered a number of simple general knowledge questions, submitted a short written essay and produced a decently carpentered towel-rack as an example of my handiwork. The one question I did not apparently answer to the interviewer's satisfaction was that relating to my religion. The other schools granted me no interview at all. Instead the London County Council offered a place at a Cordwainer's technical college, which turned out to be an institute for shoe-making near an offal yard in Smithfield market. I was the only Jewish pupil. From the very first roll-call the headmaster improvised variations on my name. It became Litintoott, Levypotsky, Levinskinoff, Litmuspaperoff and – on one hilarious public occasion – Lavatoryoffsky. For the rest of the term I endured ridicule and humiliation at the hands of both teaching staff and boys, the headmaster proving the most inventive of all. But I did not generalize from this experience. The barbarities of Cordwainer's technical college seemed localized, like the stench of decaying offal which permeated its classrooms.

As far as I can recall, therefore, the problem of identity did not begin to arise until the onset of adolescence with all its emotional and intellectual uncertainties. In my case, it coincided with the beginning of the thirties, as it must have done for many young Jews in Germany. I was then a young communist with a rather apocalyptic notion of political salvation and one day I was walking with another young communist, a big-nosed lad named Izzy Birnbaum, in the alien territory of Hoxton, where Jews were unwelcome. It was not politics that brought us there, but girls. Jewish adolescents had an idea that gentile girls were complaisant and we skirmished the neighbourhood in the hope of finding it true. Rather unwisely, Izzy had made himself conspicuous in a jazzy pullover and my hair was glistening with a dressing of margarine. Instead of attracting female attention, we ran into a gang of youth who spread themselves across the pavement and told us to get back to Palestine. It wasn't the first time in my life I'd been given that advice. The usual rejoinder was 'go to Palestine your f★★★ing self,' or 'this is my bloody country', or 'I'm as good a f★★★ing Englishman as you.' But it was somehow no longer possible to say such things with conviction, and the Hoxton boys looked as if they wouldn't stop at trading insults. We got shoved around a bit and retreated from Hoxton bruised in body and self-esteem. Uneasiness had begun.

The day of Mosley and his fascists had arrived and a frightening change came over the East End. Snotty-nosed kids with whom one had exchanged fairly harmless abuse suddenly appeared buckled and booted in black uniforms, looking anything but juvenile as they tramped through the district shouting: 'We gonna get rid of the Yids, the Yids! We gotta get rid of the Yids!' And it was even difficult to laugh at the bespoke-tailored fascists who came from the suburbs to officer these eager troops. Black was not the only paramilitary colour. A green-shirted organization which had practised woodcraft with religious fanaticism abruptly expelled its Jewish members and turned to antisemitism. Also green-shirted, the Social Credit movement took up back-street drilling with wooden rifles in preparation for armed insurrection against the international Jewish financiers of Whitechapel Road. Young communists marched to meetings in red; Zionist youth went around in blue; Jewish ex-servicemen paraded in their war-medals. Sir Oswald's bodyguarded visits to his stronghold in Roman Road, Bethnal Green, were ludicrous and, at the same time, sinister. He looked to us as we skirted the crowds with a prickly sense of peril like a comic toff playing at Mussolini; and his hot-eyed, rigid expression suggested that he derived from the slum streets and shabby onlookers an onanistic illusion of conquest. As he stood on a platform orating in a prissy upper-class English voice he aroused more derision among us than fear. We could not hate him in the way we did his followers, because we could never take altogether seriously a man with an accent like that. What came across unmistakably was a kind of hysterical evil. It penetrated to the marrow of my Jewish bones. There was something inevitable about it all; it was as if all my life I had been waiting for it to happen.

Every child of East European Jews has grown up with a working knowledge of persecution. When his elders exchanged reminiscences at the family table, there was usually a curse or two for the Tsarist police, government officials and Christian clergy. Antisemitism was a sort of unwanted inheritance: you were lumbered with it. Now it was on the doorstep again and if you were shocked, as I was, it was because it didn't seem possible that it could happen in England, the country of freedom, justice and tolerance.

When I was about sixteen I was abnormally sensitive about my appearance, having the notion that my nose was too long, my lips too thick and my walk flat-footed and ungainly. I tried to remember not to talk with my hands, but the moment I got excited they jumped out of my pockets and made un-British gestures. When I shoved them out of sight my tongue stumbled on the simplest phrases. At the same time, I had a secret conviction that people were justified in despising me.

This self-contempt made me intolerant of the imperfections of other Jews that I had begun to recognize with sickening frequency. Every time a woman with a foreign accent made a scene on a bus, or two men argued loudly in Yiddish over a business deal, or a music-hall comedian got a few laughs by jamming a bowler hat over his ears and retracting his neck into his shoulders, I was miserably ashamed. I started to look at my surroundings in a different way, although all my life had been spent in the same neighbourhood. Now the foreign names on shop fronts seemed grotesque and provocative; the kosher signs and Hebrew lettering were embarrassing advertisements of alienation; there was too much huckstering in street-markets; the flies crawling over exposed meat and groceries were proof of ingrained backwardness and squalor. I was equally affronted by the sight of a Hassid walking through the street in outlandish garb, impervious to the effect of his own strangeness, and of the herring women down the Lane, plunging their chapped and swollen fingers into the open barrels of pickled fish.

Much had changed since those innocent days when I had taken it for granted that Englishmen were simply people born in England. Until the age of ten I had not seen a country lane, a field, or the sea. England's green and pleasant land was a green and pleasant conceit in a school poem. Reality was the ghetto of East London, the only England I knew, the only place in the whole wide world to which I was truly native. And if I ever thought of it at all, what else was I but English, and what else was I but Jewish, and why should the one be inconsistent with the other? True, a hostile English tribe lived on our perimeter incomprehensibly ordering us to go back to this or that place - anywhere but here. So we were intermittently troubled: but in our teeming streets we dwelt unchallenged and secure except for the ills of poverty. I have been asked, generally by other Jews who grew up as a separate people among the nations of Eastern Europe, if it did not occur to me to wonder how my forefathers fitted into the kind of history we were taught at school. I can only reply that it did not. We got little beyond those narratives in which Canute ordered the tide to halt and Alfred burned the cakes, and what, in any case, had history to do with a boy's dreams and disappointments?

But in my early years a line was drawn through your life at fourteen and everything changed. One day you were a schoolboy in short trousers, the next a putative adult dressed like a man of forty and shoved out to earn a living. You came abruptly into contact, and sometimes collision, with the complicated society in which people competed for work, advancement and opportunity at a time when these were not easily come by. It was then that I began to learn that some were more English than others. In the first place the lesson had a class character. The kinds of occupations open to a working-class boy of little education were restricted. It goes without saying that in the thirties it was still unthinkable for anyone from Bethnal Green to aspire to become a bank-manager (or cashier), a newspaper reporter, a sanitary inspector or a commissioned military officer, even with a carefully adjusted accent.

Soon I discovered an additional handicap. Being reasonably intelligent and writing a fair hand, I hoped to break out of the tailoring, cabinet-making, fur-manufacturing, hairdressing circuit in which Jewish boys of my background sought a livelihood. Painstaking letters of application went out advising insurance companies, shipping lines, city commercial houses and similar respectable establishments that I had all the qualities required for the post of office-boy. No-one ever replied. I rushed to be first in the queue for direct interviews. Some people were frank enough to tell me that it was their policy not to employ people of the Jewish faith, others preferred ambiguity.

The 'Situations Vacant' columns of newspapers exploited the prevailing insecurity. We unemployed youths pushed and jostled around copies of the *Daily Telegraph* in public libraries, daydreaming of wonderful opportunities for salesmen, of learning to make £6 a week in our spare time, of having a healthy and interesting career with free travel all over the world in the armed forces, of becoming masters of our fate by a short course in Pelmanism. One advertisement invited the reader to obtain lucrative employment in His Majesty's Civil Service as a Grade Three Officer or something through a correspondence school that guaranteed success in entrance examinations on a money-back basis. Not having more than a shilling or two at any time, I applied directly to the authorities for the conditions of entry in the hope that it would be possible to read for the examinations in the free library. This was how I made the dismal discovery that I was not quite British enough even to empty the wastepaper baskets in the civil service. Without British-born parents, I learned, they would have nothing to do with you as a postman, a policeman, a naval rating, a customs and excise officer, a government cipher clerk or a weights and measures inspector. In fact, you weren't particularly wanted, and it seemed quite obvious to you why.

So far, my experiences had been singularly parochial, not at all lessened by a growing sense of alienation. The people I best understood were those amongst whom I'd always lived, the East End Jews, and I knew little about others with whom I was linked by fate. But more and more of them were appearing in London, uprooted men, women and children, some with scuffed cardboard or wooden suitcases, some still showing signs of recent affluence, all subdued, apologetic, unwanted.

Many hundreds of other refugees were shuffling through the wintry streets of Paris. They queued in cellars for bowls of soup, huddled for warmth in cheap bistros, hoarded their misery. In Germany thousands of others bartered vainly for passports, scurried from frontier to frontier, crawled through thickets of clawing wire towards the rifle muzzles of vigilant border guards. One could not then know that after the migrant search for a chance to live would come the enforced migration of millions to certain death. In Paris it seems to me then that the symbol of rootlessness could be taken no further. A few months earlier, I had been down, if not out, eating in soup kitchens and sleeping in doss-houses. But the umbilical cord of group and family belonging had not been severed: there was always the knowledge that friendship, or a new job, would put everything right. If Fascism conquered Britain, in what wintry city would I, too, seek transient companionship, bread, sex, forgetfulness?

A proletarian life could not prepare me for the society of the refugee artists, writers, musicians and scholars with whom I now occasionally came into contact and my East European antecedents made it even more difficult to understand them. In the Whitechapel ghetto we were never in any doubt about being Jews, but many of these new acquaintances had travelled far from their Jewish origins. Some were entirely deracinated, baptized Jews, Germanized Czechs, Marxist intellectuals, elite representatives of German culture, only the crude generalizations of Nazi racial philosophers could herd them into a common category. They were to prove far more adaptable than that earlier generation of Jewish immigrants from Poland, Russia and Lithuania who, by and large, left it to their children to assimilate. These newcomers swam in the mainstream of European culture: they had style, facility, sometimes erudition. All they required was a period of acclimatization. Within a decade, their accents perfected, there was little to distinguish them from born Englishmen, Frenchmen or Americans.

During the war I was commissioned into an alien company of the Pioneer Corps composed of these Jewish refugees. There cannot be a single civilized language for which we did not have an expert. We could easily have mustered the academic qualifications to staff a small university, assemble a decent orchestra, script, direct and shoot a movie, or launch a newspaper. One day an order came from the War Office authorizing alien personnel to change their nominal identities in case they were ever captured by the enemy. For some strange reason Scottish clan-names were most favoured and few, if any, ever reverted to their former titles.

The war, when it came, had unexpected benevolences. I travelled north to an army depot in Glasgow with a draft of conscripts from all parts of East London, young cockneys leaving the smoke with reluctance. When the train left Euston a few of the Jews grouped themselves together, exchanging glances of recognition and commiseration. There were other regional groupings, for local patriotism used to be strong in the poor districts of London. Bermondsey boys eyed natives of Shoreditch with misgiving, Hoxton stared through Homerton as if X-raying his backbone. Upper-class conscripts avoided conversation for fear of giving their class away by their accents. Once battle-dress was on and square-bashing began we were as alike as if hatched together from the same gigantic womb. For my own part, this anonymity was convalescent. The army offered little hardship. For the first time I was eating three square meals a day and still feeling hungry. I got the first warm overcoat of my life, free boot repairs and laundry, a primitive sense of well-being.

Without being a good soldier, I was skilful at tempering the rigours of military discipline and kept out of serious trouble. My Jewish neuroses vanished as I learned to turn the occasional antisemitic remark against its perpetrator with nonchalant good humour. Friendships took no account of religion or race, anyway. There was an unbelligerent war going on somewhere; if there were also rumours of cruelties, practised upon civil populations in German-occupied territory, little of it got into the newspapers, or we didn't think too much about it. In the gentle, soft-hued Ulster countryside troops played war-games and grumbled at the rain. In barrack room, canteen and village hall I stared at nothing, writing poems of frustration.

> We are the soldiers whom no gun awakes.
> Whose living fades in dumb monotony of thought,
> Whom pain gropes in the urgent thighs,
> And in the breast lies numb.
> Death is an angel who has passed us by
> To grasp another hand sailing an ocean
> Or a boy mocking the quiet stars
> While we grieve and desire.

My name appeared in anthologies with titles like *Poems From the Forces* or *Poets in Khaki*. This gave me modest status at Belfast (we had moved to Ireland) literary gatherings and may have had something to do with my subsequent selection for a commission: it did not change anything much at the time. The poems spoke of sexual deprivation and a melancholy longing for violence. It was a somnambulistic episode in many people's lives. Then came Dunkirk and one awakened to fear.

The horrible prospect that the Nazis might win the war brought home once again that I was involved in the Jewish fate. My friends, in the event of a German occupation, would have the choice of resisting or submitting to conquest. We Jews have no choice: we would die. We had not yet heard the term 'Final Solution' and the Germans were still conducting experiments to perfect the techniques of mass-murder. But the starvation and sadistic cruelties practiced in Dachau, Buchenwald and other places were known even in peace-time. It needed little imagination for a Jew to visualize what awaited him at the hands of the Nazis now that killing was licensed, hallowed by the requirements of war and patriotism.

I began to be haunted by the sufferings of Jews in Europe because these unknown victims took on the features of my own family, of my mother, my young sister and my brothers, three of them soldiers like myself, four still schoolchildren and, therefore, most vulnerable of all. It is curious and, I think, significant, that I was less worried by the immediate danger they were experiencing in the London blitz than by the fear of their helplessness in the event of a Nazi invasion. Bombs falling from the sky made no discrimination between victims: everyone had an equal chance of doom or survival. What horrified me was the cold-blooded selections practiced by the Nazis in the name of a warped ideology. I was no longer a soldier like any other soldier; I was a Jew in uniform.

About this time, a small group of Jewish fugitives - men, women and children - succeeded in escaping to the Dalmation coast and were smuggled aboard an old cargo boat, the *Struma*. It must have seemed a miracle of deliverance. Again, miraculously, they survived a hazardous Mediterranean crossing and reached Turkey, from whence they hoped to travel overland to Palestine. But there was a legal obstacle. The British authorities refused entry certificates for Palestine on the grounds that the quota allocated to Jewish immigrants was exhausted. The fugitives then applied to the Turks for permission to stay in the country. This also was refused. They pleaded that the children, at least, should be permitted to stay, but again the answer was no, and the *Struma* was ordered to leave port. Where were the wretched people to go? Back to the Nazis, who would kill them? The British and Turkish authorities were sorry, but there were rules and regulations. *Struma* sailed. Some distance out at sea, there was an explosion and it foundered. Only one survived. No-one knows what caused the explosion. Some say the boat struck a floating mine, others that the fugitives chose to die at sea rather than face torture and death at the hands of the Germans.

The sinking of the *Struma* was desolating news. It blurred the frontiers of evil. Those stony-hearted British and Turkish officials who could send people to their death because their papers were not in order were Hitler's accomplices. They were doing the devil's work, refusing children the right to live because it would upset their bookkeeping. No doubt they had consulted with superiors. Coded messages had gone from Ankara to Whitehall. Senior bureaucrats must have found it tiresome to be bothered in the middle of a war by a group of refugees who inconveniently turned up demanding to be let into Palestine. Before they escaped from the Nazis they should have found out if there was room on the quota for them. Didn't they know there was a war on?

After more than twenty years the memory is still painful. This is how I recorded it at the time in an incoherent poem of grief and bitterness.

> For everything the poets have a word.
> To everything the soldier brings his sword,
> And I who am soldier and poet only bring,
> A crushed heart and my tribal suffering.
> Too heavy are my eyes for tears, I am dumb of grief.
> They mouth the usual promises but I am deaf . . .
> Today I invoke Christ in his heavenly mansion
> To come down from the mountain and the sun
> And walk into my lowly dwelling place,
> My house of mourning, to seek out and bless
> Me for my dead, my dead for peace.
> I am Matthew, I am Luke, I am twelve Jews
> Against many whom my Master knows.
> Arrogance of Caesars and Hitlers, lies
> Streaming dark through many centuries,
> Have stormed and taken many forts of strength,
> But mine shall hold until my ally cometh . . .
> Today my khaki is a badge of shame,
> Its duty meaningless; my name
> Is Moses and I summon plague to Pharaoh.
> Today my mantle is Sorrow and O
> My crown is Thorn. I sit darkly with the years
> And centuries of years, bowed by my heritage of tears.

If it were possible to point to one single episode as a decisive turning point in one's life. the tragic sinking of the *Struma* would be that for me. Never again would I be able to think of myself as an Englishman, or face uncertainty about my identity. In the middle of this century any Jew in Europe was condemned as surely as if he was born with an incurable disease. Only the accident of geography, or astronomically lucky odds, determined his survival. And when the war was won, for me it was also lost six million times over. This exclusive sense of injury lacks generosity, even imagination. It was some time before I was able to recognize that there was no less depravity in the indiscriminate slaughter by mass bomber raids than in the selective killings practised by the Nazis, that both techniques derived from an increasing tendency on the part of people to regard other people as abstractions. But that is not my theme. I am concerned here with my education as a Jew, and it was the *churban*, the destruction, which largely completed it.

Yet England made me. When the State of Israel was established in 1948 it confronted me with a clear-cut choice and I found that I would not willingly emigrate from the English language, spoken in English ways by mild, tolerant English people. In reality I have encountered little antisemitism, most of it inconsequential, some of it the chemical reaction of over-sensitivity. I live in an urbanized English village and am not conscious of segregation from my neighbours, whose reputation for insularity has been exaggerated. I belong to them a little and they belong to me, yet they would probably be faintly astonished to learn that I feel in some ways an outsider having more in common with certain people in New York, Tel Aviv or Moscow than with themselves. They might not understand why I am sometimes overtaken by desolation watching my small daughter playing in the sunshine, why a child's discarded shoe can germinate terrible images in my dreams. But if they ever guessed these things, I would be confident of their compassion. Most of them, anyway.

Spring 1967

RUDOLF ROCKER:
Mentor of the Jewish Anarchists
Joseph Leftwich

When I was a schoolboy and an adolescent youth in Whitechapel, Rocker was a legend among the Jewish workers, who were the mass of its Jewish population. He came among them, settled among them and married one of them, Millie Witcop; he was a radical propagandist, working for the liberation of the working class and he found in the Jewish socialist and Jewish anarchist groups and in the Jewish trade union movement a fruitful field for his propaganda. Yet he was more than that. In those days the Jewish anarchist movement was as strong, or stronger, in the East End of London as the Jewish socialist movement; and certainly stronger than the Zionist movement, which had only a small following among the Jewish workers. But Rocker was to all the Yiddish-speaking workers of that time - anarchist, socialist, Zionist and non-party - the symbol of culture. They flocked to his lectures on literature and art. He was their guide and teacher. They drank his words. To the official Anglo-Jewish community, he was an agitator, a preacher of revolt and of atheism and free-thought. But to the Jewish workers, he was a man who spoke to them, in their own Yiddish, of things of the spirit and the mind about which they wanted to hear. Rocker kept them, more effectively than did the official Anglo-Jewish community, out of the Christian mission halls.

Many who were young then and are old now are transported back to their eager youths when they hear Rocker's name. Rocker is eighty this year [1953]. Jacob Botoshansky points out in the *Presse* of Buenos Aires which he edits that Rocker's eightieth birthday is an event 'not only in the Anarchist movement, to which he belongs, but in the history of the Jewish labour movement and in Jewish history as a whole'. Rocker himself writes:

During my many years of activity among the Jewish proletarians in England I had the best opportunity to see how it is possible to make people sensitive to things to which they had given little consideration before. Even today I look upon that period as one of the most fruitful in my life and the sincere and often very touching friendship of my comrades of those days, over the whole of their lives, is the best proof that the work was not wasted, was not in vain. The work was not easy. It demanded much patience. But it was done with love, and it was to me just as exciting and educative as it was to those for whom I worked. The Jewish workers who lived in England at the time, permanently or for the time being, emigrated under the pressure of the conditions in Russia, Poland, Galicia, Rumania, in order to find a new home which would guarantee their personal safety. Most of them grew up in their ghettos with no proper schooling. That they could read and write at all was thanks only to the fact that they nearly all went to *cheder* when they were young. The only language they knew was Yiddish. Most of them understood a little Russian, but far from enough to be able to draw from the rich wells of Russian literature. That was possible only for a minority of the Jewish intellectuals. Hebrew too was for most of them a foreign tongue, in which they could only read their prayers, without rightly understanding them. There were some who knew Hebrew, but their number was small. There were Yiddish newspapers, but Yiddish literature was still developing slowly. Mendele, Peretz, Frug, An-ski and a long list of others had started their literary career in Russian and Hebrew, till they realized that to reach the people they must speak to them in their own language. Thus were laid the foundations of a Yiddish literature, and of the language itself, which was clarified and enriched. The so-called 'Jewish jargon', of which the German Jews especially spoke with contempt, became a language equal to all others, and produced in the course of the last sixty years a considerable literature which can compare in every way in form and content with the creations of the smaller peoples of Europe.

Rocker is a German and, though there is no stain, no slightest fleck on his personal record with regard to Jews, he feels the heavy burden of the blood-guilt of the German people during the period of their Hitler domination. 'It is a special satisfaction to me,' he writes in the foreword to his autobiography, which deals largely with his work among the Yiddish-speaking and Yiddish-reading Jewish masses:

> that I have had the privilege at the end of my life to publish this history. It may be symbolic that the task of producing this work has fallen upon me, who come of a people which for a period of twelve years experienced the inferno of this so-called Third Reich. The barbarous representatives of this monstrous deformity of political cannibalism not only hurled half the world into an abyss of blood, tears and senseless destruction, but they also with cold calculation sacrificed six million Jews to their race-madness, and so assumed a guilt which can never be forgiven.

What brought Rocker, a German socialist and then an anarchist who had spent his early years in a Catholic orphanage, to become a Yiddish writer and editor and to throw in his lot with the Jewish working-class? He tells us that when he first came to London as a young man, he spent his time naturally in the German socialist group. He had before that met in Paris a number of Jewish socialists and anarchists, among them Sh. An-ski, who later wrote *The Dybbuk*, with whom he worked at the same bench, at their common trade of bookbinding. Some differences in the German socialist movement directed his steps, he says, more frequently to Whitechapel, where he attended the Yiddish meetings. His German was enough for him to follow the Yiddish speeches and even to be understood when he spoke German. Yet when he was offered the editorship of the *Arbeter Fraynd* and as he writes, 'so entered deep into the Jewish labour movement,' he could not read the Hebrew characters, knew none of the Hebrew or Slav words in Yiddish and the whole thing seemed to him '*oysterlish*' which means fantastic. He found himself in 'a strange world'. His first impression of the Hebrew print of the *Arbeter Fraynd* was like that made on him by the old Egyptian hieroglyphics.

It was not only the Hebrew lettering that was at first strange and alien to Rocker. Jewish life as a whole was incomprehensible. He could not at his first encounters understand why people called themselves Jewish anarchists. 'Why not Catholic or Protestant anarchists?' he asked. He listened incredulously to the explanation: 'These are not religious Jews; these are Jews who have just as little to do with religion as we have.' 'Then they are no longer Jews,' he answered, 'just as we are no longer Christians.' Finally he came to understand that 'these were Jews from Eastern Europe, Russia, Poland, Rumania, belonging to a distinct ethnic group and speaking a language which is similar to German'.

From that beginning Rocker went deeper into his Jewish contacts, until they became close and intimate and lasting – so that one of his friends writes of him as an astonishing phenomenon in Jewish life, 'a German goy, brought up as a Roman Catholic, who has for fifty-five years devoted his life to the Jewish working-class and to Yiddish language and literature.'

In his autobiography, written in his own old age, Rocker can even look back with sympathy to the tragedy of his wife's old parents when their daughter, who is still at Rocker's side, his lifelong companion and comrade, abandoned the ways of the Jewish religion. He explains how in the old home, in Zlatopol in the Ukraine where she was born, she had been extremely religious and the pride of her parents. She emigrated to London in 1894, worked in sweatshops, saved a little money and brought her parents and her three sisters to London. But meanwhile she had been drawn into the radical movement and lost her belief in religion. 'When I first met Millie,' Rocker writes:

> she was still living with her parents and sisters. She felt the distress of her aged parents. But what could she do? They behaved to her with the same warm affection, but inwardly they felt they had lost something which no one could any longer make good. The father sometimes could not stop himself from reproaching her. But the mother did not do even that; she hid what she felt in her own breast. To her, dedicated with all her heart to the fear of God, the tragedy that had hit her was God's own doing and no human being could do anything about it but accept it lovingly and be reconciled to it.

The parents tried to be tolerant also to their non-Jewish son-in-law. And Rocker was tolerant and understanding to them, perhaps more so than one of the young Jews in his group, full of rebellion against his childhood faith and the ways of his fathers, might have been. It is remarkable how this non-Jew – whose first contacts with any sort of Jewish life came when he was in his twenties – writes understandingly of the tragedy of his wife's parents.

There were many such tragedies in the Whitechapel of those days and all over the world. I knew many of the *Arbeter Fraynd* group. Of one I knew, Baruch Ruderman, I read in Reyzen's Yiddish Lexicon that he had been a *Yeshiva bokher* at Volozhin, where some of his fellow-students interested him in secular studies, in Russian and German books, so that 'he had severe clashes with his fanatically religious parents.' He came to London in 1884 and threw himself into the Jewish socialist movement. Philip Krantz, an early editor of the *Arbeter Fraynd*, came of a religious family and was a student at the Zhitomir Rabbinical Seminary before he became an anti-religious propagandist. His entry in Reyzen's Yiddish Lexicon records that 'he took an active part in the anti-religious propaganda, in the so-called Yom Kippur Balls.' Abraham Frumkin, another pre-

Rocker editor of the *Arbeter Fraynd*, came of a Zionist family settled in Palestine, was born and brought up in Jerusalem, and had been a member of *Hovevei Zion* and a contributor to the Hebrew periodicals *Hamelitz* and *Hazefirah* before he joined the anarchists. Dr Salkind, who was editor of the *Arbeter Fraynd* after Rocker had left England, had been a pioneer Zionist and a rabbi before he went to the *Arbeter Fraynd* in 1920. They were typical of their following.

I lived among that enthusiasm. I knew the enthusiasts and they infected me, an impressionable youngster, with their enthusiasm for the new world which they believed they were building. The speedy coming of the liberating Revolution seemed to have displaced the old Jewish Messianic hope. I remember Rocker in those years, when he lived in a block of tenement flats in the same street where my parents and I lived.

It was a period of struggle and ferment in Jewish life. Young Jews slipped out of the Jewish Pale and were intoxicated by the air of the big world outside; the old Jewish values seemed to them antiquated and useless. There was a new hope in their hearts. And they had been told that the new hope was bound up with the Revolution, with Marxism, the materialist conception, Godlessness. Their anti-religious militancy was part of their battle against the old forms, against oppression, against poverty. It seemed as though a blow had been struck for freedom by holding a public Yom Kippur Ball. Of course not all the Jewish workers were in the revolutionary movement. There were masses of Jewish workers who adhered to the old ways and they sometimes came into conflict. Dr Brodetsky, the son of a poor Whitechapel family who afterwards became head of the Jewish Board of Deputies, in line of succession to the old aristocratic magnates like Sir Moses Montefiore, Sir Stuart Samuel, Sir Osmond d'Avigdor Goldsmid, speaks of it in his autobiography:

> The East End synagogues were crowded. I remember as far back as sixty years ago the anarchist club with its 'intellectual' young people advertised a Yom Kippur Ball, leading sometimes to mild fights between the atheists and the religious; but Jews never went too far and I cannot remember a case where the police had to interfere.

The fact is, however, that the columns of the *Jewish Chronicle* do record such cases. In 1904 there was a clash between them in Whitechapel which ended in the police court. 'The sympathies of the community will be on neither side,' was the editorial comment of the *Jewish Chronicle*. 'What the freethinkers did was not designed to win converts, but to wound the religious feelings of others. On the other hand, the Orthodox section showed an equal culpability in taking the law into their own hands. We must not, under any provocation, have struggles in the streets on a future Yom Kippur.'

The naivety of the old days has gone. Those who do not observe Yom Kippur make no public demonstration of their non-observance. It is their personal affair. They have shed their former youthful aggressiveness. The First World War and, much more so, the Second World War, Hitlerism with its cold, calculated extermination of European Jewry shocked them out of their belief in the Paradise outside the Jewish walls. Glatstein expressed their disillusionment in his poem 'Good night, big world, great, big stinking world. I go back to the Ghetto. From Wagner's heathen music to my own Biblical chant.' In the words of the Bundist Menes, many of them decided that 'the Jewish religious way of life gave the Jew the strength to survive, qualities which enabled the Jew to overcome all difficulties'. This is a new way of looking at the old ways. They found that it is possible to cling to the old ways without lessening their passion for social justice which had impelled them in youth.

There has been disillusion too with the achievements of the Russian Revolution. Rocker has put it this way: 'Revolution in itself does not bring freedom. We see that today, how Revolution can lead to an abyss, where all freedom is at an end.'

It was not what we expected and hoped for in the days when the word 'revolution' conjured up the picture of sweeping away Czarist despotism and other despotisms, and the beginning of an era of liberty, justice and peace. But those who fought like Rocker, from youth to age, for that vision, to them all honour and respect. The book of Jewish history contains many apparently conflicting stories and Rocker's story, though it seemed at the time at variance with the normal Anglo-Jewish story, belongs to it. It is woven into the fabric of Anglo-Jewish life.

Rocker tells a fascinating tale in his autobiography of the Houndsditch and Sydney Street shootings which, in 1911, spread panic among Jews because it started an anti-alien agitation that, in those days when most of East End Jewry over school age was foreign, threatened our continued life in this country. The agitation based itself on the charge that the East End was full of criminal murderers like 'Peter the Painter' and his fellows in the Houndsditch and Sydney Street shootings, who had their haunts in anarchist clubs; the government was called upon to deport the lot. It had indeed been found that the criminals had frequented the *Arbeter Fraynd* club. Rocker makes it clear that the *Arbeter Fraynd* club was used 'freely by hundreds of people who came to our lectures and used our reading room and library'. It was impossible to check who they all were. The mystery of 'Peter the Painter' is still not clear; Rocker says that he appeared afterwards in Russia and 'the Bolshevik government made him an officer in the Cheka, of which he had been a notorious agent'.

I remember well how the official Anglo-Jewish community trembled at that time in fear of the anti-Jewish agitation that the Houndsditch and Sydney Street shootings started. Its spokesmen were in a real panic, and they tried to disassociate the community from any suspicion of being, even by sympathy, implicated. I have in front of me the *Jewish Chronicle* of 13 January, 1911, containing an editorial headed 'The Ways of Panic':

> The manner in which the deplorable outrage in Houndsditch and its sequel have been discussed in certain quarters suggests the reflection that it is as well that Parliament is not at this moment sitting. An interval is thus afforded during which it is hoped there may be a return to sanity on the part of the hysteria-mongers and which will allow the House of Commons to discuss the matter in a calmer atmosphere than at present exists. Who can say that with a rational, merely decently-civilized government in Russia, these men and men like them, instead of becoming mad desperados, would not have been rational, decent, civilized members of society? We have at least a right to ask that Parliament should not be misled into making the insane villainy of a handful of criminals the basis for new legislation directed against perfectly harmless men and women of foreign birth.

I have been reading the chapter in Rocker's autobiography about the big strike of Jewish tailoring workers in London in 1912. I remember that strike. It was a tremendous thing. It was a revolt against the horrible sweatshop system, whose effect on the improvement of Jewish working-class life in England and on all Jewish life is incalculable. The stream of destitute alien immigrants from the Jewish Pale, glad to do any work however badly-paid, whatever the hours and conditions, as long as it bought them a bed for the night and a crust of bread for the day, made them easy victims of the small master tailors, themselves not particularly affluent. The great strike of 1912 was largely led by Rocker and his comrades of the *Arbeter Fraynd*. He writes with justification that the motive which inspired him was more moral than economic. The sweating system imperilled the whole future of the Jewish population. As Rocker says: 'The sweated industry was a thorn in the flesh of the organized British workers. Most of them could not understand under what conditions this hellish system had evolved and, if they could, it would not alter the position, which made them regard the alien immigrant with distrust.'

It is strange, therefore, turning the pages of the *Jewish Chronicle* for 1912, to find that the communal organ gave very little space and attention to the strike; instead of stating the workers' case it printed a stupid story 'From a Correspondent' who said that 'considerable resentment has been felt at the flimsy pretexts upon which the agitation is based. According to the National Federation of Merchant Tailors the demand for workshop accommodation is insincere, "as many of the employees prefer to work in their own homes and refuse to come to the workshops"'. He quoted the Secretary of the London Society of Tailors, which supported the strike, as saying that the master tailors were 'sweaters, used by the big merchant tailors as a medium for sweating the workers in order to get cheap clothes for the public' – and he dismissed that as 'a rather sweeping statement offered in the heat of industrial conflict and, therefore, to be accepted with all reserve'. The whole development of the tailoring trade and of the conditions of employment of the tailoring workers in the forty years since have shown how right the strikers were. When the strike was won, Rocker writes, he could not walk in the street without being surrounded by workers expressing their gratitude for his part in the strike. He tells a story of how he found himself one day in a narrow Whitechapel street, when an old Jew, with a long white beard, came up and shook his hand and said: 'May God give you another hundred years. You helped my children in their worst need. Take a goy, but a man.' 'This old Jew belonged to a world utterly different from mine,' Rocker comments on this story, 'but the gratitude in his eyes moved me and I felt, not for the first time, that pure humanity is much more than differences of origin and conviction. It showed me what a profound effect the strike had on all sections of the Jewish population of the East End.'

Summer 1953

TO T. S. ELIOT
Emanuel Litvinoff

Eminence becomes you. Now when the rock is struck
your young sardonic voice which broke on beauty
floats amid incense and speaks oracles
as though a god
utters from Russell Square and condescends
high in the solemn cathedral of the air,
his holy octaves to a million radios.

I am not one accepted in your parish.
Bleistein is my relative and I share
the protozoic slime of Shylock, a page
in *Stürmer*, and underneath the cities,
a billet somewhat lower than the rats.
Blood in the sewers. Pieces of our flesh
float in the ordure on the Vistula.
You had a sermon but it was not this.

It would seem, then, yours is a voice
remote, singing another river
and the gilded wreck of princes only
for Time's ruin. It is hard to kneel
when knees are stiff.

But London Semite Russian Pale, you will say
Heaven is not in our voices.
The accent, I confess, is merely human
Speaking of passion with a small letter
and, crying widow, mourning not the Church
but a woman staring the sexless sea
for no ship's return,
and no fruit singing in the orchards.

Yet walking with Cohen when the sun exploded
and darkness choked our nostrils,
and the smoke drifting over Treblinka
reeked of the smouldering ashes of children,
I thought what an angry poem
you would have made of it, given the pity.

But your eye is a telescope
scanning the circuit of stars
for Good – Good and Evil Absolute,
and, at luncheon, turns fastidiously from fleshy
noses to contemplation of the knife
twisting among the entrails of spaghetti.

So shall I say it is not eminence chills
but the snigger from behind the covers of history,
the sly words and the cold heart
and footprints made with blood upon a continent?
Let your words
tread lightly on this earth of Europe
lest my people's bones protest.

Summer 1966

A HANDFUL OF EARTH
Wolf Mankowitz

Moishe he was called, and because no one had ever thought to ask what his surname was, and because he had been selling second-hand records almost from before the invention of the gramophone, Moishe Music. His stall was in one of those short dead-end streets which lead off from Petticoat Lane like forgotten backwaters in a Venice in which the Grand Canal is two hundred thousand people sluggishly flowing between banks of bargains.

As you edged your way nearer to Moishe Music past the crated ducks cackling, the fish being gutted, the smoked salmon being sliced, and bare arms dipping into barrels for herrings and cucumbers, you'd hear Chaliapin booming through the cracked horn of an old gramophone, or Gigli, his voice just a little too high and a little too fast, chirping like a canary from behind a pile of red and green water-melons.

There was nothing on Moishe's stall later than Flanagan and Allen singing 'Underneath the Arches'. In other parts of the market you could bop and swing and jazz it any way you liked from big loud Tannoys. But here you had to stand close to hear Nellie Melba singing 'Coming through the Rye'. There they were in boxes, Jack Hylton and his Metrognomes in quiet partnership with Carroll Gibbons, both at sixpence, and old red label HMV classics marked down to a shilling apiece and looking like derelict hansom cabs.

Moishe was the dustman of music and I owe an astonishing knowledge of extinct music-hall numbers to his salvage work.

I used to stand among the collectors flicking over the old discs while Moishe plugged his best-seller for the week on the hand-wound gramophone – 'The song of the Flea' it might be, or 'Softly awakes my Heart'. Slowly, carefully, considering all faults, the customers paid over their shillings and sixpences and Moishe stroked his grey-streaked beard as he slipped the coins carefully into an old-fashioned public-house till.

One Sunday Moishe was stalling-in while I still thumbed my way through a batch of early Carusos. 'Take the lot at a shilling each,' he said, 'it'll be one last bargain for you. There must be twenty-five there – here, give me a pound for the lot.'

Caruso never sang so cheap and who could resist - even if it meant stumbling home from the Underground like an overloaded camel.

'Next Sunday you won't see me here,' Moishe said as he made a parcel of the records.

'Moving to a new pitch?' I asked, thinking the parcel will weigh a ton, and what do I want so much Caruso for anyway?

Moishe handed the Caruso glut to me. It weighed a ton and a half to be precise, and the second-hand string would never last out. Then Moishe fiddled inside his shirt bringing out a small, worn, purple velvet bag.

'For fifty years I carried this round my neck. From Russia. Through Poland - sometimes I didn't have luggage, but this bag I always had. And always, right from a boy, I swore I would take it back where it belongs. To Beth Zion.'

What can a man carry around with him for the best part of his life, in a small worn velvet bag?

'Earth,' Moishe told me, 'a handful of earth from the Holy Land. Now at last I saved enough to take it back - exactly back to exactly where it come from.'

Two or three Sundays afterward habit took me against the Petticoat Lane crowd towards Moishe

Music's dead-end. Then, when no reedy ghost voice crept above the water-melons, I remembered that he had emigrated for the last time in his life. I was sorry to see him go but at the same time glad to have lost the bad habit of carrying home heavy parcels of old scratched wax.

Then one Sunday, when we were expecting for supper half a dozen elderly relatives who wouldn't be satisfied with anything less than the best herrings, I took the long creep to the best herring stall in the East End – the only other feature of interest by that dead-end from where Moishe Music had emigrated. But as I trimmed my way through towards the barrels I had completely forgotten the difference between salt herrings without and with Melba.

Then, as an old brown woman with a black scarf round her head sliced the herrings with a quick snaky knife, a Russian bass started to boom out 'The Death of Boris'. I took my slightly leaking bag of herrings and pushed through towards it. Moishe was back in the music business.

There they were, the same half-dozen careful collectors sorting over the same tattered stock, while Moishe wound the same cracked gramophone.

'Did you put the earth back?' I asked.

'It's you?' Moishe shook my hand. 'I certainly did,' he explained, 'and don't think it was an easy affair. When I got to Beth Zion the whole place was covered with concrete for a dam or something they're building there.'

'So you put the earth back somewhere else?' I suggested.

'If you think' he replied, 'that I am carrying around with me for fifty years a handful of earth from Beth Zion and I am saving and saving only to take back that handful of earth to Beth Zion, and when eventually I get to Beth Zion I am going to put that handful of earth somewhere else, then, let me tell you,' he told me. 'you are making a big mistake.'

Instead Moishe Music had given everyone a headache with his handful of earth. He nagged so many officials that eventually they decided the quickest thing was to drill through the concrete at Beth Zion and let Moishe put the earth back. Then maybe they could get on building dams without interruption.

'Why didn't you stay, Moishe? Retire there – no?' I asked him.

'No,' he explained, 'the weather was marvellous the whole time, you can pick oranges in the garden, there's a few little political problems, but who cares about politics so long as we get Jerusalem in the end. And it's a marvellous country – but it's a country for young men to live in, not for old men like me to die in. Also, I don't mean this as a criticism, but you know what I mean when I say, well – it's marvellous there, but it's not the East End.'

He put another record on the gramophone. Then, as an Italian tenor started to tra-la-la-la his way through 'The Barber of Seville', the bit every tenor always sings, Moishe fiddled under his shirt for a moment and pulled out a new velvet bag.

'Earth,' he explained, 'from the Holy Land. I couldn't leave without a souvenir.'

21st Anniversary anthology, 1974

VOICES IN THE TUNNEL
Harold Pinter

I hear voices. That's what you find in this kind of tunnel, a collision of tenors, bass baritones, counter-tenors and contraltos, like the echoes up and down the sewer in *The Third Man*.

There *is* a light at the end of the tunnel but the tunnel is like the North Circular Road, winding pitilessly to the end of its tether, fading, retreating, suddenly booming, dazzling the eyeball with fractures of light. The voices come and go.

I think they are the voices of Uncle Sam and Aunty Dolly and the girl in the deckchair which collapsed under her bottom. As she slowly decanted the appalled family gathering stared right up – or down – her skirt – black stocking-tops, thighs like lilies. She cried out and was never seen again.

Where there was Aunty Dolly there was also Uncle Mick and where there was Aunt Bessie there was also Simey from Tottenham and of course Albert and Gertie and Phyllis and Bob and Hetty and Harry, Freeman, Hardy and, in this particular case, Willis.

They're in the tunnel. Am I walking towards them or leaving them behind? Are they fading before me or falling in behind me? Are they coming or going?

I waited for Barbara whateverhernamewas for forty-five minutes under a tree in Springfield Park. When she slowly sauntered towards me, palpably bulging, she smiled and said: I knew you would wait.

She went to California.

When I bumped into Lilian whateverhernamewas in Piccadilly Circus, just behind the London Pavilion, I said: What are you doing here? I've just been with a Yank, she said. He gave me seven quid and he only went once.

She went to Australia.

Are these voices in the tunnel happening now or then?

Will they all know me when I burst out of the manhole and join them in the dark?

Autumn 2001

TWO POEMS
A. N. Stencl

For Else Lasker Schüler
I
I will nail two rockers I carved for you
on to both sides of the earth like a cradle.
You will sit beside it
and rock to sleep the world's weeping:
'On our side of the earth
things are upside down,
things are upside down,
and a mother's heart is blind,
weegele, zeegele, mine kind!'
II
With closed and hunting eyes
she reads from her body,
as if in braille script,
with understanding, tender trembling
in her finger tips.

A whip whistles a terrible song
across her tortured, tattered body,
transparent as doe-skin parchment.
Scrolled and shining in your dark sadness,
an inscribed amulet encased.

Translated from the German by Jacob Sonntag. Winter 1969

On My 80th Birthday

I am no Dante and don't know his 'hell'.
Everyone goes through his own paradise.
The only thing left to me is my hope eternal
that human suffering will end one day.

Yes, that 'mine' and 'his' should cease!

Will it happen in our day, in front of our eyes
or only when we are dead and gone?
I don't know Milton and his 'paradise',
but I know our Jewish tune, the only one.

Each tune, in turn, is genuine and true.

Of the one sound 'oy' and the silence thereafter
I made up my poems and rhymes all those years.
And the joy in them, the tears and the laughter,
I learned in *cheder* already, by my rabbi inspired.

The 'oy' in my joy – it grows more and more tired.

Translated from the Yiddish by Jacob Sonntag. Autumn 1977

THE SINGER OF WHITECHAPEL
Avrom Nuchem Stencl (1897-1983)
Josef Herman

Emotional. Excitable. Quarrelsome. Often breaking into violent temper. Would gesticulate wildly. White spit in the corners of his mouth. Would shout things which were both preposterous and ridiculous, like for instance when in a quarrel with Manger, he in the pose of an angry prophet, yelled: 'I will see to it that you never walk the streets of Whitechapel!'

Yes, this is all true, but . . . There was also another Stencl in the same body . . . A more significant one . . . He was poor but never spoke of it; his poverty became a way of his physical and emotional existence. He accepted it. He could go begging to keep up his little magazine *Loshn un Lebn* but asked nothing for himself. He reduced his personal needs to the minumum he could survive on. He would put his own, often desperate, situation against the others worse off than him and would say with a smile: 'I am quite fortunate'.

The thought of others was seldom absent from his mind . . . When friends eventually got for him a one-room council flat, Stencl worried: 'I hope this will not affect others who may need it more than I.'

He was in many ways the kind of man who would have fitted better into the fabric of medieval times. He had no need of most 'modern amenities', he could not cope with them, he could not use them. A public telephone he called a 'crazy machine'. He would walk immense distances rather than use a bus, sometimes because he could not afford the fare but also because he was suspicious of people with some degree of power over others, and this included bus conductors.

He often spoke of the 'natural courtesy of the poor'. . . 'When you are hungry, go to the poor. They will feed you. Not the rich'. . . There was also a moral austerity about his avoidance of good living: 'It can make of a good man a pig', he said.

I asked him once whether he would not be happier in Israel. He thought about it for a while and then said in a meditative whisper: 'Possibly, possibly . . . I dare say I could find in Israel too, my Whitechapel.'

Whitechapel was for him a reality and a sort of metaphysics.

He reproved me once for my atheism: 'Why avoid God when he is obviously the only reality which matters?' His God was the conventional God many Jews believe in. But Stencl also had a personal way of reaching Him, of talking with Him . . . When I asked Stencl whether he goes to the synagogue, he sighed and said, 'Not often . . . But I see God.' I asked in what language he talks with God. 'I pray to Him in the language of our prayers but I also talk with Him in Yiddish, of course.'

After his strange involvement with the poet Else Lasker Schüler in his Berlin days, he put up a wall which separated him from women, or rather, from emotional complications with women. He never married and had no affairs. He became a 'brother to all women'.

Whenever he came to my studio he always arrived with a daffodil in his hand for my wife. When he came like this the first time he whispered: 'A terrible man, Nietzsche. Nietzsche said when you go to a woman, go with a whip . . . What a terrible thing to say. . . One should go to women with flowers.' Why a daffodil? 'It is the flower of humility. Roses are arrogant.'

He never used words merely to please. He always spoke what he believed to be the truth. This made him to some people heavy and often humourless but this also inspired a great trust in all who got to know him.

On occasions he displayed a need for ceremony. One day I went with him to the Tate Gallery. Before entering the room with the Cézannes, Degas and so on, he stopped for a moment, took off his hat, bowed his head and quietly murmured: 'Respect for the masters.' Then he entered the room. He performed this little ceremony with such sincerity that I felt I should bow my head before him.

Of course, there is no single truth to a man, but there are some guiding outlines which give us insight to his singular life.

Just as he avoided good living, 'posh streets' were not for him. 'Why do people choose to live there? I feel forlorn there.'

In his shabby coat and worn-out hat, his shoulders slightly hunched, he walked the streets of the East End, making his presence felt to one and all.

He truly lived in style. This style may have seemed at times disordered but it was of monumental stature and it made sense.

Spring/Summer 1983

STANDING STILL: STILL STANDING
The Synagogue at 19 Princelet Street
Sylvia Paskin and Jane Liddell-King

'A house is a palimpsest on which successive generations have left their mark, and all of them, in principle, are worth preserving' - Raphael Samuel

'As many of you may be aware this is an extremely delicate subject for me to discuss. While I cannot bring myself to refuse our shores to persecuted foreigners, I would do all in my power to dissuade these foreigners from coming to our shores' - Arthur Sebag-Montefiore, Anglo-Jewish Conservative candidate, at an election meeting in Bethnal Green, 10 January 1889

Handsome, austere, dignified, the exterior of 19 Princelet Street, London E1 appears to have much in common with the other Georgian townhouses in this Spitalfields street. It is an architecture that beguiles – sensitive to the scale of human beings, offering proportion, elegance, harmony and containment. But nothing quite prepares you for the emotional impact of the interior of No. 19 – housing, as it does, in a 16 by 40 foot extension, the last remaining example of an Eastern European *stiebel*, a deconsecrated shul whose gaping Ark, piled-up empty pews, broken and missing panes of stained glass and dust-covered, splintering *bimah* bear witness to the absent ritual and liturgy that once filled this tiny, high-Victorian gem. 19 Princelet Street is a particularly important building since it encapsulates in its very structure the whole history of Spitalfields, an area shaped and informed by successive waves of immigrants. Immigrants who for three hundred years sought through their endeavours to graft a life onto that of the host culture, to obtain bread, work and a roof over their heads in a new, 'promised' land – a land far from the religious and political persecution which menaced the Huguenots and Jews and the threat of poverty which brought the Irish and Bangladeshi communities to Spitalfields.

Spitalfields was always a 'place on the edge', an area just to the east of the City marking a boundary between those who control and those who provide, and it was identified early as a perpetually simmering cauldron of unrest. The introduction to the volume on Spitalfields and Mile End New Town in the *Survey of London* (1957) reads:

> The 'liberty' immediately east of Bishopsgate Street was a refuge for dissidents and Spitalfields as a whole was a stronghold of Nonconformity. Baptists settled early here and an important Quaker meeting was established during the Commonwealth. In 1684 the officers of the hamlet were imprisoned and put in the pillory for refusal to take the required oaths. The State Papers of that period contain frequent references to dangerous opponents of the government in Spitalfields, some thought to be involved in the Rye House plot, particularly in and about Brick Lane . . . The area [is] closely associated with the history of the Huguenot silk weavers [and] very largely built up by the time of the Revocation of the Edict of Nantes in 1685. Aliens were present in Spitalfields before the middle of the century and two years before the Revocation, French weavers were sufficiently numerous in Spitalfields to attract the hostility of the English apprentices. In 1718 and 1753-4 the hamlet and parish scavengers could speak no English. The history of Spitalfields was . . . marked from an early period by industrial distress which was sometimes expressed in violent rioting . . . The 1730s were marked by repeated riots by weavers against their masters, requiring troops to be sent from the Tower and similar acts of violence marked the 1760s and early 1770s.

Nevertheless, it was in the spirit of prestige and personal confidence that the terraced house itself was built in 1719 by Samuel Worrall, a prominent local builder. He was a master carpenter who did much of the work at Nicholas Hawksmoor's superb Christchurch as well as at the Rectory at 2 Fournier Street. Two years after building 19 Princelet Street, Worrall had created sufficient wealth for himself to build his own house between Princelet and Fournier Street. The entrance to the yard is opposite the former synagogue and his house survives to this day. Number 19 became home successively to a draper, a drugster, a glover and, in December 1722, a needle-maker. From 1743 onwards it housed a different kind of inhabitant. It became the home and workshop of a Huguenot and Master Weaver, Peter Abraham Ogier, one of thirteen children of Pierre Ogier who came originally from Bas Poitou. His nephew, another Pierre Ogier, joined the Livery of the Weavers company and five years later he was a director of the French Hospital. Perhaps it was Peter Abraham who put in the window with the leaded lights at the top of the house which constitutes the airless weavers' attic (airless, incidentally, to prevent the silk losing weight). Subsequently, his niece Louisa married Samuel Courtauld whose family proved crucial to the London silk industry and whose descendants ultimately created a vast textile empire. In 1745 Peter Abraham's firm proved its allegiance to its adopted country and the established monarchy by offering some thirty of its young male employees to fight the Catholic Young Pretender.

For all Ogier's successful integration into London life, he first arrived in London as a Huguenot refugee. The word refugee (from the French *réfugié*) was first used to describe the Huguenots, French Protestants who were persecuted by the Catholic establishment and who eventually fled to other lands. The major exodus was in 1685, after Louis XIV revoked Henri IV's Edict of Nantes which allowed the Huguenots freedom of worship. Some 50,000 made their way to England, bringing with them their skills as clock and instrument makers and their expertise in the silk industry. They settled for the most part in Spitalfields.

Samuel Pepys, whose wife Elizabeth was herself of Huguenot descent, liked to go and hear the French services, in order to keep up his French. On 30 November 1662, he wrote:

> In the afternoon, I to the French church here in the City, and stood in the aisle all the

sermon, with great delight hearing a very admirable sermon, from a very young man, upon the article in our creed (in order of Catechism) upon the Resurrection . . .

In October of the next year Pepys describes another, very different religious service:

. . .After dinner my wife and I, by Mr Rawlinson's conduct, to the Jewish Synagogue – where the men and boys in their vayles, and the women behind a lattice out of sight; and some things, stand up, which I believe is their Law, in a press, to which all coming in do bow; and on the putting on their vayles do say something, to which others that hear him do cry Amen, and the party doth kiss his vayle, their service all in a singing way and in Hebrew. And anon their Laws, that they take out of the press, is carried by several men, four or five, several burthens in all, and they do relieve one another, or whether it is that everyone desires to have the carrying of it, I cannot tell. Thus they carried it round, round about the room while such a service is singing and in the end they had a prayer for the king which they pronounced his name in Portugall, but the prayer, like the rest, in Hebrew. But Lord, to see the disorder, laughing, sporting and no attention, but confusion in all their service, more like Brutes than people knowing the true God, would make a man forswear ever seeing them more; and indeed, I never did see so much, or could have imagined there had been any religion in the whole world so absurdly performed as this. Away thence, with my mind strangely disturbed with them . . .

Disorderliness and brutishness were accusations leveled also at the Irish, another group of immigrants to Spitalfields. Having conquered and despoiled Ireland, the English were nonetheless rather surprised to find themselves visited by a continual influx of poor Irish people seeking a respite from constant hunger. The surplus population came because the Poor Law operated in England and, though it gave little and harshly, it still kept starvation at bay. The Irish were consistently greeted with hostility, prejudice and suspicion. There were laws throughout the sixteenth and seventeenth centuries restricting Irish movement in England. Spitalfields, near the docks, was an obvious place for the Irish to live – just outside the City where they could form a pool of cheap labour for the trading and financial families and businesses. The influx of the Irish led to competition for work in the docks, market and textile trades. There were anti-Irish riots in Spitalfields in 1736, when the weavers protested that the Irish were undercutting their wages, and these were followed by others in Wapping, Shadwell and the docks. A comment in a newspaper from much later typifies a common reaction: 'The quarrelsome, riotous and indeed, bloodthirsty disposition of the lower orders of Irishmen, who intoxicated with gin or whisky, has long called for exemplary punishment.'

After Waterloo, Irish immigration into the East End was at its peak, and the residue of 'respectable' inhabitants of Spitalfields had left. The area now became known as a notorious and nefarious slum and the very houses that had been graced by the elegant and successful Huguenots had degenerated into lodging houses (the silk industry collapsed in 1826) and fetid workshops inhabited by 'The People of the Abyss', as later chronicled by the writer and adventurer Jack London, who called the East End 'the hell-hole of humanity'.

In 1869, exactly 150 years after the house was built, the Loyal United Friendly Society adapted and extended 19 Princelet Street as a synagogue. These founding fathers were small businessmen from Eastern Europe who had established themselves to some degree. They created their society specifically to help fellow Jews beginning to arrive in Spitalfields from the same region. The synagogue was extended across the garden, demolishing a Huguenot workshop that had stood there. The basement was adapted for use as milk and meat kitchens, the room under the prayer hall served as both a meeting and eating room and was completely excavated below garden level. A ground-floor room served as a school room. On the first floor they built a Ladies' Gallery which sat on slender cast-iron columns. A small fireplace with engraved roses stands at the entrance to the Gallery for the ladies' delectation. The upper floors survived for the use of the caretaker and other tenants.

More and more Jews from Lithuania, Poland and Russia were now arriving in the area, fleeing pogroms, the threat of military service and other persecutions of Czarist Russia. There were already Jews (mainly of Sephardi descent) living in the City – affluent merchants, bankers, dealers in stock and lawyers, most of them upwardly mobile and anxious to assimilate into the wider culture. The influx reached a peak in the 1880s and put pressure on scarce working-class accommodation – the Irish were pushed towards Bow and Poplar. In 1889, Charles Booth, author of *Life and Labour of the People of London*, wrote of the Jews: 'they fill whole blocks of model dwellings; they have introduced new trades and new habits and meet their fate independent of the great stream of London life surging around . . .' These incoming Jews set up around a hundred places of worship in the East End – alongside a few major synagogues such as Sandys Row, Bevis Marks, Machzike Hadass, Spitalfields Great, there were now many smaller domestic *chevras* where *landsmann* (fellow townsmen) could worship together:

> It seems that a dozen or so poor foreigners have clubbed together to form a *minyan*. They subscribe twopence a week and pay the occupier of the house in Hanbury Street where I was visiting two shillings a week for the use of his kitchen as a shul. Relatively to the humble surroundings the Ark looked rather imposing. It only contained small *Sepher* (and a little religious lumber such as a *Tallis* and an *Aleph Bes* card) but it was large enough to hold two or three scrolls . . . The walls were decorated with an *Hanosen Teshuah* in which the name *Kveen Victoria* appeared as large as life (yes, our foreign Jews are thoroughly loyal to the queen in whose blessed land they have found asylum from foreign persecution).

From this time forth, the *Jewish Chronicle* (as this quotation makes clear) and other organs patronized and criticized the new immigrants. Jews already established often resented these incomers – it drew too much attention to them – who were advised to 'Eschew your Yiddish language and customs. Adopt the English language with its civilizing customs.' Those intent on being 'acceptable' were seldom comfortable with those whose sense of religious and social autonomy resisted assimilation.

During the 1920s and 1930s, with increased economic status, Jews began to leave the East End for the leafy suburbs of Golders Green and beyond. The Blitz gave a further impetus to their departure. When the various synagogue buildings came onto the market, they were not recognized as culturally or architecturally important and were allowed to become derelict and abandoned – to become parking lots and mosques. Religious artefacts were sometimes found in nearby street markets. 19 Princelet Street managed to avoid the fate of other synagogues and it continued to have a small struggling congregation well into the 1970s, although some of the later services took place only in winter. In 1980 the building was sold to the Spitalfields Historic Buildings Trust and until recently stood empty and unused.

By the 1960s only a remnant of the once thriving Jewish population remained in the East End. Much of the tailoring, fur, cabinet-making and dress factories had also gone and the sweatshops had turned into no less unhealthy leatherwear workshops. Around this time a fourth major wave of immigrants arrived in the Spitalfields area. From the late nineteenth century on, there had been a steady stream of men from the region of Sylhet, in the north-east corner of India, arriving on these shores. They worked on British merchant vessels and were known as lascars. Many jumped ship and obtained short-term employment in the East End. Some found work and lodging among East End Jews, who were sympathetic to those subject to prejudice like themselves. These early Sylheti migrants were joined by many others in the 1950s and 1960s, all driven by poor economic circumstances in their own country and the promise of job opportunities in England. These were mainly young single males often supplied with some money from their families or local village communities. In 1971, after a bitter civil war, Sylhet became Bangladesh.

Those who were in England had planned to remain only for a short period and to provide their families back home with money or acquire a little capital to buy land, give better marriage dowries, start businesses back home. But the economic situation in England proved tougher than anticipated and dreams of merely being sojourners and making an early return faded. The face of Spitalfields changed once again as these new immigrants moved in, some straight from Bangladesh, others down from the Midlands after suffering redundancy. Spitalfields now houses around some 36,000 Bangladeshis. Many opened restaurants, some took over the leatherwear and clothing businesses that the Jews had abandoned. This time there was little conflict or competition, as the Bangladeshis simply filled the vacuum left by Jewish migration to the suburbs. As with the Huguenots, Jews and Irish before them, there was a rapid expansion of low-paid, unskilled employment. There are now innumerable Indian restaurants in Brick Lane and Commercial Road, food markets, travel agents specializing in South East Asia and some large leather shops. It is impossible to walk in Spitalfields without noticing that the street signs are written in Bengali. In the words of the late historian Raphael Samuel:

> The Bangladeshis are re-enacting the original patterns of migration to this area. They settled most heavily in the self-same streets. They took up the same trades. They practised it seems the same kind of family economy in which self-exploitation was a very condition of survival. Like the Jews they formed, within their own precinct, an ethnic majority, treating the streets and pavements as communal places and the shops and restaurants as meeting places.

Now the workmen are busy everywhere, adding yet more faces and fascias to the shops, houses and market. Brick Lane has its bagels and Balti restaurants, there are new design shops and artists' studios, bars and clubs for the young entrepreneurs who are moving in. The City financiers are encroaching and prices have risen astronomically in the area - pastiche Georgian houses stand next to historic buildings saved from demolition. Against this dynamic and vibrant backdrop, 19 Princelet Street is a moving reminder of the past reality of the East End - a place where survival happened against the odds and had to be fought for. What clings to Princelet Street, what is intrinsic to a place which has been the site of hope, loss, abandonment, decay and deconsecration, is a sense of suffering and of struggle, of life as a daily challenge which must be met and overcome.

An urban myth has attached itself to the disappearance of David Rodinsky, the last inhabitant of 19 Princelet Street. Rodinsky, a mysterious self-taught linguist who read Russian, Sanskrit, Hebrew and French, lived at the very top of the house in the weavers' attic. A twentieth-century Jewish refugee seeking a perch, he seems to have stayed under the eaves for many years until one day in the late 1960s, when he left Princelet Street and was never seen again. His room was left as it was when he abandoned it, a table set for dinner, a bedcover turned down with pyjamas still on the pillow. The calendar on the wall with a picture of Millet's *Angelus* is dated 1963. The story of the quest to discover what happened to him was told in *Rodinsky's Room* (Granta, 1999) by Rachel Lichtenstein and Iain Sinclair. Meanwhile his room has been packed up by the Museum of London to be preserved and perhaps one day put on display.

One can muse on the beauty of the synagogue (even try to count the last glimmers of the painted gold stars on the azure ceiling over the empty Ark), on its rich and diverse history, on the community that was, on why it was, and is, standing still. Raphael Samuel lived all his life in nearby Elder Street and he once wrote about his own house:

> The mezuzah on the doorpost of my basement kitchen . . . is no less a part of the history of this house than the coin of the London Corresponding Co. found in the floorboards, likewise the mid-Victorian range and rather warped Georgian shutters.

Common if knotted threads unite the immigrants, the Huguenots, the Irish, the Jews and the Bangladeshis. All were once immigrants, spoke different languages and worshipped God in various ways. All these communities have lived and worked in these streets, all faced conflict and prejudice from compatriots.

Now 19 Princelet Street synagogue is to become 'a living museum of immigrant life exploring why people have sought refuge and freedom in this area'. Plans for the Spitalfields Centre will give the building an expressive totality in which we can all share. It should be a powerful and enduring source of understanding of the communities that established themselves in Spitalfields and those yet to come, both an extraordinary reminder of the past and a significant beacon for the future.

Winter 1998-9

GENOCIDE IS A CHEESE SANDWICH
Working with victims of torture and persecution
Sonja Linden

'Are you Jewish?' The questioner was Black and British and in the split second of hesitation before my reply, my mind hurtled down a series of mean, dark corridors - the souring of relations between Blacks and Jews, the relative failure of the Black immigrant population to thrive, as compared to the more successful Jewish one, the consequent shift to the right of British Jewry. Down one corridor I flashed past Maureen-BT-Lipman and Vanessa-over-the-top-Feltz. Down another I sped past an image of myself in my questioner's eyes: a Jewish, middle-class, middle-aged softy with pretentious liberal aspirations. Yet the question was asked of me in the staffroom of the Medical Foundation for the Care of Victims of Torture, and it came from the lips of a young Afro-Caribbean woman caseworker, one of a hundred volunteers and employees whose dedication and commitment is nothing short of inspirational. The mere fact that her job brings her into daily contact with victims of ethnic cleansing should have been enough to quell my incipient paranoia; she of all people was not going to be small-minded about my being Jewish.

Why had she asked me though? Ah, of course, the conversation I had just had across the room with Alex Sklan, the clinical director and ex-Head of Jewish Care, had been peppered with Jewish 'in' references. Now that he had left the room, she had turned to me and said 'Are you Jewish?' meaning 'too'. And I said yes. 'Like Helen and Alex,' she commented. And indeed Helen Bamber, who started the Foundation in 1985, and group analyst John Schlapobersky, who set it up with her, are both Jewish. So too are a good many more staff at the Foundation, I told her. 'Really?' she said. And then, uncharacteristically, I went a step further, and volunteered something of my background as a 'second generation' person, daughter of refugee parents from Nazi Germany. It is no coincidence, I told her, beginning to wear my badge with pride, that quite a number of Jewish people are working at the Foundation. There are points of identification for us in this work and, more important, it is a way of putting our history to use. Fifty years after the Holocaust, the time for wringing hands is over, now is the time to use our experience to help other persecuted peoples, now is the time to make good come from bad.

This was one of a number of 'second generation' moments I have had since starting my work at the Medical Foundation as their Writer in Residence. When I tell people about this work they are often either baffled or aghast or both. Baffled because many do not know what the Medical Foundation does (or what a Writer in Residence is), and aghast when I tell them. The Medical Foundation exists to enable survivors of torture and organized violence to engage in a healing process. It offers, free of charge, medical, psychiatric and psychological consultation, assessment and treatment. Equally important, it offers rehabilitation over months or years, through social care, casework, physical and psychological therapies, group and family work. It also performs a vital service in providing forensic medical reports to document torture and ill-treatment in support of claims for asylum. It is the only organization of its kind, brainchild of its founder-director, Helen Bamber, whose life was indelibly marked by her arrival at Belsen shortly after the war at the tender age of nineteen as a member of one of the first rehabilitation teams. Remarkably, the organization relies almost entirely on donations from members of the public.

In addition to the individual treatment offered, dozens of the Foundation's clients, including adolescents and children, participate in therapy groups centred around art, gardening, cooking, dance, storytelling and now writing. As a professional writer, primarily of plays and short stories, I received an Arts Council National Lottery Award for one year to set up the *Write to Life* project to help victims of persecution and torture gain relief from their past traumas through the process of writing testimonies, poetry, fiction or any other form.

It is here that people are often aghast. 'How can you bear it?', 'I don't think I could do that' and 'Isn't it terribly depressing?' are typical responses. More often than not their faces have by now crumpled into an expression of such anguished sympathy that I fear I will shock them when I say that, on the contrary, I find the work exhilarating - because it takes me to the very edge of human experience.

The people I meet have not only faced death, which often beckoned to them as a welcome relief, but pain, grief and degradation that one would imagine to be unendurable.

In short, they have looked into the abyss of human suffering and, like Helen Bamber, their lives have been indelibly marked. But the fact remains that they have survived, and this is also where the exhilaration comes in, for each story of suffering is by definition a story of human endurance and courage. The people I meet have returned from the abyss and are now sitting next to me, alive. They are scarred, of course, emotionally and often physically, but they have lived to tell their story and it is the telling of the story, we now know, that is the first stage in restoring harmony to a fractured human existence. My exhilaration comes from the privilege of sharing these darkest moments of human experience with survivors. But it also comes from the knowledge that I, as a helpless, often impotent citizen, can actually offer some respite, can make a difference. In a world where we are daily assaulted in our living-rooms with images of political brutality, television has made bystanders of us all. Rwanda, Kosovo, Bosnia, we either watch with grim disbelief and mute compassion or switch off, because to watch and not to act is beyond the human. My receiving of these grim tales at the Medical Foundation is the very least I can do. It requires neither courage on my part nor risk of life. It takes place far from the firing line and the torturer's lash, it is recollection in tranquillity, albeit fragile tranquillity, and it offers balm.

The sessions I give are one-to-one and can run for up to two hours at a time, if need be. It is clear that the opportunity to talk freely in a sympathetic and non-clinical context, to be listened to and thus to be recognized for a couple of hours, is as valuable as the exercise of honing a piece of writing. Unlike the psychotherapist, I do not have to be a neutral listener, I can express surprise and shock, in other words respond as a fellow human being in a natural and untrammelled way. In this respect, and importantly, I can also be seen as a representative of the host community, on whose behalf I offer a listening ear. Some people know what they want to write. Others don't and it has to be teased out of them. In every case, however, we start with the ephemeral, words in the air, and end up with the tangible, words on a page.

One Iranian doctor came to me with poems, written in very simple language, his first attempts in English, but mostly we talked. He told me about his three years as a political prisoner and only after I took him to a PEN Writers in Prison meeting at Chelsea Town Hall did he start writing up his experiences. He was a gifted writer. The first piece he wrote for me was entitled 'The Green Groove'. The mere title impressed me. Here was a man who had been in the country barely three months, for whom English was still a struggle, yet the poet in him had driven him to the dictionary to discover the word 'groove' and link it alliteratively with 'green'. For a brief period in his incarceration he and his cellmates had been allowed out to the bathroom three times a day for minutes at a time. In place of a window there was an electric fan embedded in the bathroom wall and he noticed that there was a vertical chink alongside it, a gap in the wall through which he could get a tantalizing glimpse of the outside world. What he could see for the few seconds he dared risk standing in front of it was a courtyard shaded by some trees in a neighbouring garden:

> Other prisoners were not interested in my green groove but I was obsessive about it. It was only about 20 centimetres high and three centimetres wide and yet as far as I was concerned I could see the whole world through it. Try and imagine what it is like to be behind bars, seeing nothing but grey walls, angry guards and tortured prisoners and to see these pictures over and over again. The green groove was like a key that opened the prison door for me and let me go outside for a while, even though this was only in my imagination. This tiny view, which I managed to glimpse through the narrow groove, lifted my spirits tremendously. It gave me hope and made me feel that I really would one day be able to go though to the other side - and I did.

What I found both moving and fascinating about this particular client was that he had the capacity to find moments such as these, moments of redemption. His writing was always focused on such moments of light. (Another of his pieces appears in the anthology assembled by the Medical Foundation, *Captured Voices*.) Subsequently he told me that I was the first person he had ever told these stories to. Later I was to discover that this was not unusual, as there is a reluctance on the part of victims of torture to inflict any further emotional burden on their nearest and dearest. Moreover family and friends have often refrained from asking - a conspiracy of silence well known to the 'second generation'. Frequently, then, they make the difficult entry into our unfriendly society with their stories still locked inside them, and although it is painful to relive them in the act of writing, to do so, they tell me, offers both validation and relief. Writing can give coherence to what feels like an incoherent life.

I often find myself telling people that my own parents suffered persecution under the Nazis, as a way of connecting with them. Sometimes I am a bit self-conscious about this when I am with clients from the Middle East, but it never fails to be an important bridge and it is always interesting for me to discover just how much or little people from cultures outside Europe know about the

Holocaust. The doctor from Iran, it turned out, had been inspired by Viktor Frankl's book *Man's Search for Meaning*, and I lent him a copy of Simon Wiesenthal's *Sunflower*. To another client I lent Primo Levi's *If This is a Man*, which she has read with enormous interest. There is no doubt that my own background and reading of Holocaust literature informs my interaction with the clients I meet in important ways.

A few months ago the Oscar for Best Foreign Film was awarded to Roberto Benigni for *Life is Beautiful*. For many Jewish people, the film did not work, but I was one of those for whom it did. The essence of the story - a father using humour and imagination to shield his very young son from the horrors of the Nazi death camps - reminded me of some of my clients at the Foundation, for whom imagination and humour were vital tools of their survival. One client told me that, immediately after being tortured, he would sometimes find himself laughing out loud in his solitary cell. Everyone thought he was mad. In fact, he told me, he was conjuring up for himself the wildest and funniest scenarios as a way of distancing himself from the horror. Only his body was in the cell, he told me, his spirit was mostly somewhere else, on the other side of the 'green groove'. 'Without imagination,' he said, 'I would not have survived.'

Earlier this year, I was invited to give a short talk about my work at a conference. I brought along with me P, a woman who had served an eight-year sentence in her country for belonging to a left-wing organization. She entered prison a beautiful young woman of twenty-four and within two years her hair had turned completely white. Her psychotherapist at the Foundation, who had worked with her with enormous skill and patience over a number of years, gratifyingly told me how P had been transformed as a result of the writing sessions, for until then she had been 'emotionally blocked'. P told the conference that, before working with me, she had tried to write on her own in her own language but that it had not helped her. 'I wrote it like a person in prison. Nobody read it. Nobody gave me feedback.' In this first attempt at writing she just poured out all the negative feelings that existed between prisoners, as she had suffered a lot as a result of this. Currently, at her request, we are co-writing a book about her experience. This leads her to think about her time in prison almost every day, as she tries to recall incidents, and she is amazed at the detail with which she remembers things. But whereas, in the past, remembering this time used to give her a lot of nightmares, which cast a shadow over the whole of the next day, since working with me, she told the conference, the nightmares have stopped.

Currently I am working with a young Tutsi woman from Rwanda, who is a recent arrival in this country, having tried and failed to make a new life for herself in Rwanda since the genocide in 1994. The Tutsis, like the Armenians and the Jews, have undergone one of the most blatant genocides of the twentieth century. Two distinctive features stand out: the time-scale and the proportion of the population directly implicated in the killings. Just under a million Rwandans, an eighth of the population, were slaughtered in a mere three months. Vast numbers of 'ordinary' members of society, civilians, took up arms against the Tutsi population, often families living next door to them, whose children had played with their own children, whose parties they had been invited to. When radio stations put out the call to the Hutu population to wipe out the entire Tutsi race, not only did neighbours kill neighbours, but doctors killed patients, teachers killed pupils, Hutu husbands killed their Tutsi wives and mixed-race children. The 'tall people' had to be cut down to size - like the Jews, the Tutsis were seen as physically distinct as well as elitist and arrogant - and what better way to do this than to chop off their feet, to the laughter and cheers of jeering Hutu crowds? If the Holocaust was carried out in cold blood, murder by proxy, the genocide in Rwanda was carried out in hot blood and was a hands-on operation, directly involving the majority of the Hutu population.

The entire family of Martine, the young Rwandan woman I met, had been murdered. The Hutus who had burnt down her family house started threatening her again, at which point she decided to try and make a new life for herself outside her country. I went to see her in her hostel accommodation in Camberwell a few days after she had been moved there from a bed and breakfast place in Earls Court. I was moved not only by her history and her mission to write a book about it, but also by her plight in this country. She had paid an agent to escort her out of Rwanda, asking him to take her anywhere, as long as it wasn't an African country, 'because in all Africa there is trouble'. He accompanied her on the plane, announced they were going to Britain and promised to take her to a place of safekeeping. At Heathrow they boarded a minicab, which took them to East London. At this point he turned tail, declaring that he had to go straight back to the airport in order to catch his flight home. 'Go to a mosque or a church,' he said, 'They will help you.' And he left. Stranded in the middle of an unfamiliar city with no money or contacts, she saw people coming out of the mosque – as a Muslim, she knew it was Ramadan. She approached a number of people and asked in her very poor English if they could put her up for the night.

Eventually an Indian family took pity on her and she stayed with them for a week. They enlisted the help of a solicitor and she was put in touch with the Home Office and the local council. She had barely come to terms with her traumatic arrival in London when the council packed her off to 'a very bad place' in Hastings, Kent. This proved too much. Five years after witnessing mass slaughter in Rwanda, the desolation of her new life, with no human contact or financial resources, drove her to the edge, literally. She started to walk to the sea. She wanted to end her life. The manager of the hotel ran after her, asked her what she was doing and urged her to talk to him instead. He phoned the council in London and she was transferred back.

Since being moved to Camberwell, she lives on food vouchers that will not extend to such things as toothpaste, soap or sanitary towels. Her ability to distract herself from her nightmarish memories is severely limited, since she is not entitled to work until she has been here six months nor is she given any money. She cannot travel or make a phone call. The only money she has received are small amounts from the Medical Foundation, who have also supplied her with the only clothes she possesses. She is forced to spend most of her time in a bare little room dominated by a huge fridge, which was empty when I visited, since, quite apart from the fact that she is too depressed to eat, the food vouchers hadn't arrived that week and the council had not provided her with anything to cook with, no saucepan, no cutlery, no dishes.

Had Martine been called Martin, her plight could have been worse, since women asylum seekers are given preferential treatment in terms of housing, and men often end up sleeping rough. Under the proposed Immigration and Asylum Act, all asylum seekers will be subject to this harsh regime, so that not only will they be living below the poverty line, but robbed of their dignity and autonomy by a dehumanizing voucher system with cash handouts of a pound a day. (Currently this state of affairs applies only to those who claim asylum after gaining entry into the country.) The blanket 'disincentive effect' sought by this New Labour government, with its shameful old Tory rhetoric about 'bogus' asylum seekers, seems aimed primarily at appeasing a xenophobic tabloid press.

The most poignant moment for me was Martine's account of how she spends her nights. She has enormous difficulty in sleeping, because of what happened to her:

> Every night, every night I crying. But you know if I want to make my head very good, I just thinking this thing: that they didn't kill my parents, that they're still in Rwanda, I just pretend, I imagine my mother she's calling me, 'Come on, Martine, do this, do that,' you know? And my Dad, I pretend he's sitting over there, in his armchair. And that's how I get to sleep. But then I have bad dreams, *cauchemars* you know . . . I wake up very, very, very,

very early in the morning. I don't know what to do. There's no TV, there's nothing. If I get something to do maybe like it will be better. In the morning all the time I just watch from the window and I don't see anybody except cars and I just start smoking, smoking. I know is bad, my life is very bad . . .

Martine wants to write a book about what happened in Rwanda 'to take it away from my heart'. Another young Rwandan woman came to see me at the Foundation a year ago with a similar history and a similar mission. I saw her for the first time again very recently, and was amazed at the transformation. She is no longer depressed or wracked with nightmares and feels she has to come to terms with what had happened. She attributes this to the writing of her book. It took her two years to complete it – she got up at five every day to write and cried most of the time. Very often she would destroy the previous day's work, as she felt it was no good. She also reported that the nightmares stopped when she was about halfway through the book. I asked her if she was ever tempted to give it up, since it was such a painful process. Only once she said, but she had the most tremendous support from the doctor treating her at the Medical Foundation, who inspired her to keep writing throughout the years she was treating and counselling her: 'That's why I love her very much.' She listed a number of reasons that had compelled her to complete the book. One was to give a message to other people not to give up, people addicted to drugs or drink, people anywhere in the world who are feeling hopeless. Another reason was to broadcast the injustice meted out to her people, and not just by the Hutus:

> Since I was young, my father taught me that there are some big organizations which help protect people, like the United Nations. Can you believe that the UN knew that we were going to die a month before the genocide, and that half our people died in front of the UN and no action was taken, nothing, they just saw people dying and buried them?

I was reminded of Primo Levi's reasons for writing his account of his time in Auschwitz. In his preface to *If This is a Man*, he described how he and his fellow-inmates in the Lager had been overwhelmed by 'the need to tell our story to the rest of the world, to make them participate in it'. His book, therefore, had first and foremost been written to achieve 'an inner liberation'. The young woman from Rwanda told me that, having completed her book, she now felt 'clean'.

'Genocide', according to one American military intelligence officer, 'is a cheese sandwich.' He was talking in a Kigali bar to fellow American, Philip Gourevitch, while the latter was researching his remarkable book on Rwanda, *We Wish to Inform You that Tomorrow We Will Be Killed with Our Families* (Picador, 1999):

> 'A cheese sandwich. Write it down. Genocide is a cheese sandwich.' When asked to explain, he said, 'What does anyone care about a cheese sandwich? Genocide, genocide, genocide. Cheese sandwich, cheese sandwich, cheese sandwich. Who gives a shit? Crimes against humanity? Where's humanity? You? Me? Where's humanity? Who's humanity? You? Me? Did you see a crime committed against you? Hey, just a million Rwandans. Did you ever hear about the Genocide Convention? That convention makes a nice wrapping for the cheese sandwich.'

Summer 1999

THE ARRIVAL AND DEPARTURE OF ADAM AND EVE AT DOVER

Dannie Abse

I

At the gate, expelled from the fable
of the East, the man's profile turned towards
the ullulating distraught woman.

And behind this couple now stumbling forward
– she half-bent over in her weeping –
the distant blitz-light of an angel.

II

So many thousands of centuries passed
and, in their innocence, new friends eased them
of the bdellium, the onyx stone,
and the little gold acquired in Havilah.

So many more miles of thorns and thistles,
so many more winters howled away,
before they came, at last, penniless,
to the alerted paparazzi at Dover.

The fuss! The fuss! The woman moaned on,
inconsolable, but the man seemed composed
until secular officials decreed
they faced no danger in their native country.

The Home Secretary (appealed to) said,
'At the end of the day' and 'God is merciful'.
Ceremonious duty done the two
'economic migrants' were repatriated.

On TV newsreels see them stepping from
a police van, discharged from this little world,
this scepter'd isle, this other Eden,
still in disgrace, coats over their head.

Summer 1998

THE GOLEM OF GOLDERS GREEN
Jonathan Treitel

I am searching in the attic of my family house.
Next to the dust, the rafters, the historic Readers Digests,
the retired armchair with leaking upholstery, the roll upon roll
of wallpaper leftovers, the speaking doll that doesn't . . .
is a box stacked with my unused barmitzvah gifts: books,
mostly – and here's one that will do to begin with:
The New Standard Jewish Encyclopedia.
I thumb through its alphabetical order: discover –
jostled between Golgotha and Sam Goldwyn who said:
Begin with an earthquake and rise to a climax –
what I have been looking for.

The rusted catch on the leaded window jiggles;
undoes. My head protrudes
into London. There, to the right, I see –
were it not for the blocks of flats, the line-ups of semi-detacheds,
poplars, horse chestnuts, and the lie of the land –
clear to the artificial lake on Golders Hill Park.
Around it, an old woman in a wheelchair is pushed;
a Filipina servant jogs on her day off;
a Hassidic father crouches, lowering his earlocks
for his son to tug; a park keeper shouts a warning to
too-eager kids coming close to the brink
as they throw their bread on the water.
The ornamental birds lap it up. Ripples overlap like chain-link, and part
magic-trickily. I observe
iridescent mallards, the superficial paradox
of black swans imported from New Zealand,
a hunger of ducks, an implausibility of flamingoes . . .
and, by the edge, on a patch of shining mud,
an old man with a book and a stick in 1573.

He is Rabbi Yehudah Loew, the Maharal of Prague.
Times are bad. The Inquisition sputters on. Sephardim are still
leaking away from Spain. News is coming through
of the troubles in Mainz, not to speak of
the events at Worms. Somebody stepped out
the other day onto Golders Green Road without glancing left
and was run over: I had been at school with him.
A friend of my parents has a growth in the rectum.
Rudolf II has an air of tolerance, but . . .

We need a messiah – or failing that
at least an odd-job-man to do the rough work.
A flaming brand
glimmers smokily on the banks of the Vltava
at midnight four centuries ago where the Maharal,
high on fasting and chanted penances,
scratches with his stick on a silted shore. He sings
Genesis 2:7 – God breathes
into Adam's nostrils. He sketches
the shape of a man. He paces around it,
clockwise, seven times. He scrolls his manuscript of the Book of Formation.
He reads
an alphabetic acrostic which I,
with my torso in an attic and my head
in open air, and you,
moving your finger down this page,
are reading:

Atta
B'ra
Golem
Dovek
Homer
V'sigzor
Zeidim
Chaval
Torfei
Yisroel

(You create the Golem, made from mud,
to defeat the wicked, the ravagers of Israel)

The torch gutters out. The mud glows, sizzles,
swells into some-
thing or
body who
arises,
naked, male soul-free – amazing
the Filipina, the Hassid, me, the park keeper, the wheelchair woman
and the kids scattering crumbs.
The scared birds flap to the far end of the lake.

Let's dress this Golem, then,
in a skein of old legends. Give him the dark heart
of Mary Shelley's Frankenstein's monster. Lend him an oblong suit
stripped from a flickering black–and–white Boris Karloff.

Equip him with the brute power of Karel Čapek's Robot.
Assign him the mindless intelligence of Isaac Asimov's UNIVAC.
Stamp a Name of God on his brow – *Emes* – Truth –
as in the Habimah Theatre's long-running blockbuster.
Or just kit him out with second-hand rags:
a holey cloak; too-big boots, slightly punctured
(as the Maharal did); and beckon.

The Golem follows. His boots' iron tips,
ringing on the cobblestones, strike sparks.
A yellow star is pinned over where his heart's not.
He takes the path through the vegetable market and the meat market
rising to the Ghetto in the shadow of the Castle. Or he saunters
through Golders Hill flower garden. He admires
the brilliance of daffodils and the impertinence of snowdrops.
He lowers a stiff paw to stroke a crocus. He squeezes
a sprig of lavender: it gives up its perfume. He nods to an old tune
that an oompah band on the bandstand is banging out. Or he stands at the back
of the Altneu shul while the Maharal is intoning Kaddish.
The rabbi rests his palms on the creature's head.
'This is a mute I found by the river. Let him stay. I will care for him.'
The Golem tells the time by the horloge on the Ghetto Town Hall
(its hours are marked in Hebrew; its hands move counterclockwise)
or the Cenotaph by the Golders Green bus station
(its face is fixed permanently at midnight).
He is assigned commandments:
sweep the rabbi's floor; guard the Ghetto gate;
drop into Grodzinski's for a kilo of Israeli couscous in a cellophane bag
He pauses under where the sign was: Buy Bloom's Best Beef.
He scrapes the mud off his soles on the welcome mat of the Public Library,
finds himself under bars of fluorescent lighting. Past
General Fiction, Crime, Psychology, Selected New . . . and ends up in the corner,
kneeling beside Judaica. He is used to his dark niche
in the Maharal's study, brooding on nothing but his rabbi at the lectern
assembling Talmudic commentaries - wonderful pensive wrangles -
which I have the Golem pull from the stacks, along with stories
by the Brothers Singer and the Brothers Grimm,
by Poe and Shelley, by Ozick and Aleichem,
Winkler's (New York, 1980) monograph on the Golem mythus . . .
Hump them to the light-pen operated check-out . . . and up
to here and now in the attic.
Volumes multiply around me in towers and crenellated walls
like a Build Your Own New Jerusalem construction kit
not assembled according to instructions.
Bookmarks, trapped in the jaws of closed books, flutter.
Books flap open on deliberately creased pages. Flick and browse.

My pen squawks. My notes rustle. Variant legends congregate . . .
There is a good Jewish virgin: there is a wicked Christian priest.
There is a pig and a dead baby, Pesach and Easter,
a small corpse dumped in a ghetto yard, a charge of ritual murder
which the Maharal refutes by dint of superior wisdom
and his Golem's strength. . . . And what of history?
No blood libel stuck in the age of Rudolf. So they all lived happily, ever . . .

Conduct a wordsearch under 'GOLEM' on a database of rabbinical responsa.
1. Can a Golem speak?
2. May a Golem form part of a quorum for prayer?
3. Has a Golem a soul?
4. Will a Golem be resurrected at the end of time?
5. Can a Golem father a child?

1. Only living men can speak.
2. No – because he is not one of the Children of Israel.
   Yes – because he is an adopted orphan. Both replies are given.
3. His soul is not like ours; but he has a spark of the divine – and so
4. He will be resurrected.
5. Adam, moulded from earth, was a Golem before he was a Man.
   A Golem is the father of us all.

In the topmost storey of the Altneu shul,
the Maharal erased the aleph from the Golem's brow, making
Emes into *Mes* – meaning Death.
The creature became mud and wormy dust again.
The Maharal slammed and locked and double-locked the door after himself,
staggered to ground level,
and proclaimed
that never again should anyone ascend the turning staircase,
unlock the attic door, and disturb the Golem's remains.
And in every generation since, we have been climbing
the stairs and twisting the key in the lock.

Summer 1991

A PALESTINIAN IN GOLDERS GREEN
Ghada Karmi

My father knew little of London. Arriving in 1948 with no knowledge of the city's ethnic composition, he had unwittingly stumbled on the least suitable and, in the circumstances, the most ironic choice of address. Quite funny, really. He found a house to rent in Golders Green, then the main area of residence for German Jewish refugees. It is still known today as the most Jewish part of London, even though many other nationalities and races live there. Jokes are made about the Jewishness of Golders Green and, in the 1950s, when one took a bus to go there, the bus conductor would often shout out to the passengers 'Anyone for Tel Aviv?' I can remember that the upper floor of the house next door to us was let to a German-Jewish doctor whom we often consulted informally for some minor illness. Inevitably, my secondary school, Henrietta Barnett in nearby Hampstead Garden Suburb, was full of Jewish girls – or so it seemed then.

Not that I understood the significance of any of this at the time. I suppose, looking back, it was the combination of my parents' preoccupation with sheer survival in those early years of exile and the unthinking assumption of many adults that children know much more than they really do which led them to give me little information or, when pressed, ambiguous messages about our origins and history. Thus, I knew that the loss of our home and our flight to England were due to what Jews had done to Palestinians – but I didn't know the details. And yet I had to reconcile that with the fact that here I was in London, going to school with Jews, freely mixing and making friends with them, regardless. Had I but known it, this was in a way a reflection of my parents' genuine lack of acrimony against the Jews, despite their loss. They were hurt and sad but, surprisingly, not vengeful (even today, many Palestinians cannot bring themselves to speak or meet with Jewish people). I could not have understood that at the time and it only confused the issue for me. Not surprisingly, by the age of fourteen, and in the absence of any directions to the contrary, I decided that whatever the Jews in Palestine had done was irrelevant to me here, and if anyone had asked me at that time what nationality I thought I was, I would almost certainly have said: English.

That cosy assumption was soon put to the test by a small incident which took place at about that time. I came home from school one winter afternoon to find a dismal scene in our kitchen. Now our kitchen, as indeed the rest of our house, was in any case usually dark and gloomy. In those days, we had no central heating and no carpets. The curtains were never drawn and the steam which formed against the dark window panes streaked down in rivulets to pool on the wood at the bottom. This and the weak bulb in the ceiling light made our kitchen look unwelcoming and a little sinister.

But on this occasion the atmosphere was much worse than usual. My mother was sitting in an armchair, her head thrown back and her eyes closed. My father was there too, which was in itself unusual since, if he were home early from work, he would normally be reading in his tiny study upstairs. He sat uneasily on the edge of his chair, frowning deeply.

As I came in and took in this grim scene, I said, 'What's the matter? What's happened?' When there was no answer, I said in some desperation, 'Has someone died?'

At this, my mother half-opened her eyes and said, with a touch of Arab drama, 'If only she had!' and promptly fell silent again. Now thoroughly alarmed, I turned to my father. 'Please, tell me what's going on.'

Still frowning, he sighed heavily. 'It's the Dajani daughter' – referring to a Palestinian family who were close friends of my parents – 'she's just told her mother that she's engaged to marry an

Englishman.'

'Is that all?' I cried with relief, 'what's wrong with that?'

My mother cast me a venomous look. 'What a stupid girl!' she muttered and closed her eyes again. 'Please,' I persisted, looking at my father, 'what's wrong with it, why are you so upset?'

'Don't you know,' said my father with some irritation, 'that it's wrong for a Muslim woman to marry a non-Muslim man? This Dajani girl should have known better. I gather,' he was now addressing my mother, 'that he's offered to convert.'

'Oh?' snorted my mother angrily, 'who's that supposed to fool?' She shook her head sadly. 'After all that mother's done for them, to be repaid like this. And she a widow who sacrificed her whole life to bring them up.'

No one noticed that I was agape with amazement. 'Do you mean,' I said to my father 'that no Muslim girl, like me say, can ever marry someone who isn't a Muslim? That I can't marry Fuad, for example?' Fuad was a Christian Palestinian friend, who worked at the BBC with my father.

'No!' my father shouted in exasperation, 'You cannot. You should know these things without having to be told.'

But I didn't know, since no one had ever bothered to tell me. In those days, I knew scarcely another Muslim of my own age from whom I could have learned what my parents never taught me. I found out much later that, under Islamic law, marriage between a Muslim woman and a non-Muslim man was unlawful, but not the other way around. While conversion of the man to Islam would satisfy the legal requirement for a valid Muslim marriage, social custom meant that such conversions were dismissed as mere ploys designed in effect to permit an outsider male sexual access to a Muslim woman.

'Marrying out' like this was regarded as a sin not ameliorated by conversion, and the people who contracted such marriages were usually either ostracized or spent the rest of their lives apologizing for what they had done. In extreme cases, the woman was disowned, expelled from the family circle and regarded for all intents and purposes as having died. In addition, the non-Muslim suitor might face direct threats or even physical attack from the men of the woman's family. In the Britain of the 1990s, very little of this would have been news, but in the 1950s the country had not yet become home to the thousands of Muslim immigrants from the Indian subcontinent who came later and made Islam a familiar creed.

I remember how on that dark winter afternoon I went up to my bedroom, leaving my parents downstairs, and sat on my bed, thinking. I had a sense of revulsion and horror. 'I am nothing to do with these people,' I finally decided. 'They're intolerant and primitive and I do not belong with them.' I comforted myself with the knowledge that I was part of a higher order of being, liberal, free, English, where such bigotry would not be tolerated.

And there it was left until two or three weeks later, when I had occasion to go to Patricia's house one afternoon. Patricia was one of my three best friends at school and she and I were very close. She was a Jewish girl, pretty and petite with long blond hair, ivory white skin and china blue eyes. With my dark eyes, dark hair and olive skin she and I could not have looked more dissimilar. There was, I remember, at that time a popular TV advertisement for DAZ soap powder which showed how muddy garments washed with this soap were dazzlingly transformed. To the amusement of our school friends, Patricia and I once enacted this advertisement by crouching behind a desk in the classroom, labeled DAZ. They saw me crawl behind the desk first and, while I hid there, Patricia emerged from the other side to loud applause from the others.

She had joined the school one year after me and I remember her as shy and waif-like. I felt sorry for her and we soon made friends, telling each other secrets and visiting each others' houses after school. My parents grew fond of her and were especially charmed when she learned a few words of Arabic, which she used whenever she saw them. Her family likewise took warmly to me and made me feel at home. Patricia's father was a businessman who lived in Jersey – 'for tax reasons', they always said mysteriously – and came to visit the family from time to time. Her mother, a short, dark dumpy woman of Rumanian origin, maintained the family home in London perforce on her own. She resented her husband deeply for this and, young as I was, I could sense the unhappiness and tension in Patricia's house from the first time I ever went there.

Not that her parents were ever anything but the soul of kindness and affection towards me in those days. Patricia's father was a witty, amusing man who looked and behaved like the stereotypical Jewish comedian. He would hunch his shoulders and move his hands about when he spoke – 'hand signals', as they were known – in a way which I found very funny. He always greeted me with a hug and a kiss whenever he saw me, and he would usually say something to make me laugh. When, years later, I became a doctor, he would invariably quip whenever he met me, 'Well, how's the abortion business going?' (this was in the days before the Abortion Act of 1967, when such operations were illegal).

Later still, after my first marriage broke down, he would say, 'So tell me, are you going to marry again or did you decide to stay happy?' Likewise, Patricia's mother was like a mother to me too. I used to eat in their house, stay the night, join them on occasions when the extended family of Patricia's aunts, cousins and their husbands and wives got together, and became as intimate as if I had been one of them. When I grew up, two of them who worked in the rag trade used to offer me clothes at wholesale prices just like the other family members. Amazingly, I think looking back that I was the only 'goy', or non-Jew, with whom they associated so closely and, ironically enough, the only Palestinian they ever met.

On that afternoon when I went to see Patricia I had forgotten all about the mixed marriage incident at my home. As Patricia let me in, she put her fingers to her lips and, almost walking on tiptoe, ushered me into the kitchen, where everyone normally sat. But, whereas I was used on such occasions to a warm greeting from her mother followed at once by tea and a large plate of cakes, this time, there was no such welcome. I could see that I had intruded onto a tense family scene and I think I was there only because I was 'family' too. Patricia's mother was pacing the kitchen floor, wringing her hands and looking more round and plump than usual, while Patricia's elder sister, Claire, sat at the table her eyes cast down as if in shame.

'How could you do it to me? How?' wailed the mother. '*Oy, yoy, yoy*, what a problem, what a trouble!' I looked at Patricia, mystified, who did not look back. 'It's all your father's fault, of course. Take them to London, he said, they might meet nice Jewish boys there, which they're not going to do in Jersey. And I came, I believed him.' She was now tearful. 'And for this? Why couldn't we have stayed in Jersey, so quiet, no temptations?' She stopped by Claire's chair threateningly. 'Look up, look me in the face and tell me what I did wrong? Didn't I give you girls everything, clothes, food, time to see your friends while I slaved here? And me all alone, your father never home, too busy enjoying himself to worry.' She suddenly noticed me hovering just inside the room. 'Come and sit down, darling,' she said, 'I hope you're never going to be a trial to your mother, like her.' She jabbed an angry finger at Claire.

The latter spoke for the first time. 'It's not a crime, we've only been out a few times,' she murmured in a small voice. This invoked an instant redoubling of the mother's rage. 'So, this is supposed to make me happy?' she demanded. 'First, you go out, then he comes here, then I get used to the idea, then you speak to your father who's not here so he should worry, then you get married! Let me tell you, it's never going to happen.' To my surprise, Claire suddenly burst into tears. She was older than Patricia, and had always seemed to the two of us self-possessed, even hard. She was as dark as Patricia was fair – an endless source of innuendo in the family about the alleged role of the milkman – vivacious and attractive. She often talked down to Patricia and me as if we were annoying pests who should be invisible. To see her crying now was strangely upsetting.

'Yes, you should cry,' said her mother relentlessly, 'Just as you made me and your aunt Ruby cry. You better do a little thinking next time you want to go against your mother, your father, your whole family.' And, with that, her tough manner seemed to collapse and she also started to cry.

In the small pause that followed, Patricia signalled to me and we both quietly slipped out of the room. Upstairs, as we sat down on Patricia's bed, I could hardly wait to find out what the scene which we had just witnessed was about. 'What on earth?' I began. Patricia shushed me and went nervously to the door to make sure we were not overheard. She then came back to the bed, sat down and sighed.

'Well, you see, it's this English boy my sister's been going out with. I knew about it, but Claire never told anyone else. And then my dear mother had to go and find out, because she picked up the phone when they were talking this morning.'

'Well, so what,' I said, 'who cares? I mean why should it matter if she goes out with an English boy? And what's this about being English? I thought you were English?'

Patricia looked searchingly at me. 'We are English, but we're still Jewish,' she explained unhelpfully. 'Don't you know about being Jewish? You're not supposed to marry anyone who isn't Jewish as well. Even going out with anyone who isn't Jewish is bad, because you might get hooked on him and get married. That's why my mother's so upset and, as my dad isn't here, I think she's scared he's going to blame her for it.'

I stared at her in bafflement, memories of an earlier scene stirring in my mind. 'Do you mean to tell me that a Jewish girl like you, say, can't marry a non-Jewish man?'

'Of course not, silly', she said, 'and the other way around. Didn't you know that?' But I didn't, any more than I had known about the Muslim version of the same story.

'And what would happen if Claire went ahead and married her boyfriend just the same?' I asked.

'Well, I'm not sure,' said Patricia, 'I know it can be pretty nasty, like no one will speak to her or visit her. She won't be one of the family anymore.'

'What about if he converts, you know becomes Jewish? Is it all right then, can they get married?' I asked.

Patricia's brow puckered in thought. 'I don't think so,' she said uncertainly. 'My cousin Ruth's friend married a goy who converted. All I can tell you is that no one likes him and her family doesn't let him visit. She always goes on her own, and I don't think they're very happy.'

I looked at her. 'And what about you, are you going to accept it? Aren't you going to marry who you like?' To my dismay, Patricia hesitated. 'I don't know, maybe not.' And in answer to my shocked intake of breath, she said defensively, 'Well, it's not very nice, is it, to have your family throw you out and all your aunts and cousins never speaking to you again. How would you like it?'

Perhaps I wouldn't, I thought, but it was not that which bothered me at that moment. It was much more what I had heard in both houses, mine and Patricia's, which really confused me. The parallels were striking, the reactions disturbingly similar. And yet Palestinians and Jews were supposed to be formal enemies. To us, they should have been alien, another species, with other customs and other ways and feelings. But apparently they were not so different, at least in these respects. And my parents accepted without demur my friendship with Patricia and other Jewish girls like her.

They knew that I stayed with her family and they welcomed her into ours, although they themselves would no more have socialized with her parents than flown to the moon - a polite nod if they happened to come across one another in the shops was as far as either side was prepared to go. For them, the lines of demarcation were seemingly clear.

But for me at that time there was no such clarity. However it was that my parents explained away the paradox of their lives - refugees from Jewish persecution in Palestine, only to end up in the bosom of a Jewish community in London - I had no explanation for myself. I could only feel bewildered and uncertain about who I really was. I suppose, looking back, my valiant try at being English and thus belonging to neither camp was only paper-thin. I loved Patricia and her family and others of my Jewish friends and I wanted this to be a straightforward emotion, uncomplicated by a politics and a history which I neither knew nor understood.

But then I was only fourteen and did not realize that such simple aspirations were not for the likes of me. Although I scarcely felt it then, I was already marked by dispossession and exile and, like all Palestinians, would grow to live a life whose every parameter was defined by history and politics.

It was a problem whose complexities I would only understand years later. The subsequent history of my relationship with Patricia's family encapsulates its unique nuances. My friendship with her remained lifelong, despite two Arab-Israeli wars and my political activism, but not so her parents. These dear people who had known me throughout my childhood, had seen me through the break-up of my first marriage to an Englishman - 'Marry one of your own next time, my child,' had cautioned Patricia's mother to me sympathetically at the time, 'if only I could introduce you to a nice Jewish boy, I would' - and had always been glad to take me into their home; these same people ended up shunning and avoiding me, as if I had become their sworn enemy.

This happened during the 1970s when, following the spate of hijackings in Beirut, Palestinians began to be labeled everywhere as 'terrorists'. I resented this crude condemnation of a whole people and expressed my feelings vociferously. It never occurred to me at the time that what I took to be the self-evident truth of my cause and the legitimacy of my striving to express it could have borne any relation to the sensibilities of a little English/Rumanian Jewish family living in Golders Green. I saw them as wholly outside the framework of my conflict with Israel, which had never impinged on our friendship throughout my childhood. To me, they were human beings whom I liked and valued; I did not see them as a category to be defined according to my political predilections and then condemned. In the 1970s, my feelings for them were as warm as they had always been and so it was with surprise and pain that I noted their avoidance of me and their evident embarrassment if we ever happened to meet. It was finally Patricia who put me in the picture. To my anxious question about the meaning of their behaviour, she said placatingly, 'Look, they're both pretty old and pretty batty. Don't take any notice.'

'No, but there must be something, some reason,' I persisted.

She sighed. 'If you must know, they think you're going to go round the Underground, lobbing bombs at people. There, I told you it was silly.'

But 'silly' is not the word I would have used. I felt ineffably saddened by what she had told me and suddenly nostalgic for the way it had been between us during my childhood. I had no quarrel with Patricia's parents, nor they with me. It made no difference in the end. They never saw or spoke to me again until the end of their days. Patricia's father died first, and five years later his wife. I was not told of either funeral until the day had passed.

Autumn 2000

2

COMMUNITY

'A London Synagogue – the Feast of Tabernacles' rom the **Graphic** 2 November 1872 / *Spring 1990*

THE CURIOUSNESS OF ANGLO-JEWS
Frederic Raphael

'What curious attitudes he goes into!' 'Not at all', said the king. 'He's an Anglo-Saxon messenger and those are Anglo-Saxon attitudes. He only does them when he's happy.'

That quotation was used by Angus Wilson as an epigraph for his novel, *Anglo-Saxon Attitudes*. I trust that its pertinence to my theme will authorize its perversion: if for Anglo-Saxon you were to read 'Anglo-Jewish' throughout, you might, I think, agree that the curiousness of Anglo-Jews is hardly less remarkable than that of Anglo-Saxons. Very probably, it stems no less from their happiness.

If Anglo-Jewry has had its rough times, it has, on the whole, enjoyed a remarkably untroubled existence. Anglo-Jewish attitudes, however strange or maddening, are bound to have been influenced by the Anglo no less than the Jewish element in the environment.

I visited England first when I was about three years old. Unlike many, I did not cross the channel to get here: I crossed the Atlantic. I was, in almost all respects, a typical American child. When I looked at Harrods, I compared it unfavourably with Macy's. I was shocked and scornful at the lack of skyscrapers. I said bâth, not barth. My father was born in London and I was, in fact, of dual nationality. I was, however, certain that I would grow up in God's own country and that I should never take a barth in my life. The Raphaels, so my father said, were among the first families to return to England on Oliver Cromwell's invitation and it was appropriate that my English grandparents lived in Cromwell Road, even though the family appeared to have derived no large advantage from their early start. They had not acquired any choice properties or founded important banks or businesses. Their names appeared in the record of certain synagogues and can be deciphered in antique cemeteries, but only my great-uncle Jessel Benson was ever a manifest toff.

My grandfather worked for Raphael Tuck's, the Greetings Cards people. I had the childish illusion that the Raphael in the firm's name was a tribute to his participation, whereas in fact it was the Christian name, as it were, of the founder. In much the same way, I believed that the Renaissance painter was some distant relative, although his Raffaele was indeed literally a Christian name. Man cannot live by truth alone: we are supported, as we seek to secure ourselves against chance, by all sorts of comforting myths and reassuring illusions. Benjamin Disraeli, faced with the serried smugness of the English aristocracy, promoted the idea that the Jews, by virtue of their biblical provenance, belonged to a nobler house than any inhabited by the Earl of Derby or even by the Hanoverians themselves. The insolence of the arriviste's imposture was seconded by a wit that contrived to argue his case with ingenuity and, at the same time, conceded that he did not really believe that the Jew was a superior form of life. His path was made, if not smooth, certainly less bumpy by the great speech by Lord Macaulay in which the liberal historian called for the emancipation of English Jews, but Disraeli could not have made his primrose way to the seats of power had he not accepted formal baptism.

Benjamin's father, Isaac, was a distinguished *littérateur*, the author of Byron's favourite books. He was a collector of literary oddities, a connoisseur of human foibles, a man of eclectic tolerance, you might say, who found nothing human either alien or lacking in a certain absurdity. No one could accuse either Isaac or his son of turning his back on Jewishness; it does not seem to have occurred to them to change their proud name. But seeking admission to the Church of England was a necessary prelude to taking part in English social and political life and I doubt if the Disraelis felt much shame in the process. Isaac D'Israeli was a child of the Enlightenment; he admired Byron no less than his Lordship admired him. After Byron's death at Missolonghi, he gave employment to Tita, Byron's legendary gondolier, and in due course Benjamin found the genial and hirsute

Venetian a job in the public service and, eventually, a pension. It would have seemed ridiculous, I am sure, to someone of the Disraelis' background and culture, to allow allegiance to an outmoded cult to embargo a bright young man from access to fame and fortune in the modern world. English, indeed European, society in the nineteenth century appeared to be moving inexorably towards a homogenized political synthesis. Disraeli's rhetorical denunciation of 'The Two Nations' accorded very well with his own personal predilections.

I suspect that it was not until the mass immigration in the last decades of the nineteenth century that English Jews became generally aware of their foreign brothers or of the consequences which the Jewish condition elsewhere might have on their own prospects and attitudes. In this parochialism they had much in common with the British population at large: Englishmen, of whatever persuasion, have rarely been remarkable for their willingness to believe that they are as other men are. Pharisaism has long been an endemic condition in the sceptred isle; if the British loved the underdog, they were rarely slow to keep him under. Disraeli's imperialism, with all its affectations of principled guardianship, could be read as the ultimate attempt to achieve a kind of world-wide assimilation.

If the British could indeed command the seven seas and most of the continents and if only lesser breeds were to be 'without the law', in Kipling's cunning phrase, there would be no call or case or distinction on the grounds of race or religion: all men would be equal under the crown. Heaven on earth would be staffed by Anglo-Saxon angels. British dominion over palm and pine would revive, at least, the Roman model under which the Jew Paul of Tarsus could, without anomaly or foolishness, assert that he was a Roman citizen and entitled, like any other, to appeal to Caesar. There was nothing necessarily sly or ignoble in Disraeli's sentimental opportunism. He was not acting in his own or his racial brethren's partial interests: was it not good and fair that all men should be equal under the law and that the law should be, wherever possible, British?

Disraeli's brilliant success could hardly fail to excite and reassure British Jews, or to set a standard for them. Single-handed, he seemed to efface the darker pages of local history. I am not concerned here to rehearse tales of medieval outrage, but I should perhaps mention the case of Rodrigo Lopez, Queen Elizabeth I's doctor, whose terrible execution, on a trumped up charge of treason, is recounted with grisly relish by Lytton Strachey in his *Elizabeth and Essex*. Although Lopez had converted to Christianity, the rumours about him were believed not least because he was a Jew, as well as because he was a Spaniard. We have echoes in modern times where German Jews were regarded as Germans, although they were refugees, and their dubiousness was redoubled, rather than negated, by their Judaism. The Queen began by affirming her trust in Lopez, but she could not protect him. I shall spare you the details of his protracted agony, but the most poignant moment, for us, was his cry from the scaffold that he was 'as good a Christian' as any of those who gloated over his sufferings. There is small doubt that he was innocent, but Elizabeth could not save him from the mass psychosis which commanded her subjects. Lopez's naive notion that swearing his fidelity to Jesus could influence the mob can, of course, be made to endorse the arguments of those who claim that it is futile ever to seek to escape the allegiance - or the taint - of the blood. What was rare in England was a commonplace in Spain: the Inquisition was notoriously vigilant, not to say vindictive, in its examination of the genuineness of conversions from Judaism to Catholicism. It is a matter for deeper analysis to decide why Jews are so often suspected of dual loyalties, as if such things were not common in many ways in many societies.

The demand that a man decide absolutely and definitively where all his loyalties lie is both impertinent and crass. A Jew in Britain is no more obliged to put all his eggs in one basket than is any other citizen, though it is a choice he can elect to make. What some may see as a lack of commitment is surely more happily to be regarded as a liberal conscience. Disraeli's social strategy may have been a clever one - in that it integrated him with a society that he challenged to exclude him and also renovated the ethos of the Tory Party - but it was neither shabby nor dishonest. Religious partisanship cannot provide a basis for a just or democratic society; no theocratic enterprise can lead to the sort of world in which cultivated people would want to live. It is true that we cannot have the world we would choose, but that does not require us to choose a world that panders to narrow minds or subscribes to savage orthodoxies.

When I was seven years old, a New York kid who liked Eddie Cantor and Jack Benny and Jones's Beach, Buicks, Macy's, the Good Humour Man and the Empire State Building and who had heard, vaguely, of the German-American Bund and Father Coughlin, my British father - who wore seersucker suits and loved to dance in Harlem - was transferred by the Shell Oil Company to their London office. It was 1938. Our time in London was expected to be brief. My father's career was in the States and he was to be in England only to gain experience of the American department in London so that he could then take over a better job in New York. His temporary transfer may also have had something to do with the antisemitism which he had been encountering in Radio City.

I accepted the move without regret: life would presumably not change all that much. When we arrived in London, my parents avoided the obviously Jewish suburbs. We found a flat in Putney. My English grandmother was not happy: 'I should say Roehampton, if I were you', she said. My parents were not seeking to conceal their Jewishness, but they did not wish to immerse themselves in it either. We had lived on Central Park West in New York and we had many Jewish friends, but even in the States my parents, with a typically liberal attitude, avoided exclusiveness. We lived near the Spanish and Portuguese synagogue, but my only memory of it is of the day when I got frost-bite and clung to the railings to avoid being dragged away by the icy wind. In New York there were so many Jews that ostentatious pieties were an irrelevance. All the usual contradictions were in the melting pot: while my Lithuanian grandmother viewed all non-kosher food with disgusted suspicion, her husband - who had been born in Bad Kreuznach, near Munich - was not above a good old ham sandwich when we went to the ball game. My father still preferred cricket, though he was a considerable enthusiast for the American way of life. His accent and attitude, however accommodating, remained decidedly British. He had been to St Paul's and to St John's College, Oxford and such things mark a man, if he is lucky. Justifying what he could not alter, he elected to embrace rather than bemoan his posting to London. He did so in terms I shall never forget: 'Well, Freddie boy', he said, 'at least you'll now be able to grow up to be an English gentleman and not an American Jew.'

Is there something comically dated in his confidence? He genuinely believed in the values of the English gentleman - they are not, after all, evidently shameful - and he also believed, no less ardently, in a Jew's right to embrace them. He had seen American Jews, many of them apparently irretrievably foreign in language and manners, treated as second-class citizens, refused admission to clubs and restaurants and denied easy access either to power or to places of learning. The American Jew, in the 1930s, was uncertain of his title to citizenship: he was constantly menaced by the oafishness of the mob and the superciliousness of the nobs. It might be true that Jews were making a great impression in the arts and in political thought, in certain areas of manufacture and marketing, but they seemed fated to remain on the margin, like the metics of Periclean Athens, sharing in the prosperity and the glamour of a society where they could never quite be at home. My father's family was thoroughly at home in England, although some of them may have been more at home than others. He had been the first of the Raphaels to go to Oxford, but his father, Ellis, was a man of gentle dignity who played golf at Sudbury and whose appearance, in black coat, striped trousers and bowler hat, no more distinguished him from his SW7 neighbours than did his accent or his haircut. He belonged to a synagogue in Paddington and he had married a Jewess, but he would have been surprised and offended had anyone accused him of being anything but an ordinary Englishman, not that there was necessarily anything ordinary in that. He went to synagogue on High Days and Holy Days, but he did not, I think, refuse to eat bacon. My father did so, on one occasion at least.

In 1918 he was recruited into the army, being of the same age as the century, and was sent to camp on Wimbledon Common. The food was revolting and the breakfast involved sausages and bacon of a particularly unpalatable kind. My father could not stomach it and decided to mount his protest on religious grounds, since none other was likely to impress. His *démarche* resulted in his being served with a boiled egg, while the rest of the squad got the same old bacon. A mass conversion to Judaism seemed to be on the cards, but the entrance fee turned out to be unendurable for the company and he continued to eat his egg in solitary, Semitic privilege. Evidently it did not occur to my father to conceal his origins or to fail to take whatever petty but proper tactical advantage of them was available. I must confess that I should almost certainly not have had the nerve to do the same thing a generation later. Allowing for the probability that I lacked his boldness, I still think that it is fair to say that a Jew in England in 1918 was not the same article as a Jew in England in, say, 1948. In between came Hitler, Mosley and the British mandate in Palestine.

One of the happy oddities of Jewish history in England is that, while there have been scandals and atrocities, the English Jew cannot point to any signal act of injustice which supports a glum view of his prospects in this country. If there is anything in British attitudes to cause us disquiet it concerns, so far as I can see, foreign rather than domestic policy. We know, of course, that antisemitism has occasionally reached nasty proportions, but we have nothing here to compare with the Dreyfus case. That sense of scandal which drove the onetime assimilationist Herzl to conclude that Zionism was the only recourse could hardly have been kindled in England. Indeed, when Palmerston rattled his sabre on behalf of Don Pacifico, a Greek Jew who had been ill-used and who just happened to be a British subject, he served notice that the meanest Brit might expect support from the heaviest artillery Her Majesty's government could mount. Palmerston's motives may have been cynical or vainglorious, but he made it conspicuously obvious that no Briton was to be abused by foreigners, however foreign his own provenance.

On the other hand, Jewish life in France has been profoundly, and ineradicably, marked by the Dreyfus case. Indeed, the egregious connivance of Pétain and Laval with the architects of the Final Solution can be seen as the revenge of the anti-Dreyfusards. Dreyfus' corrupt condemnation polarized French society in a way from which it has scarcely recovered today. The Jews, who had once declared themselves '*heureux comme Dieu en France*' were alerted to the fear and revulsion with which they could be regarded by those with whom Napoleon's emancipation had supposedly made them one. Recent studies suggest that even at the highest levels, where French Jews seem wholly at home in the machinery of Gallic intellectual and economic life, a sense of apprehension and alienation persists. The final irony is that the French Jews might have fared better had the unfortunate Captain Dreyfus indeed been a spy. From a mythical point of view, he is a scapegoat who failed: the guilt he might have taken with him to Devil's Island has, however grotesquely, remained to fester and pollute those who were courageous enough to secure his vindication.

In England, there is nothing comparable. Instead, we have a comedy. The Marconi case is the obverse of the Dreyfus affair. Rufus Isaacs was accused, among others, of having used inside information to enrich himself by the purchase of Marconi shares. The most distinguished Jewish lawyer of his day was saved from disgrace by somewhat disgraceful means. He told the House of Commons that it was not true that he had used his position to buy shares in the British Marconi company at a nice price. His assurances were accepted and his career took him on to the heights: he became both Lord Chief Justice and Viceroy in India. But if his assurances were indeed true, they were only just true: the shares he and his colleagues had chosen to buy were in the *American* Marconi company. A sharepusher with a phoney prospectus could scarcely hope to get away with it on a finer point of law. It is a sorry but comfortable irony that the French attitude to Jews has been more poisonously influenced by the conviction of an innocent man than have British attitudes by the acquittal of a guilty one. However, it would be rather too blithe to claim that the accusations of sharp practice leveled against 'international financiers' by Oswald Mosley and his fellow-ranters were not primed, and to some degree justified, by the behaviour of Rufus Isaacs and his colleagues in Lloyd George's government.

The high comedy of Rufus Isaacs was repeated, as low farce, in the case of Sydney Stanley, in the 1940s. Those who were not alive, or adult, at the time will probably not even remember that lively little item of English social history. Sydney Stanley – a stateless person – was paraded as the man who corrupted honest politicians and received favours in return for whisky and clothing coupons and cigars. He did little that is not now a commonplace of business entertaining, but he signalled the re-emergence of the despicable Yid as a figure in the post-war bestiary. It was lucky, perhaps, that he was also a comedian of rare talents whose replies before Mr Justice Lynsky's tribunal almost made a fool of Sir Hartley Shawcross, one of the most deadly cross-examiners at the bar. Nevertheless, Stanley's banal machinations embarrassed a Jewish community for which, despite the Holocaust, and Britain's manifest failure to prevent or inhibit it, the gentile population felt scant sympathy. The conflict in Palestine caused a cleavage inside the Jewish community and between the Jews and their neighbours of a kind that had rarely existed before. Until very recently, when religious and racial fundamentalism once more became respectable, if not *de rigueur*, it was more or less assumed that one did one's best to become assimilated to the dominant culture and ethos. The ultimate tribute to that ethos was, of course, apostasy. My American mother will never forget how my great-aunt Minnie, who had violet eyes that glowed in the dark, and a voice deeper than the basement, once told her that there was no such thing as a Jewish lady. 'But you're a lady, Minnie,' retorted my innocent parent. 'I was never a lady, Irene', boomed my great-aunt, 'until I became a Christian.'

The English side of my family was riven with extravagant prejudices of all kinds; antisemitism was only one among many. My grandmother disliked Russians and Americans with equal venom. She did not think much of the working class either, nor yet of the medical profession which insisted that her heart condition was not terminal and was probably indigestion. She did manage to die of a heart attack eventually, but she waited till she was eighty-seven. Her antisemitism was not quite as aggressive as her sister Minnie's but they and their handsome third sister, Rosie, formed a trio of Graces whose pleasure it was in their youth, and beauty, to sit in the lobby of the Grand Hotel, Eastbourne, and scan the incoming faces with searching malice. Should Minnie spot a Hebraic countenance, she was in the habit of hissing, in a carrying whisper, the one word 'Fish!', their easily-broken codeword for Jew.

My grandmother's long-serving maid, Winifred, whose last name was, by pure coincidence, Stanley, though she was no relation of the infamous Sydney, was a subscriber to *The Watchtower*, but she never failed to remind certain members of the family of their pious obligations by sending them Jewish New Year cards. Minnie, an intimidating character, was exempt from these promptings, but Winifred considered it her Christian duty to keep the rest of us up to the mark right until her ninetieth birthday. I suspect that she favoured only the males of the family with her promptings, perhaps because she had a feeling that only those of the male sex were really Jews, an unspoken, perhaps unconscious tribute to the hold that circumcision has on the gentile imagination. Although Winifred, who had much in common with Proust's legendary servant-figure Françoise, insisted on wishing a different New Year on us, she did not, I am sure, doubt the family's claim to be thoroughly English.

Certainly my father would have been infuriated by any allegations of foreignness of any kind, even spiritual. Assimilation did not stand in the way of antique pieties, but nor did the latter in the way of assimilation. Zionism was unappealing to him in his youth and irrelevant in maturity. If he admired the State of Israel when it came into being, he would never, I am sure, have dreamed of living there. It was a refuge for the unfortunate, not a haven for everyone. I am bound to say that the excessively fervent Zionism and Israeli patriotism of some English Jews sometimes strikes me much as it would have struck him; the lack of wholehearted belligerence in the Anglo-Jewish attitude may not satisfy the militants but it is not necessarily evidence of a faint heart or an empty head.

My father never complained of being Jewish and he would never have stooped to concealment, but his friends were often gentiles (he would never have used the vulgarism goyim to refer to them, even behind their backs) and he was wholly at home in the land of his birth. Yet he was often aware of antisemitism and sometimes shared the apprehensions of the Jewish Board of Guardians that improper behaviour by newcomers might test the tolerance of the British. He winced at queue-bargers or black-marketeers for the same reasons that he never failed to stand a round of drinks or to pay his debts promptly. He was a good loser and a genial winner. Courteous to women and correct with men, he never waved his hands or raised his voice. He endured pain with a stiff upper lip, and he knew a great deal of pain, and he believed that it was best to make light of things. If he told a joke, he never laughed at it; if you told one, he would certainly smile, even if he had heard it before. He may have been disgusted that even here there were golf clubs where he could not be a member, but he would not dream of seeking to impose himself on company which did not welcome him. He never thought England a perfect place, but if he criticized it, as any Englishman might, he took it to be as decent and just a society as one might hope to find. In the event, he never returned to America to live and I do not think that he regretted it. He liked the good manners of the British, in the days when they had good manners, and he assumed that those of his own middle class were men whose word was their bond. The way in which he respected the religion of his fathers was of a piece with the conventional decency with which he tipped his hat when he passed the cenotaph or listened to the Queen's speech or had a bet on Derby Day. It was not a matter of earnest belief or deep feeling but of rectitude and decent habit.

He had been a World Champion Ballroom Dancer in his youth and he carried himself with the aloof modesty of someone who had once been the best there was. He never alluded to his triumphs, just as he sought to keep quiet about his disappointments. He liked to think that he exemplified the Greek ideal, of Nothing In Excess. It is not, I should like to believe, a disreputable ambition. I am tolerably certain that he was indeed what he thought he was, an English gentleman who happened to be Jewish.

Not everyone in our family considered it possible to reconcile Jewishness with gentility. A young man wrote to me not long ago claiming cousinage. We had, he told me, the same great-grandparents. He was, and is, the grandson of my very rich great-uncle, Frederick Jessel Benson, after whom my father named me, hopefully, not that it ever did me much good. Young Roderick, whom I have since met, had already come down from Oxford before he had any idea that there was, as one of his female cousins put it, a 'skeleton in the family cupboard'. Although Jessel actually died on the Day of Atonement, after returning from synagogue, his descendants had worked with furious ingenuity in the effort to conceal all traces of their Jewish connections. Typically enough, they became sneering antisemites and inveterate snobs: Jessel's widow went to live in Monte Carlo and relished the Proustian acquaintance of dethroned royalties. The reasons for her recoil from Judaism are inaccessible to me, but they seem to have held good for her daughters and that whole side of the family. It is interesting to observe that young Roderick, whose researches into the whole background have already turned up some choice items, is delighted by the discovery of his Semitic genes, and genesis. It is for him to analyse in depth what it means for a routine Englishman, whatever that means, to discover that he is a Jew, whatever that means. What it means will depend, I suppose, on what he makes of it, or it of him, in an intellectual or social or religious sense.

Jewishness, George Steiner has observed, is 'a club from which, in the twentieth century, there can be no resignations'. This is perhaps a more British observation than one might expect from Steiner, for it suggests that it is a matter more of honour than of racial allegiance or religious commitment. To be a Jew is, I think, to accept, in the existential sense, the absurdity of the human predicament rather than to rally to a demanding series of rituals or to the chauvinistic vanity of Zionist fundamentalism. I concede that this is probably an Anglo-Jewish attitude but then, for all my American birth and childhood, I have to admit that it is with difficulty that the apple falls far from the tree.

Autumn/Winter 1983-4

THE ENGLISH COUNTRY COTTAGE
Ruth Fainlight

A Jewish poet in an English village:
incongruous and inappropriate
as a Hindu in an igloo, a Dayak in
Chicago, a giraffe at the South Pole.

That shadowy yew in the churchyard, only
a few steps away from this cottage door,
was planted in the centuries between
the Lincoln pogrom (when little St. Hugh,
they claimed, was murdered by the Jews, and all
Christ-killers left alive were banished)
and the year when Oliver Cromwell changed the law
to grant honourable men of Israelite persuasion,
with their prudent wives and obedient children,
the privilege to be legally present in England.

As a youth, my father was a patriot,
a Labour-voting true blue. But though
he felt entirely English, the problem was:
to certain natives of whatever class
he was a wily, greasy Levantine
and always would be. His solution was
to leave the country, go far enough away
to `pass for white`, somewhere he could play
at being pukka-English through and through.
(Yet still more proud to be a Jew.)

Maybe because she came from Bukovina,
my mother had no illusions. She was used to
rejection, born to it. First, the shock
of Ellis Island: another world, another
language (I knew how hard she tried). Then
further uprooting; though the nineteen thirties
were not exactly propitious, her restless husband
— handsome, dreamy, unpolitical —
felt the lure of home, dragged her to England.

I ran straight into the fire`s centre,
towards the focus of trouble, glamour, danger;
danced, like Esmeralda, on the Round Table
as desperately as if to save my life.
Such were my tactics in those distant times.
Now (though mimicking the locals dutifully),
thatch and cruck-beams cannot camouflage
the alien. The carillon rings mockery.

Sometimes I wonder if I should have known better:
to sweetly smile and eat the mess
of pottage – but never sell my birthright
for an English country cottage.

Spring 2000

CHAIM SUPERMAN ENCOUNTERS
A JEWISH INTELLECTUAL
Barnet Litvinoff

★ *Chaim Superman had been pressed for an article for the first issue of* Words Within Worlds, *a publication intended to cater for the interests of Higher Brows in the Constellation of Neptune. He consented to do so with the stipulation that he would retain copyright and suffer no editorial censorship. He also asked that his fee be sent as a donation to the Asimov Hostel for Single Parent Families in the neighbourhood complex of the Milky Way. We are privileged to reproduce the article by arrangement, with the usual acknowledgements-Ed.*

During my time on Earth I was always rather proud of our Jewish intelligentsia, declared Chaim Superman (who in his previous existence resided in the Hampstead Garden Suburb district of London, and now dwells in Outer Space on the Fifteenth Horizon). We were especially favoured in having so many outstanding minds in our community. This accounted for our concentration on the things of the spirit, and the high standard of our communal newspapers.

We also had a little parliament of our own in Great Britain, called the Board of Deputies of British Jews, and its tone of debate was so elevated it could put the House of Commons to shame by comparison. Of course, some of our intellectuals were members of the House of Commons too, and when they spoke you could immediately detect the change of mood there. Sometimes Mrs Thatcher was so impressed with their arguments that she was lost for words.

The Jewish intellectuals to whom I refer were usually born, like myself, in dire poverty in the slums of the East End of London. However, this is where the similarity ends. I wasted my young years chasing girls over the bandstand at Shoreditch Buildings, and playing pitch and toss for pennies in the side streets, or sneaking off on Saturday afternoons to watch the Spurs. Not our young intellectuals. They were preparing themselves to be leading intellectuals, and were already writing their avant-garde poetry and solving intricate problems of mathematics in the Reference Room of the Whitechapel Public Library. They won scholarships to Oxford and Cambridge by the time they were fifteen, and collected Nobel Prizes in all subjects on offer.

Some of them became the great intellectuals of the Conservative Party where, provided you knew your place, it was no great disadvantage to bear a physical resemblance to Trotsky. Others gave Labour the benefit of their abilities, but these mostly came to England from the Continent after Hitler had decided they were surplus to requirements, and they had strong Hungarian accents. One thing none of them forgot, and that was to visit their old mothers still living in the East End, to whom they brought autographed copies of their newspaper articles, translated if necessary into Yiddish.

Switch on the BBC Third Programme and sure enough you would hear our intellectuals speaking on a host of different abstruse subjects, the Dual Image in Karl Marx, say, or the Twilight of American Society. When they delivered a lecture on the transition to feudalism in Merovingian Gaul it was as though they had been there in medieval France when the excitement began. I used to be amazed at the way they could ring the changes. One day it was an analysis of Dublin's Jewish problem as illustrated in the *Ulysses* of James Joyce, the next it was a discussion on class divisions

★ *By authorization, I have in various places toned down the more colourful language, inappropriate to a Jewish publication, employed by the intellectual − C. Superman.*

among the Kirghis tribes. Where did they find the time to do all that research!

What was specially gratifying for us was the appearance of Visiting Jewish Intellectuals from France or America or Israel on our TV programmes, when they had a book to sell. This happened if a non-Jewish intellectual could be found with an equally great mind, for example Terry Wogan, to interview them. All this was very good public relations for my people, I might say. It took the attention of the Press for a moment off our property developers, and that anti-Israel propaganda that actually suggested the Arabs had a case.

Now I have never shied away from a good read. I had seen the articles in the *Jewish Chronicle* and that very superior magazine *Commentary* (my wife Betty made me a gift subscription for my seventy-fifth birthday, which entitled me also to attend three lectures free if I happened to be anywhere in the neighbourhood of the Jewish Theological Seminary of New York), so it was no news to me that the intellectual was much concerned with his Identity.

Questions of identity loomed very large with our Jewish writers, and they could be most informative about it. As I understand it, they felt a heavy responsibility to their people because, through an accident of birth, they had escaped the Nazi Holocaust in Europe. They intended to do something about this, perhaps write a great Holocaust Novel if they could get a decent grant from a rich foundation.

Our intellectuals were above all humanitarians. I am very proud to inform you that they never failed to make a point of this. Humanitarianism was good for Jews. Apartheid in South Africa troubled them no end (though not so much if they happened to live in Johannesburg). They could not bear the thought of oppression, no matter how far away it occurred. They were always generous in allowing their names to be used in letters for publication in *The Times* about the way the Soviet Union was treating those of its citizens who had themselves discovered their identity and wanted to get to America, which is a very free country as far as identity is concerned, particularly for the intellectuals.

Well, I never had an opportunity to meet a Jewish intellectual down below. Our paths didn't cross - not socially at any rate. We sometimes invited one of them to speak on the subject of his identity at the annual Brains Trust concerned with 'Jewish Culture, What Now?' held by the Garment Manufacturers (Wholesale and Export) Lodge of the B'nai B'rith, and I had a few signed copies of books by Jewish intellectuals on the top shelf of my walnut book-case. So when I was invited to meet some Jewish Super-intellectuals at an Inter-Galactic Reception on the Fifteenth Horizon to mark the publication in satellite-recorded English translation of a small anthology by a group of young Hebrew poets - it was called *Towards New Concepts of Jewish Identity* - I leapt at the chance. I had in fact paid for the translation, which was why I was invited to the Reception.

One of the intellectuals was jostled into a corner of the bar, so I thought it would be interesting to engage him in discussion and obtain some insight into his attitude to his identity. He very graciously agreed to do this on the record, and for publication. I promised him a dozen copies for his files. Here is our discussion verbatim, polished up for your easier comprehension.

Chaim: Will you, as a Jewish intellectual, give me your views on the restoration of our nationhood, after many centuries of dispersion, in the reborn State of Israel?

Intellectual: I have strong views on this. I believe Israel is the most significant event to have occurred in Jewish history for two thousand years. They have devised a new, humanitarian form of society over there. It is called a kibbutz, and is based upon self-labour, self-help, strict equality in the distribution of razor-blades, and the brotherhood of man - woman too. Most people in the kibbutz double in two jobs. The first is tilling the land, the second is working for the Secret Services of the Free World. So while they make the desert blossom with one hand, as it were, with the other they are protecting humanity from a neo-Nazi plot to dominate the earth, or tracking down some nut with a plan to blow everyone up with a nuclear bomb. I have in fact read a book or two about these exploits.

Chaim: So have I. Nine of them made the list of top ten paperbacks in 1980.

Intellectual: Right on! The Israelis alone live a truly free and uninhibited Jewish life. They're not afraid of antisemitism over there, you know. No-one gets persecuted, not even the crooks and black marketeers. That's because Israel is the only real democracy in the Middle East. All the countries around there are one-party states. But I would challenge any contention that Israel is a one-party state. Why, at the last count there were seventy-six.

Chaim: Yes. You are evidently not counting the various sub-parties within each party. I am very gratified that you think this way.

Intellectual: Another thing. I envy the Israeli intellectual because he has been able to come to terms with his identity. Yes, I love Israel.

Chaim: They must be greatly encouraged over there for your support. With such admiration for the young state did you never have the urge to go and live there?

Intellectual: Funny you should ask, because that was always my intention. But in my younger days all my energies were concentrated on my literary work, and I could never have found time or strength for the task of reclaiming the soil, which of course had been neglected by the Arabs for centuries. It was, I suppose, a feeling of inadequacy, that I was not good enough for Israel. Then I became busy bringing up a family, and organizing my Zionist lecture tours in America and other countries where the Jews lived oppressed existences and had plenty of money. My spare time was spent meeting other intellectuals at seminars, and in giving talks about the East End to people living in the West End, which required considerable research.

I think I can say I did my bit, as you will see from my plays and novels. I placed the Jews in a very favourable light, showing that we had a wonderful sense of humour in the midst of our sufferings and persecutions. If I included a bent Jewish character in one of my stories, I always took care to include a bent gentile character also, to correct the balance. Even when I grew older, and more successful, and had less trouble organizing my grants from the Arts Council, and made sure my children got into decent universities - not those dumps like Newcastle and the College of the Distributive Trades - I continued to support Israel with all the talents at my disposal. Am I talking too much?

Chaim: Not at all. I presume you visited Israel frequently, to maintain contact with the intellectuals living their free Jewish life in Tel Aviv and Jerusalem?

Intellectual: As a matter of fact, no. I was asked several times, but mostly the invitations seemed to clash with other invitations to visit China, and Cuba, and Hungary, and the Edinburgh Festival. There was one occasion when I was able to accept. This was arranged by the Western Hemisphere Division of the Jewish Agency's Absorption Department's Office of Inter-Cultural Relations, which was run by a small staff of sixteen led by my friend General Shimon 'Two-gun' Tinpotsky, hero of the Six Day War. Unfortunately a small technical problem came up as far as I was concerned, and I'm sorry to say Shimon proved most uncooperative.

Chaim: What was this technical problem?

Intellectual: They wouldn't pay the travel expenses of my wife and three children! My family was due for a holiday and the kids were really looking forward to it, it was pitiful to disappoint them. But I wasn't going to spend my own money to bring them to Israel.

Chaim: As a successful Jewish intellectual you could have afforded it, I suppose?

Intellectual: I'm not saying yes, I'm not saying no. But that's beside the point. I was concerned with the principle of the thing. There are, after all, so many demands on an intellectual's time. It's unreasonable to expect us to be out of pocket just because we have a crucial role to play in cultural life. When these gentile intellectuals are invited to Israel they are treated like lords, though they spend most of their time boozing at the Hilton at public expense. I'm not in the habit of running around looking for freebies, but why should I be discriminated against just because I happen to be of Jewish origin? None of my children drank anything but fruit juice, which I understand flows through the irrigation pipes.

Chaim: But Israel is a poor country, isn't it? What with its heavy arms expenditure, all those new immigrants to be absorbed, reclaiming the desert and sending goodwill delegations round the world, there's not very much left over.

Intellectual: Is that my concern? Up here in the Mega-System I'm constantly bumping into types who went to Israel bukshee: rabbis, bishops, Labour Peers of the Realm, Conservative Peers of the Realm, Independent Peers of the Realm, Friends of Israel, Enemies of Israel, Musicians for a New Israeli Music, sociologists to investigate the mystery of why the Arabs don't like the Jews. Don't tell me they didn't take their families along. It's aggravating! Let's change the subject.

Chaim: I recall from your terrestrial writings and speeches that you have a profound admiration for our culture.

Intellectual: No doubt about that. Culture has been the Jews' consolation and strength in all times of adversity. It sustained them in their wanderings, and enabled them to survive as a humanitarian people. And that's what culture is really about, not the bourgeois stuff passed round with the port by those pee aitch dees. Why, a Jew would go without food in the old ghetto to give his children culture. I'll send you a xerox of the article I wrote on that subject for the *New Statesman*.

Chaim: In what form might it be said that you yourself cherished this culture? You must have a profound understanding of the Hebrew language.

Intellectual: Well, I learned a little as a kid, but have forgotten it.

Chaim: You are familiar with the Hebrew masterpieces in translation, then?

Intellectual: Is that the stuff they drummed into me for my bar mitzvah?

Chaim: You doubtless took care that your children grew up with a thorough grounding in the classical writings of their people, so as to safeguard the Jewish heritage for future generations?

Intellectual: My wife used to take them to Hebrew classes at the synagogue Sunday school near where we lived. The rabbi didn't make too much fuss that I never joined his synagogue. He was glad to get the children of a big name like me, and I offered to open their Jewish Book Week with a major keynote speech.

Chaim: You spoke earlier of your concern for your children's education, so I am sure it was a first-class Hebrew school, or you wouldn't have sent them there.

Intellectual: I will say this for it, it was handy; a convenient place to leave the kids on Sunday mornings when we like to take a walk over Hampstead Heath and meet our friends for a drink at the Bull and Bush.

Chaim: There can be no question but they received a fundamental Jewish education at that Sunday school, to prevent their alienation from the cultural tradition of their people.

Intellectual: Do you think so? I couldn't judge, and I never asked. As a matter of fact they didn't stick it out for too long. I could understand that, for they had lots of homework from their proper schools, and they were entitled to a lie-in on Sundays.

Chaim: But it was considerate of you to provide for their schooling nearby, to spare them a tiring journey every day.

Intellectual: What makes you say that? I used a bit of influence to get the girls into this exclusive place specializing in art appreciation, which I was keen on, on the other side of London. Our son went to Westminster, as a day boy of course. My strong Jewish family instinct wouldn't allow me to enter him as a boarder, and my wife liked the idea of his being seen round the neighbourhood in his topper. But it's true they were never tired out by long arduous journeys on the bus, because I spent my mornings for years taking them in the Volvo. This meant they were quite fresh starting the day. My boy would never have got into Oxford otherwise. Nothing like a bit of class in education.

Chaim: Then may I ask a more personal question? It concerns the Talmud, which I am sure you will agree is one of the world's great works of literature and ethical teaching, and after the Bible our most precious inheritance. Which portions of the Talmud have you found most relevant to yourself as a Jewish intellectual?

Intellectual: Pardon?

Chaim: Which Tractate of the Talmud has most inspired you in your work, and determined your moral path?

Intellectual: What's a Tractate? I told you I have forgotten all the Hebrew I ever learnt.

Chaim: But it's translated into English!

Intellectual: How was I to know that?

Chaim: You mean you haven't read any part of this masterpiece? After all, it embraces lore and history and the wisdom of our forefathers, and guides our conduct towards our fellow-men.

Intellectual: Do you mind! I've read the whole of Proust, naturally, and in the original. I have made a detailed study of the literature of Greece and Rome. I'm familiar with Tolstoy, Turgenev and Dostoevsky, Shakespeare, Milton, T. S. Eliot, Spike Milligan, Goethe, Schiller, Saul Bellow, Philip Roth, Kierkegaard, Harold Pinter, Jacques Maritain, Freud, Marx, Damon Runyon, the Bloomsbury Group . . .

Chaim: But not one word of the Talmud?

Intellectual: I happen to be a busy creative artist. Isn't that stuff for those characters with curly sidelocks and fur hats?

Chaim: You have no religion, then?

Intellectual: I never said that, did I? I have great respect for the Jewish religion. It's a complete way of life. I went to synagogue once, when my young brother got married. And when my dear mother, bless her memory, died, I said the Kaddish. A rabbi wrote it out for me phonetically in English.

Chaim: It's a very moving prayer, isn't it?

Intellectual: Is it? The rabbi never translated it for me.

Chaim: So you have no interest in your religion otherwise than at a funeral?

Intellectual: A man's personal beliefs are a matter for his conscience. I won't answer that one.

Chaim: Of course. Please forgive me.

Intellectual: Look here, I've never created a degenerate, lecherous Jewish character in any of my novels, like Roth and Heller. My Jews are well-read, well-behaved, innocent victims of antisemitism, and hardly ever rich. Some of them actually work for a living. I'm interested in good race relations, as you will see from my short story about the Black tennis-player whose girlfriend's father became leader of the National Front. It won an award from the Wolfson Foundation, and Woody Allen bought the film rights. Isn't that enough?

Chaim: May we now talk about your interest in the affairs of our community?

Intellectual: I've never in my life denied I was a Jew. The reason I changed my name was because I didn't want to be typecast as a Jewish writer, but as a writer who happened to be a Jew. When Pinter went to cocktail parties people didn't point at him and whisper 'There goes that Jewish writer Pinter,' but 'there goes that humanitarian writer Pinter.' He got away with it, so why shouldn't I? Look what happened to Dylan Thomas, playing the Taffy around the Camden Town pubs. I felt sorry for Dylan, always required to rake up that Swansea crap. After all, my publisher wanted my books to sell.

Chaim: I am referring to the contribution you made to our rich communal life on Earth. Youth work, helping the Jewish aged, committees in support of Israel, the struggle against discrimination. Perhaps you were a member of the Intellectuals' Lodge of B'nai B'rith. Were you active in our famous communal parliament, the Board of Deputies of British Jews?

Intellectual: Is that what it's called? I thought it was the Board of British Janners. One of that family invited me to a lunch once, of the Intellectuals Against Ken Livingstone Committee. I didn't join.

Chaim: But you are surely against intolerance?

Intellectual: When I saw the kind of mob gathered there I preferred Livingstone to the intellectuals. And the grub was pretty monotonous, that kosher spaghetti Bolognese washed down with half a glass of Carmel Passover wine. Not like the hospitality accorded us writers and artists at the lunch table of *Punch*.

This terminated our discussion. I felt that the insight I had gained into the mind and heart of this Super-intellectual should help my readers to understand the soul-searching, the loneliness, the restless quest for truth, that will ever be the lot of those who must obey the commands of the spirit. And when they are Jews, only more so. There's no intellectual like a Jewish intellectual.

Autumn 1985

THE YOM KIPPUR SWIMMING GALA
Alexander Flinder

Soho's Berwick Street market has changed very little from when I first knew it in the 1930s. Still the familiar smells and sounds, the cockney banter of the market people and the stalls terraced high with fruit and vegetables. The market has changed little and so, for that matter, has my old school just around the corner. Walk to the top of the market, step between the piles of discarded fruit boxes, turn right into Peter Street and there it still stands, brick-built, solid, typical of the elementary school of its time and seemingly indestructible. Nowadays it houses the Westminster College of Modern Languages, but I knew it as the Pulteney School, a name of which the Headmaster of the Boys School was immensely proud.

J. C. Whitebrook instilled this pride in his boys, a pride exemplified in the school song:

We are some of the Pulteney boys,
We are some of the boys,
We know our manners;
We spend our tanners,
We are respected wherever we go.

Author anonymous; cockney certainly, but with something I think you will agree of a Jewish flavour. It follows because 95 per cent of the boys of the Pulteney were Jewish. With St Anne's, St Peter's and the Pulteney to choose from, most of Soho's Jewish parents seemed to opt for the school without any obvious religious affiliation.

It also so happened that, with the exception of Bunky Stear and Nobby Clark, the School's swimming team was wholly Jewish. A trivial statistic were it not the basis of my story.

You see, J. C. Whitebrook was passionately fond of swimming. He pursued its promotion with an almost evangelistic fervour. He would often declaim, 'It is my purpose that no boy shall leave the Pulteney without having achieved some competence in swimming, and desirably a knowledge of life saving, and the Schaefer Method of resuscitation and respiration'.

This passion did not always go over well with the parents: 'What sort of *meshuggas is* this? My boy is going to be a tailor, not a sailor.' And you can imagine the average Jewish mother's neurosis about wet heads in the middle of the winter. None the less it was tolerated for, as my own mother put it with a sigh and a shrug of the shoulders: 'Well, what can you do? Mr Whitebrook is a very good man, and if it means so much to him?'

We were approaching the summer holidays and the Head brought the swimming team together to give us the details of the Westminster School's Swimming Association Championships which were to be held in the month of September following our return. 'Now boys,' said the Head, 'I want you to train very hard when you are away, we have an excellent team, our best ever in fact. I believe that at the Championships Gala we stand a very good chance of achieving something that we have never done before, that is, to beat our arch rivals Buckingham Gate Central in the overall Championship.' He then went on to give us the dates of the heats and the Final Gala and asked whether there were any questions. There were none. And the class was about to be dismissed when a voice came from the back of the class; it was my friend Gordon Yospa. 'Please, Sir.' 'Yes, what is it, Yospa?' 'Please, Sir, we can't.' 'We can't?' repeated the Head, 'what do you mean 'we can't'?' 'Please, Sir, we can't, it's Yom Yippur, the Day of Atonement, Sir, it says so in my diary, Sir.'

There was a moment of stunned silence, broken by a gulped '*oy vey*' from Sidney Koss. 'Blimey,' gasped Bunky to Dusty, 'they can't swim on that day, it's their Black Fast and they'll be in their church all day.' 'Are you sure?' said the Head. 'Yes Sir, when our *cheder* teacher gave us the date I put it in my diary, here Sir, look.' The Head took Gordon's diary and his expression confirmed the worst. 'This is outrageous, how could they?' 'They' presumably being the officials of the Swimming Association. 'I must look into this straightaway; dismiss boys and I shall call you together again when I have investigated this.'

For the next two days we hardly saw the Head; even his set classes were taken by other teachers. Rumour had it that he was out seeing different people; we didn't know what to make of it all and our buoyancy of a few days earlier developed into a deep gloom. At last we were called together, this time to the Head's study. You were only summoned to the study for the most serious of admonishments or for the imparting of serious confidentiality. The Head sensed our glumness. 'Sit yourselves on the floor, lads.' The term 'lads' was used when the Head was at his most friendly: 'Cheer up, lads, I think we may have found a solution.'

'Now listen carefully,' he continued, 'and I shall tell you what I have been up to. First of all, the Swimming Association Officials have expressed their apologies, it was a genuine mistake. Unfortunately the date of the Finals cannot be moved, but all is not lost. I have consulted with my good friend the Reverend Amias of your synagogue in Manette Street, and he took me to see your Rabbi Ferber with whom I have had a long discussion.

'Now I understand that your Yom Kippur service ends at 7.15 pm. Well, the Gala officials have offered to delay the commencement of the races until 8 pm. As a result of my discussion with

Reverend Amias and Rabbi Ferber who, I must say, have been extremely understanding, they have advised me that there is no religious reason why you cannot take part in the competition once the Day of Atonement terminates. However, they pointed out to me that many of you will have fasted for twenty-four hours and it is customary to return home after the service to a feast. Therefore the understanding and co-operation of your parents is essential. I shall therefore approach all your parents and Reverend Amias and Rabbi Ferber have allowed me to say that I have their support in what I propose.

'My plan is this: you will leave your synagogue promptly at the termination of the service and make your way to the Haymarket where I shall have two taxis waiting for you outside the Theatre Royal. Mr Fitch and I shall be there with some light refreshments, not too much, mind you, as you will be racing shortly afterwards. We will then proceed to Great Smith Street Baths in time for the first race at 8 pm.' The negotiations with our parents were not easy, but what finally did the trick of course was Rabbi Ferber's advocacy.

So that is how I came to be sitting in the West End Talmud Torah Synagogue in Manette Street on Yom Yippur with my *tallis* on my shoulders and my swimming costume in my *tallis* bag. Nearby sat Gordon Yospa, Alfie Strohlitz was on the other side together with the Feldman twins, Lou Walters and the Goldshaker brothers. Around the corner in Soho Square was the Beth Ha'Safeh Synagogue with some of our chaps and there were others in the two synagogues in Alfred Place, the Western and, next door in the West Central Girls Club, the Liberal Synagogue. Sidney Koss had to come from the big synagogue in Great Portland Street.

The last *shofar* blast was as a shot of a starting pistol, and we were halfway down the rickety wooden staircase with the *shofar* still reverberating in our ears. Tumbling into the street we charged down Greek Street just behind Solly Goldshaker who had forgotten to take off his *tallis* which streamed behind him like an exotic scarf. Trying to slalom through a group of prostitutes standing on their regular pitch on the corner of Old Compton Street, Solly charges head first into one of them who collapses on top of him, fox furs and all. Her companions come to her rescue with flailing handbags and Gordon and I dive into the melée to extract our best junior free stylist in one piece. We escape down the road followed by the lingering scent of perfume and face powder and English curses that we understand well and French curses that we can't.

Up Shaftesbury Avenue, short cut by the Trocadero, over Coventry Street and down the Haymarket where the taxis are waiting by the Theatre. Funny how I can still recall that the play advertised on its hoarding was *The Ten Minute Alibi*. 'Well done, lads,' said the Head as each breathless competitor arrived to be presented with a packet of crisps, an apple and a bar of Nestlés milk chocolate. Arriving at Great Smith Street Baths behind Victoria Street we tumbled out of the taxis into the large wash house where the local housewives would bring their laundry; no washing machines in those days. On Gala nights the wash house served as the changing room. 'What are the Yids dressed up for in their Sunday best?' No time to explain before the Head brought us together for our customary pre-Gala pep talk. 'Do your best, lads. As usual Buckingham Gate are the favourites, but I think that we can beat them this time; good luck.'

Points were awarded for each event on the basis of three for a first, two for a second, and one for a third, but we hadn't reckoned with Burdett Coutts who turned out to be the dark horse so that from the first race there were not two schools battling it out, but three, and there was hardly a point between us as the evening went on. Records fell like nine-pins and the water frothed as boys churned up and down the pool as if their lives depended on it, all to the accompaniment of the cheering spectators.

By the time the last event was reached, Buckingham Gate had thirty-two points, with us and

Burdett Coutts on thirty-one each. The last race was the Giant Relay comprising six swimmers in each team, awarding six points for the first, and four and two for the second and third. Our star was Lew Walters. He had already won the Individual Free-Style and we calculated that with Lew as our last leg our plan must be to at least keep up within reach of the leaders on each earlier leg.

There was little in it on the first leg, but as each boy took over, Buckingham Gate gained a few inches over Pulteney and Burdett Coutts who were neck and neck all the way. Buckingham Gate's last man took off with a good yard lead on the other two. Lew's style was all power, his chunky arms swung in wide arcs slamming the water with his head turning only slightly to breathe, his legs flaying rhythmically, the water churning in his wake. The Burdett Coutts swimmer in the next lane matched Lew stroke for stroke, but with a seemingly effortless smoothness. Steaming up the pool as one the two swimmers cut down the leader's advantage; onlookers went wild shouting and cheering on their team. Two yards from the end, the three swimmers were dead in line when suddenly Lew seemed to lift himself bodily out of the water, as dolphin-like as any human could possibly be, to touch a clear six inches ahead of the others. The Pulteney had made it; they had won the Everett Cup and for the first time J. C. Whitebrook actually joined in with 'We are some of the Pulteney Boys'. In his retirement the Head loved to reminisce about the Yom Kippur Gala.

But my tale has a sequel for, some years later when I was in uniform and on leave, I called on Chazan Amias and this is his version of Rabbi Ferber's involvement in the Yom Kippur Gala:

> Yes, indeed, I do remember when my good friend Mr Whitebrook came to see me with his problem about the swimming competition. He needed support in getting the parents' permission. So I took him along to see Rabbi Ferber and I thought that I would have to act as interpreter because, as you will remember, the Rebbe speaks Yiddish and very little English. But much to my surprise and delight this wasn't necessary because your Headmaster spoke German which he had learnt during the Great War. So there the three of us sat together talking about our work in Soho and then touching on matters of religion, philosophy and so on, and you know it was quite obvious that the Rebbe and the Headmaster warmed to each other. As you know the Headmaster got the Rebbe's support and when I told the Rebbe afterwards that the school team had won, he chuckled with delight and then you know what he told me? It was this: 'Amias, did you ever wonder why I was so ready to give the Headmaster my support? I will tell you. Do you remember that in the Talmud, in *Gemara*, it says "it is the duty of every man to teach his child to swim"? Now tell me how many fathers in Soho you know can teach their child to swim or even have time to teach their child to swim? But here we have a Headmaster who is performing that *mitzvah* for hundreds of boys and their fathers; so of course I gave him my support, it was the very least that I could do.'

Summer 1992

OUR DESTINY IN WHOSE HANDS?
A modest proposal for democratizing the Jewish people
Jonathan Freedland

More than three years have passed since I met the man who changed my life. I haven't spoken to him since that day, but I've spoken about him quite a bit. His name is Marvin Manning, he's probably eighty years old by now and he lives in Sunny Isles, Florida.

I met Marvin during the 1996 presidential election campaign, when I was trekking across the United States covering the battle of Bill Clinton versus Bob Dole for the *Guardian*. I had pitched up in Florida to write about a new force in American politics: the pensioners who spend their twilight years as political activists. They were famously effective in Florida, where elderly residents of the large apartment blocks known as condominiums had become the crack troops of 'grey power'. Most of them were refugees from New York or New Jersey, fleeing to Florida to the year-round sunshine. But they weren't ready for the lawn-chairs just yet. They wanted to get busy.

They spent their days replicating the old-time techniques of machine politics they'd learned in their youth. They would knock on doors, getting out the vote. In the argot of Florida politics, they were 'condo commanders'.

Manning was one of them, regularly hitting the phones or organizing lifts to the polling station. One of his duties was the printing up of 'palm cards', slips of paper small enough for the condo flock to smuggle into the voting booth, reminding them which way to vote – just in case their aged memories had let them down. He showed me his latest offering, a yellow square endorsing one Alex Penelas for mayor, with a reminder to 'Punch 38' on the voting machine. Marvin reckoned he delivered about four hundred votes that way.

I wanted to know what Mr Penelas had done to catch such a lucky break, winning such valuable backing. It turned out the candidate had undergone a grilling from Marvin and his fellow condo commandos, facing questions on everything from health insurance to beach renourishment. His opponent had done the same, but it was Alex Penelas they liked. And this was no one-off. Marvin's 'concerned citizens' committee' inflicts the same ordeal on all contenders for public office, including the local congressmen and even the Governor of Florida himself. 'It's like a job interview,' Marvin explained. 'They work for us, so they have to pass an interview.'

And those were the words that changed my life. I filed my story on the condo commandos, left Sunny Isles and moved on to the rest of the campaign – right up to Clinton's victory in November. But Marvin's words stayed with me. I realized he had put his finger on the entire American philosophy of power. In his view, it was all very simple: the people are in charge, and the politicians are their servants. They are the boss; the candidates they elect are mere hired hands. Marvin had summed up the entire founding ideal of the American republic, captured in the first three words of the US Constitution: 'We the People'. In America, sovereign power is meant to belong to the people – and nobody else.

I thought about that notion long enough to make it the basis of a book I wrote in 1998 called *Bring Home the Revolution: How Britain can live the American Dream* (Fourth Estate). This argued that America's founding ideal of popular sovereignty was one Britain should steal for itself. Except it would not really be stealing. For the founding fathers of the new United States were, in fact, British radicals, either by birth or parentage: men and women who had wanted to work their revolutionary magic in Britain but had ended up shipping it across the Atlantic. Now, I argued, it was time to bring home the revolution.

Once the book was out, I travelled across Britain, speaking at public meetings, conferences, even the odd literary festival – trying to spread the word. I argued that the Britain of the twenty-first century should adopt the ideal of popular sovereignty, even if that meant taking some radical steps: an elected second chamber, a written constitution, a bill of rights, a vast programme of devolution and, most controversial of all, the abolition of the monarchy and its replacement by a republic: after all, if the people are Sovereign, there can be no other pretender to that title. Underpinning it all was the belief that had animated those first Americans, along with the radicals of every era: the conviction that human beings do not merely inherit a world – they have the power to shape their world anew. The exiled British radical Thomas Paine put it best in 1791, when he wrote *The Rights of Man*: 'Government is for the living, not the dead . . . Every age and generation must be as free to act for itself, *in all cases*, as the ages and generations which preceded it.'

That was the message for my fellow Brits. But what about my fellow Jews? Several friends, and some readers, challenged me on this point. Here I was urging Britons to have the confidence to declare themselves sovereign over their own affairs, to realize they – and no higher force – controlled their destiny: would I ever dare say the same to the Jewish people? Such a stance would be even more radical than the argument I'd asserted about Britain. At least *Bring Home the Revolution* had only demanded British independence from the House of Windsor and the top-down institutions which govern in its name: a Jewish version of the same argument would surely mean independence from the 'higher force' which governs us – and we all know what that is.

Yet this is precisely the case I want to make. It is time for 'We, the Jewish people' to declare ourselves masters of our own fate and to govern ourselves. The democratic revolution which swept across much of the planet in the last century seems to have left the key institutions of world Jewry all but untouched. This is the unfinished business of the *Haskala*, the final task of Jewish enlightenment. It is our very own challenge for the millennium.

The starting point is the claim that we are a people. This is not as uncontroversial as it sounds. Eavesdrop on any sixth-form Jewish identity seminar, and you'll hear some Jews identify themselves as part of a race, and more as a religion. The racial designation is defeated easily enough: just glance at any of those UJIA appeal ads, showing a mosaic of Jewish-Israeli faces – some black, some white, some Indian, some Slav. There are few more multi-racial peoples on earth than the Jews.

Religion doesn't quite cut it either. If to be a Jew is to be a subscriber to a faith, then how do we account for the millions of Jews who have next to no religious belief? If Woody Allen, Jerry Seinfeld and Harold Pinter all declared themselves atheists, would we say they were no longer Jews? We would not. Yet what kind of religion is it that sees non-practice and non-belief as no bar to membership? No, religion will not do.

The simplest solution is to use the only words that fit: we are a people. Our culture may have begun as religion, but it is also the product of our history, our wanderings, our encounters with the other nations of the world. More than a religious sect, we are a civilization.

This is not a polemical point. It is a factual statement of Jewish demography, a description of the people we have become. The mountains of statistical data assembled in Israel and beyond all point in the same direction: roughly thirty per cent of world Jewry identifies itself religiously. The remaining seventy per cent have moved on, defining their Jewishness as a matter of secular culture.

So we are a people. But here lies the contradiction. However much we Jews might regard ourselves as a people, we have never taken that founding American step – never declared ourselves sovereign over our own affairs. Instead, like the loyal colonials of the 1770s, we still defer to a higher authority. To the American loyalists, the mighty power demanding submission was the Government of King George. To the Jews of today, the sovereign power is the sacred texts of Judaism and the rabbis who interpret them.

Those subject to this higher authority are not solely the Orthodox Jews who happily submit, volunteering to live their lives in accordance with the letter of *Halacha*. I'm talking about the great mass of world Jewry, including that seventy per cent who have moved away from observance. For they too are ruled from on high.

The most obvious illustration comes in Israel, where rabbis still take the key decisions about individual and family life. Marriages, divorce, burial and conversion are all in their hands. No one elects these decision-makers to their posts, and they certainly do not command a majority of the electorate, yet they exercise crucial powers. This goes beyond the familiar business of political influence exercised by a major interest group – a practice common to democracies everywhere. This is not like the gun lobby swaying politicians in America. For what the rabbis enjoy in Jerusalem is monopoly, sovereign power over key aspects of ordinary Israelis' lives. They and they alone decide matters of birth, death and marriage: the institutions of the civil Israeli state have no role. It is as if the National Rifle Association did not merely exert pressure on the US Congress, but was granted formal control over the distribution of gun permits. Put simply, the Israeli state has contracted out a chunk of its jurisdiction to an unelected priesthood. So a Russian immigrant can die for Israel, wearing the uniform of the Israel Defence Forces, but he is denied a burial spot among his fallen comrades – because an unelected rabbi deems him insufficiently Jewish. An abused woman can beg to be divorced from her violent husband and, even if most Israelis would support her right to be free, she and they are powerless: *Halacha* gives the wife-beater the final say, ruling out any divorce until he's happy to grant a *get*. Israeli civil law has no voice in the dispute: the matter is in the hands of an Israeli rabbinate with no accountability and no democratic standing whatsoever.

One point has to be stressed. To be angered by this state of affairs does not amount to an attack on religion. Nor is it any kind of denial of the rich, vibrant heritage of our tradition. It is simply a rejection of religious *coercion*. One can live a life enriched by the precepts of Judaism without believing our religions leaders should also enjoy political authority. It is a clear enough distinction, but an important one. If the Jews are a people, then they should surely be sovereign over their own affairs. In democratic terms, that means Jews choosing the people who write and implement the laws governing them. This is a basic condition of democracy and popular sovereignty, as the authors of the American Constitution understood so well. Israel's surrender of so-called domestic matters to an unelected rabbinate fails that test.

Sadly, the problem is not confined to the Jewish state. Jews across the world are even less able to make their own decisions. Consider this: if a poll were taken of world Jewry, asking if women deserved equal rights to men, what do you reckon would be the result? My guess is that, led by the liberal, Democrat-voting Jews of the United States, the answer would be a resounding Yes. Yet Jewish law and practice reflect no such thing. In short, there is a democratic deficit in the Jewish people. We are bound by texts a majority no longer regard as divinely ordained, which are then interpreted by a select priesthood none of us choose.

A useful way to see the problem is to imagine its opposite. Picture an election for the post of Chief Rabbi of Great Britain, the *de facto* leader of Anglo-Jewry, the man invited on the programme to speak for our community. Let's say one of the candidates for that job ran on a platform which declared homosexuality an abomination, believed that a woman's singing voice was a dangerous temptation to weak-willed men and should therefore never be heard in public, and condemned the late Hugo Gryn, rabbi and Auschwitz survivor, as 'an enemy of Judaism' – do you think such a candidate would win a secret, postal ballot of all Britain's 300,000 Jews? My hunch is that he would not. Yet Jonathan Sacks is the Chief Rabbi.

This is a particular riddle for liberal-leaning Jews. Why do we tolerate standards in our own people that we would condemn in, say, the country where we vote? I often used to have fun imagining telling a group of progressive New York Jews about this strange sect which demanded women sit apart from men, regarded them as unclean when menstruating and 'chained' them into unhappy marriages. Just as they would be rustling their cheque-books, offering their donations to the struggle against the Taliban, I would reveal that the sect in question lived not in Kabul nor even Tehran, but right here at home. These are the laws of the Jews, even if few Jews would ever endorse them. The challenge, then, is, to bring the Jewish rulebook into line with the rest of our values, to write laws which reflect the people we have become - not the one we used to be millennia ago.

A case in point would be conversion. The only way to become a Jew today is through a religious procedure, whether Orthodox, Reform or Liberal. Yet those born Jewish can be as non- or anti-religious as they like: no one will deny they are Jews. This is a glaring contradiction, born of the mismatch between the Jewish rule-book and the way we actually live: the Jewish people is now a cultural entity - yet the only route open to newcomers is through a turnstile marked 'religion'. If we were to devise a new process, one suited to the people we actually are, we would solve what may well be world Jewry's most pressing, painful question. At present we are shrinking through a definition of Jewishness which counts out all but those with two Jewish parents. It is a definition which interprets an event other people might consider expansion and growth (extending our reach beyond the narrow Jewish gene pool) as assimilation and disappearance instead. Instead of counting in, we count out - voluntarily describing ourselves as a people which is shrinking. If we counted in, we would actually boost our numbers by accepting willing newcomers. Such a move would have a further benefit: it might begin to reduce the untold heartbreak currently being wrought on the Jews and non-Jews who love each other.

What's stopping us? Why can't we issue our own declaration of independence, insisting that we are a people ready for self-governance, ready to use the time-honoured device of majority rule? At least three forces are holding us back.

The first is our own sentiment and insecurity. Failing to distinguish between religion and religious coercion, even liberal secularists are prone to a nostalgic, *Fiddler on the Roof* feeling about the Jewish world, one which makes them loath to attack the black-coated, bearded men who seek to rule over them. Rather than take on the religious authorities - as they might, say, the last Tory government - they tend to forgive the rabbinic establishment. If an MP or minister held the views voiced by Sacks, many Jews would rush to denounce him. But we make an exception for Sacks and the rest of his rabbi chums: after all, we feel, when push comes to shove, we're all Jews together.

Moreover, if we're honest many officially secular Jews secretly rely on the Orthodox as keepers of the Jewish flame. 'I may have abandoned the tradition,' thinks the secular Jew, 'but at least I know someone is keeping it alive.' It's a vicarious form of dependency. We don't want to fight the rabbis: we find their presence too reassuring.

Besides too few of us have the confidence to attack the rabbinate the way we might have rounded on Portillo or Howard. We fear we are too ignorant of our own tradition, we can't possibly know enough to take on these wise men. We don't see that this has been the response of ordinary people in the face of ruling elites through the ages: to feel blinded by jargon, ritual and mystery. Read Bagehot's brilliantly-knowing description of the British constitution, in which all the 'dignified' magic, flummery and ceremony of monarchy served to keep the people confused. The message was clear: government is a task for a select caste of initiates; the ignorant masses should know their place. Today's Jewish leaders do not set out deliberately to baffle - though one should always be vigilant when faced with the right-winger who refuses to debate until you have studied as much as he has - but the effect on rank-and-file Jews is the same. Unable to penetrate the code, they absent themselves from the discussion, leaving it to those who know best.

We need to cut through these sentiments, seeing both the nostalgia and the mystery for what they are. We should let the latter, in particular, intimidate us no longer. As Paine wrote, 'There is no place for mystery, nowhere for it to begin' when people govern themselves. Once the Jews take their destiny into their own hands, the old superstitions and mystification - the barriers to democratic participation - will soon melt away.

A second brake on a Jewish demand for self-rule is our own laziness, our own yearning for a quiet life. Think of those seventy per cent who have drifted from *Halacha*. They have voted with their feet, taking a decision to ignore those Jewish rules they deemed out-of-date. They have ignored them, yes - but they have not sought to change them.

It's a seductive position, one that's been put to me often. When I spoke at the 1998 Limmud conference on the subject of reforming our conversion laws, I was astonished by one response from the floor: 'Why are you even bothered? If someone wants to marry out, let them marry out. If they don't like the rules, they don't have to keep them.'

Those words were a plea to walk away, not to try to make a change from within. As such, they were a direct denial of the Jews' status as a collective entity: if a member of the Jewish people objects to one of its rules, his or her only option is to break away completely. The same logic applied to Britain would demand that anyone anxious to change anything not get involved in democratic politics - where they might persuade a majority to their view - but instead either break the law or emigrate. Don't like Britain's divorce laws? So break them - or move to Australia. No one would argue that, yet in our Jewish lives this is precisely the reasoning we live by.

The last bar to action is the most fundamental. Religious Jews would argue it most keenly, but plenty of others would sympathize. Put simply, what possible right do we Jews have to decide our own laws? We are not a people like the founding Americans, for in our case there really is a higher authority: the divine word of *Ha'Shem* handed down on Mount Sinai. Of course Judaism is not a democracy; how could it be? It is a theocracy.

Yet even this argument has an answer, from deep within our own tradition. For Judaism is not antithetical to humanism - on the contrary, a strong strain of the one runs through the other. Our tradition tells the story of a dispute on a point of law between two rabbis, Eliezer Ben Hyrcanus and Gamliel. Eliezer was so convinced of his rightness, despite the majority ranged against him, he told his rival the stream by their feet would soon flow backwards to prove it. And so it did. But Gamliel would not budge. Eliezer then predicted that the walls of the *Bet Ha'Midrash* would crumble. So they did, but still Gamliel was adamant. He said the trees would uproot themselves, which they did, but it did no good. Gamliel and his supporters would not be swayed. Finally God himself spoke - in Eliezer's favour.

Now whom does Judaism record as the victor in that dispute? Why, Gamliel, of course - for he had the majority on his side. The lesson thereafter was that decisions were to be taken *lo b'shemaim, can b'aretz* - not in the heavens, but here on earth. Even the Almighty agrees. As the sacred texts tell it, after Gamliel's victory God laughed, chuckling that 'my children have beaten me'.

So this is our tradition, one in which a Jewish majority has the right to decide the Jewish future. That is the ancient view - and that must be the view today. It has been renewed in this last century, in the form of the Zionist revolution. For the real obsession of those first pioneers was not so much states or borders, but the assertion of peoplehood: their contribution was to persuade their fellow Jews that they were not a religious sect, but a people, with national rights. We persuaded the rest of the world of that, too: why else would the United Nations have accepted the notion of a Jewish state?

That declaration has some serious implications. It means we have to govern ourselves as a people. The first Zionists imagined that as a simple matter of ensuring all the Jews lived in the same territory. Today it will have to mean something else: we will have to find ways for a globally dispersed people to govern itself. That will require genuinely fresh, imaginative thinking. Perhaps one day it might even entail some sort of worldwide Jewish election - with Jews everywhere choosing a single leadership, one not defined by the old notions of borders and territory. Globalization is already happening and, as a Diaspora people, we Jews are readier for it than most. The communications revolution and the Internet could soon make the old nation-state mode of thinking a thing of the past. Jewish self-governance beyond the confines of Israel alone may one day be possible. But first we have to want it.

We have to wait to wear clothes that fit us, shedding the medieval garb of a religious sect and replacing it with the democratic robes of a modern people. We have to bring our Jewish lives into harmony with the rest of our existence. We have to let Marvin Manning, who believes people like him can be in charge of their own destiny, believe that as a Jew as well as an American. It is a tall order, but we Jews have plenty of experience of such things. We have made so many revolutions before: it's time to make another one now.

Autumn 1999

TRYING TO BE JEWISH
Michael Rosen

I
When I was seven
David Kellner came up to me at school and said,
You are, aren't you?
What?
No, you are, I know you are, you are aren't you?
I'm sorry, I don't know what you mean, I said.
My mum says you are and she knows,
she says she knows you are from your name.
What?
You're Jewish aren't you?
I think so, I said.
There you are then, David Kellner said...

well, my mum says you should come to the synagogue
and do Hebrew Classes.

So I went home and I said,
Er David Kellner says I should go to synagogue
and do Hebrew Classes.
I see, mum said.

Hebrew classes were run by Mrs Kellner
but there wasn't a synagogue yet.
It was a corrugated iron Methodist chapel
without any Methodists in it.
Zeyde thought it was hysterical;
So Michael's going to cheder! Michael's going to cheder!
Zeyde didn't go to shul either,
he went to Hackney Downs instead
and stood around with a lot of old men in dark suits
with shiny bits on the tukhes of their gatkes.

At Hebrew classes Mrs Kellner who was very small
and had a huge and very wonderful bosom,
taught me the letters.
I could only remember two of them.
They both looked like the letter seven
but they each had a dot in a different place.
One of them had the dot over the top
and the other one had the dot in the middle.
How do you tell the difference, said Mrs Kellner?

I'll tell you.
(I never told David Kellner
that I loved his mother's wonderful bosom.)
What happens, she said
when you get hit by a football over your head?
You say OH!
And what happens
if you get hit by a football in your belly,
you say OOOH!
There you are
that's how you tell the difference.
One says OH! And the other says OOOH!

This, I remember
but I left Hebrew classes
after they shouted at me on the outing to Chessington Zoo.
You don't have to learn Hebrew
from people who give you tsurres at Chessington Zoo.

II
The second time I tried being Jewish
was when Mr Adams the maths teacher came out.
None of the experts on Jewishness had spotted him
but he announced that he would run a Jewish assembly
and Marshall, Serlin and Stoll went straightaway.
Cheeps gave it a miss on ideological grounds
and I joined him.
They didn't run assemblies for Jewish communists.
I'd heard about the conscience clause
that said that schools have to lay on assemblies but no one has to go to them.

I went to see the severely depressed deputy head.
I won't be going to assembly any more, I said.
Is this so that you can come to school even later than usual? he said.
No it's because I'm an atheist.
There is another assembly, he said.
I know I said. But I'm not going to any assembly.
Yes, I heard you say that, he said
but there is another assembly, you know.
Yes I heard you say that
but I'm an atheist.
He wasn't impressed
but said that I would have to bring a letter from home.

I told my father
that I wasn't going to go into assemblies any more.

He said, is this so that you can go to school even later than usual?
I said it was because I was an atheist
and so was he and so was mum
so it was fair enough.
He said, kvatsh!
He didn't believe a word of it,
but he wrote the letter and I got out of assemblies.
I had stood up for atheism.

Then I became wild about Lynne.
There was only one thing for it.
Jewish assemblies.
I went back to the severely depressed deputy head.
I would like to go to Jewish assemblies, I said.
I thought you did, he said.
That's a much better idea.

So every day,
I sat with Stoll, Marshall, and Serlin
and we said the Shema
and I tried to get as near as possible to Lynne
but she always sat next to Rebecca Feinstein
who it was rumoured had been having it off
since she was thirteen
(was this possible?)
The breakthrough came just before Jesus Christ's birthday
when a whole mob of us
took part in that traditional Jewish custom,
carol-singing.
Sometime between We Three Kings and
Oh Little Town of Bethlehem
me and Lynne swapped jumpers.

Spring 1996

THE NON-JEWISH JEWISH FEMALE CARTOONIST and Other Confusions
CORINNE PEARLMAN

I WAS WANDERING IN *LIFE'S DARK WOOD*...
Who am I? Where do I belong? Should I have a child? Shall I go to Waitrose?

...WHEN I WAS ASKED TO CONTRIBUTE TO **Jewish Quarterly**.
I'm afraid I haven't seen your work...
...but Carol Bennett suggested...
Pearlman! Pearlman! It must have been my name!

I'm a great admirer of **Spiegelman's** work.
Well, I can't compete with **Mauschwitz**...

YOU SEE, THE TRUTH IS — I'M NEITHER THE **CHILD OF A SURVIVOR**...

...NOR A **LONG ISLAND ÉMIGRÉ JAP** LIKE ALINE KOMINSKY CRUMB...
...AND I HAVEN'T EVEN CONTRIBUTED TO THE "**KVETCH**" ISSUE OF **WIMMIN'S COMIX**!

In fact, m..my parents are **assimilated**!!
I must ask Caroline what she does with **hers**!
It's different **soil**, darling!

*Maus by Art Spiegelman (Penguin '87) *Love That Bunch by Kominsky Crumb (Fantagraphics '90)

But isn't it **obvious** to people, when they see Daddy's **nose**?
Of course it is!
We just don't **talk** about such things!

Coming from **you**, darling, I'm so **surprised**! Surely you don't expect us to go to **shuel**?!
No! I just wondered, that's all.

I mean, Daddy takes it all with a **twinkle** in his eye!
Not a bad drop of Gevrey, eh?
He's marvellous, but we thought **she** was **off**!
People **know** that it's just a **game**.

I'll just take these **Horti** society minutes round to **Biddy's**!
Remember we're going to dinner with **Bysshe** and **Tottie**!

Your father **loves** playing the **country squire**!
But when the chips are down..?

OF COURSE, ASSIMILATED JEWS HAVE A **NOBLE TRADITION**...
...BUT SOME FRIENDS TAKE CONVINCING...
Stop playing the **Jewish card**! You're just **middle-class**!
But I'm not English the way **you** are!
DENY THY FATHER...?

...**REFUSE THY NAME**?
Make me a cup of tea, Jew!
It's sick!
An identity! I have been labelled!
Did you hear what he called her?!
How appalling!
How anti-semitic!
*"But he's only a little Chinaman!" Grandma, 1973

Of **course** she's Jewish! Just look at those **flanges**!
PRIDE
It's true! I have flanges!
...AND I'LL NO LONGER BE A **CAPULET**!!

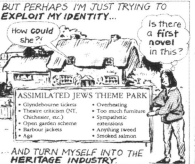
BUT PERHAPS I'M JUST TRYING TO **EXPLOIT MY IDENTITY**...
How **could** she?!
Is there a **first** novel in this?
ASSIMILATED JEWS THEME PARK
• Glyndebourne tickets
• Theatre criticism (NT, Chichester, etc.)
• Open garden scheme
• Barbour jackets
• Aga
• Overheating
• Too much furniture
• Sympathetic extensions
• Anything tweed
• Smoked salmon
...AND TURN MYSELF INTO THE **HERITAGE INDUSTRY**.

SO I **CONTINUE** TO WANDER IN LIFE'S DARK WOOD (THERAPY'S TOO EXPENSIVE)
Who am I? What **is** a Jew? Perhaps I **will** go to Waitrose after all...

Waitrose, hmm...
What kind of a name is **Waitrose**?

3
VANISHED WORLDS

Yehuda Abravanel, from the title page of a French translation,
Philosophie d'amour de M. Leon (Lyon, 1595) Woodcut / *Winter 1992-3*

THE TYRE-CAIRO LETTERS
Liz Cashdan

Expanded from a fragment of parchment in the John Rylands Library, Manchester

Sadaka to his father: Tyre October 1090
Father, they've given the post of cantor
to someone else –
do you remember the blue day of hope
I left Cairo with the oarsmen singing?
– to a pimply youth who intones without feeling
and an abominable accent.
Today is the first of Ramadan and the town
is on edge. The Jews keep close.
The streets are wet with the first
of the winter rains.
Give me your blessing. I am married now.
(You hoped Bathsheva Bat Eliahu
would be your new daughter.)
But give me your blessing even so.
It is Elisheva Bat Shmuel who has
found favour in my eyes.
Now the name of Sadaka Ha-Levi will
sound here in Tyre over the generations
when our sons and our sons' sons
are called in the synagogue.
I am in good health. I sing every day.
I send a son's love to my mother.
Sadaka Ha-Levi Ben Solomon.

Bathsheva to Sadaka Ha-Levi: Cairo October 1090
Cairo is hot and I long for you.
Since you left I have done nothing
But weaving every day till my back aches,
My finger joints stiffen.
Today, my little brother pulled the threads
Now they lie tangled on the floor tiles
Making new patterns where the old are worn away.
I cannot sort out the wools:
Mother has cut the knotted lumps out
Like some hideous growth
But the frayed ends hang forlorn
She will beat Isaac for what he has done
But Father will praise him because he learns so well.
He will not see the red and blue bruises on Isaac's back.

Now I am sad.
I want my weaving ready for your return
But I do not know how to finish it.

Aviva Bat Solomon to her brother Sadaka: Cairo December 1090
Distant brother, you say you are married now.
How I wish you could unsay those words.
Father has received your letter but he will not reply
His wrath is the wrath of a jealous God:
the women of the family keep silent
while his anger roars through the house,
a hot wind in the season of the chamsin.
He walks the streets alone, his head to one side
unable to face Bathsheva's menfolk.
Your news is whispered from hearth to hearth
and the bales of wool that should have come
as Bathsheva's dowry gather dust in her father's shop.
Mother fears for Father's business
dreads that hunger will be the guest at our table.
I have no blessings to send you
only the wailings of a sad sister
who curses the white boat and those singing
oarsmen who rowed you to Tyre.

The matchmaker to Sadaka's father: Cairo December 1090
Honourable master, it is seven months now
since you visited me with your son
I found him an excellent match
a young girl well-provided for.
Her father's storehouse has silks and woollens,
you could not do better.
She is comely into the bargain:
her skin the colour of olives
her teeth white as a sheep's fleece
her eyes blue as the blown glass of Tyre.
Why has your son gone to that far off city
where the young girls are lewd and ugly?
The marriage has been arranged
and you must pay me the ten gold coins.
I am old now, I have waited too long:
my house needs a roof
before the winter rains destroy me.

Elisheva Bat Shmuel to her mother-in-law: Tyre January 1091
Strange Mother, whom I have never met
I send you greeting from Tyre.
Now that I am one with your son
I shall love you as a dutiful daughter.
As the new moon pulls the tides of the sea
so each month my body will be prepared
and when my hopes are washed away
in that unclean flux
I shall be cleansed in the Mikvah
and my womb will be dedicated
to the grandchildren you desire.
Greet Ya'acov, the little brother whom I do not know
and kiss Aviva, my new sister
whom I long to meet.
How I envy the white birds who fly
to strange lands and new homes.
Though I cannot fly, my heart has wings.

Solomon to his son Sadaka: Cairo April 1091
Since you left, my fortunes have run dry
and I long for your return.
Today we have had the ceremony to mark
the rising of the Nile.
Kettledrums have sounded these three days,
trumpets have blasted our ears.
The stones of Cairo echo the hoofbeat
and march of the Caliph's army.
Men of wisdom have ridden with the princes
and your Uncle with the doctors of the court.
The Caliph dismounts at the head of the canal,
hurls his spade to make the first breach
and the slaves attack with pick and shovel:
the Nile floods. The waters are blessed by the giving of alms
to the deaf-mutes in the first boat.
Now the markets of the city will swell
with the fruits of the earth,
but in my hearth there is an emptiness.

Bathsheva to Sadaka: Cairo July 1091
So you are married. I wish you well.
Now I am without the ties which held
me to you, I am a new person.
The days of weaving are gone, the lengths
of cloth which might have been my dowry
are sold and I am glad. Some other

woman can enjoy those coloured threads
which bound me for so many months.
I have opened a school. Women from Fustat
leave their blind teachers, come to our house.
I have collected flowers and herbs
and your uncle has named them for me.
Today I used tincture of iodine for a cut hand,
kaolin for a stomach that cannot keep its food.
I have begun to study the oculist's art.
Soon I shall see into the ways of men.

Sadaka to his father: Tyre April 1096
There is bad news from Constantinople:
They say the Franks are moving east
Travellers speak of massacres in Blois
a thousand Jews killed in Mainz.
The Franks want Jerusalem for their
three-in-one god and I fear for our safety.
The Caliph has increased our taxes
to pay for the defence of Tyre.
The town is full of snorting horses
and the flash of Muslim scimitars.
If you are willing to receive us in your house
we shall leave this threatened town
sail the blue road back to Cairo.
The curse of war will be lifted from us,
you will greet your granddaughters
and their shining faces will bless your old age.

Sarah to her son Sadaka: Cairo September 1096
My dearest son, your father is dead:
he died in the quiet of the night
in the new moon of Tishrei. We have sat on low stools,
said Kaddish every day for seven days.
Now I must put aside my mourning:
there is work to be done.
Your sister Aviva has a good head for sums,
today she counted, sorted the bales.
I have employed three men from Fustat,
dyers who have brought their own vats,
Installed them in the outside sheds.
The wood is rotten and I fear we shall have
dye leaking into the courtyard.

Worse still, Ya'acov spends his time
with these men when he should be learning.
There is no-one to tell him – if only your father –
but such thoughts are useless:
dyed cloth makes a good profit.

Elisheva Bat Shmuel to her sister-in-law: Tyre December 1096
Sister, Aviva, I write to you
though we know each other only by name.
One woe follows on the heels of another.
Sadaka is dead.
The Franks fired the synagogue in Antioch:
he had gone there to sing Kaddish.
The rabbis tell us we should not grieve:
the dead have found a safe harbour
but his was too short a journey.
Now I shelter with the widow, Leah,
but fear of the Franks is all around us.
I do not know how long Tyre will be safe.
Leah has ships bound for Cairo
with cargoes of tabby carpets
rose and violet-water in Tyre glass.
We will cross the sea that brought Sadaka here.
You will have a new sister to help
with the dyestuffs and your mother a new daughter.
As women we shall be strong, give each other comfort
and my daughters will grow in a place of peace.

Winter 1991-2

A COMPLAINT AGAINST THE TIMES[1]

by the sage **Don Yehuda Abravanel**

(may his memory be blessed and live forever)[2]

In which he recounts all the troubles which befell him from the day of his birth, his wanderings, the abduction of his first born son to whom he writes this testament.

1   These times have cut through my heart with a sharp arrow
and cleaved asunder the kidneys within me.[3]

They have wounded me and the wound is incurable;[4]
they have crushed me and made my pain everlasting.[5]

They cast me down and scarred my flesh;[6]
grief has devoured my blood and marrow-juice.

They gnawed at my bones in their anger
and leapt against me and set on me like a lion.

5   It was not enough that they should toss me like a ball[7]
and turn me into an exile, a wanderer in my youth.

They made me wander like a mercenary[8] through the world
and drove me to the farthest ends of the earth.

It is now almost twenty years
since my horses and chariot have known any rest,

And my step has measured the waters and the dust[9]
of every land, and my youth has been taken from me.

They drove my friends and comrades into exile too,
and they sent away the people closest to me.[10]

10   I can no longer see those with whom I had sweet counsel[11]
nor my mother, nor my brother, nor my father.

They scattered my dear ones, one to the north,
another to the east, and another to the west,

So that my thoughts would be troubled
and I would not find peace in my meditations.

And when my face turns to the east[12]
solitude bruises my heel[13]

1. The word '*zeman*', 'time', is in the singular and has a variety of meanings drawn from the poetic tradition of Hebrew poetry in Spain. Yehuda lists both the concrete and abstract meanings of the word. For the latter see distich 87.
2. This sub-heading is probably by the late eighteenth/early nineteenth-century scribe, and is included in the first edition of the poem by R. Kircheim and E. Carmoly in *Otzar Nehmad* vol. 2 (1856), pp 70-75. The sub-heading is also included by N. Slousch, 'Poésies hébraïques de Don Yehuda Abrabanel'-Revista de Estudos Hébráicos vol. 1 (Lisbon, 1928), pp. 192-230 (p. 199), but is omitted by later editors, for instance, Carl Gebhardt, *Leone Ebreo. Dialoghi D'Amore. Hebraeische Gedichte, Herausgegeben Mit Einer Darstellung Des Lebens und des Werkes* (Heidelberg: Societatis Spinozianae, 1929), pp. 3-30 (3).
3. *Job*, 16: 13.
4. *Micah*, 1:9.
5. *Jeremiah*, 16:18.
6. *Lamentations*, 3:4.
7. *Isaiah*, 22:18.
8. Some editors read this as 'drunkard'.
9. *Isaiah*, 40:12.
10. *Psalms*, 148:14.
11. *Psalms*, 55:14.
12. Jerusalem.
13. *Genesis*, 3: 15.

And my foot slips and my mind is unquiet and goes astray,
and I do not know whether I go or come.

15   Ah indeed, these times have consumed my heart and rent it
and dismembered me as would a bear or a wolf.

The times have lashed me with sighs and terror,
with pillage and looting and imprisonment.

Yet this was still not enough. They sought
to snuff out altogether my little flame.[14]

There were two boys who were born to me
sons of rare beauty, the crown of my pride.[15]

The smaller of the two I named Samuel,
but the times, lying in ambush, snatched him from me

20   And struck him down at the age of five,
leaving me to anguish and ague.

The elder I named Yitzhak Abravanel
so that he would know the rock from which I myself was hewn,[16]

His forebear being a mighty name in Israel,
the son of Ishai, the everlasting light of the west.[17]

At his birth I wished to implant in his heart[18]
wisdom and to teach him the best from his fathers.

But at the age of one, ah me, he was taken from me
and turned from his course by my pursuers.

25   When the children of Sepharad were driven out
the king ordered a trap to be devised for me:

So that I should not take flight and escape through the gorge[19]
he ordered my only son[20] to be taken – the one who had drunk my milk

To force him to follow the king's religion.
But a good man, one trusted by me, revealed this plan to me.

As if he were a thing I had stolen,
I sent the child, with his wet nurse, in the deep of the night,

14. *Job*, 18:5.
15. *Isaiah*, 28: 1.
16. *Isaiah*, 51:1.
17. The reference is both to the house of David, as Y.A. claims a royal descent, and to the ever-burning western light in the Temple.
18. *Deuteronomy*, 33:9.
19. *Psalms*, 136:13. A reference to the flight from Egypt; see also *Genesis*, 15:17.
20. *Genesis*, 22:2.

To Portugal. There also a king ruled with hands defiled by blood[21]
who had once sought my destruction.[22]

30   For great had been the honour and wealth of my father there,
during the reign of that man's father.[23] (He had been the king I admired.)

But then this one came to power—vicious, cruel,
greedy, a man filled with lust, doglike.

So when his ministers and his brother plotted against him,
he falsely accused my father of being a conspirator too,

And after murdering his own brother sought to kill my father.
But He Who presides over the cherubim saved him from death,

And he escaped to Castile,
his birthplace and ancestral home.

35   But as for me, he destroyed everything I owned
and robbed me of all my goods, silver and gold.

And when he learned of my son's coming to his kingdom
and that I was about to flee to my father's house in Italy,

He imprisoned the boy and held him, and ordered
him never to return whence he had been exiled.[24]

And after the death of that king there came to power a witless one –
a fanatic in his religion, a hollow man.[25]

He persecuted the community of Jacob and enforced
conversion on them, the children of my noble people.

40   Many of them took their own lives rather than break
the laws of He Who gives us succour.

And my son, the apple of my eye, was still held, and even his name,
taken from the rock whence I was hewn, was changed.

He is now twelve and to this day I have not seen him.
Thus I am punished for my covetousness[26] and error.

And I weep, and my anger is upon my head,
and against my own soul is my complaint and my lament.

It was my fear that chased him into the trap;
to save him from a flame I sent him into the pyre.

21. *Isaiah*, 59:3.
22. João 11 (1481–1495),
King of Portugal.
23. Alfonso V (1449–1481),
King of Portugal.
24. *Jeremiah*, 40:12.
25. Manuel I (1495–1521),
King of Portugal.
26. *Isaiah*, 57:17.

45   Still, through slow time, I wait to see him.
Why do you linger my beloved hart? [27]

Why do you oppress he who gave you your life,
and send arrows to strike his side?

Why do you darken the light in my heaven[28]
and turn dawn into sunset before my eyes?

The moon darkens forever in my sight
and the stars are sealed among clouds.[29]

Not the smallest fragment of sunlight brightens my misery
nor does it shine through the windows of my heart.

50   My lily of Sharon flowers not[30]
nor does rain fall on my grass.[31]

The memory of you steals sleep from my eyes,
and I cannot tell the hours between waking and sleeping.

I take no pleasure in what I eat, honey is bitter
to my palate, a cup of poison would be sweet to me.[32]

I eat a hard cake of grief baked on coals[33]
and weep over each dry morsel.[34]

I mingle tears with the water I drink,
and the blood of grapes[35] does not enter my mouth.

55   Only water crosses my lips. I have become a Nazarite
and am taken by all to be a Rechabite.[36]

But when I dream of your return and see
your image in my mind's eye

My torments change into sweetness[37]
and my face shines like gold.

I sleep and my sleep is sweet to me,[38]
and I awake filled with well-being.

I drink and the water is sweet to me,
and the clods are soft in the thought of you.[39]

27. *Song of Songs*, 2:91.
28. *Isaiah*, 5:30.
29. *Job*, 9:7.
30. *Song of Songs*, 2:1
31. *Micah*, 5:6; *Deuteronomy*, 32:2.
32. *Zechariah*, 12:2.
33. *Kings I*, 19:6.
34. *Proverbs*, 17:1.
35. *Genesis*, 49:11.
36. *Jeremiah*, 35:2.
37. *Psalms*, 16:1 literally: "The boundary lines fell for me in pleasant places."
38. *Proverbs*, 3:24; *Jeremiah*, 31:26.
39. *Job*, 21:33.

60   But then, when I recall your exile, like a fire
      my heart burns, and the desert wind smites me.[40]

      I am like a man dazed and confounded,
      my back is bent, my stature shrinks.

      Joy and sorrow mingle when I recall you.
      You are my balm, yet you are my oppressor and foe.

      Your image is sculpted in my heart,
      your absence from me is carved in my inmost mind.[41]

      Not for a moment can I forget your absence;
      the hope of seeing you gives me no joy.

65   Your distance turns my wisdom into foolishness,[42]
      your exile twists my path like a snake.

      For you is the summit of my tree bent to the ground,
      for you my pride is prostrated.

      So the sycamore has risen higher than the cypress,
      and even a hyssop is now taller than the cedar.

      The bat soars higher than the falcon,
      and a fly above the wings of eagles.

      My limbs are as weak as a child's;
      even a lamb could now overcome this lion.[43]

70   I scorn song and have broken my lute,
      my harp I have hung on the willows.[44]

      My song has turned into loud wails
      my pipes howl with the sound of the banshee.[45]

      My peacock is changed into a porcupine
      and my turtle dove into a jackal.

      I have come to despise the palaces of kings
      and long to dwell in the Arabian desert.

      My son, your exile has made breaches within me.[46]
      it has bruised my heel and set traps around me.[47]

75   It has put fear and anger into my heart,
      and rot in my thoughts and my bones too.

40. *Isaiah*, 49: 10.
41. The imagery of sculpting
or carving is related
to Renaissance Platonic
philosophy.
42. *2 Samuel*, 15:31.
43. A pun on his Italian name,
'Leone' (lion).
44. *Psalms*, 137:2.
45. Literally the sound of a
ghost, from *Isaiah*, 29:4.
The Irish word implies the
lack of an English one.
46. *Job*, 16:14.
47. *Genesis*, 3:15.

I hear your mother weeping every day
as she calls you the darling of her heart, her suckling babe:

'Who has stolen you from my bosom,
who has caused the fruit of my womb to be lost?'

I have no strength to bear her complaint,
I cannot conceal my own anguish.

Though I had gone off to serve yet another king,
whom God my benefactor gave to me,[48]

80   I wandered still and had no rest,
dwelling in Edom[49] among the people of fire.

But I have found no cure for my sores,[50]
nor one who will straighten these times.

I hold in contempt the days and nights of my travail:
to them I prefer death – oh let it come.[51]

Life is heavy on me, and the days
are like the sands on my shoulders and back.

What avails a life of grief?
The portion allotted to me has come to an end.

To one filled with bitterness life is like death,[52]
and a short time is as long.

What avails my hope to see better things
when a cubless bear lies in ambush for me?

The children of this day, the sons of the quiver, have their bow high above,
and Time is aiming and shooting at me.[53]

I have been marked as the target of these arrows;
they have enclosed me in a deadly circle.

I will now address my only son,
(let him no longer be the cause of my grief!):

90   'My first born, open your heart, know you are the son
of sages who were as wise as prophets.

48. Alfonso II, King of
Naples.
49. Italy.
50. *Hosea*, 5:13.
51. *Job*, 34:36.
52. *Psalms*, 79:11.
53. The 'children of the day'
are the children of Time.

Wisdom is your heritage, and I pray you,
let not the days of your youth be wasted, my beloved.

Follow now, my son, a desire for learning,
read the Scriptures and understand my writing.

Read the *Mishnah* and study the *Talmud,*
according to the *Thirteen Principles*, by questions and answers.

How else can I bear the thought of his conversion?
This is my sickness, this my fever, this is the sword [54]

95   Which rends the cage of my heart
with the hireling's blade—no barber's razor![55]

To whom shall I pass on the sum of my knowledge,
to whom shall I give to drink the juice from my wine press?

When I am gone, who will taste and feed on
the fruits of my thought and writing?

Who will understand the testimony of the books
written by my father, who is my pillar?

Who will draw the water from my spring,
and who will drink it in the dry land?

100   Who will gently[56] gather the fruits of my garden[57]
and prime my tree of knowledge and pick from it?

Who will continue my work and complete it,
who will do the cross-weaving on my loom?

Who will be ornamented by my knowledge when I die,
and who will drive my mule and chariot?'[58]

Who else but you, my heir the delight of my soul?
I owe a debt to my Rock[59] and you are the bond.

My soul thirsts for you, my body longs for you,[60]
in you I will quench my thirst and hunger.

105   It is for you to advance my teaching,
for you to carry the light of my knowledge and wisdom[61]

Which I inherited in part from my father and teacher,
the father of my learning, my guide and rabbi.

54. *Isaiah*, 2:4;
Deuteronomy, 28:22.
55. *Isaiah*, 7:20.
56. *2 Samuel*, 18:5.
57. *Song of Songs*, 5:1.
58. *Isaiah* 66:20
59. God.
60. *Psalms*, 63:2.
61. *Isaiah*, 59:19.

The rest I obtained with my own labours,
and conquered with my bow and sword.

So that the power of my mind made the wise men of Edom
no more than locusts compared to me.[62]

I visited their schools of learning
and there were none who could engage with me.

110   I vanquished all who rose in argument against me,
and forced my opponents to surrender, putting them to shame.

Who would dare to argue with me on the secrets of creation
and the mysteries of the chariot and its rider?[63]

I have a soul which is higher and more splendid
than the souls of my worthless contemporaries.

My form has been moulded by the power of my God
and my soul is imprisoned within its cage.[64]

It never ceases in its yearning to ascend upwards,
and my wish is that you, my son, will climb even higher.

115   My friend, why are you there among people with impure hearts
like an apple in a forest of carobs?[65]

Why is your pure soul among these Gentiles
Like a lily among thorns and weeds?[66]

Arise and flee, come to me in my exile,
escape, and be for me like a roe or young hart.[67]

Come to your father's house, to the Rock Who begat you,
and may He, my God, my strength, sustain you.

Let Him straighten your road,
and lead you from the rough ground to the level.[68]

120   May He place mountains of blessings on your head,[69]
among them the blessings of my father and grandfather.

May He put light in the darkness of my mind,
and in His benevolence put right my own crookedness.

I commit my seed to God my shepherd
and entrust my hope to God my father.[70]

62. *Isaiah*, 40:22.
63. *Isaiah*, 66:15. A reference to the Kingdom of God in kabbalah.
64. This refers, to a kabbalistic and Platonist image of the soul which forever aspires to break out of the matter that holds it down.
65. *Song of Songs*, 2:3.
66. *Song of Songs*, 22.
67. *Song of Songs*, 2:9 and 17; 8: 14.
68. *Isaiah*, 40:4.
69. *Genesis*, 49:26.
70. *Psalms*, 55:3.

May He grant me to see my beloved;
may I address my darling and he will listen to me.

I will then sing to my Creator a song of love
I will sing it to Him while I have my being.[71]

125 I will bring Him my offering;
I will prepare gifts before Him.

Thus I will be joined to the most Holy One:
soul, eyes, head, and heart.

May my God be more pleased with my hymn of praise
than with any sacrifice.[72]

May He reveal to me the splendour of Zion,
the glory of its kingdom, the Messiah to be anointed by cherubim.[73]

And on Zion's summit[74] may there shine forever
the two beacons, the sons of David and Tishbi.[75]

130 Then no enemy will defile Zion[76] from generation to generation,
and nor shall the Arab pitch his tent there.[77]

*Translated from the Hebrew by Dan Almagor, Barbara Garvin and Dan Jacobson.
Winter 1992-3*

71. *Psalms*, 104:33; 146:2.
72. *Isaiah*, 1: 11.
73. *Ezekiel*, 28:14.
74. The site of the Temple in Jerusalem.
75. Tishbi: Elijah.
76. *Psalms*, 55:13.
77. *Isaiah*, 13:20.

SOL
A.C. Jacobs

'See the sun redden towards evening'

Near Malaga, I see the sun
Reddening, yellowing into the blue sea
And think of Shlomo Ibn Gabirol,
Malagueñan, who wrote that line.

And this afternoon I drank a cup
Of sweet wine in a hidden square
Where Lorca drank and is remembered.

It is the time of *El Cambio*,
Changing. The Moors are gone,
The Catholic realm is gone,
The heady dictatorships are dregs.

The other end of the Mediterranean,
Where I have also been, fumes.

The poems sing their lusts, their elegies.

Cordoba, Granada, sierras, exile.

Old passions cry in measured times.

Torre del Mar, January 1988
Winter 1988-9

THE LEGEND OF THE WANDERING JEW
A New Interpretation
Hyam Maccoby

The legend of the Wandering Jew began as an insignificant anecdote. Gradually, however, the story acquired accretions which gave it significance and mythic status; and, in its full-blown form, the story is the reincarnation of a very ancient archetype.

The legend is known to have developed out of a medieval (13th century) tale, or rather 'tall story', about a man called Cartaphilus, who was neither a wanderer nor a Jew. However, some of the main features of the later story are already present in this first version. Cartaphilus was a Roman, Pilate's doorkeeper. He struck Jesus, on his way to his Crucifixion, and told him to hurry; Jesus answered, 'I go, and you will wait for me until I return'. By these words Jesus conferred on Cartaphilus the curse of immortality; an immortality of remorse, since Cartaphilus became a devout Christian. Cartaphilus was not a wanderer, for he lived through the centuries in Armenia. The German name for the Wandering Jew is '*der ewige Jude*' – 'the Eternal Jew' – and this name is more faithful to the earliest version of the story than our 'Wandering Jew' or the French '*le juif errant*'. The gift of immortality remained, however, as an essential ingredient of the fully-developed story.

In the next century, the figure appears in Italy under the name of Johannes Buttadeus ('John-who-struck-God'). He has now become a Jew, instead of a Roman, and has become a Wanderer; part of his curse being that he is always restless and cannot remain in one place for long.

However, it was not until the beginning of the 17th century that the Wandering Jew legend really achieved popular success. His name has changed to 'Ahasuerus'. The legend now proliferates all over Europe. Sightings of the Wandering Jew are reported in much the same way as flying saucers are reported nowadays. Ahasuerus was once a shoe-maker by trade, a native of Jerusalem. He is now a convinced and repentant Christian, but must expiate the curse pronounced on him by Christ; he must live and wander until the Second Coming. The name 'Ahasuerus' is rather a strange choice. The Biblical Ahasuerus was not a Jew but a Persian king, probably to be identified with Xerxes. But we may guess that this name was chosen because it was not too Christian and not too Jewish. Names like Simeon or Matthew (or even John, the original but rejected choice), though Hebrew in origin, had too Christian a ring, while names like Solomon or Moses had acquired villainous or comic Jewish associations inappropriate to a noble penitent. An Old Testament name like Ahasuerus would sound vaguely Jewish to people not too well acquainted with the Old Testament story, just as Shakespeare's choice of the non-Jewish names Tubal and Chus, from the Old Testament, seemed appropriate enough for his Jewish characters in *The Merchant of Venice*. But 'Ahasuerus', with its kingly associations, would also sound dignified.

Thus, even in the 17th-century folk-tale version, the Wandering Jew is a dignified figure. The description of him as tall and stately, with a grave, sad expression, reinforced this impression of dignity. Later, in the elaborations of Romantic literature, this dignity becomes greater still, since the Wandering Jew is credited with supernatural knowledge and mystic powers. We may ask the question: 'How was it that, in the 17th century, at the time of the greatest degradation and humiliation of the Jewish people, a folktale grew to popularity in which a Jew is represented as a noble, dignified and even awesome figure?' This was the time when, after centuries of anti-Jewish legislation, designed to expel the Jews from every honourable, dignified employment, they were at their lowest point. They were continually harassed and moved on from place to place; there was in fact a large-scale migration of Jews to Eastern countries. They were in sober truth Wandering Jews at this time, and this historical fact has been adduced to explain the growth of the Wandering Jew legend. But it does not account for the dignity of the Wandering Jew, which is so much at variance with the Jews' position of humiliation and with the figure of the Jew in other Christian folk-tales such as the Jew's Beautiful Daughter story, which reached literary status about this time in Marlowe's *Jew of Malta* and Shakespeare's *Merchant of Venice*.

In the Wandering Jew legend we have an unexpected aspect of the Christian image of the Jew; an aspect which reflects a need of Christians to build up their image of the Jew as well as to break it down. It is as if the very success of the Christians in humiliating the Jew in the world of reality has led to a need for a more reverential image in the world of fantasy. As long as Christians feared the Jews, regarding them as figures of established power, they resorted to the weapons of ridicule and vilification. But when it became clear that the Jews were defeated and had become harmless objects of contempt, it became necessary to restore some of the lost awesomeness. The Wandering Jew represents both the defeat of the Jews and the restoration of their dignity.

We must remember that the aim of the Christians was never merely to beat down the Jews. If this had been so, the Jews could have been annihilated, like the Albigenses. One of the strongest beliefs of medieval Christians was that the Second Coming of Christ could not take place until the Jews were converted to Christianity. (Marvell's 'till the conversion of the Jews' means simply 'till the millennium'.) The Jews, therefore, had to be preserved; otherwise the Second Coming could not take place. This was the point of the Disputations which were held periodically to convert the Jews. When Luther reformed the Christian religion, one of his first thoughts was that now at last the Jews could be converted. When medieval Church dignitaries, such as St. Bernard of Clairvaux, intervened with the raging mob to save the remnants of Jewish communities, their chief argument was not humanitarian but that the Jews were necessary for the Second Coming. This belief was not merely an outcome of St. Paul's pronouncement (*Romans* XI, 25) that the Jews would be converted in the last days. The matter goes much deeper than the interpretation of an isolated text. The Jews were never put on the same footing as the other heretics. They were the representatives of the Old Religion, against which Christianity had rebelled, and there was a feeling of bad conscience about them. The Jews were father-figures, and rebellion against the father is never a straightforward expression of hatred. There is the residual feeling of love, the desire for approval, the desire to gain, after all, the father's blessing. Even the accusations against the Jews were an attempt by Christians to convince themselves that the Jews, despite all their appearance of indifference, really did believe in Christ. Why did the Jews steal the Communion wafer and stick pins in it, thus making it bleed, unless they believed, after all, that the wafer was the body of Christ?

The Wandering Jew aroused such passionate interest because he was a witness to the truth of Christianity – a witness sorely needed in the millennial excitements and conflicts of the 17th century. Only a Jew could give Christianity its final confirmation. The Wandering Jew was the very Jew whom centuries of Christian persecution had been designed to produce; dispossessed and beaten into humility and repentance, but retaining enough of the dignity of the Father to give his blessing and his clinching testimony to Christianity.

But the Wandering Jew also has a more universal significance. This Christian Jew-image is a relatively recent manifestation of a very ancient theme. It is interesting to compare the Wandering Jew with some figures of ancient mythology in order to discover what he means apart from the context of the Jewish-Christian conflict.

The essence of the Wandering Jew is that he is someone who has sinned deeply and is, therefore, condemned to punishment. But his punishment is an ambivalent one; from some angles it can even be regarded as a reward. He is cursed with eternal life; but this is also the reward of heroes, such as Arthur, or Frederick Barbarossa, or the Biblical Elijah. Indeed, the Wandering Jew derives directly some of his characteristics from the Christian hero, John, the favourite disciple of Jesus, who was also told by Jesus 'Tarry till I come' (*John* XXI, 22), and whose name is attached to some versions of the Wandering Jew ('John Buttadeus' and the Spanish 'Juan Espera en Deo'). Even the condemnation to wandering cannot be regarded as wholly a curse. To wander is more interesting than to stay at home. The Wandering Jew visits all lands, meets with exciting adventures and acquires strange knowledge. He has the romantic aura of such wandering heroes as Hercules, Dionysus, Odysseus and the Hebrew Patriarchs. He is one of those mythical figures who express the stay-at-home agriculturist's yearning for the lost freedom of the era of nomadism.

If the punishment of the Wandering Jew is equivocal, we are forced to the conclusion that there is something equivocal about his crime too. What is this crime which is also a heroic act, so that its punishment is also a reward?

One of the most interesting ancient analogues of the Wandering Jew legend is the biblical story of Cain. In this story, Cain, after committing his terrible crime, is condemned to be a wanderer: 'A fugitive and a vagabond shalt thou be in the earth'. Instead of being condemned to death, Cain is condemned to life, and in order to ensure that his life should not be a short one, God 'set a mark on Cain, lest any finding him should kill him'. Yet we are then told that Cain 'built a city', and that his descendants were the founders of the arts. Jubal was 'the father of all such as handle the harp and organ,' and Tubal-Cain was 'an instructor of every artificer in brass and iron'. If, as modern scholars think, Cain was the eponymous ancestor of the Kenite (Rechabite) tribe (a fact which the Biblical narrative purposely obscures), his descendants were a highly-respected Arab clan of nomadic smiths who accepted Judaism but retained their own tent-dwelling, ascetic way of life, for which the Prophet Jeremiah commended them (*Jer.* XXXV). The wandering life which was decreed for Cain as a punishment eventually became a sign of sanctity. The whole story is permeated by the ambivalence which we noted in the Wandering Jew story. Cain's crime and punishment are terrible; but in the outcome, he is shielded from death, acquires special gifts and talents, contributes in a distinguished way to civilization and becomes a holy person.

It may be objected that the Wandering Jew's crime of jostling Jesus on his way to crucifixion is too trivial to be compared with Cain's fratricide. In the original story of the Roman Cartaphilus the crime was indeed relatively trivial; but as soon as the sinner became not a Roman but a Jew, the significance and seriousness of the story were transformed. The crime became a symbol of the deicide of which the whole Jewish people was held to be guilty. Christian writers of the early Church, looking for allegorical meanings in the Old Testament stories, saw both Cain's murder of Abel and Joseph's betrayal by his brothers as foreshadowings of Jesus's betrayal and murder by his brothers, the Jews. So the crime of Cain and that of the Wandering Jew are not, after all, dissimilar.

In the wider field of mythology, the story of Oedipus presents some parallels with that of the Wandering Jew and Cain. Oedipus, having discovered that he has killed his father and married his mother administers his own punishment. He blinds himself, and sets off on wanderings, which eventually lead him to Athens. He has acquired the gift of prophecy; he announces the place and time of his own death, and that his bones will bring prosperity to Athens. Though the gift of a charmed life is lacking in the story, we have the Wandering, the special gifts and the eventual sanctity. There is the characteristic ambivalence, the feeling that the awesomeness of the crime confers heroic status.

There is an even more interesting parallel between the story of Cain and that of Adam (Edmund Leach, in *Genesis as Myth,* has suggested with some plausibility that they are variants of the same story). Adam, as a result of his crime, is thrust out from his true Home. The ground (as for Cain) becomes cursed for him. And yet his crime brings him gifts; he has acquired 'the knowledge of good and evil'. Without his crime he would have remained an innocent child; now he has grown up. The gift of immortality comes into the story too, for if Adam had sinned even further and eaten the Tree of Life, he would have become immortal. As it is, the punishment of death pronounced for eating of the Tree of Knowledge (*Gen.* III, 3) is not carried out. The crime of the sinner has made him into a hero; God Himself says, 'The man is become as one of us.' The theory that Adam's sin brought death into the world is late, and is in contradiction to *Gen.* III, 22.

The Hebrew story of Adam (which has been much distorted and misrepresented by Christian exegesis, especially in connection with the doctrine of Original Sin) is a profound parable of the human condition. It is primarily about the acquisition of knowledge and the guilt associated with this. The Wandering Jew story, however, like that of Cain, is primarily about violence; but the 'violence' story has its 'knowledge' aspect too, the idea that guilt and knowledge are intermixed, that a terrible crime of violence enables the criminal to break through to a higher state of awareness. 'Knowledge through sin' is the common denominator of all these stories; though in some of them knowledge arises as a by-product of the sin, while in others the acquisition of forbidden knowledge is itself the sin. The Adam story is of the latter type; others of this type are the stories of Prometheus, and of Faust. Another example is Teiresias, who was punished because he found out too much about sex; blinded, like Oedipus, he acquired the gift of prophecy and prolonged life. The Adam story too, according to some interpreters, is concerned with the acquisition of sexual knowledge (see especially Theodor Reik's *Myth and Ritual*).

It was primarily the 'knowledge' aspect of the Wandering Jew which interested Romantic writers such as Shelley (see *Queen Mab* and *Hellas*). Shelley saw the Wandering Jew as one of those rebels against authority, such as Adam, Prometheus and Faust, who defy the tyranny of God in order to acquire independent status and knowledge. The Wandering Jew certainly has this aspect, and from this point of view, he can be regarded, like Adam, as a symbol of mankind in general. Every man is a Wanderer, who has been ejected from the warmth of the Eden of childhood because of the sin of curiosity and desire for independence. But his punishment is his reward. The world of adulthood brings hardship, unrest, a life prolonged in agony, but it also brings responsibility, freedom, skill, sense of achievement, adventure and morality. This is the theme of the stories of Adam, Prometheus and Faust. (In the case of Adam, there is a great difference between the Adam of Judaism and the Adam of Christianity, the knowledge-guilt association being so much stronger in Christianity that the heroic aspect of Adam's sin is virtually obliterated.)

The Romantic universalization of the Wandering Jew story, however, is not entirely satisfactory as an interpretation. This rendering omits the specific content of the story; the Jewishness of the Wandering Jew, the flavour of the Christian-Jewish conflict and the wider significances of that conflict. Shelley used the Wandering Jew as part of his attack on Christianity — or rather on organised Christianity, for Shelley, like other Romantics, was really re-asserting the antinomian essence of Christianity. Shelley, in fact, placed the Wandering Jew on the Cross; but that is not his place. He is the Crucifier, not the Crucified. (Coleridge's Ancient Mariner, based partly on the Wandering Jew and partly on Cain, retains more of the essence of their characters, since the Ancient Mariner is guilty of a genuine crime of violence.) Shelley wished to abolish Sin altogether from the story. The Wandering Jew is for him, like Prometheus and even Satan, not a sinner at all but a pure-souled revolutionary. But this is to by-pass the main point of the Wandering Jew story, which is that it is concerned with the problem of guilt. It is a Christian story, and it expresses the Christian method of dealing with the sense of guilt.

The role of the Jews was to take the blame for the Crucifixion. The Christian method of dealing with guilt is by the sacrifice of Jesus, who by suffering torture and death, rolls away the burden of sin from mankind, or at least from those who identify themselves with the sacrifice. This, of course, is a very old, perhaps the oldest, method of coping with the problem of guilt; the only thing new about Christianity is the unwillingness of the devotees to admit exactly what they are doing, though they come very close to it at times. The drawback of human sacrifice, as a purge of guilt, is that it sets up a new burden of guilt in connection with the human sacrifice itself. Who is going to take upon himself the guilt of carrying out the human sacrifice? The answer is to arrange, mythopoeically, for the sacrifice to be carried out for unworthy motives by someone who can then be regarded as evil. In this way, the devotees who benefit by the sacrifice can wash their hands of responsibility for it, and drive away with pious horror the wretch who performs the sacrifice for them. Pilate, washing his hands of responsibility for the blood of Jesus, is thus, the perfect and prophetic symbol of the Christian Church, for whom the Jews took over the responsibility of performing the sacrifice which was indispensable to the salvation of all Christian believers. An exact formulation of this solution to the problem of guilt is found in the Gospels: 'The Son of man goeth as it is written of him: but woe unto that man by whom the Son of man is betrayed. It had been good for that man if he had not been born'. (*Matt.* XXVI, 24; see also *Luke* XXII, 22.) The man spoken of is

Judas, but the text applies to the Jewish people as a whole, and to their symbol, the Wandering Jew. The human sacrifice has to be performed, but woe unto the man who performs it!

Thus the Wandering Jew was essentially an Executioner, who like the hangman once in England, was shunned by ordinary people and banned from their homes, just because he performed for them an act which they regarded as necessary, but had not the courage to perform for themselves. If this was true of the hangman, who executed people found guilty of great crimes, how much more so was it true of the Wandering Jew, who (as representative of the Jewish people) executed an innocent man! For Jesus was not only innocent; he *had* to be innocent, or the whole sacrifice would have been inefficacious. Only a 'lamb without blemish' would be a sacrifice acceptable to God. And Jesus was not just an innocent man; he was God Himself. (The apotheosis of the victim, who represented the people, is a feature of all rites of human sacrifice, since the intention is to promote unity and identity between the people and the god.)

We must not confuse Christian mythology with the facts. As a matter of historical fact, as far as modern scholars are able to recover it, Jesus was executed by the Romans, at the instigation of certain Jewish quislings, on a political charge of sedition against the Roman occupying power. Jesus himself was not a Christian but a Jew, who would have regarded with horror any attempt to endow him with the mystique of a pagan sacrificial cult. But this cult was superimposed upon the historical facts after Jesus's death, and it is with the mythology of this cult that we are now concerned.

The cultic role of the Jews, then, is to take upon themselves the guilt of performing the sacrifice of Jesus. The satisfaction with which Christians contemplated the sufferings of the Jews in their exile was not a matter of simple sadism or sense of victory. Nor did it derive merely from the thought that the Jews, in suffering for their sin in rejecting Christ, proved the truth of Christianity. The real satisfaction lay in the hidden thought that the suffering of the Jews showed that they, and they only, had to pay for the guilt of performing the indispensable sacrifice. Christians could benefit to the full from the Crucifixion while regarding the perpetrators of the deed with horror. Whenever the suffering of the Jews appeared to diminish, a feeling of panic would grip the Christians. If the Jews were prosperous and flourishing, someone else would have to pay for the deed. Perhaps, moreover, the whole sacrifice would prove inefficacious, and the huge burden of sins which the Crucifixion had rolled away would rush back upon them. If only the Jews would stop complaining about their sufferings as if they did not deserve them! If only they did not insist so on enjoying their lives, whenever they were given the opportunity! If only they would say, 'Yes, we crucified God, and we are willing to pay the penalty! We embrace our sufferings!' Then the Christians would have regarded the Jews almost with love. This is the Christian fantasy which is embodied in the story of the Wandering Jew.

It is interesting to compare the role of the Wandering Jew with that of Jesus himself. In some ways, the two roles are similar. Jesus takes upon himself all the sins of mankind: it is as if he has actually committed all these sins. And then, by his sufferings on the Cross, he atones for all the sins which are now on his head, and thus he saves mankind from the necessity of paying the penalty of eternal damnation. The Wandering Jew takes upon himself one sin only, that of being the Executioner, but this is the greatest of all possible sins, the murder of God. By his suffering he atones for this sin and relieves other people of all responsibility. He is, in fact, a kind of Christ-figure himself. This observation is by no means new. Indeed it is quite a fashionable attitude nowadays for Christians to regard the Jews as a Christ-nation who, by God's design rather than out of wickedness, were burdened with the guilt of the Crucifixion. 'We are all guilty of the Crucifixion, but the Jews were elected to bear the burden.'

The Jews, of course, have traditionally regarded themselves as a Chosen People, but not as one chosen to be an emblem of Man's sinfulness. The Jews have even regarded themselves as a Christ-nation, who suffer for the sins of mankind. The whole passage of *Isaiah* (ch. 53) about the Suffering Servant, which Christians regard as prophetic of Jesus, is regarded by Jews as descriptive of the historical role of the Jewish people. But there is a great difference between the Jewish Christ-people and the Christian Christ-hero (even the difference between the idea of a heroic community and that of a heroic individual is full of significance). The Jewish Christ-people suffers because it knows how to live, not because it knows how to die. Its sufferings are not desired; they are the inevitable consequence of its moral stance, its insistence that man's destiny is in his own hands, a message. which the world rejects with horror and persecution. The Jewish people suffers not because its sufferings are essential to mankind (as Christians think); when the Jews cease to suffer the world will have grown up. And as long as the world has not grown up, the Jews will suffer. This, at any rate, has been the Jewish interpretation of the role of the Jews.

In some pagan cults, the human sacrifice was carried out without guilt. The performer of the sacrifice was a Priest who was regarded with honour (examples are the priests of Moloch, and much later the priests of the Aztecs). But as civilization progressed, people began to see human sacrifice as something shameful. In Hebrew religion, this shame led to the complete abolition of human sacrifice and the substitution of animal sacrifice. The story of Cain, as remodelled in the Bible from earlier sources, is an allegory of this tremendous step forward in human civilization. (Another such story is that of Abraham's cancelled sacrifice of Isaac.) Abel is an animal sacrificer, and thus gains God's favour by being free of the guilt of murder; Cain refuses to sacrifice animals, and therefore stains his hands with human blood. But in other cults, the shame felt about human sacrifice did not lead to its abolition. It was thought that human sacrifice was too necessary ever to be abolished; but expedients were found by which the newly-experienced shame could be appeased. Someone else could be blamed for the sacrifice. A bizarre example (which shows that guilt attached even to animal sacrifice) is the Buphonia sacrifice by the priests of Athens, who killed Zeus in the form of a bull. After killing the bull with an axe, they fled without looking round. Later they held a trial in which the axe was tried and condemned for the murder of Zeus. The story of the killing of the Norse god Balder by the blind Hother suggests that another expedient was the use of a blind man as Executioner, so that inadvertence could be pleaded. A parallel to this story can be found in the Midrashic legend of the killing of Cain by the blind Lamech. (In both stories the killing is performed by shooting with an arrow, ie a remote control execution, which further lessens the feeling of responsibility.)

The story of Cain points to another expedient that must have been common. The man who performed the sacrifice would be solemnly excommunicated. A curse would be pronounced on him, and he would be sent away to wander in the desert. However, his sacramental role as officiating Priest at the sacrifice would not be entirely forgotten. A holy mark would be put on his forehead, so that, though an outlaw, he would be immune from violence. And he would be credited with magic powers of divination and with supernatural skills. (What was the 'mark of Cain'? Robert Graves, adducing *Ezekiel* IX, 4, has conjectured plausibly that the mark was a cross in the shape of a capital T, symbolizing the name of the god who was sacrificed and resurrected, Tammuz. On a cross of this shape the human sacrifice in early times was performed. Later, sacred kings escaped being sacrificed by substituting criminals for themselves. The cross eventually degenerated, in the hands of the Romans, into a mere method of executing dangerous political prisoners. But when Jesus died as a rebel on a cross of this very same design, the ancient Tammuz Cross-cult, still alive in Adonis-worship, was included in the cult of Jesus. The Wandering Jew, in some versions, had the mark of a cross on his forehead.)

In Judaism, a remnant of this expedient of excommunicating the Sacrificer may survive in the Day of Atonement ceremony of the Scapegoat (see *Leviticus* XVI). On this solemn day of release from sin (probably originally a day of human sacrifice), two goats were involved in the ceremony. One was sacrificed in the Temple, but the other, the Scapegoat, was cursed and sent away alive into the desert. (This, at any rate, was the Biblical practice, though later the Scapegoat was killed in the desert by being thrown over a cliff.) The first goat represents the human sacrifice itself; the Scapegoat (how he reminds us of the Wandering Jew!) represents the Sacrificer. Actually, the word 'Azazel', wrongly translated 'scapegoat' on the basis of a fanciful Rabbinical etymology, is really the name of an evil spirit of the desert. Just as Satan entered Judas when he became the Betrayer of Jesus, so the evil spirit Azazel once entered the Executioner, who then became his wandering devotee. Indeed, the expedient of blaming someone for the human sacrifice may account, historically, for the creation of the figure of the Devil. The cult of Osiris, for example, originally human-sacrificial, gave rise to the dark Murderer-figure of Osiris's enemy Typhon or Set. Christianity, with its revival of the concept of human sacrifice, led to a great revival in the status of the Devil-figure Satan, who had been relegated in Judaism to a lowly position as a minor angel obeying God's orders as kind of counsel for the prosecution.

Christianity prides itself on having abolished the Hebrew rite of animal sacrifice. Certainly, animal sacrifice (as the Hebrew prophets pointed out) was not an ideal solution to the problem of guilt. But it was a great advance on human sacrifice, which represented such an enormous need that it could not be abolished without trace. The proof of the inescapability of this need is that Christianity was forced to re-institute human sacrifice, not in the old form of a periodic literal event, but in the form of an interpretation of the death of Jesus, ritualized in the Mass. This was human-sacrifice-in-the-head, which was in some ways even worse than actual human sacrifice, since it required a permanent communal Scapegoat instead of a periodic individual one.

This Scapegoat was the Jewish people, who, however, refused to accept the role or even to understand what was required of them. So the fantasy-figure of the Wandering Jew was created to fill the Christian need for acceptance by the Jews of their role in Christianity. In this way, in 17th century Europe, an ancient myth was revitalized. It derives from a period of pre-history when devotees were beginning to awake to the horror of human sacrifice, but were still unable to abandon it.

Spring 1972

IN THE WARSAW GHETTO - SUMMER 1941
Rafael F. Scharf

When the German army entered Warsaw on 20 September 1939, nearly 400,000 Jews were living in the city, roughly a third of the population. Immediately, they become the target of mounting repression, subjected to forced labour, prohibited from using railways and other public transport, made to wear the Star of David, stripped of their possessions. Virtually without protection of the law, they fell to the mercy of hooligans, sadists, and robbers, of whom there was no shortage. The daily food ration for Warsaw's Jews became 184 calories, compared with 669 for a Pole and 2,613 for a German.

On 2 October 1940, the Germans established an area into which all Warsaw Jews - roughly

138,000 people – along with persons of Jewish origin and Jewish refugees from the provinces were herded; some 113,000 'Aryans' living in that area had to leave.

The Germans then declared the district a 'plague-infested' zone, and the Jews were required to build a wall around it. The Germans did not like the word 'ghetto' and forbade its use; they referred to it as the 'Jewish residential district.' (*Wohnbezirk*). Indeed, the comparison with a medieval ghetto is totally inappropriate, as it implies a degree of normality, where people were born, pursued their interests, died in their beds. In that 'district,' surrounded by a ten-foot-high wall and a parapet of barbed wire, in a space of approximately 1,000 acres, a population of about 500,000 had to sustain itself, thirteen persons to a room, and many thousands without a roof over their heads. Nearly sixty percent of the population was left without a means of making a living.

In Warsaw, as in other occupied towns, the Germans designated a *Judenrat* (Jewish Council) as the body responsible – with their own lives – for the enforcement of orders in the Jewish community. After the establishment of the ghettos, the *Judenrat* was given control of the police, economic management, and all matters of food supply, housing, and education. Although this seemed to be giving Jews a great deal of managerial autonomy, in reality the Germans created the *Judenrat* solely for their own convenience. *Judenrat* members had no option whatsoever but to respond to every command or caprice of their masters. They were often charged with collecting punitive contributions, one method of reducing the Jewish population to penury. As might be expected – and this indeed was part of the German plan – the *Judenrat* often attracted the fierce hostility and hatred of the Jewish population, deflecting these emotions from the real executioners. The role of the *Judenrat* remains a subject of controversy in the study of the behaviour of Jews under German occupation.

The Germans appointed Adam Czerniakow as head of the Warsaw *Judenrat* – it mattered little to them who would act as their puppet. Czerniakow kept a diary in which he noted his daily dealings with various German officials – a diary that remains a most important source of knowledge of that period. It shows Czerniakow, much maligned by his contemporaries, as an almost heroic figure, pleading and arguing with his implacable masters with great courage and dignity, wringing from them small concessions here and there, trying to persuade himself and those around him, in the face of mounting evidence to the contrary, that the worst would not happen. When it become clear, even to him, that 'resettlement' was a euphemism for murder, he refused to put his signature to a directive ordering the deportation of children, and took his own life. He was condemned by many as a coward, and his contemporaries comment bitterly in their diaries: he should have warned the ghetto, he should have issued a call for resistance. Later judgments are kinder to him. This points to the agonizing moral dilemmas that often faced people in those apocalyptic times, dilemmas to which there was and is no answer.

The Warsaw Ghetto was a vast concentration camp with a simple ultimate purpose – to exterminate the Jews through hunger, through cold, through disease. As time went on, it become common to see corpses on the street. Bands of children roamed the alleyways searching for food scraps. Even though the gates were guarded and the penalty for leaving the ghetto without permission was death, the residents tried to survive by smuggling food from the outside. Risking their lives, children proved the most effective smugglers and supporters of their families. The German governor, Hans Frank, stated in a report, 'It is not necessary to dwell on the fact that we are sentencing the Jews to death. If the Jews do not die of starvation, it will be necessary to step up anti-Jewish measures, and let us hope that, too, will come to pass.' Frank's vision soon materialized in the fulfilment of the Wannsee Conference decision on the 'Final Solution'. In July 1942, under the pretext of 'resettlement,' a mass deportation to the death camps began and continued, with

Willy Georg *Two photographs from the Warsaw Ghetto* (Summer 1941) / *Summer 1993*

short pauses, until mid September. During those seven weeks some 265,000 Jews were transported to Treblinka and murdered in the gas chambers. Some of the victims, lured by the promise of food, presented themselves voluntarily at the Umschlagplatz - the railway siding from which the human cargo was packed into cattle trucks and dispatched to the death camps. The deportation drastically reduced the ghetto population; 35,000 inhabitants were permitted to stay - mainly workers employed in German workshops and their families. In addition, some 25,000 Jews were hiding in the ghetto illegally. Under such conditions, as a defiant gesture and in a quixotic attempt 'to die as human beings', Jews organized a resistance. A few hundred desperate people, gathered from the whole spectrum of Jewish society, formed battle units, arming themselves with a few pistols, submachine guns, and Molotov cocktails. In all, their defense amounted to very little. On 19 April 1943, when German troops entered the ghetto to liquidate the last remnants of the population, they met with armed resistance. To their surprise and shock, the Jewish fighters inflicted losses on them and forced them to retreat. The outcome of the battle was, of course, never in doubt for a moment. General Juergen Stroop crushed the uprising with tanks, heavy artillery and flame-throwers. Avoiding open street combat, he systematically burned the houses, block by block. German bombs and hand grenades killed the fighters huddled in bunkers and canals. In spite of that, the battle continued sporadically until 8 May 1943. As a final, triumphant act in the war against the Jews, General Stroop blew up the Great Synagogue in Warsaw and wrote in his report: 'The Jewish residential district is no more.'

The Warsaw Ghetto uprising had an enormous effect on the morale of the Jews and non-Jews around the world. The longest battle against the Germans in occupied Europe before April 1943, the uprising story has become a legend.

We owe a great deal of our knowledge of that period to the effort and initiative of one man, Emanuel Ringelblum (1900-1944). A teacher, historian and social worker, he is one of the unsung heroes of our time. From the initial outbreak of war, he became one of the chief organizers of Warsaw self-help and mutual assistance committees. He kept a chronicle of events and, at his inspiration, in the autumn of 1940, a group with the cryptonym 'Oneg Shabbat' (the Joy of the Sabbath) started writing bulletins describing and documenting the situation. Under his guidance, Oneg Shabbat developed a network of reporters all over the country who collected information in response to a prepared questionnaire. They thought, rightly, that every scrap of paper relating to Jewish life would be of inestimable historical value. Thus they collected official posters, public announcements, diaries, letters, advertisements, packaging, copies of the monitored foreign radio broadcasts and, above all, newspapers and news sheets of the many underground groupings. They commissioned special reports on various aspects of life and fed news items to the Polish underground press.

The Germans took little interest at first in what the Jews were doing among themselves. Jews could write, talk, curse and gossip almost openly. They could discuss in the streets and cafés the illegal news-sheets that circulated freely in the ghetto. Semi-official and clandestine committees sustained the fabric of communal life on all levels, alleviating hunger, providing education, organizing cultural events, setting up projects for medical research, generally keeping up the spirits and the morale of the population. Behind the facades of the tenement houses, around the large, typical Warsaw courtyards, cultural and religious life took on new forms adapted to the unprecedented, immediate needs.

The network of the Oneg Shabbat was the first to obtain eyewitness reports of the mass murder by gas in Chelmno, the first to raise the alarm in the Polish underground press and, finally, abroad. On 26 June 1942, the BBC broadcast news of the extermination of Polish Jews, based on reports sent by Ringelblum. He noted: 'By alerting the world to our fate we fulfilled a great, historic mission. Maybe this will save some hundreds of thousands of Polish Jews. The near future will show. I don't know which one of our group will remain alive, whom fate will choose to make use of our archives, but of one thing we are certain – that our sacrifices, the risks taken, the tension of constant danger, our toil and suffering, have not been in vain.' As the noose tightened, the danger of losing the archives caused serious concern. A few months before the liquidation of the ghetto, all materials were assembled, packed into sealed milk churns and metal containers and buried in a cellar deep under the ghetto buildings. After the war, in 1946 and 1950, two parts of the treasure were found under the mountain of rubble which was all that remained of the ghetto. The third part must be considered beyond retrieval, and the sense of its loss is haunting.

The recovered collection consists of some forty thousand pages, mostly still awaiting analysis and publication. The largest and the most important archive of the era, it remains a priceless source of what we currently know and may yet know about the life and death of the Warsaw Ghetto and the destruction of Polish Jews.

Ringelblum gave of himself unstintingly to the last. In March 1943 he was persuaded to leave the ghetto and find shelter on the 'Aryan side.' On 18 April, the day before the last deportation and the eve of the ghetto uprising, he re-entered the ghetto, wishing to spend Passover with the last survivors. He was caught in a roundup and sent to a concentration camp near Lublin. When his location become known, a team smuggled him out of the camp and brought him back to his Warsaw hiding place, reuniting him with his wife and son. He continued writing; amazingly, without access to books and sources, he wrote one of his key studies, *The Relations Between Poles and Jews in the Second World War*. In March 1944 the Gestapo discovered Ringelblum's hiding place, which reputedly housed sixty people. All of the Jews and the Polish family who sheltered them were taken to the Pawiak prison and shot – within a stone's throw of the ghetto.

In one respect, at least, the Germans were unlucky in their choice of victims. The Jewish people were determined to leave a trace of their fate, at whatever cost. Feeling abandoned by God and man, they were haunted by the thought that the world would not know how they lived and died. Writing made dying easier. The last entry in Chaim Kaplan's diary before his deportation to Treblinka was his anguished cry: 'If I die – what will happen to my diary?'

Primo Levi, in *The Drowned and the Saved*, imagines members of the S.S. taunting their victims: 'However this war may end, we have won the war against you, none of you will be left to bear witness, and even if someone were to survive, the world would not believe him. There will perhaps be suspicions, discussions, research by historians, but here will be no certainties, because we will destroy the evidence together with you. And even if some proof should remain and some of you survive, people will say that the events you describe are too monstrous to be believed; they will say that they are exaggerations of Allied propaganda and will believe us, who will deny everything, and not you.'

Because of these writers and scribblers, the truth has been recorded, has become known to the world, and no one but a maniac or pervert will deny it. These testimonies give us a picture of consummately hideous times. They show us the depth to which humans can descend, and they document how hatred can bring hell on this earth.

The photographs on these pages were handed to me by Willy Georg, a former soldier in the German army, to whose doorstep I was led by friends who knew of my consuming interest in this field. Willy Georg is now over eighty years old – of a generation of Germans with whom I am not at ease without further probing. I am satisfied that he is not suspect: a man of good education and a fairly prosperous background, a professional photographer; at the age of thirty, when these photographs were taken, he was still in the humble rank of Funke-I radio operator. This does not point to someone who was favoured by or benefited from membership in the Nazi party.

How did these photographs come to be taken? Willy Georg has a clear recollection. He was stationed with his unit in Warsaw (in a district called Mokotow, he thinks). Known to his colleagues and superiors as a professional photographer, he was earning extra money to send home by taking snapshots of his fellow soldiers. One day, in summer of 1941, his officer called him and said, lightheartedly: 'There are some curious goings-on behind that wall. I am issuing you with a pass to enter the enclosed area through one of the gates. Take your Leica, and food for the day, and bring back some photos of what you find.'

He did as he was told. He entered the ghetto, walked around, snapped what he saw on four rolls of film, loaded the fifth. Toward evening a German police detachment entered the ghetto, spotted him, and told him to hand over the camera. They opened the back and removed the film; Georg said nothing about the four rolls in his pocket. His credentials verified, he was led outside the gates. He developed the film himself in a photo laboratory in Warsaw. He is proud of his professionalism: after half a century, the film looks as crisp as new. He sent the film home, to his wife in Munster. He gave it little thought in the intervening years, until lately, when he felt the time was approaching to make his final dispositions.

He felt shocked to the care, he says, when he saw these photos anew and recalled those times. It would have been tempting to ask him how he felt then, fifty years ago, when he came unprepared upon that horrific scene, unlike anything he could have encountered before. But there would have been no point in this: all he would have said is what he thinks of it now, or, rather, what he thinks would be appropriate to say to me now. He remembers how polite these people were to him. Although he might not have known it, they had to be polite: a Jew encountering a German was obliged by order to doff his cap and step off the pavement.

This photographic record is not unprecedented. Other photographs still exist that were taken in the ghetto by the Germans around that time and later. (The most famous image – of a small boy in a peaked cap, with his hands raised – stems from one such source.) A team from the German Propaganda Ministry assembled a collection that is now in the official German archives in Koblenz. These photographs were made with the explicit purpose of showing the degradation of that subhuman race, of their indifference to the suffering of their brethren (look how they pass the corpses lying on the street without batting an eyelid), of people allegedly enjoying themselves playing cards in coffee houses. These photographers and their masters were clearly unaware of the reverse effect of their work ultimately, the images degrade not the victims but those who created them.

Willy Georg's snapshots, on the other hand, were totally spontaneous; they simply record the passing scene. The people caught in these photographs – busy, feverish, emaciated, oppressed, but still living a life of sorts – are unaware of the unthinkably cruel end that awaits them shortly. Virtually none will escape a horrible death. One's instinct is to shout a word of warning – Run! Hide! – but it is too late. At that stage nothing, but nothing, they could have done or left undone would have had the slightest effect on their fate. To many of us who grew up within or next to that human landscape and who remember it lovingly, these people – shameful to confess – did not at that time look attractive. These misty eyes, beards, sidelocks, crooked noses – one looked away, embarrassed by what a non-Jewish onlooker might feel or say. It now seems clear that these faces, etched with worry and wisdom, lit with inner light, otherworldly, Rembrandtesque, were inexpressibly beautiful. Set against that rogue's gallery, the flowers of the 'master race' – Goebbels, Goering, Streicher, Frank, and Hitler himself – little more need be said. These photographs give a lost glimpse of a people to be murdered, leaving the world forever and irreparably the poorer for it. The lessons of their lives become more valuable as the time approaches when there will be no living witnesses, and future generations might find such things beyond belief.

This is an expanded version of an article from Summer 1993

ON THE TWENTIETH ANNIVERSARY OF THE MURDER BY THE NAZIS OF JANUSZ KORCZAK
Emanuel Ringelblum

Janusz Korczak (Dr Goldschmidt) was a medical doctor and a well-known pedagogue. He began as an assimilationist. Under the influence of the new currents he came ever closer to the Jewish masses and renounced his earlier assimilationist tendencies. He was a very talented writer for children. His books were read by thousands of children, with bated breath. They made him famous not only among Jewish but among Polish children as well. His books helped to shape their character, accustomed them to the good, the refined, the clean, the modest. His best known work is *Król Macius Pierwszy* ('King Macius the First'). *Joski, Moski, Srulki* (popular names of Jewish children) is a reportage about a children's colony, a report on the achievements in the field of education, a kind of advertisement and recommendation of children's colonies as a vital educational means. That same book was adapted for the Polish scene and appeared under the title: *Jozki, Jaski, Franki* (names of Polish children). In addition he wrote: *Spowiedz Motylka* ('Confessions of a Butterfly'), a book about children's life in a Russian school; *Antek* and *Koszalki Opalki* ('Stuff and Nonsense').

Parallel with his literary work which earned for him the reputation as one of the best writers of children's books in Poland, he practised the pedagogic ideals which he preached in his books, when he took over the administration of the orphanage on Krochmalna 92, which brought him renown as a great children's friend, a superb educator, an inspired pedagogue who penetrated deep, very deep, into the souls of the children. Good, normal relations between the educators and the children prevailed in the institution. All activities in the orphanage were carried out by the children themselves. There was no paid personnel as in other orphan homes. The concept of children's self-administration was realized to the fullest degree. A children's court would adjudicate all infractions of the institution's rules. In Korczak's children's home a painstaking cleanliness was observed and the relations between teacher and children were of the best.

The institution cared for its pupils even after they had gone. The graduates from Korczak's home lived in a students' hostel under educators' supervision. Seldom does one find such attachment of pupils and graduates to an institution. Years later, when the graduates were already abroad, scattered over the seven seas, they continued to keep in touch by correspondence with their beloved teacher Dr Korczak and the rest of the teaching staff.

With the outbreak of the Second World War, Korczak was faced with the difficult task of maintaining the institution at its pre-war level. After the establishment of the ghetto boundaries it had to move from Krochmalna 92 to Chlodna 33. With painstaking and laborious effort the institution was transferred to its new location. But there too it did not find peace. That part of Chlodna was later excluded from the ghetto area and the children's home had to move again to a new address, on Sienna 16, the headquarters of the former Association of Polish Business Employees. From there the institution was transferred to that place from where there is no return – to Treblinka.

Dr Korczak, together with his right hand, Mrs Stefania Wilczinska, spared no efforts to obtain the substantial means necessary to maintain several hundred children. The old friends of the famous Warsaw institution were gone. It was necessary to recruit new members and friends who would care for and concern themselves with the hundreds of orphans and street urchins. Dr Korczak alerted all social institutions, and first of all *Centos* (Children's Welfare Organisation), about aid for his Home.

In Korczak's institution the children did not suffer hunger even in the bitterest days of the ghetto. The great children's friend did not limit his concern to his own institution. He took under his wing the entire community of Warsaw's Jewish children. He was their defender, their passionate advocate. He roused the entire population to the need of the destitute children, and where the danger was especially great he intervened personally. This was the case with the children's home on Dzielna 39. In that Home children dropped like flies. All of Warsaw was aroused. Dr Korczak took over the Home and put an end to the mismanagement that prevailed there. He did not content himself with merely alerting the Jewish institutions about the plight of the children. Together with his teaching staff he organized concerts and literary events for the purpose of raising funds and enrolling friends for the children's homes.

Dr Korczak was the type of rebel who stopped at nothing and would not conform to his surroundings. When the Germans introduced the band of shame (arm band with the Star of David compulsory for Jews) he insisted that as a Major of the Polish Army he was not compelled to wear it. The Germans, however, placed little stock in this view and arrested him. It took much effort on the part of his friends and students to set him free.

During the war Korczak kept a diary. He also wrote a three-volume work, *Dziecy z Eretz* (Children of Eretz) as a result of his trip to *Eretz Yisroel*. These works were probably saved because Korczak had passed them to his friends and students on the Aryan side.

Both before and during the war, Korczak worked together with Mrs Stefania Wilczinska. They went to their death together. Everything connected with Korczak's name, the children's home, his teaching of love for children, was the common contribution of both. It is difficult to say where Korczak begins and where Wilczinska ends. They are twins merged into one soul, one idea: love of children.

Wilczinska introduced the system employed in her children's home to other children's institutions. She would inspect other schools, instruct the teachers in the love of children and how to educate them in accordance with the most modern principles of pedagogy. Even in the most difficult war years Mrs Wilczinska would organize children's excursions to the summer home in the nearby vinage, Gaclewski. She possessed excellent organizational abilities. She was a wonderful pedagogue herself, loved and respected by hundreds of graduates from the children's home, appreciated by hundreds of educators and thousands of children.

That model institution, famous both at home and abroad, did not escape the general fate of extermination of the entire Jewish population during Warsaw's first *Aktion* - liquidation. The *Juden-Sieger,* the S.S. murderers and the Ukrainians came and took away the children together with the teachers and maintenance personnel, with Dr Korczak and Mrs Wilczinska at their head.

Korczak's path to Treblinka is described by the former secretary of the Warsaw *kehillah*, Nachum Remba, who saved hundreds of people in his work on the Umschlagplatz (transfer point for deportation to extermination camps). Remba writes:

> It was a day that crushed me completely. The small ghetto was being blockaded. We had been warned that the nurses' school, the apothecaries, Korczak's orphan home, the children's homes on Sliska and Twarda and many others, were all being taken away. It was a terribly

hot day. I made the children sit down near the end of the building. I had hoped they would succeed in winning a reprieve for the afternoon and thus hold out until the next day. I proposed to Korczak that he come with me to the *gmineh* ('Jewish Council) and persuade them to intervene. He refused. He did not want to leave the children alone for one minute.

The loading began (into the trucks heading for Treblinka). I stood near the head of the *Ordnungsdienst* (Jewish Ghetto Police) that led the people to the trucks. I stood there and with thumping heart watched to see whether my plan would succeed. I kept asking myself about the state of the trucks (that is, whether they were not already full). The loading continued but the quota had not yet been fulfilned. A closely packed, driven mass was harried on with truncheons. Suddenly Mr Sh. (Shmerling, the Jewish commander of the Umschlagplatz, to whom the Germans referred to as *der jüdischer Henker*), gave the order for the children to be led away…

At the head of the procession was Korczak. No! I shall never forget that scene. That was not a march. That was an organised, silent Protest against the banditry! In contrast to the herded mass that went to the slaughter like cattle, here was a march the like of which is hard to conceive. All the children were grouped four abreast. Korczak, erect, eyes uplifted and holding two children by their hands, led the procession.

The second group was led by Stefania Wilczinska, the third, by Barniatovska, her children carrying blue knapsacks, the fourth by Sternfeld of the children's home on Twarda. These were the first Jewish cadres who went to their death with honour, hurling looks of hatred at the barbarians. They presaged the coming of the avengers of our tragedy, who will avenge the evil deed.

Even the *Ordnungsdienst* stood at attention and saluted. Upon seeing Korczak the Germans asked, 'Who is this man?' I couldn't control myself any longer, tears began streaming, down my face. I hid my face in my hands. I was overcome by deep pain at our being so helpless, at our inability to do anything but stand there helplessly and look on at the murder.

At night I imagined that I was hearing the thump of children's feet, marching in cadence under the leadership of their teacher. I heard the measured steps, tramping on and on without interruption to an unknown destination. And to this day I see that scene in my mind. I see clearly the figures, and I see the fists of hundreds of thousands that will come raining down on the heads of the henchmen.

Translated from the Yiddish by Yuri Suhl. Spring 1962

50 JEWS AND A DEAD CAT
Yuri Suhl

Based on an entry in the Ringelblum Diary

The Herrenvolk strutted through the square
eyeing the Slavic trash
they felt called upon to rule
when they stumbled on a dead cat
lying in the gutter.

Goddamn Jews! spluttered one
spitting on the carcass
they'll pay for this!

They fanned out into the streets
and returned with fifty bearded Jews.

Bury that cat, Jews!
a shot rang out in the square
and next to the cat's carcass
lay the fresh corpse of a Jew.

The Jews, now forty-nine
pondered the command
here, one asked, or on some vacant lot?
the Germans replied with another shot.

The Jews, now forty-eight,
got down on their knees
and using fingers for a spade
clawed the ground
buried the cat
flattened the mound.

Give us a prayer, Jews!
a shot rang out in the square
a prayer for the cat's hereafter!

The Jews, now forty-seven,
closed their eyes and
swaying to and fro said the Kaddish
while the Germans rocked with laughter.

But the Jews –
conniving to the last -
fooled them
the Kaddish they said
was for their own dead.

Autumn 1975

A LETTER I WROTE IN 1945
Vera Elyashiv

This is a letter I wrote to my aunt (my father's sister) shortly after my liberation from the camps in 1945. I was then not yet sixteen years old. I wrote it very reluctantly and under repeated pressure from my aunt who understandably was anxious to know what happened to her parents, her brother and her niece – myself. When I eventually did write, I did not attempt to give a full account of what really happened in all those years, only indicating some of the landmarks which bore the answers to her immediate questions. I wrote in German without the remotest thought of publication.

When my aunt translated the letter into Yiddish and had it published in a memorial volume to the perished Lithuanian Jews, I was naturally upset and embarrassed.

It remains the only thing I have written about those years. More and more I am reaching the conclusion of the impossibility of writing about what really happened there. Those who have not been there are not equipped to grasp an experience of such intensity; those who have been there are unable to write about it because they have gone through an experience which has put them on an entirely different plane of perception. All they can say about it now in retrospect must sound like rationalization, a self-apology, a tortured reconstruction of an intimate dream, a negative wishful-thinking trying to outwit the truth.

I tried to explain this to the editor of *The Jewish Quarterly* when he asked me to write about my personal experiences in the Concentration Camps. I agreed, however, to translate into English this one and only letter I wrote then, which, with all its imperfections, has at least some of the directness of documentary evidence. In doing so I have taken the liberty of being more precise in some descriptions which as a child I could not bring myself to utter.

I hope that it will be remembered that it was written by a bewildered little girl, with neither writing nor publishing ambitions, about how her father and entire family perished and she alone survived, without really trying, but feeling guilty and ashamed for that.

V. E.

On 27 October 1941, when I was eleven years old, the ghetto police in Kovno announced that everybody, including the bed-ridden, invalids and cripples were to gather at 5 am in the 'Big Square'. No one undressed that night in the ghetto of Kovno. I was put in three dresses, one on top of the other, and put to bed. At half past three I was woken up. It was dark and very cold. According to the orders no one was allowed to stay in their homes. When we went out into the street we could see huddled and bent shadows emerging from all directions. All were going – the old and the crippled, some limping, some hopping, sick ones and paralysed ones carried with their bed. But you could hear hardly anything but the uneven shuffling of feet – it was like a speechless funeral.

It was dawn when we reached the square. The cold October morning had covered the ground with thin, white frost. The S.S. in their black uniforms were already waiting; cursing, abusing and hitting about with the butts of their rifles. They organised us in long narrow columns. Then the sorting out started. We didn't know then the significance of the two groups into which they divided us; right – left. At least now I think we didn't know. We saw them coming closer and closer. I stood there clinging to my father's arm with one hand and grandmother's with the other, her other hand being held by grandfather. Then a terrible and incomprehensible thing happened: grandfather and grandmother were thrown to the left and father and I to the right. Of all the terrible moments that were to follow, this was one of the worst for me. I don't think I'll ever forget their big helpless eyes. They kept turning to us with outstretched arms and their lips were moving but no words came out.

Two Gestapo officers pushed them brutally away. Only when I saw them joining the other separated group I started to cry. Father told me not to move and he ran to the officer. He returned after a few minutes, his face bleeding. I shut my eyes and let myself be dragged on by him. The first snow started to come down. Large wet flakes covered our shoulders, heads and faces.

That day 10,000 people were taken away by the S.S. and killed on the Fort, outside the town.

We, the remaining, were kept in the square until the evening. When eventually the orders were given to leave, many dead bodies remained behind on the snowy ground.

Father and I returned 'home' to the tiny flatlet we had in the poor Jewish quarter of Kovno, which had become the ghetto. All the cupboards and drawers were open and turned out. Father undressed me and put me to bed – he didn't talk to me that night. I slept in grandmother's bed. There was no need any more to sleep two in a bed. I squeezed grandmother's pillow in my arms and cried myself into sleep.

Early next morning I was woken up by strange cries coming from the street. I looked out of the window and saw lots of people running in all directions, calling names of their missing ones, some accusing one another, some wringing their hands, beating their breasts and crying, crying, crying. This was one of the first big scale shocks, the things that came later didn't have the same impact.

Nearly three years of similar 'actions' followed. The ghetto shrivelled by killings, raids, and 'natural deaths'. Gradually we were also stripped of almost all our possessions. Using our few remaining ones, extra ingenuity, and under the risk of heavy punishment, we sometimes managed to get an extra piece of bread or even a piece of butter from the Lithuanians outside the ghetto. During all this time my poor father took care of me through all the risks and dangers. He even managed to smuggle me out of the ghetto and paid to hide me with a Lithuanian family he knew, but after a short while I ran away and returned to the ghetto. Father was grief-stricken.

In July 1944, the remaining population of the ghetto was informed that they were to be deported. We were ordered to leave the ghetto and forbidden to take anything with us. The ghetto, we were told, would be burned down and whoever tried to hide and remain there would get buried under the debris. I tried to insist on staying in the little hidden cellar, 'bunker' in our terminology, where in the past I managed to survive a special raid on children and several other raids. Father wouldn't hear of this, and so after a long struggle we joined the others gathered in a square outside the ghetto walls. We were told to wait there for trains to take us into Germany. It seemed that there was a scarcity of trains. We waited there for three days, without anything to cover us even at night. From the square we could see the houses of the ghetto exploding and burning. We knew that thousands of people were inside. I cried for the few I knew and for hope that was going up in smoke.

On the fourth day we were woken up at four in the morning. Heavy rain was falling and we were drenched to the bones and shivering. The guards formed us up into a long column and 8,000 starving, stiff-limbed people dragged themselves to the railway station. We were thrown into trucks – the tiny windows and doors were closed and bolted after us. Once moving we soon found ourselves lying one on top of the other, half suffocating. The wet clothes were steaming. Some of the women whimpered or lamented. Some of the men broke the little windows and jumped outside. Through the cracks between the boards it seemed that one fell under the wheels of the train and a second was hit by a bullet when he got on his feet and started to run. In the other wagons similar scenes must have taken place.

At a certain point the Germans announced through the closed doors that we had crossed the border and were in Germany and that there was now nowhere to run. For some reason this had a tremendous effect on me. The silent stupor in which I must have been most of this time left me suddenly and I started to beg father to kill me. I screamed that it was his responsibility since he brought me into the world, and it was his responsibility to free me from all this.

There were those who got hysterical and some screamed in a terrifying way. People started to hit the wagon walls with their fists. This actually had the effect of calming me down. Father was holding me firmly in his arms.

By now two days had passed since we left. Two days with no food or drink. There was a terrible stench and I think I was half faint. On the third day the train stopped. The door was slid open and framed in a blinding sky was the fat face of an S.S. officer. He seemed quite revolted by what he saw. Withdrawing a little he announced that all the women and children must come out and that the men remain inside, so that they could be counted separately.

Soldiers' hands and rifle butts got the reluctant, frightened and by now weakened women and children out of the wagons. I, as with most of the others, could hardly stand and hardly knew what was happening when suddenly the doors of the wagons were closed. I could hear father crying out my name, his cry almost drowned by the noise of the engine and the other cries. I must have tried to run, because I fell and when I got up I could see the back of the fast disappearing train. This was the last I saw of my father.

I don't think we then fully realised what this occasion meant, as we never fully did, and thought that we would be reunited soon, though there was a terrible gloom. We found out that we were in a place called Stutthoff. From the railway station we were taken by a little train of open wagons in which we were standing up, to what turned out to be the concentration camp. I don't remember how the road looked, nor the arrival in the camp. The first thing I saw consciously was a double barbed-wire fence. It must have been about five metres high. There were warnings that it was electrified. High above it there was a tower with guns sticking out in all directions. Lots of long huts stretched before and around us, and we did not at first see the other towers and installations. We discovered these later.

We were brought to a building with two separate wings. I think one had the word 'bath' the other 'steam-bath' on it. Again we were sorted out, right to the bath – left to the steam-bath. All the older frail and ill-looking women and all of the few children who survived till now were sent left.

German guards with batons guarded the separate lines. Others came with large baskets and confiscated all the money and valuables, like the remaining watches, bracelets and rings, those few possessions people managed to salvage and hide from all the other raids, including little bleached and crumpled photographs of the family. Even my attempt to salvage a little ring of my mother's I had managed to keep by pressing it into a piece of soap failed. My piece of soap was flung to the ground and heavy boots trampled on it.

The grown-up women were one by one put on a table with their legs spread out and to my horror and consternation were examined inside – for hidden treasures, I learned later. This was my first view of a gynaecological examination. All of us were examined externally, in the hair, between the fingers and toes.

From there, stripped naked, we had to go through a door into the steam-bath. One of the traits people developed in those years was to push forward to get in first. In the end, being small and shy, I found myself the last, and alone standing before a locked door. The white-frocked German who saw me there, naked and trembling, said something about my being able to do some work and sent me as I was over to the other bath. Only later was I told that those that went in through that door never came out anywhere alive. They were gassed and burned. I don't think I fully grasped this then, and who knows whether I can now.

In the other bath almost everyone was through by now. Even the 'hairdresser' who shaved the women's heads was gone. I was pushed into a shower bath and there, without being given a towel, somebody threw me a heap of rough cloth, which turned out to be a male prisoner's garment – since the dresses were all gone. I got a pair of big trousers and a shapeless jacket in blue and grey stripes and a striped flannel, collarless shirt – no underwear. It turned out to be a blessing compared with the big, shapeless, rough wool dresses which was all the adult women got.

It was already dark when I was pushed out bare-foot into the yard and with a few other remaining women forced over the cold and stony ground into an army-type hut full of continuous rows of bunk beds. This was to be our home for the next four months. They were months of starvation and strange semi-military drilling with parades, marching, and counting, all accompanied with heavy blows and kicks from the guards of our group – prisoners themselves, but criminal ones. We got starvation rations of food for which we had to march in pairs. Abuse and beating up were as much part of this routine as of the others.

At the end of the four months another selection took place. The group in which I found myself was sent to work. Our prisoners' clothes were replaced by a strange array of summery 'civilian' clothes including sandals, some pink or gilded, and with high heels. We were given some kind of pot or pan for our daily food – some ended up with chamber pots.

Thus equipped we were transported to the Province of Elbing (Eastern Prussia) to dig trenches for soldiers and later for tanks. We were housed in tents and slept, ten women to one little tent, with freezing ground underneath us and damp freezing canvas touching our heads and shoulders.

We were about 1,200 women, again guarded by the S.S. with a vicious sadist as their commander, who chose amongst the women one to assist him as a 'Kapo' and three to assist at her side.

Winter came. Women got wounds and abscesses from malnutrition which in the frost became gangrenous. The death rate was accelerated by typhoid and dysentery. At last overcoats were sent. In spite of the ugliness I considered myself lucky to be in a big and heavy man's coat. By now our tents were covered with a thick layer of ice and snow and the ground underneath was frozen. Our feet were wrapped in straw held with wires, but this did not prevent most of us getting chilblains which became infected and never healed. Our hands grew all blue and purple.

We moved to a third labour camp as the trenches had to be extended. By now only 513 women had survived out of 1,200. From early morning to late evening we dug in the hard clay with pick-axes to complete our stint of the 1.8 metre deep trenches. Women died whilst they were working and on the march home. We were not allowed to stop and pick them up and so their bodies were trampled on. Not a sigh, not a tear was shed for them. Each knew that tomorrow it could be their turn.

As time went by, water became scarcer and scarcer. We could not wash. But sometimes I tried to wash with my ration of morning coffee – burnt chicory water. Parasites dug into the flesh of the weaker ones. On our way to and from trenches we sometimes passed fields of potatoes, beetroots or turnips and in spite of the inevitable beatings women would fling themselves into the fields where they managed to dig out with their fingers one or two vegetables before the guards and their rifle butts got at them. No morals or scruples or even fear would hold them back. I think it was fear that restrained me.

Most of the women had bodies black and blue, torn, scratched and infested, their ribs poking through and bellies swollen. My secret selfish pride was that I avoided being like that. I conducted my own kind of war against the Germans in which every day I came out the victor. I avoided doing anything that would give them an easy pretext to beat or touch me to the extent of refusing extra food or better conditions when these were offered by Germans who took pity on the only girl who spoke German and reminded some of them of their own children. Four seemingly endless years had passed and somehow in spite of everything I was still alive. Alive in filth, blood and amidst corpses. I was almost sixteen by now.

Normal life – my beautiful white room on Kestucio Street 55, my Fräulein Elia from Königsberg, the dog, grandmother and grandfather, father – all this seemed much more unreal than the squalor I lived in. Yet in spite of everything I treated this time partly as a dream and I was sure that soon I would be re-united with father.

By now we found ourselves in Poland midway between Torn and Bromberg. Early one morning, it was at the beginning of May, 1945, we saw that the roads were packed with refugees; cattle ran about the fields in frightened confusion and the usual *'alles aufstehen!'* (Everybody to get up!), had a different sound. Before our columns were ready to march to work the camp commander appeared and announced that we would not be going to work but be evacuated into Germany, since the Russian troops were advancing and were close to our position. He said there was no reason for us to rejoice since none of us would reach the Russians alive. We were ordered to take with us our only possession – our food container – and we set out to what he threatened was to be our last journey.

We marched for about a fortnight. All this time we did not get bread or any other food. From time to time, especially when the roads were being shelled, we managed to take some vegetables from the fields or gardens we happened to pass. Sometimes I was given potatoes or carrots by the women – I didn't dare go myself for fear of being beaten by the Germans when the shelling ceased. All this time we were leaving corpses on the roads. One German officer always tried to help me and often offered me his own rations which I proudly and stupidly rejected. He also sometimes managed to drag me into hiding when the aeroplanes appeared and he tried to comfort me; the road seemed without an end.

After two weeks on the road we reached a rather big forest. There our guards suddenly disappeared. We dared not go further. Next day a German *'fieldgendarmerie'* (rearguard) appeared. They surrounded us and waited for the order to liquidate us. But it never came. A messenger arrived breathlessly on a horse and announced that the Russians were a couple of kilometres away. They all fled in panic.

And that is how the Russians found us. It was quite a romantic moment since 'the Russians' in this case was one beautiful Russian Captain, Jewish, with a fur hat and riding on a steaming horse. Soon more Russians arrived. This was the long-awaited and never really believed moment of liberation. We were very quiet, a few were completely petrified and others cried quietly.

Soon afterwards we marched again. In a strange way we were more tired and weak now. We were guided to some gathering place, I hate to use the term 'concentration point' as it was really called. It was an abandoned hotel. There we found groups of survivors from other 'liberated' camps; and there we stayed for eight more months under the Russian command. 'Command' because that is what it really was. During this time, of which I have very little recollection, we were questioned by many commissions and investigators to establish whether or not we were fascist collaborators. That is how we were received by what we then thought was 'the free world'. Later, together with some other women from Lithuania, I was transported back to Kovno. But most of the women did not go back and decided to stay outside the Soviet Union.

Back in Kovno I did not find my father. I was told by somebody that he witnessed his death in Dachau. This is all I could find out about it then.

I know this letter does not tell you what really happened. Forgive me its style and lack of coherence. I know it will be difficult for you to really follow it. I do not have the necessary talent and lack even the appropriate vocabulary. Ask me for clarification if something does not make sense to you. Give my best regards to my uncle and cousin Sasha. I kiss you all.

Autumn 1970

HOMAGE TO SALONIKA, THE CAPITAL OF VANISHED WORLDS
Mark Mazower

From the text of a Greek leaflet issued by the *Organismos Politistikis Protevousas tis Evropis-Thessaloniki* 1997:

> Thessaloniki, classical city, Hellenistic city, Roman, Byzantine and Balkan, city of the East, city of Europe, a remarkable city with a presence through history...

The money has been pouring in: warehouses down by the station now house trendy jazz venues; the old mansions are getting a face-lift; new cafés are opening by the minute. Browsing in a smart central bookshop, my attention is caught by a work on the world Jewish conspiracy. Its blend of capitalists, communists and Zionists is illustrated by the usual money bags and hooked noses. 'How can you sell this rubbish?' I ask the manager. 'Many people ask for it,' he replies.

> Thessaloniki, the city which Kassander founded, has embraced in its culture every kind of religion, custom and tradition. Occupied or occupier, it insisted upon providing a home to whoever chose it for the quality of its soil, its links with the sea, and the roads which link it with other worlds.

In November 1996 we held a conference there on the fate of Greek Jewry during the German occupation. It was the first ever devoted to the subject, with speakers from a number of countries. But most of the city's professors, journalists and commentators stayed away. It was as if the Jews had lived in another city, not theirs. These were not their ghosts.

Or maybe it was just an unusually warm autumn day, or the publicity had not been good enough.

> The succession of civilizations is marked in Philip's gold, in the royal buildings of Galerius, in the Egnatian Way and the cupolas of churches, in their mosaics and frescoes, in the complexity of fortifications, the houses of the Upper Town, the Ottoman shrines and the Art Deco architecture of the city's buildings. Temples, markets, palaces, hippodrome, basilicas, churches, baths and shrines. Traces of Hellenism, Rome, Byzantium, the Ottomans ... Traces of a remarkable city!

Looking for the site of the old 151 neighbourhood, home to hundreds of poor Jews in the 1930s, we stopped a couple of men of about the right age. 'Yes, you're not far.' They gave us directions. 'That way. Opposite the electricity offices. But there's no trace of it now. It's all new buildings.' The traffic roared up Markos Botsaris street. Did they remember the Jews? Of course. They all went to school together, they were friends. They used to do chores for them on their day of rest. Did they remember the day they had to leave the 151? That too. The whole area was surrounded by police and Germans. They weren't supposed to go in. Did you? 'Sure, we were kids.' The rooms were just as they had been left. They took a few bits and pieces and got out.

> The first recognized settlement inside the Thermaic Gulf was neolithic, the prehistory of Thessaloniki, a city which took its name from the sister of Alexander of the Macedonians. In its long history, today's capital of the Greek North has been distinguished as foundation of the Hellenistic world, as royal seat of the Roman Empire, as joint capital of Byzantium and, more recently, as metropolitan centre of the Balkans.

On the plane home, Elisabeth showed me her new game. We must have played about twenty times. She and her mother had spent the summer with her grandparents in the city and were flying back to Canada. They were good company. Her mother had grown up in Salonika, in 40 Ekklisies, just overlooking the university campus. Did you know that the old Jewish cemetery lay on that site, I ask. Sure, she says. When we were little, we used to play there down in the sandhills. The new buildings were going up. Sometimes we found bones and things. We had this game, looking for treasure. What the Jews were supposed to have buried before they were taken away.

All these stories just under the surface, waiting their turn.

★

From *A Handbook for Travellers in Greece, describing the Ionian islands, the Kingdom of Greece, the islands of the Aegean Sea, with Albania, Thessaly and Macedonia* (London: John Murray, 1854):

> The inhabitants of Salonica amount to 60,000, of which a moiety is nearly equally divided between Greeks and Turks, while the remainder are Jews, the descendants of those expelled from Spain at the beginning of the 17th century. Their language is still a corrupted Spanish. Their outward dress consists of the fez, or turban, and of a tunic reaching to the ankles, and bound at the waist by a shawl or sash. The dress of the women differs but little from that of the men. A few Frank merchants are settled at Salonica, besides the consular body. There is a pasha, a Turkish garrison, and a Greek archbishop. There are steamers to Constantinople once or twice a week, in about 36 hours.
>
> The commerce of Salonica consists in exporting the corn, cotton, wool, tobacco, beeswax and silk of Macedonia. A British Consul resides here. Salonica is subject to malaria, and the whole country at the head of the Gulf is miserably unhealthy. There is excellent shooting in the neighourhood, including pheasants, woodcocks, wildfowl etc.

★

'Through the door opening on the *varandado* comes the sound of voices and the tinkle of silverware. Sarica, the maid, is setting the table. Father will soon be coming home. He wishes Nono would return from the country.

'From somewhere he hears his name called. He peers down into the garden, now full of shadows, but does not answer. The hubbub in the street has now subsided. A cavalry officer, coming from the Konak, the government offices, trots by, followed by his orderly. The storekeepers have already lit their kerosene lamps, and on the darkened background of grey walls little squares of yellow light appear. Snatches of a softly crooned song drift to his cars:

Decild'a la morena que lla me va ir,
La nave lla 'sta'n vela y lla va partir.
(Tell my dark-haired one that I am going
The ship has set sail and is leaving.)

'Again he is being called. The same voice, a woman's voice, clear and musical, sounds, this time from the *varandado:* 'Where are you, my soul?' The little boy hesitates for a moment. He looks at the minaret, now a shaft of white reaching to the sky. With a sigh he leaves the balcony for the brightly lighted *varandado.*' From *The Minaret*, which forms the prologue to *Farewell to Salonika, Portrait of an Era*, by Leon Sciaky (London: WH Allen, 1947).

★

Occasionally in the archives one encounters some more or less forgotten figure whose life seems to sum up the hopes and disappointments of a vanished world. One such was Avra'am Benaroya, who died in a suburb of Tel Aviv in 1979 aged well over ninety. In April 1950, while still resident in Greece, a letter from him was published in a daily called the *Evraiki Estia,* (Jewish Hearth), which enjoyed a small circulation among the country's much-depleted post-war Jewish readership:

> Dear Editor,
> I read with interest your piece on Ben-Gurion's stay in Salonika, where he studied law, and since I remember this period well, I'd like to supplement these memories with a very characteristic episode in the career of today's prime minister of Israel.

The letter recalled events which had happened nearly forty years earlier. Benaroya, who was born into a Sephardic family in Bulgaria, and started off teaching Bulgarian in a Jewish school in Plovdiv, settled in Ottoman Salonika in 1908. He more than anyone helped turn the city into the home of the most important workers' movement in the Balkans. There was a *Club Ouvrier*, a journal printed – naturally - in four of the city's leading languages (Judaeo-Spanish, Bulgarian, Greek and Turkish), and a powerful union organization known as the *Federaciòn Solaridad Obradera*. It was, in all, an exciting atmosphere for the young Jewish man who would later call himself Ben-Gurion.

'In 1910 exactly', Benaroya's 1950 reminiscence continues,

> the future Prime Minister of the State of Israel settled in Salonika where he registered as a student in the law faculty of the Turkish university. In early 1911, at the initiative of the present writer, we organized in the offices of the *Federaciòn* a special debate on the Jewish question. We invited Ben-Zvi and Polin, together with Green (Ben-Gurion) and the Zionists. Surviving Zionists and socialists will remember well the long discussion in which Ben-Zvi and Green spoke Hebrew. Florentin and others took part on behalf of the Zionists. The speeches were translated into Judaeo-Spanish.

At this time it had briefly seemed possible that the many different ethnic and religious communities of Macedonia might live and struggle together. But only briefly. As in Western Europe, nationalism was more powerful than class solidarity. In 1911 Benaroya was sent into exile by the increasingly nationalist Turks. In 1912 the Greek army marched into Salonika and made the city Greek. Benaroya's world was transformed, and narrowed.

From that point on the Zionist workers' movement gained energy and creativity. But the international situation of the times and the lack of a coherent Jewish mass in Palestine did not allow the leaders of international socialism to appreciate the whole value of the positions adopted by Ben Zvi and Green.

After 1912 this strong-willed man carried on, working for socialism inside Greece. He met the Prime Minister, Venizelos, and was instrumental in founding the Greek trade union movement. But then he became impatient with the limited horizons of the Greek left, and became a marginal figure, respected as commentator and theorist but of little political weight. In inter-war Salonika he enjoyed great prestige as a journalist and union organizer. Recently, in the Saoul Modiano Old People's Home in the city, I met a man called Moise Bourlas who remembered him from those days:

> He was the soul of the workers' movement in Salonika. A good man, and much loved. Because if you bear in mind that he was Jewish, he enjoyed - how to put it - great love among the working people - from all, from everyone. He was very fair-minded, not just in his views, but in his manner of expression. When he said something, you thought it was made of pearl. He was direct, a man who knew how to talk on the level with each kind of man - cultured with those who were educated, a worker with the workers, illiterate with the illiterate. He had a knack of understanding people so that he got close to them and they felt at ease.

Benaroya survived the war as a political prisoner in a German camp, but lost a son, as well as what was left of the Jewish world in which he had grown up. During the Cold War, his brand of independent leftism attracted persecution in Greece from both Communists and right-wing nationalists. In 1953 he finally left and emigrated to Israel where he lived in poverty, continued to write and helped set up a small group of like-minded Ladino-speaking socialists with their own newspaper, *El Tiempo*. To this heroic point had shrunk the energies of one of the greatest political minds of Balkan Jewry, active to the end.

'It needed the Second World War', Benaroya's letter concludes,

> and the historically unprecedented persecution of the Jewish race, the disappearance of millions of martyrs and the heroism of a few thousand representatives of socialist Zionism, to bring into being the State of Israel and to make the combination of national liberation and the social transformation of the Jewish people fruitful and beneficial.

Salonika in the early part of this century hosted many remarkable individuals. There was one of its own sons, Mustafa Kemal, who later - as Ataturk - achieved fame as the founder of modern Turkey. There was Ben-Gurion himself, and his fellow student Ben-Zvi. Avra'am Benaroya is a less familiar figure than any of these, his achievements outweighed by his disappointments. Historians are prone to glorify history's success stories, but let us spare a thought for Benaroya, a man who understood all kinds of people 'so that he got close to them and they felt at ease'.

★

The archives of the University of Thessaloniki contain a small offprint which - so says the librarian's stamp - was catalogued in 1939 and has not been much read since. Its title is *Etudes Saloniciennes* by Mercado J. Covo; it is dated 'Eloul 5688 - août 1928', and was presented by the author as an offprint from the yearly publication, *El Maccabeo*.

A dedication, written in ink: 'A la Bibliothèque de l'Université de Salonique, "Alma Mater" de la Grèce, Sept./ le j'offre ce . . . opuscule. M. J. Covo, Professeur de français au Talmud Thora, 38 rue Sparta, 38 Salonique.' I cannot make out the penultimate word of the inscription. At least one of the 38s must refer to the year of the gift.

The essay presents Covo's initial researches into the Jewish printers of sixteenth-century Salonika. He stresses the glorious history of the community, as well as its regrettable lack of interest in its own past, and asks for assistance in his own scholarly endeavours: *L'histoire d'une Communauté comme la nôtre, deux fois millénaire, ne s'écrit pas en un jour et ne saurait être l'oeuvre d'un seul chercheur.* He describes his joy at a new discovery, and accepts with calm the fact that certain obstacles to scholarly knowledge may be insurmountable. He ends with a plea:

> En attendant, je serais très reconnaissant à tous ceux qui voudraient bien me signaler des éditions rares de Salonique et me procurer contre argent des brochures parties en notre ville sur nos Ecoles, nos sociétés etc. (Comptes-rendus du Talmud-Thora, Alliance isr. Univ., Etz-ha-Haim, Hessed Ve-Emet, Kadimah, Hôpital etc. etc.).

En attendant – the words of a true scholar, for whom the pursuit of knowledge is cumulative, and collective, and requires true patience and commitment. And the best touch of all – a postscript which the author cannot resist, betraying his reluctance to wind up:

> PS: Ce court essai de l'histoire de la typographie hébraïque à Salonique au XVIe siècle était déjà sous presse quand de nouvelles recherches m'ont permis de découvrir de nouveaux documents sur la production littéraire des juifs d'ici et leur impression en cette ville au 16e s., documents que j'utiliserai très prochainement. M.J.C.

I have not been able to find out whether Covo continued to publish his researches in the short time left before war broke out. Nor do I know what he made of the German professors who arrived in his city in 1941 with the *Sonderkommando* Rosenberg to ransack the scholarly riches of the community. They seized 10,000 volumes and sent them to the Reich for the new advanced research institute into the Jewish Question which was being set up by Alfred Rosenberg himself. And what too would he have made of the news which broke half a century later, in the spring of 1995, that these volumes had been discovered in Moscow? Perhaps all this would have simply seemed to him among the vicissitudes of scholarship.

★

AA 4209 18.30 from Chicago O'Hare landed on time. Waiting for me in the terminal building was a man called Mike Vogel. He came over unhesitatingly and held out his hand. I apologized for keeping him waiting: he had come specially. It was nearly nine in the evening, and the lounge was almost empty, but a snack bar was still open, and we sat ourselves down at a table.

> We used to call them 'Saloniki'. *'Saloniki! Atras, Saloniki!'* 'Look out, Saloniki!' They had such a language, none of us understood. We didn't understand it. We knew there were Greek Jews coming. The Nazis would tell us: You're going to have some Grecos. They'd tell us: 'Today we're gonna eat cheese' - that meant Dutch; sardines and paté, French; Hungarian salami, Hungarians. With the Greeks it was figs, olives and a few bananas. They were dressed also different, but the dress didn't last long 'cos they were undressed.

Miso Vogel was born before the war in Slovakia. Today he works in Indianapolis. In March 1942 he was deported as a slave labourer to Auschwitz 1 where he was consigned for a time to the so-called *Kanadakommando* which helped unload the trains as they came in from all over Europe. As a result, he is one of the few people in the world alive today who saw the transports arrive from Thessaloniki in the spring of 1943:

> When they brought the Greek Jews in, this was the most chaotic transport to be unloaded. First of all, none of us spoke Ladino. They came in terrible physical condition because it took so long. It was the worst transport. They'd brought figs and olives with them. We had to take everything away from them. They didn't understand the selection. It was hard to assemble the Greek Jews. You see, if you had an Ashkenazi Jew you could speak to them. Ladinos don't speak Yiddish. We had to physically take them and separate them. It was so chaotic that there were a lot of beatings by the Nazis. They couldn't get them into line by speaking so they started beating and hitting them ... The Greeks didn't understand. '*Geht rechts, Geht links!*' didn't mean anything to them.

Did he mind me taking notes? Far from it. He wanted to tell me. His memories of the Jews from Salonika were succinct, but strong and vivid. 'They and the Ukrainians had it worst. Yet they had a good sense of humour. They used to say in French – referring to the Germans – "*Cochons*"'. After a few minutes more, we walked downstairs to the luggage area, and I found my driver. He was impatient to leave, so Vogel and I said goodbye. His wife was not well and he had to get back. Soon we were on the freeway out of the city.

> The worst thing that happened to the Greek Jews was in May 1944, when they started to bring the Hungarian Jews to Auschwitz. The *Sonderkommando* was expanded by 400 people. Otto Moll got a number of Greek Jews to work the gas chambers. They worked in the pits. Hungarian bodies were burning in pits and the Greeks had to stomp on the coals to trample down the bodies. I remember ...

Summer 1997

THE DANCING BEAR
Frederick Goldman

Because I speak the language, my editor at *Stars and Stripes* had assigned me to check on a report that forty Jews had been murdered, and sixty wounded by Poles, on 4 July 1946, in the village of Kielce. This was the latest in a series of stories which had reached us - *after the Germans retreated west in 1945* - about violence against survivors when they returned, after the war, to reclaim their homes. The Kielce incident, if true, boosted the total of deaths to over 1,500. The Jewish victims were sometimes accused of using the blood of Christian children in the baking of Passover matzos, or profanation of the Host, or other blasphemies.

It was a juicy story, but I had no wish to see my native land again. I felt the sour taste of anxiety rise during the tedious flight over the graveyard of Germany and western Poland. In Warsaw, I learned that the event in Kielce had attracted wide attention in the European press, after the *New York Times* headlined its interview with the Catholic Primate of Poland, Augustus Cardinal Hlond, 'Cardinal Puts Blame on Some Jews for Pogrom'. The embattled prelate had been forced to consent to a media gang-bang. Surrounded by microphones and repeatedly assaulted by exploding flashbulbs, his composure eroded as rapid-fire questions implied church incitement in the slaying of death-camp survivors. He rebutted by charging that rising antisemitism was 'to a great degree due to the Jews'. They were becoming prominent in the post-war Communist government, he said, so violent reaction by Polish nationalists was understandable. Then he abruptly withdrew, referring further inquiries to Bishop Stefan Wyszynski, head of the Lublin diocese, which included Kielce.

As the press conference disintegrated, I had a joyful reunion with David Andrews, whom I'd last seen in Bastogne at a Chopin recital which was aborted when Panzer divisions encircled the town and we rushed to defence posts. David was now with *The Times*. We agreed to go to Lublin together. A young Russian journalist arranged a ride for us early the next morning, so we were there before the rest of the press gang, and were accorded a long private interview with Bishop Wyszynski. We talked in awkward German and awkward French for hours. He was a charmer, obviously well-educated and intelligent, projecting a forceful personality. (It was easy to understand why he was, soon after, named Primate of Poland and to the College of Cardinals. He would become the immovable object against which the assumed-to-be irresistible force of successive Communist regimes exhausted themselves.) Although the bishop assured us that he was looking into the 'rumour' himself and already had investigators in the village of Kielce, he volunteered to put a car and driver at our disposal so we could pursue our own enquiry.

Hours later, in my bleak hotel room, I reviewed the notes made during our interview, and memories of life in Poland before the war. Sleep was difficult; my emotions were agitated. When I finally succeeded in dozing off, a childhood nightmare returned.

I found myself in a vast white-walled room without doors, cold as a glacier. The floor shook with the thunder of a giant, dancing bear; its monstrous shadows raced over the ceiling and walls. As a boy, I had first seen the creature in the barnyard of a peasant's farm some miles from my birthplace in Oshmiana just before Passover. Oshmiana was a small village midway between Vilna and Minsk. Then, 20,000 Jews lived there. A stone's throw from the main street – the only one that was paved – could be found the homes of Jews on muddy lanes, with geese, ducks, chickens and children waddling in puddles around every water pump.

We lived cheek-by-jowl with Christian neighbours; they were as familiar with our customs as we were with theirs. We heard their 'Hail Marys' on Sunday mornings and we stayed off the streets when they came out of church. They saw us parade to our synagogue every Friday evening and heard our songs through the open windows. Just as we knew their liturgy, Christians were familiar with ours. This intermixing of Jews and Christians in eastern European villages like Oshmiana was normal – except once a year, when the atmosphere thickened, as before a storm.

Towards Easter, tensions appeared. Reminded in church of Christ's Passion, some Christians became angry as they saw and heard their Jewish neighbours preparing for the joyous festival of Passover. Latent hostility could easily become belligerence. We Jewish children were reared on tales of abuse; we were told of pogroms. Bred into our psyche was the expectation of violence. Even prominent Jews were no exception: the teacher, pharmacist or merchant. So when Jews met a Christian on the sidewalk outside the train station, where we picked up our mail and newspapers, we would step aside, even though there was ample room for two. We lifted our hats and inclined our heads.

Such were the norms which early defined my sense of self and the social rules which prevailed. When I was twelve, I started to work in the family store. We sold dry goods, yard goods, notions, trimmings, hosiery, gloves, work clothes – practical things needed by gentiles as well as Jews. In addition, my grandfather stocked costume jewellery, music boxes, clocks and watches – the big ones with heavy chains and German gothic numerals on their faces. We had many rolls of embroidered tape which women adored – farm women particularly – to fancy up their dresses and smocks. Occasionally grandfather would invest in a semi-precious stone, or a filigree gold or silver brooch, hand-painted enamels, porcelain pins with cameos.

The year of my bar mitzvah, I was thrilled by grandfather's offer to take me along on his annual spring 'rounds' of farms and estates in our *gubernia*. It was just before Passover and Easter, when customers were minded to dress up for the holidays. The roads had been churned by carriages, horses, carts and herds of cattle into a muddy morass, streaked by ribbons of melting snow. Since dawn we had ridden many hours through forests and fields and had visited many farms. It was past noon as we approached an elaborate fence encircling the barnyard of a good customer, whom grandfather said he knew well and liked. In eastern Europe, after harvest, peasants would carve new fence slats and create fanciful new arches over the gates. Every one was different: the fence design itself and the slat-patterns were unique to each property, as was the ornamentation of roofs, windows, doors, shutters.

To the side of the wide barnyard gate for the animals, there was a small one with a bell-pull. Servants inspected us through the close-set slats and reported to their master. Finally, we were admitted to the courtyard which stretched between the towering barn and the farmer's two-storey house. Mud in the courtyard was almost as deep as on the road. Wagons were parked to the side and there were two dozen men, women and children at a trestle table which had been set near the house. The women and the girls wore embroidered holiday dresses; the men and boys had handsome sheepskin vests, also decorated. Couples were dancing clumsily, arms wrapped around each other. A balalaika was being strummed softly. Vodka jugs were numerous.

Grandfather and I stood at some distance until we were invited to approach the table. A space was cleared. Grandfather spread out jewellery, trinkets and lots of new novelty items we had just received from Warsaw – embroidery tape, multi-coloured shawls, silk flowers, gorgeous buttons. Many things were passed from hand to hand for examination. Then the farmer, high cheekbones curled into a broad smile under pale blue eyes, threw his arm around grandfather's shoulder and shouted, 'What news from Jerusalem, Moses? Has your messiah arrived yet?' Everybody laughed, but I was shocked when grandfather cackled too. I had never before seen this dignified man treated so familiarly – let alone have his beard tugged, which the farmer did next, to more laughter.

It was bewildering. In our large family, grandfather was revered. In the Jewish community, he was admired: he was president of the *kehilla* - the civic association - and a member of the *Chevra Yosher*, the Association for Justice. (Jews did not take legal matters to gentile courts in those days; disputes were settled among ourselves.) He had a beautiful baritone voice, and acted as cantor at Sabbath services.

Before my eyes, this tall, stately man seemed to shrink as the laughter continued. Then, the farmer banged on the table with a jug of vodka, poured a mug for grandfather, and shouted: 'Sing, Jew! Sing for us your Sabbath song, "How Beautiful You Are!" And dance for us as you did several years ago - like the bear that performs when the carnival wagons come!'

My grandfather drank from the mug, then started slowly to sway and hop, from foot to foot. The driving rhythm of the balalaika, the clapping hands, the fists pounding the table accelerated the tempo. Faster and faster, grandfather whirled, beard flying and a grimace masking his features. His eyes were squinted shut. His skullcap flew off.

The sun blinded me. It was a time of dread. In a paralyzed trance, I was sick at heart, scared by fear and shame and fright - pain which haunts me still, through all the years since that long-ago springtime in that long-lost world.

But for the celebrants, the performance was a great success. Everybody was in a good mood. The vodka circled the table with the jewellery and other goods. Buying was enthusiastic. Most of the stock was sold. What little was left, grandfather and I packed up. The long ride home was through an immense grey, cold silence, and we didn't look at each other.

Weeks later, grandfather explained that the farmer had meant no malice. What had happened 'was not the first time – it was as normal as expecting Jews to tip their hats when meeting a Christian on the street'. The story came out in bits and pieces during long walks – punctuated by gentle reminders not to kick my left ankle, a peculiar habit I'd recently acquired.

With many interruptions, the story would continue. 'After King Casimir the Great, in the fourteenth century, invited Jewish immigration to develop trade,' he explained, 'Polish and Lithuanian nobles were not averse to enjoying the increased prosperity produced by the middle-men from their great landholdings, but they were firm about maintaining social distance. One way they did this was to invite 'their' Jews for special entertainments and disguise them as Tartars or Gypsies; or costume them as Turks; or even Africans with blackened faces. The dancing bear tradition acted out a role-relationship between us and our Christian patrons.' This onerous practice, when Jews sang and danced to order, he went on, acquired the name '*mayofis*', a bastardization of '*ma yofit*', the first words in Hebrew of the Sabbath song – 'How Beautiful Thou Art'. Pronounced by Christians phonetically, the words also became a name for people who accepted compromises and concessions as part-payment on the price for survival.

In the years that followed, I came to understand the symbolism whereby our lovely liturgy, counterpointing the individual's love for God with God's love for His people, was transformed into a travesty – and a victory. The challenge is not heroism but endurance.

In the airless Lublin hotel room, awakened by my nightmare from restless sleep, I tried to calm myself with the thought that the legend – and my memories of childhood – were about people and places long ago and far away. Then I remembered details of the interview with the bishop. We talked of many things: of the democracies' past mistakes; of the developing political dilemma; of chances for Polish independence.

Finally, he got around to the reason David and I had asked to see him. Though he had, as yet, no facts on the 'Kielce incident', as he called it, he assured us that the position of the Polish church was clear: antisemitism was 'contrary to the spirit of the Gospel'. He added that he had made an 'exhaustive study' of ritual murder accusations in Europe from the Middle Ages into the twentieth century and would brook no such disturbances in its diocese. Then, in a casual aside to his secretary, he switched from French to Polish, muttering that on this subject, 'the evidence is inconclusive'; he was – I remember him saying – 'left in doubt about the truth'. I assumed he didn't know that I understood the language. Until, as he ushered us out, he put his arm around my shoulders and asked in Polish, 'What news from Palestine?'

My thoughts shuttled between rural barnyard and episcopal mansion, between peasant and prince. Just as there had been no malice in the farmer's teasing of grandfather, I assumed there was no ignorant bigotry in the bishop's words about ritual murder. Just an atavism, as indelible and implacable as the appendix. Dark and evil, it entwined and choked, like wisteria. I had to face reality: as human nature doesn't change, why should human behaviour?

After breakfast, I asked David to wait in the hotel lobby for the diocesan automobile, which the bishop was providing to take us to Kielce. I thought I'd have a better chance of finding a pharmacist in Lublin. I needed moleskin for my left ankle, which somehow I had bloodied yesterday, walking back to the hotel.

Summer 1994

THREE POEMS
Nelly Sachs

Chorus of the Dead

We, hollowed like sieves
by the black sun of fear –
Run-offs of the sweat of the minute of dying we are.
Withered on our bodies are the deaths
done to us,
like field-flowers withered on a sandhill.
O you, who still greet the sand as a friend,
who, sand speaking to sand, can say:
I love you.

We, we tell you:
Torn are the cloaks of the secrets of dust.
The air which was choked within us,
the fires in which we were burned,
the earth into which they threw our remains,
the water pearling away with the sweat of fear,
burst forth within us, in a flash.
We, Israel's dead, we tell you:
By now we are one star ahead,
reaching beyond and into our hidden God.

Translated from the German by Jacob Sonntag

Chorus of those who were saved

We who were saved
Out of whose hollow bones death had already carved his pipes,
Across whose sinews death had already drawn his bow –
Our bodies still reverberate mournfully
With their crippled music.
We who were saved
The nooses braided for our necks
Still hang before us in the blue air
And the water clocks measuring the hours
Still fill with our dripping, dropping blood.

We who were saved
The worms of fear still gnaw within us.
The constellation of our stars is buried in dust.
We who were saved
Beg you:

Be slow in showing us your radiant sun.
Lead us from star to star in single step.
Softly, quietly, let us learn life anew.
For otherwise, the song of a bird
Or the filling of a bucket at the well
Could break open our pain –

So poorly sealed within us –
And carry us away in its flood.
We beg you:
As yet, do not show us a biting dog.
It could be, O, it could be
That we would fall apart into dust
Before your very eyes.
What is it that holds our frame together,
We whom the breath of life has left
Whose soul fled unto ADONAI out of that midnight
Long before they saved our bodies in the Ark of the Here and Now?
We who were saved
We press your hand
We acknowledge your look –
But we are only bound together by the farewell.
The farewell in the dust
Binds us . . together . . .

Translated from the German by Albert Hoschander Friedlander.

Chorus of the Orphans

We lament to the world:
They hewed down our branch
And they threw it in the fire –
Firewood they made of our protectors –
We orphans lie in the fields of loneliness.
We orphans lament to the world:
At night our parents play hide-and-seek with us –
From behind the black folds of the night,
Their faces gaze at us
And their open mouths speak
Drywood we've become in a woodcutter's hand –
But our eyes are the eyes of angels,
Looking at you,
Penetrating the black folds of the night –
We orphans,
We lament to the world:
Our toys became stones.

Stones have faces, of fathers and mothers,
They don't fade like flowers, they don't bite like beasts –
And they don't burn like drywood, when thrown into the oven.
We orphans lament to the world:
O world, why have you taken from us our tender mothers,
And our fathers who say: my child, you are my likeness.
We orphans are like no one in the world any more.
O world,
We accuse you!

Translated from the German by Jacob Sonntag. Winter 1966-7

FATHER, JEW, POET
Shimon Markish

Let us, first, turn to Peretz Markish's creative journey – as it looks to a son's eye, granting that he, the son, is neither objective nor unbiased.

Markish broke into print in 1917, at twenty-two, and was noticed and appreciated almost immediately. Nor did it take him long to show the principal attributes of his poetic gift. First, there was an astonishing abundance and richness of poetic imagery, an abundance that seemed to press the limits and lose control of itself. But this was an illusion: in fact, it was the conscious device of an expressionist. Second was his revolutionary quality which in literary terms meant Modernism – the breaking of traditional aesthetic and stylistic norms. Third – and in obvious contradiction to his Modernism – was his deep rootedness in the national past, in traditional Jewish themes and images.

He began in the so-called 'Kiev circle' or 'Kiev triumvirate' which also included David Hofstein and Leib Kvitko. All three went down the path of Expressionism. They demanded a new life for Yiddish poetry which, though young in years, was already bogged down with doleful complaint and provincial imitation. All three enriched and renewed both the poetry and the language. And all three were shot on the same black day.

In 1921 - already a well-known poet and the author of four collections of verse, and two long poems - Peretz Markish left Soviet Russia for Warsaw. If the work of later periods provokes controversy, then the verse and long poems of this early period seems to provoke only delight. The poems *'Volhynia'* and *'Die Kupe'* ('The Heap') show two of Markish's themes. The first is a farewell to the past, to the home that is dilapidated, uncomfortable and doomed, but nonetheless one's own. Even the mockery and the decisive rejection are suffused with quiet grief, the forerunner of a future nostalgia for the claustrophobia of the shtetl, and the source of the poem's agonizing lyricism. The second, about the pogroms in the Ukraine during the Civil War, is a desperate cry of pain and anger: anger not only at the murderers but also at the victims for submissively offering their throats to the knife. Its angry pathos links it with Bialik's poem, 'In the City of Slaughter', written, literally, on the bloody tracks of the Kishinev pogrom of 1903. In this link between Peretz Markish and Bialik, the founding father of modern Hebrew poetry, I see yet more proof of an incontrovertible and, for me, exceedingly important truth: Jewish culture is a single unit, independent of the languages in which it is expressed.

The new poetry in Yiddish showed many other points of resemblance with new poetry in Hebrew. I will name only one: a lighthearted and playful joy in living, so characteristic of Markish and, say, Shaul Tchernichowsky, a joy forgotten in the Jewish world since the great trio of Spaniards: Halevi, Ibn Ezra and Ibn Gabirol.

Of the five years that Markish spent abroad, the most productive were the ones in Warsaw. Although he formed unforgettable and priceless literary ties and friendships in other places - in Paris, for example, with Marc Chagall and the writer Oizer Varshavsky - in Warsaw he worked with the cream of Yiddish literature, the genuine 'stars' of its prose, poetry and criticism. And the results of their association, the fruit of those years, will remain in our culture for a long time. The literary journal *Khaliastre* became such a landmark in Yiddish literary history that Chone Shmeruk called 1922, the year of its first issue, 'the *Khaliastre* year'. It seems particularly noteworthy that one of the co-editors of the journal was Uri Zvi Greenberg (1896-1981) who was to become a great writer of the new Hebrew poetry, as well as an ultra-nationalist, a mystic and an extreme political rightwinger. But no matter how far he moved from the leftist, 'proletarian' ideals of his youth - ideals he shared with Markish - Greenberg always preserved the warmest memories of Peretz Markish and the work of their Warsaw days: he spoke about this to my mother and brother when they arrived in Israel in 1972. Is this not because even their youthful thoughts were more about Jews and Jewishness than proletarian internationalism?

In any case, this was apparently the conclusion that the guardians of proletarian ideological purity reached when Markish returned to the Soviet Union in 1926. For at least six years without pause, they upbraided and 're-educated' him, accusing him of all possible anti-proletarian sins, including 'Zionist contraband'.

At this point, one asks the hardest and most tormenting of questions: Why did he go back? What drove him? Why didn't he stay in Europe? Why didn't he go to America, as apparently had been agreed between him and Peretz Hirshbein? The main reason was that the new Russia appeared to him to embody the hope of Yiddish culture for the whole world. He shared this illusion with a vast number (if not the majority) of Jewish writers in the late 1920s. The network of Yiddish schools, newspapers, magazines, publishers and theatres seemed to be a guarantee of a long and stable future. Markish was not the only one to return. The 'Kiev Triumvirate' returned in full. So did the two major prose writers, Der Nister and David Bergelson. There was even a sizeable group of immigrants from various European countries. None of them could foresee what awaited them and their nation in the 'hospitable homeland of socialism' after Hitler's destruction of European Jewry. But nobody at the time could foresee the magnitude of Hitler's threat either.

A second question is even more tormenting: What happened to Markish's talent, what happened to the poet and man during the fifteen years (1926-1941) of the consolidation and triumph of Stalinist totalitarianism? He was neither killed nor arrested in the years of the Great Terror - on the contrary, they arrested and killed the enthusiasts of proletarian purity and vigilance who had hounded Markish after his return from abroad. And he didn't stop writing; on the contrary, the late 1920s and 1930s were for him a time of heightened creativity and many publications. Nor was he passed over for government honours: when in 1939 writers were given decorations (for the first time in the history of Soviet power), he, alone among Jewish writers, received the highest award, the Order of Lenin. In a society that conformed inflexibly to the strictest protocol, this meant that in the official hierarchy Markish was Jewish Writer No. 1.

This is the way it was. I don't intend either to deny or to hide it. Nor will I hide his inevitable acts of compromise with those in power. Their burdensome inevitability may be hard for the western reader to understand, but it is more than understandable to those who had the opportunity to warm themselves under the sun of Stalin's constitution, including Akhmatova, Pasternak and

Mandelstam. Markish's *'Poeme Vegn Stalinen'* ('Poem about Stalin'), published in 1940, belongs in this category. And still, in my opinion, one can't talk about either a degradation of his talent or his capitulation to the totalitarian regime.

If he sang the praises of Soviet power, his fear for his own life and the lives of those close to him was not the only stimulus – and not, by far, the most important. I remember an episode from another, already post-Stalinist epoch. We were at the funeral of a university professor, a cold and dry man who was an obedient conformist in scholarship and in life. And his funeral was dry, without sympathy or tears. Only one of his former students wept bitterly. When it was over I asked him why he was so upset. And he answered me with a reproach: 'How could you of all people not understand? He wasn't an antisemite!' One mustn't forget that until the Hitler-Stalin pact of August 1939, Soviet power stood alone in opposition to the antisemitic frenzy in Europe (not only in Nazi Germany, but in Poland, Rumania, Hungary) and to the whole world's indifference to the fate of the Jews. I am convinced that for Peretz Markish the Jew, this was the deciding point in his political orientation. (In the same way, for Markish the Yiddish poet, the deciding point was not censorship and proletarian critics, but the existence of good books in Yiddish, his native, singular and endlessly beloved language; that is how he described it in a letter to a close friend in America, the writer Joseph Opatoshu.)

In any event, the 'Poem about Stalin' was concluded and sent to the publisher *before* the Hitler-Stalin pact. After it, Markish wrote the verses *'Tsu a yidisher tentserin'* ('To a Jewish Dancer' – in the Russian translation, 'The Ghetto Dancer'), which were not only impossible to publish during the period of Communist-Fascist peaceful coexistence, but impossible even to show to a publisher.

If he retreated from the Expressionism of his early years, it is not because necessity dictated to it. It was part of his personal evolution, organic and natural, like that of his older contemporary and good friend Boris Pasternak. But was it a retreat at all? Was it not simply a matter of maturation? The rebellion, the extravagance departed, but the strength remained, if it did not in fact increase. This strength comes through unerringly in the Russian translations; Markish had many admirers among Russian poetry readers.

In general, if Peretz Markish wrote lines and verses that I am ashamed of today, hundreds of his works, written during those fifteen years, will nonetheless remain in our poetry for a long time. And that is without reference to their subjects and titles. I will cite only two poems: *'Brider'* ('Brothers'), about the Civil War in the Ukraine, and *'Dem balgufs toyt'* ('The Death of a Stout One', in Russian translation 'A Kulak's Death').

His war verse will also remain, as will the monumental verse epic *'Milkhome'* ('War'). This is not simply because the war against the Nazis saved a considerable part of Soviet literature from Orwellian 'doublethink', and Markish, in particular, could raise his voice in a torrent of pain and hatred. More important is the fact that the Markish of the war years is probably the most Jewish, having been freed once and for all from his blind youthful negation of the past, and recognizing anew the eternal values of Jewishness.

After the war, when the centre of global antisemitism had moved from vanquished Germany to victorious Russia, when it became impossible to breathe and you could feel with your fingers the oncoming pogrom, when there were only two or three years left to write (which meant – to live), Markish wrote what might well be his finest lyrical cycles, the most perfect examples of his philosophical, romantic and nature verse. He was not torn from life and poetry during his decline, but at the height of his seemingly inexhaustible creative powers.

It is, however, no accident that poetry has the last place in my title. For me, Peretz Markish has always been a father and a Jew first of all, except that the 'Jew' and 'father' are merged indissolubly.

At first glance, the children in our family were one-hundred-percent assimilated. At home we didn't speak Yiddish: my mother didn't know it at all, and my father spoke perfect Russian. We heard Yiddish when my father's friends came to see him and when relatives came from the Ukraine. Yiddish was father's language - and only that. We didn't get any Jewish education at all, in any form. There's no need to talk about a religious education; not only my father and mother, but even my grandmother (on my mother's side – we didn't know my father's parents) were utterly indifferent to religion. Nor did we have a non-religious, secular education, a kind of introduction, say, to Jewish history with a pedagogical goal. And still we grew up as Jews. For me it was as natural to be a Jew as to breathe or love my grandmother. I was a Jew – and that was that. A Jew from birth and forever, in the same way that I was a boy and not a girl. This completely organic sense of belonging to Jewry I have retained all my life in exactly the same form that I received it as a child from my father. The belonging was exclusive in the sense that it excluded any supplements – I could not be, let's say, both a Jew and a Russian - but for all that it was neither self-satisfied nor aggressive: it didn't try to prove anything either to itself or to anyone else.

In the morning *Shema*, which I read for the first time when I first said Kaddish for my father – that is, already in freedom, in the West – I was struck by what seemed to be familiar words from *Deuteronomy*: 'Thou shalt teach them diligently unto thy children, speaking of them when thou sittest in the house, when thou walkest by the way, when thou liest down and when thou risest up.' My father never taught any of us in any way, but I am certain that it is impossible to give children a sense of loyalty to Jewry in a better or more effective way than Peretz Markish did through his very existence.

First I see him with the eyes of a small boy; later with those of an adolescent. Father is almost always busy. 'Shh! Papa is working!' – that is, he's writing, tapping on his typewriter. But not the same way as his neighbours in our building, which was just for writers: Papa was writing in Yiddish. He had a different, special profession: the neighbours were writers, but he was a Jewish writer. Papa's study is quiet, Papa isn't home. He's at a meeting at the Writers' Union, or at the theatre, or on a business trip. I have no doubt that if he's at the theatre, then it's Mikhoels's Jewish theatre; if he's on a business trip then it's to Minsk, Kiev or Birobidzhan; and if he's at a meeting at the Writers' Union, then he's shouting and waving his hands in the company of the same people who were always at our house: Dobrushin, Nusinov, Bergelson, Halkin, Wiener, Rossin. In any event, when he returns home and tells Mama the events of the day, I can't catch any names except Jewish ones. Now father is home, we have guests. In the study, and then in the dining room, and then back in the study, there's a fearful *kvalt*: everyone is talking at the same time, and all of it in Yiddish. That's the way it had to be; I couldn't imagine it any differently. Looking back, I realize that I didn't merely grow up in a Jewish atmosphere, but in the very thicket of communal life, communal interests and anxieties. Even if the community no longer was what it had been in the recent past, still the spirit and tradition of the Jewish community as a special organism, separated from the surrounding world and unmixed with it, were alive, animated and healthy. The people making a noise in the home of Peretz Markish were not arguing about their personal interests or about the interests of their 'international socialist homeland'; they were talking about what one thing or another meant for the Jews, for Jewish culture, the Jewish fate and the Jewish future.

This sense of separateness from the surrounding majority was demonstrated with special clarity in a short toast that Markish made, in his own home and at his own table, in the first days after the war. Our guests were writers (this time not Jewish ones), actors and a dozen or so famous generals; the wife of one of them was a good friend of the family. After innumerable glasses in honour of the victory and the victors, Markish stood up and said: 'I want to drink to the hospitality that the Russian nation has offered my own Jewish nation.' 'How can you say that, Peretz Davidovich?' objected one of the generals. 'What do you mean, hospitality? This is your home!' But Markish was insistent: 'To your hospitality!'

During the war my 'instinctive' Jewishness became conscious – I recognized my own ignorance and demanded a Jewish education. I told my father that I wanted to study the Jewish language; in our house, that could only mean Yiddish. I don't doubt that my father was pleased, but he took my request as something completely natural, flowing necessarily from both my life and his life, from our common life. He found me a teacher but never tried to help me himself. Why should he? One fine day his son would certainly address him in his, in their, language with the same spontaneity and lightness that he possessed when he had addressed his own father. And if that truly fine day never came, then it was the fault of the blackest day of my life [27 January 1949], when my father was led away, out of my life forever.

I don't have to repeat that Peretz Markish was a passionate Yiddishist, but it was from him, from my father, that I first heard Hebrew – in our Ashkenazi pronunciation, of course. I had read Bialik in Jabotinsky's Russian translation and told that to my father. He asked what I liked best. I said, 'The Tale of the Pogrom' (which is how Jabotinsky titled the poem 'B'ir ha'harega' – 'In the City of Slaughter'). He took a volume of Bialik from the shelf and began to read aloud. He read for a long time with obvious delight, more for himself than for me since I couldn't understand a word; he read the same way he read his own work, with the same inimitable passion. In the final analysis, though, it was for me, because ever since that day I have felt a timid reverence for Hebrew. This may not help me in equalling the fluent speech of my Sabra nephew, Peretz Markish the younger, but it has become another cornerstone in the fundament of my Jewishness.

I don't recall that my father ever spoke about God, about commandments or about holidays. But when thinking over his behaviour many years later, particularly his reactions to my childish mischief, I understood to what extent it was motivated by religious tradition and how – in a completely unconscious and unintended way – it led us, the children, to that same tradition. Once as a joke I referred to Moshe Rabeinu by the Germanic name 'Moses'. Father yelled at me: 'Don't you dare! How can you be so flippant! Either use the Russian Moisci or the Jewish Moishe!' I didn't understand the reasons for his anger and explained myself. I had read it in a collection of Jewish folk songs. 'You're lying! Or you got something mixed up! And if it's true, then there are more Jewish fools out there than there should be!' The image of Moses was for him something sacred and inviolable; and thus the unfamiliar Germanic form, innocent in itself, struck him as an affront to divine greatness.

Another time, playing with my sister, I pinned on my mother's dressing gown, stepped into her high heels and used her lipstick. My father emerged unexpectedly from his study and saw us. I can still see his face, white with anger. He tore off the gown, pulled me out of the shoes and dragged me to the bathroom to wash my lips. He could hardly have explained anything coherently, but the point was made: it was absolutely forbidden for men to dress in women's clothing. (Only many years later did I notice the verse in Chapter 22 of *Deuteronomy*: 'A woman must not put on man's apparel, nor shall a man wear woman's clothing; for whoever does these things is abhorrent to the Lord your God.')

Trifles? Of course. But what sculpts the wax of a child's soul if not trifles? And so, after the war, when my sister and I had grown up and he had grown older and closer to us, more interested in us, he began to tell us about his childhood, about the *cheder* in Polonnoe, the synagogue in Berdichev where he sang in the boys' choir until his voice broke – these stories about the Jewish past sit in my soul and memory like bricks atop an indestructible foundation.

My father didn't teach me to pray, and I remained an unbeliever, an agnostic. He didn't teach me faith but he taught me faithfulness - faithfulness to the Jewish past and the Jewish future. This is the centre that holds my life together, and it was secured by his hand. I know I am only a weak spark from his generous flame. But I am from him and am turned towards him: I look back at him constantly and forever. Not so long ago I heard from the French-Jewish philosopher Emmanuel Levinas that memory is already a kind of prayer. My God, how true that is! Forty years have passed since I began to pray, not even realizing it - I pray for my father, about my father and about myself, a small portion of my father. And when, as an unbeliever, I join believers four times a year at the memorial Yizkor service and ask the Almighty to remember the soul of my father and teacher who departed into eternity, I am not lying or being hypocritical. He did more than give me life; he placed me on the path that I am following to this day. And this memory of him, my prayer, I would like to share with everyone on earth and prolong to the edge of time.

Translated from the Russian by Alice Nakhimovsky. Summer 1992

A MIRROR ON A STONE . . .
Peretz Markish

Now that my sight comes back to me again,
I see, and feel it with my body's every part,
that, like a mirror on a stone breaks up to bits,
so, breaking with a bang, did break my heart.

Each of the pieces surely does not cease
to be a witness to my being until I'm gone.
- Don't trample on me yet in judgement, Time,
until I have picked up the splinters, one by one.

I'll pick them up and piece them, bit by bit,
together till my blood-stained fingers hurt.
However I may try to make them fit,
they will show up my face forever blurred.

Now only, in my sadness, as I comprehend
the painful process, I begin to feel the pain
of wanting once to see myself reflected whole in these,
the scattered splinters cast upon the seven seas . . .

Translated from the Yiddish by Jacob Sonntag. Autumn 1956

TWO POEMS
Lotte Kramer

for X
In Prague

I

When talking of his town
He translated poetry,

He was so much in love
With each stone, each house,

Not one nerve of history
Deserted his eyes,

Not one line of literature
Questioned his hands,

He was like the river:
Open and always.

II

I wonder how his grief
Can confide in tight walls,

How his lost city
Can continue in bare light,

His hands holding dead pages
Across the broad bridge

From the leaning sorrows
Of the old cemetery

To the tall steps
On the gothic hill.

Jewish Cemetery in Prague

Roots creep and coil themselves
Round skeletons, eight deep,
Inside the dust of Prague.
Trees roof the narrow space.

So, tightly packed, the generations
Keep their silence here.
The wise man and the teacher★
Fold away their mysteries.

The Golem's shadow haunts
The deep, while hundreds come
To touch these witnesses, to find
Some faith with ancestors.

And underneath the Vltava
Has stretched her arms
To gather back the seeds of souls
Into a central European sea.

While stones, some leaning on each other,
And heavy with inscriptions,
Are slowly sinking every year
Towards the rooted dead.

★Rabbi Loew, creator of the Golem.

Winter 1980-81

BECAUSE OF THAT WAR
James E. Young

It has been said that the Holocaust turned every survivor into a witness, every witness into a writer. This is not true. Some became writers, others graphic artists, others filmmakers. Still others fell silent altogether and went to work as farmers, mechanics, shop clerks, engineers, businessmen, bureaucrats and parents. Given the very bookishness of Jewish tradition, the number of witness-scribes telling their stories may not be surprising. But not all survivors are born rememberers or gifted story-tellers. In fact, the great majority will probably live out their lives without having transmitted a fraction of their experiences. Except for the day-to-day pockets of memory opened in interactions with family or in response to daily tribulations, most survivors may leave their pain, bitterness or gratitude for life itself largely unexpressed. This is one of the reasons why the listener's task has never been to deny the survivor his medium of expression – whatever it may be. In light of the growing volume of second generation literature, some of it remarkably idiosyncratic, attempts to restrict the artistic expression of the survivor's children are no less misguided.

The range of possible responses to the Shoah by the children of survivors grows with every generation. In an age dominated by popular culture, survivors' children are as likely to distinguish themselves as Abstract Expressionists as they are portrait artists, or as likely to play rhythm-and-blues as they are classical piano. Israeli novelist David Grossman has responded brilliantly to his parents' generation through the allegorical indirection of his fiction. By remaining true to his medium, Art

Spiegelman did not trivialize his parents' experiences so much as wondrously expand the 'comix' art form itself. In the cases of both Grossman's *See Under: Love* and Spiegelman's *Maus,* the artist redefined the borders of his respective medium, creating forms that allow a powerful self-scrutiny of both the survivor's story-telling process and the child's attempt to respond. Like Spiegelman's *Maus,* filmmaker Orna Ben-Dor-Niv's *Because of that War* captures the very essence of relations between survivors and their children, between their stories and their children's capacity to assimilate and eventually transmit them. As a child of survivors, Ben-Dor-Niv has turned for her subject to the music and lives of two of Israel's most popular rock musicians, Yehuda Poliker and Ya'akov Gilad, both children of survivors. In a deeply personal look at the making of their celebrated 'Ashes and Dust' album, this film explores both the children's artistic response to their parents' lives and their attempts to retell their parents' stories in their own idiom. Because the children of survivors are, in this case, rock musicians, this film is also about (there is no other way to put it) 'Holocaust rock 'n roll'. As writers write and artists draw, rock musicians make rock music: how else should they respond?

As we discover in this extraordinary film, even the seeming facetiousness of such an idiom cannot obscure the subtle interplay between a parent's story and her son's music, the non-verbal bond created between generations and between singers and their audience. Both Ben-Dor-Niv's film and the folk-rock of Yehuda Poliker and Ya'akov Gilad challenge critics to rise above archaic high art/low art distinctions to explore the multiple kinds of understanding created in popular culture. Like *Maus* or *See Under: Love,* both film and music succeed here, partly because together they force us to re-examine so thoroughly our assumptions regarding the ways we learn about the Shoah.

As a child of survivors, Orna Ben-Dor-Niv admits to growing up among a generation of Israelis that still sniggered approvingly at the approbation, 'Don't take seriously a person from Auschwitz'. She was a Sabra with all the Sabra's contempt for the Galutnik, exemplified by the Holocaust Jew. Only later would she have the patience to listen to the survivor's story – and begin to understand her own place in the world in light of her parents' past. As it was for Spiegelman, Poliker and Gilad, the story of the Holocaust for this child of survivors remains enmeshed in the story of her relationship to her parents.

With this in mind, the film-maker aspired to tell the story on her terms, but without patronizing her parents' generation: 'I had to tell it in my generation's voice which included new-wave music and film.' A generation of young Israelis had moved from resisting their parents' stories to unselfconsciously retelling them in forms uniquely their own. Questions of this music's propriety or seemliness have not preoccupied Israelis as they have others. For in Israel, the Shoah is not hidden from view or compartmentalized as it is in other countries. It is rather a part of daily life in Israeli consciousness, its monuments and survivors part of a shared landscape.

As a result, both the film and the music at its core are built on an intricate web of relations: between Poliker and Gilad; between the children and their parents; between the parents and their stories; between the children and their parents' stories – and finally between the children and their musical response to their parents' stories. In addition, several levels of narrative also weave themselves into the film: the parents' story-telling, the children's putting these stories to song, the music itself, and the linear movement of the film. Words, images and sound are then interlaced in Poliker's riveting performance of the music, which functions as meditative interlude during which the stories are assimilated, their emotive content objectified in sound.

Our first glimpse of Yehuda Poliker in the film is an angry, bitter one: he practically spits out the words, *'Biglal hamilchama ha'he* . . . Because of that war, my family takes big bites of their food now. Because of that war, I have no relatives. Because of that war, I was born. Because of that war, you were born'. As related by lyricist Ya'akov Gilad, the first expressions of his parents' experiences came not in his mother's stories, but in everyday parent-child relations: 'Because of that war,' Gilad tells us, 'I was an hysterical child. Mama, where are you going? How long? Are you coming back? When? I had a basic abandonment anxiety.' The parents weren't any better: they wouldn't let the children out of their sight, wouldn't let them go on youth group *tiyulim*. Call, come back, don't go there: the world is a dangerous place.

This is less the casting of blame, however, than it is the recognition that their very lives and music are inextricably bound to their parents' experiences during 'that war'. Poliker's considerable reputation as lead-singer and guitarist in the Israeli rock band, Benzin, had been built on a brand of hard-rocking party music. An exuberant light-heartedness in songs like '*Yom shishi*' ('*Yom shishi aht yoda'at, yesh ba'ir mesibah*', Friday you know there's a party in the city) seemed indifferent to the cloying heaviness of his parents' memories. But between the early and late 1980s, he and his songwriter gradually ceased denying the shadow their parents' stories cast over their lives.

For Poliker at first, it meant learning the music and instruments of his father's boyhood home in Salonika: a language he could share with his parents. Between his own stutter and his parents' rudimentary Hebrew, it was almost as if Poliker had sought an alternative medium, something deeper than words to convey his father's pain and his own response to it. In turning to the music of his father's early home, he would simultaneously give his father voice and speak to his father. The Greek folk melodies and themes he introduced to Israel's rock music scene were immensely popular during the mid-1980s. In 1987, he took the next, excruciating step and began incorporating the story and pain of his father's Holocaust remembrances into the music itself.

Poliker's father, Jacob, was the only one of some fifty in his family to survive the Shoah. Filmed at his kitchen table in Kiryat Bialik, Jacob sits next to his wife and describes how he, his relatives and the rest of the community were rounded up by the Nazis in Salonika, how the children died during the eight-day trip to Auschwitz and how the remainder, save Jacob and his brother, were sent immediately to the gas. Jacob makes a brave on-camera attempt to relate the story of his brother's eventual death, but the pain overwhelms him and he dissolves quietly, stoically, into tears. His wife asks someone off-camera for a glass of water, so he can finish. 'Where was God?' Jacob asks and then replies, 'he was a goy'.

Jacob is not a born story-teller: he is only semi-articulate, his Hebrew rough and elemental. The power of his expression is no less effective for that, however. For in capturing the choppiness of his telling, his long pauses and searches for the right word, the film's images, sounds and silences are eloquent. One story, in particular, stands out: his eldest son's bar mitzvah in Israel. Jacob recalls watching the guests drinking and dancing, when he is reminded of all his family who are not there to share this *simcha*. 'I suddenly threw a glass to the floor and turned over a table,' he said. 'All these people and none of my family.' Unconsciously, perhaps reflexively, he had enacted the ritual of the broken glass, the recollection of acute pain at the moment of greatest happiness.

Gilad's mother, Halina, on the other hand, is a professional Holocaust story-teller, a travelling minstrel of the Shoah. Sitting in front of her computer, tapping out little dots of light, she polishes her stories, her script, to an art. 'Never do I feel so strong, so alive as when I tell my story,' she says, and we believe her. 'It started when I had to tell my son all about it,' she recalls, 'for with every telling came a victory. I am alive. When I'm alone, without listeners, I cry.' So from school to school she goes, speaking to hundreds of students, holding them rapt. We watch as she stands before an auditorium of teenagers, her story seeming to tell itself in an unstoppable torrent. Her words, her hands' movements, her expressions, her dramatic pauses have all been honed in hundreds of such tellings. Her eyes alternately flash in fury and well up in tears: telling the story is clearly her *raison d'être*. She feels life most acutely, most powerfully, in the midst of these tellings, in the remembered moment of separation from her mother and young lover, at the edge of her own near-death.

At one point in the film, the two musicians bring Halina to visit Poliker's parents. Sitting next to Jacob at the kitchen table, Halina describes how she once tried to write Jacob's story for him. After taking copious notes, transcribing them and then weaving them into narrative, Halina concedes that she wasn't sure where Jacob's story ended and hers began. To some extent, every story-teller makes another's story his or her own – which is what these survivors' children have done in their music. For both Poliker and Gilad have drawn verbatim from their parents' lives and stories, putting Halina's words to the music of Jacob's childhood. What Halina has written and spoken, her son Gilad puts to music composed and sung by his mate, Poliker. Survivors write the libretto, their children the musical score.

The resulting songs, collected in 'Ashes and Dust', thus meld the parents' story to the children's retelling of it, the parents' experiences to their children's musical response. The melodies of these songs range from soothing and lyrical to sharply dissonant. An angry, piercingly stretched high-E string bends until our hearts break, before quietly retreating. Like someone with a trauma too grave to tell, Poliker stutters badly, in his interviews with Ben-Dor-Niv. Only when he sings does the stutter disappear: his raspy voice, made for hard rock, also suits his new music. For his are blood-throated songs, some choked out, others whispered, some alternately torn from Poliker's throat, others chanted like prayers. Some songs are screamed with rock music intensity, four-count beat intact, accompanied by pounding drums and guitar; others are almost crooned in something approaching sweet pain.

On the one hand, lead guitar riffs remind us that these are still rock musicians, now grown up. On the other hand, even a densely metallic tune carries these words aloft, keeping them lighter than air. In fact, rock lyrics by themselves almost never withstand an overly-attentive ear: they are meant to be part of the music, their sense overwhelmed by sound. Without music, even the survivor's words here, once abstracted from their source, seem pedestrian and banal. They demand the voice of the singer, in whose breath they are re-animated, in whose song they are borne aloft.

Of the eleven songs comprising 'Ashes and Dust', all refer either directly or obliquely to the child's growing awareness of his parent's past, of its effect on him. *'Halon l'yam hatichon'* ('Window to the Mediterranean Sea') laments an unwritten letter and then suggests an immigrant's arrival and first home in Yaffo, the dreaded loss of new happiness there. In *'Shir achrei hageshem'* ('Song after the Rain'), perhaps the most beautifully arranged melody on the album, Poliker sings for both himself and Gilad:

> A song after the rain
> An old song mother taught me to sing
> A song after the rain, a song after the rain
> An old song that curls upward and out the window
> It awakens memories in me
> In the streets after the rain
> The life of a recent past
> Doubt still accompanies me

Once learned, this song simultaneously lends expression to the rain and protects the singer from it, consoles the singer and sustains his doubt. The entire album is, in effect, 'a song after the rain, a song mother taught me to sing'.

Only one song refers explicitly to the killing process itself. *'Hatachana hakatana Treblinka'* ('The Little Station Treblinka'). The most haunting song on this track is actually put to the words of a poet, Wladislaw Schlengel, which had been recited to Halina in the Warsaw Ghetto. She remembered the poem, recited it to her son, who put the words into a rhythmic story-song of the train ride from Warsaw to Treblinka. In Hebrew, the song is more incantation than song, its hypnotic metronome laced intermittently with the wall of Poliker's guitar:

> *Kan hatachana Treblinka*
> *Kan hatachana Treblinka*
> On the line between Teluscz and Warsaw
> From the railway station Warsaw east
> They leave on the train and go directly
> The trip takes sometimes
> Five hours and forty-five minutes . . .
>
> And a normal sign says
> *Kan hatachana Treblinka*
> *Kan hatachana Treblinka*
> And there's not even a ticket window

Here is the station Treblinka, he repeats, reverberating to the echo of a broken chord. As Poliker recites these words, a shiver of tambourine passes through, punctuated by a monotone bass, counterpointed by drums. Only the refrain is sung: *'Kan hatachana Treblinka'*. Poliker's guitar cries once, twice, and pulls us back into the refrain. This is a long way from Benzin's rocking dance music: the camera turns around to face Poliker's audience and they are sitting bolt upright, transfixed.

In her memoirs, Simone de Beauvoir wrote: 'The evening after a massacre, I was listening to a Beethoven *andante* and stopped the record halfway in anger: all the pain of the world was there, but so magnificently sublimated and controlled that it seemed justified.' We remind ourselves that it was also music and poetry – Schoenberg's 'Chorus of the Warsaw Ghetto Survivors', Celan's 'Todesfugue' – that inspired Adorno's similar, if far more notorious, response to art after Auschwitz. What it is in music that stirs the soul so deeply, that cuts to the quick of our emotional reserves, remains that which makes music so suspect as an expression of pain. By inflaming emotions around themes of such enormity, music runs the risk of creating runaway feelings, of generating pathos for its own sake: one definition of kitsch. At the same time, only music, in its elixir of chords and notes, can express the pre-articulated sound unavailable to words. In this medium, we share another kind of understanding, itself impossible to articulate in prose, whose complexities, textures and resonances are lost to images or narrative alone.

Conventional critical categories distinguishing high culture from low, serious art from popular, break down in the face of iconoclastic or avant-garde forms of expression. In response, the critic's role continues to evolve from arbiter of taste to curious cipher of meanings created in texts. We are no longer content merely to legislate good art over bad or to apply socially constructed models of criticism as if they were divinely ordained. Likewise, the critic's job is not to dictate the story-teller's medium so much as it is to explore the ways it organizes meaning and memory, how it leads to or inhibits further understanding of this time. Instead of merely patronizing popular culture or dismissing it altogether, we might better recognize the unique understanding passed down to us in every generation's aesthetic responses to the Shoah no matter how unexpected they may be.

THE WHITE JEWS OF COCHIN
Ron Taylor

For years they trusted in a familiar
who held out in alleyways
and other shady places,
escaping the headachey sun

but who faded from the picture, following
a more reasonable sun
back home in Oporto or the Algarve.
Unreasonably alone

they stayed hot centuries, unwelcome
among the old Anjuvannam,
Black Jews carried there by the navy
of Tarshish, who pretended

to remember Solomon. No escape from sun
and mosquitoes, no room in
the black synagogue, despite the Jews Deed
giving them a sort of king.

Jewtown built at last, the sun shimmered now
on a white synagogue
until time and history ceased to apply.
With eager tourist camera

dodging from the Cochin sun, you will see
they have not prospered,
their cool white temple tinkling emptily
with coloured glass globes

like fragile archaeology. And hastening
once more for shadow
back in Jewtown lanes, you are amazed
to meet their pale faces.

Winter 1994-5

4

ON WRITERS
AND WRITING

Josef Herman *The Storyteller* (1940-43) ink on paper

THE ROAD TO MYSELF
Aharon Appelfeld

I was born in a town named Chernovitz. Until the First World War, it was part of the Austro-Hungarian Empire. A very Jewish town and very assimilated too. For my generation, assimilation was no longer a quest - if one may speak in such terms - it was a way of life. True, some displaced remnants of Jewish life still existed, but they were devoid of life. Middle-class Jewry considered its sons to be liberated from the ancient tradition.

The grandfathers still maintained religious practices, but to inspire us with their belief was beyond them. The assimilated Jew was a believer. His belief made him partially blind. His concepts of life were mainly in abstracts: humanity, progress, beauty - the benefits they would bring to society. He could not imagine that such concepts would arouse hatred, brutality. The assimilated Jew was a naive person, blind to the demons which surrounded him, and if he saw them he denied them. He accused himself. Our old grandfathers knew of this demon by instinct, but it was beyond them to convey to us the message to save us. We were blind.

The Holocaust pressed us into the depths of suffering without distinguishing between the believers and the estranged. Perhaps for us, the children, it was easier. Our suffering was mainly physical and did not involve any soul-searching. For our parents it was the end of their world. Everything they believed in was suddenly destroyed. All they had left was their naked Jewishness. The Jewish secret, which no longer existed and flickered so dimly, suddenly exacted both emotion and judgement.

The accusation was clear but unbelievable. You are Jewish because your mother and your grandfather were Jewish. It does not matter if you are a believer, a communist, a Bundist, a Zionist, a convert. The Jewish blood in your body condemns you. You are a danger by your very existence. You are deserving of death. It was like in *The Trial* of Kafka, beyond rational arguments. The assimilated Jew is a rationalist by nature. He denies mystics, demons, superstitions. His view of life, if generalization is permitted, is built up clearly, somehow uprooted and beyond reality, but steadily, reasonably. Suddenly, he was presented into a world where no reason existed.

Our parents could not save themselves. Saving our lives was their main concern. We were the meaning in their lives. Even then, while making our escape, when we saw how they jeopardized their lives while seeking a safe place for us, we knew that in this imperilment, at the edge of death, they were not only commanding us to life but handing over to us the very meaning of their lives.

The suffering brought us back to Jewishness. In the alien forests and villages, we felt the secret of our Jewishness. It was a sweet secret, like the smell of snow which draws you slowly to the edge of death. We knew that because of that secret we were fair game for every axe and rifle. But without it our existence would have been even less. In the forests, it seems a hard knot was tied between us and the thin flame of our Jewishness. The Jewish secret became the only warmth in our misery. Our shelter. There we cherished thoughts of home, parents; at times, of course, this shelter was life's final resource.

And so fate supplied a precautious and harsh entry into both our inner consciousness and the world of our parents. Our parents were suddenly taken from us, leaving us in a hostile environment, raw-natured. Our Jewishness was far from any social method. We learned Jewishness through our bodies. For years our bodies were in danger because our bodies were a target for all kinds of brutal and violent intentions. Our very existence became a secret. It was not that our homes had not had an influence on us, but what came afterwards was so powerful and so brutal that all traces of this influence were erased. All along we knew that our Jewishness was a kept secret, but it was also a catastrophe. There were moments when we despised our fate, the fate of the persecuted innocents. In moments of weakness we turned our back on it.

Our childhood, in an assimilated environment, followed by camps, forests, hostile gentiles, fashioned us as Jews. It is a wave of memories, revulsions, guilt feelings and obligations that we never dared examine in depth. It is hatred and love which are inseparably bound together.

The years of suffering passed and in 1944 the Soviet armies liberated us. We were twelve years old. The long war years had left their mark on our faces, our bodies, our movements. Even more so on the way we felt and the way we thought. First of all suspicion and complete lack of trust, from the most innocent object to any person. The enemy lurked everywhere. You had to watch out. Some of us were completely dominated by this feeling. The war years shaped the movements of a boy I remember in such a way that he moved slickly like an alert animal. He would not touch anything before peering at it at length.

In 1946 we came to Palestine. We were fourteen years old. What could we boys of fourteen do with so many memories of death? Relate to them, live them? We learned to keep quiet. The experience was too great for us; the soul was incapable of assimilating so many themes. Great catastrophes left us down. We were full. An oppressive fullness beyond meaning. Many of us turned to business, entertainment, studies, all kinds of activities, but no one dared to look into himself. The attempt to understand, to give expression, to form, seemed not only impossible but even pretentious. To be silent, to maintain an inner silence – that would have been the best. That was but a fleeting wish. Of course, the desire to say something never left us even in our darkest moments. But what we were able to say came out of us in a stutter. Worse, they were words from their own vocabulary.

I turned to literature. Why had I turned to literature? Probably to open the darkness and chaos within me. A deep desire to break up the old vocabulary, to say something of my experience. Many dangers lurked in my way. Modern Hebrew literature created by our native writers could not help me. It was a fresh and naive literature that fitted very well the heroic time of Israel's War of Independence. Again, I realized that my soul was not capable of accepting the normalest norm. Consciously or otherwise, we had a different norm, an apocalyptic one. Then came years of struggle, years to seek words and rhythm that would fit my experience. Anyway, the new words were not born.

Help came to me from an unexpected source. It came from a man who had not experienced the Holocaust but who had already foreseen the horrors during the calm days of the declining Habsburg monarchy: the Jew Franz Kafka. I had glanced at a page of *The Trial* and the feeling that he had been with us in our anguish never left me. In Kafka's language I found, on the one hand, suspicion and scepticism, and on the other, deep yearning for meaning. The thought that I had not been alone in my experience not only eased my burden but introduced me to the wider space of spiritual suffering.

Our parents were in conflict with their heritage. We were born into that conflict. Their world, the world of the assimilated Jew, the modern Jew, if interpreted positively, was a struggle for a new form of life. It was a bitter struggle, and by denying their Jewishness, it became tragic. Their painful soul-searching was for us not only a bitter memory but a guiding lesson.

Kafka's Jewish heritage was concealed even in his Diaries where he allowed himself to speak freely. Kafka's intimate interpreters, who were also his friends, emphasized that Kafka was not only a Jew by birth but also in his way of thinking. His metaphysical yearnings are but the expression of his Jewish inwardness. The path to *The Castle* is but the cry from the depths for meaning. The accused K., sensitive and alert, is not man in general but a cover for his Jewish origin. Is there any truth in this interpretation? This is how it has been interpreted by me. At times, we imagine that only by us – we who were pitched into the Holocaust from the depths of assimilation – are Kafka's twisted corridors understood.

Everything dear to Kafka was dear to me: the Prague circle, the spiritual affinity to East European Jewry, the Jewish theatre, Kafka's desire to settle in Israel, the revulsion at the modern Jewish petit bourgeois, the search for a spiritual Judaism. If Kafka gave me words, tone, rhythm, a way to express myself, Jewish mysticism in its Hassidic embodiment gave me fundamental comfort. When I speak of mysticism, I am not referring to its source but to that expanse of ideas which Martin Buber and Gershom Scholem elaborated upon. Just as I felt in Kafka the deep longing of the assimilated Jew trying to get to the core of his being, I found in mysticism a religious language which was most appropriate to my experience and my perceptions. The breaking of the vessels, the release of the force of evil, the aggressive demons, the sparks demanding their redemption.

If Kafka's vision is interpreted as a path leading to a religious faith, then this outlook is very close to me. I have not managed to go beyond it. There were years of course when I thought that our experience during the Holocaust would transform us completely. But the shock apparently was too great, the wound too deep, and the tools of our consciousness too weak to bring about a transformation.

After the war a group of Jews wandered about the desolate beaches of Italy. They refused to stay in the shacks and supported themselves by seasonal labour in the villages. Sleeping under a roof, surrounded by domestic objects and going about making money, seemed to them, after the Holocaust, not just absurd but a renewed agreement with the cultural illusions which called forth the demons from the depths. They preferred wandering to petit bourgeois comfort. It was a kind of protest, perhaps a hint of the kind of life which suited us best after the Holocaust. I spent a few months with them. We were wandering along the beaches – the simple food, going barefoot, sleeping under the stars, the pauses, the immersion in thought, the silence. I recall it as an afterglow of a religious experience which stays with me.

On that long beach, the refugees made their separate decisions. Some of them cut themselves off, rejecting their past. Others clung to every remnant, every trace of their Jewishness. The desire to escape, to run away from yourself and your fate, and the desire to cling to every trace were bound together. I am not judging anyone, but let this be said: He who chose to go up to Israel saw more than just the rehabilitation of the body.

Autumn / Winter 1984

VAY IZ MIR – WHO'D BE A JEWISH WRITER?
Howard Jacobson

From the title of this lecture, which I regretted no sooner than I'd suggested it – that being the nature of Jewish writing – some of you may already be thinking this is going to be not so much a lecture as a kvetch – a kvetchture. Well, that isn't my intention, though I will remind you that complaints do run deep in Jewish culture. What is a Jewish prophet but a complainant, a *klogmuter*? What have so many of our fallings-out with God been, if not expressions of vexation that we cannot stand before Him in order to get what we have to say to Him off our chests? Remember Job:

> Oh that I knew where I might find Him! that I might come even to his Seat! I would order my cause before Him, and fill my mouth with arguments.

I wouldn't be the Jewish writer I am – wouldn't be a Jewish writer at all - if I didn't wake each morning with a mouth *full* of arguments.

To be Jewish is to demur. In one sense the Talmud is the longest and most creative demurral in all literature. The word I use more than any other word - except perhaps the word 'Jewish' itself – is 'but'. Reading gentile writers, I am always astonished at how long they can go without using the word 'but'. The day breaks, the sun shines, the hero has his breakfast (unless he's in an Irish novel, in which case he can't afford breakfast), the heroine arrives, they fight, they make up, the sun goes down. Not a 'but' in sight. But me – *but* me - I am constantly demurring. From whom?

Well, from the day breaking, for a start, because it never *fully* breaks the way you want it to, and from the sun shining for similar reasons of dissatisfaction. But of course what my 'buts' are really taking exception to is whatever has gone before them in my sentence. I demur, grammatically, and as a matter of cultural necessity, from myself.

The literary critic F. R. Leavis, with whom I studied in the 1960s, used always to describe the critical procedure as one party saying, 'This is the case, is it not?' and his respondent answering, 'Yes, but . . .' Leavis had a Jewish wife and was himself sometimes taken to be Jewish. 'Leavis' - it had an austerely Hebraic ring. In fact he wasn't Jewish, he was of Huguenot extraction, but the something Jewish about his critical practice - rigorous textual analysis, belief that the text itself held all the meanings there were, a marked fondness for disputation, and a certain obduracy which always kept him beyond the pale as far as high-table politics went - explains, I think, why a Prestwich grammar school boy such as I was, an inveterate chooser who felt controversialism to be a sacred calling, found him so congenial. I didn't realize that at the time. I thought I was escaping the parochialism of Manchester Jewish life; but in fact, without knowing it, I was digging deeper in.

'Yes, but . . .' Not just a refusal but an ingrained incapacity to go very far down the line of agreeing with anyone. I don't doubt I overdo this. It is now constitutional with me, if I encounter upwards of two people of the same mind about anything, to take it for granted they are wrong. Concurrence of any sort makes me physically ill. Jews don't think about hell much; but if I were to put my mind to hell, it would be a place with no wine in it (or only Pesach wine), and where everybody agrees with everybody else.

'I don't care what you have to say,' sang Groucho Marx in the 1932 movie *Horse Feathers*,

> It makes no difference anyway,
> Whatever it is, I'm against it!
> And no matter how you changed it or condensed it
> I'm against it.

Whatever it is, I'm against it, as though some property of profound unintellectualism, some infection of wrong-headedness, inheres in being *for* it. Very specifically, I get this 'being against it' from the half of my family who came from Lithuania. To be from Lithuania is to be numbered among the *Mitnaggedim,* or opponents, a name that was given to us by the Hassidic Jews of central Russia, Hassidism being the thing we were opposed to most. Uncouth costumes, dancing, drinking, turning cartwheels in the snow, calling ecstatically on the Messiah - none of this was our idea of being Jewish. 'Moshiach is coming!' was and still is the rapturous cry of Hassidic Jews. 'Yes, but...' was and still is the reply of we *Mitnaggedim,* we enemies of whatever is not severely rational, not of the intellect, not strictly within the law of God.

The other side of my family, though not Hassidic, come from Hassid country, and still behave at family functions in the Dionysian manner abhorred by *Mitnaggedim*. They dance, they sing, and if it weren't for not wanting to split their dinner-jackets, would turn cartwheels on the snowy wastes of that great steppe of Tartary we call Didsbury.

So I enjoy in my own person this momentous argument between two branches of Eastern European Judaism. I am at once Apollonian Jew and Dionysian. Add the fact of my choosing to be a Leavisite to the accident of my being born a *Mitnagged* and a secular Hassid - a congenital opponent to myself - and you get an extreme case.

Extreme or not, I don't expect you to take issue with me when I say that the butting and demurring I have described, the extravagant stylistics of analysis and disagreement, are characteristic of the way Jews have been thinking since we have evidence of their thinking at all. Call it dialectics, and you can see why people have detected the methods of the Talmud even in the work of such a determined Jewish rejectionist as Karl Marx.

'The young Marx likes to show off in brilliant antitheses,' wrote one contemporary commentator. 'These also indicate the characteristic casuistry of Jewish thought patterns.' 'Casuistry' is a rather poor translation of the German word used to describe Marx's style here - *Spitzfindigkeit* - meaning oversubtlety, quibbling, nit-picking, pettifogging.

Of course one man's over-subtlety is another's necessary method of procedure. There's a moment in David Hare's, to me distasteful, one-hander, *Via Dolorosa*, when the self-aggrandizing playwright explodes with impatience, worn down by the amount of quibbling indulged in by a table-load of Orthodox Israeli settlers putting their wits to the inconsistencies surrounding the age of a particular biblical bride. Is she three or is she thirteen? If she's three, how can she be strong enough to water the camels, if she's thirteen . . . Hare sits there 'marvelling' that 'it never occurs to anyone here that maybe the story is simply wrong', thereby showing that not only the *Spitzfindigkeit* - the love of hair-splitting - but also the intellectual conscientiousness of the Jewish mind, will always be beyond him. By 'intellectual conscientiousness' I mean a vivid apprehension of a problem no less than the ingenuity to solve it; I mean that extraordinarily dynamic capacity to feel the perplexities of an ancient story as though they are every bit as urgent now as they were however many thousands of years ago, when the story was first told. And I mean that unswerving conviction, essential to any critic worth the name, that the text is the text and nothing else is admissible.

This sort of intellectual conscientiousness, a determination to lay hold of every meaning that a text may hold, because the meanings are of now, because the meanings to now, is one of the distinguishing features of the Talmud. Without doubt the dialectical method of the Talmud - *pilpul* - can sometimes bewilder itself. Even so distinguished a Talmudic scholar as Adin Steinsaltz cannot resist retelling the famous parody of the exhausting mental dexterity you routinely find in Talmudic dispute:

> A rabbi asks his disciple why the letter *peh* [p] was needed in the word *korah*. When the disciple replied that the letter *peh* did not appear in the word *korah*, the rabbi persisted: 'Let us just assume, for the sake of argument, that the letter *peh* is placed in the word *korah*.' 'But rabbi,' asks the disciple, 'why should the letter *peh* he needed in the word *korah*?' 'My original question precisely!' relies the rabbi.

But then isn't this one of the cornerstones of the Jewish joke - an over-subtle acknowledgement of our own over-subtlety? Just think how many Jewish jokes there are which entail torturing the bearer with demonstrations and counter-demonstrations of logic, exactly as one Talmudist would torture another, with the aim of getting to the bottom of God's meaning.

So is a Jewish joke also a way of getting to the bottom of God's meaning? For the moment, I let that question hang in the air . . .

Not every Jew likes Jewish jokes. Add the tortuous satires of Jewish comedy to the *Spitzfindigkeit* and obduracy I've been discussing, and then mix in the extreme rationality, the nay-saying, the hyper-criticality, the self-consciousness of which this lecture is a shameless example, and you have a version of the Jew which Jews themselves have been squabbling about for centuries.

Behind every argument Jews have had with Jews since the dispersal - what sort of Jew to be, where to be it, how conspicuously to be it, how self-sufficiently to be it, how religiously or secularly to be it - lies this one fundamental question: has our nature been distorted by the fact of exile? Is the ingenious, joking Jew the Jew in essence or the Jew of the ghetto and the *galut*? Otherwise positioned, out in the world, with a country of our own or assimilated into someone else's, as we seemed to be assimilated into Germany a hundred and fifty years ago, would we still suffer these mental contortions, or wouldn't we rather stand up straight and tall and blond, yea-sayers not nay-sayers, lovers of the clean open spaces of the mind rather than its narrow twisting passageways and airless ante-rooms?

In the opinion of the great Jewish historian Heinrich Graetz, you could trace much of what was wrong with the pre-Enlightenment Jew to Talmudic study itself.

> The perverse course of study pursued by the Jews since the fourteenth century had blunted their minds to simplicity. They had grown so accustomed to all that was artificial, distorted, super-cunningly wrought [sounds like our friend *Spitzfindigkeit* to me] . . . that the simple, unadorned truth became worthless, if not childish and ridiculous, in their eyes.

Or you could blame the barbarities of the shtetl, as the critic Ba'al Makhshoves powerfully did in his description of the work of the Yiddish novelist Mendele. Castigating shtetl Jews for the narrow life which they had consented to lead, forever conjuring new fears and placing new yokes upon themselves, believing themselves to be the Chosen but giving themselves up to nothing but child-rearing, ritual and the scrutinizing of sacred texts, an Eternal People dying of hunger three times a day, Makhshoves wonders that the Jew was not able, *somehow*, to rise above these circumstances, but − but

> among his atrophied senses there remained vivid only the sixth one: an overly sharp intelligence which tended to laugh and jeer at the contradictions of the life he was leading . . . A sharply critical intelligence that hangs suspended over a dead body feels the agonies of life as though in a dream; they pass through the dust-covered sense and reach the mind like some distant flicker of lightning without thunder . . . In Jewish wit one can hear the voice of self-contempt, of a people who have lost touch with the ebb and flow of life. In Jewish mockery one can hear . . . the sick despair of a people whose existence has become an endless array of contradictions, a permanent witticism.

The response to which superbly poetical analysis - to the degree that it is true - has, for many Jews, been Zionism. 'The central purpose of the entire Zionist experiment,' writes Isaiah Berlin of Chaim Weizmann, 'was designed to cure the Jews of precisely these wounds and neuroses that only their enforced rootlessness had bred in them.' Those 'wounds and neuroses' being? The usual: cynicism, vulgarity, bitterness, fanaticism, black humour, knowingness; the corrupt and destructive cleverness of slaves, the aimless, feckless, nihilistic restlessness inherited from too long a sojourn in the ghetto.

It fascinates me that whether the perceived remedy is to enter sophisticated society, as the Jews of Germany did, hoping to pass as something you are not, or to sail across the seas to a country which is yours alone and where you no longer have to be or feel a slave, the description of the illness is always the same: over hundreds if not thousands of years of exile the Jew had grown emotionally bent instead of straight, contradictory instead of unified, and the clearest manifestation of this bentness was the highly wrought comedy with which he viewed his condition. The unforgivable element in this comedy, over and above the usual difficulties which comedy poses to serious men, being that it betrayed self-hatred.

Self-hatred, there we have it. You will still hear the charge levelled against Woody Allen or Philip Roth. Would you believe that it has been levelled even against me!

But I ask you which is the self-hating Jew – the Jew who makes a permanent witticism of the imperfect, not to say contradictory, life he leads, or the Jew who winces at such satire, recoiling from an ancient Jewish recourse, and therefore from an important ancient aspect of Jewish genius? Is it a mark of self-*love* in a Jew to remove all references to Jewishness from his conversation, from his mind, and if only he could – ah, if only he could – from his physiognomy?!

I don't know whether it's an unvarying rule of social psychology that whoever accuses a member of his group or religion of self-hatred is in fact only betraying a still deeper level of self-hatred of his own, but I have always found this to be so in my group. When I proposed *Roots Schmoots* as a travel series for television, why was it that only gentile television executives were interested? And why, when it was made, was it Jewish television executives who told me they wished I hadn't done it? Was it my conspicuousness they blushed for? Or was there something I had done that made them fear for *their* conspicuousness? And if so, which of us disliked himself so much he couldn't bear even a version of himself to be seen?

That there are Jews in our intellectual community who would do anything rather than look or sound Jewish, or who fancy that if they don't mention it nobody will notice, I find more regrettable (when I don't find it almost tragically absurd) than perhaps I reasonably should. You aren't obliged to notice in yourself an endless array of contradictions. If you don't feel them, you don't feel them. And I am certainly not going to embark on a campaign of 'outing', though I often think I would like to. Who am I, anyway, to say what a Jew should or shouldn't look like or aspire to look like intellectually? And if I complain that it isn't strictly Jewish to grow up straight and tall and jokeless, am I not perpetrating that version of Jewishness which every enlightened Jew since Moses Mendelssohn and every Zionist since Herzl has been trying to ditch?

Yes, I am. For the simple reason that that's the Jewishness I like and admire and value and see the point of and see a future for, most. And this, if you like, is the crux of my lecture. Not *'Vay Iz Mir* - Who'd be an English Jewish novelist whose first concern is not the Holocaust?' but *'Vay Iz Mir* - Who'd be a Jew of any sort that didn't want something of the shtetl, of the exile, of the long tragic but also exhilarating experience of negotiating foreignness, to sing in his blood forever?' If you'd like me to put that more succinctly, *Where's the fun in being an unmarginalized Jew?*

In fact, I suspect we have no choice. I suspect too much has happened for us to be any other sort of Jew. Israel was meant to normalize us, but what's 'normal' about Israel? And I'm not entirely certain that being a Jew ever was very different to this anyway. Chaim Weizmann, like Heinrich Graetz and Ba'al Makhshoves, put our mental subtlety, our butting and demurring, our subservience to the life of the mind, our twisted laughter, down to a misfortune of history. But who were we before? How do we find ourselves before we were wrongly placed? Putting his mind to Moses – or, more particularly, to the Mosaic prohibition against graven images, the prohibition against bodying God forth as an idol or making any other physical representation of Him – Freud notes that it elevated God to a higher degree of intellectuality . . . All such advances in intellectuality have as their consequence that the individual's self-esteem is increased, that he is made proud – so that he feels superior to other people who have remained under the spell of sensuality. Moses, as we know, conveyed to the Jews an exalted sense of being a chosen people. The dematerialization of God brought a fresh and valuable contribution to their secret treasure. The Jews retained their inclination to intellectual interests.. The nation's political misfortune [and when wasn't there one?!!] taught it to value at its true worth the one possession that remained to it – its literature.

There is much to ponder in this. A God one cannot see may not in Himself explain the sorts of subtlety that came to accrue to the Jewish mind at the time of the Talmud and thereafter, but a theology of invisibility is bound to make some demands on a people's ingenuity. Add to that the pride Freud speaks of, and a certain over-and-above intellectual preening becomes more likely. We all become subtle when explaining what we cannot see, and subtler still in the company of those so lost to sensuality that they can apprehend only what their eyes deliver to them, people for whom a God can only be a God if He looks like a stone animal . . . or a pop star. As for the contempt we will sometimes feel for those prosaic sensualists our neighbours, and the nostalgia we will sometimes feel for the sensuality we have got the better of in ourselves, all the makings of satire – at our neighbours' expense and at our own – are to hand. If that means I'm saying that a refined sense of the ridiculous is a natural consequence of monotheism, then that's what I'm saying. Blame Freud.

The other cause and effect to look for in Freud's account is that of national misfortune and literature. Would we be less the people of the Book if things had gone swimmingly for us? Do we have a book – *the* Book – precisely because things were *not* going swimmingly for us? The Book, after all, is as much the story of our dispossession, of destruction and disinheritance, as it is the story of our creation. Are we therefore bound in some matrix of suffering and hyper-literacy just about from the start, long before we found ourselves in the shtetls of Poland and Lithuania?

Let me throw in another thought from Freud's *Moses and Monotheism*. Not so much a thought, actually, as an aside. 'Why the people of Israel,' he wonders, 'clung more and more submissively to their God the worse they were treated by him – that is a problem which for the moment we must leave on one side.'

'*Submissively*', '*clung* more and more submissively'. Since this is Freud, we wouldn't expect him to have missed the erotic nature of the figure – the people of Israel, often called the children of Israel, clinging to the feet of a cruel father, or a cruel lover, or both. An act of erotic submission which feeds upon itself, one submission encouraging another. *Masochism*. Masochism and monotheism – wouldn't you say there was a connection of inevitability between the two? One God, against any sort of bodying forth of whom there is a prohibition, one invisible God who chooses you but who doesn't answer when you call, who is all goodness and who therefore cannot be responsible for any harm that befalls you – that being all *your* fault – how can devotion to such a deity not have, at the *very* least, particles of masochism in it?

Now masochism, if you will allow it is just one word for a complex of emotional strategies, is surely what so many of our critics of the twisted shtetl Jew have been complaining of. A lack of any decent sense of self-worth. A desire to see oneself punished. An attitude of mind, a turn of bitter humour, in which one metes out one's own deserts. The very thing that is meant to vanish when we become sophisticated citizens of the world or go to live in Israel.

I'm interested in masochism. I'm interested in the nexus between belief, masochism, intelligence and the joke. I have found myself reasoning, from time to time, that masochism is the glue of comedy, and when that doesn't quite work, that masochism is the glue of Jewish comedy at least.

The key text on this subject, if it hasn't yet been written by me, is *Masochism in Modern Man,* by Theodor Reik, a student of Freud's. What Reik is particularly good on are the strategies whereby the masochist turns defeat - a defeat he himself has set about orchestrating - into victory:

> The masochist does not accept punishment and humiliation, he anticipates them. He not only demonstrates their impotence to withhold the forbidden pleasure, but he affirms and demonstrates that it was they which helped him to it . . . By taking the place of authority and chastising himself he suspends it. By punishing and disgracing himself, he transforms punishment into an enticement . . .

Among the tools of the masochist's trade, Reik discerns defiance and a sullen derision. It is by these means that the masochist preserves his personality even in surrender, remains stubborn while yielding, stays haughty in his humility:

> The derision represents a step beyond defiance. Having become prouder through humiliation, more courageous through pressure, the masochist becomes a spiteful scoffer. His sabotage assumes the form of complete docility. His resistance consists in not-resisting. His blind obedience becomes rebellion. There are nations in whom such a masochistic manner produces the most malicious and most biting jokes against their own national peculiarities and weaknesses, jokes that in their accuracy of aim expose their own communities . . . However, such self-humiliation and self-derision do not exclude a hidden pride in national merits that are unknown and inaccessible to strangers. The jokes, while deriding the shortcomings of one's own people, yet secretly praise the virtues of these defects . . .

In those strategies of scoffing which Reik describes - sabotage through docility, resistance through non-resistance - we may hear the echo of representations of Jewishness we would rather not be reminded of. Shylock, the Jew of Malta, Fagin - the Jew as depicted by those who haven't read Theodor Reik.

But I think we can also recognize in Reik's account the *modus operandi* of the Jewish joke as we enjoy it, when we do. It explains at least why, communally, all together in the right place at the right time, we derive such pleasure from the spectacle of one of our own - a Mel Brooks, a Jackie Mason - taking us, again and again, through every refinement of our national shortcomings. And why the experience leaves us not at all humiliated, but invigorated.

But I also see that if masochism is a neurotic strategy born of too much anxiety, we might not welcome it, however cunningly it turns the tables on its real or imaginary enemies. Better not to be in need of such a resource in the first place. Maybe. Maybe better not to be submitting to an invisible God who seems not to be there when we need Him. Maybe the condition of neuroses to which we give the name masochism is an inevitable consequence not of being pushed historically from pillar to post, but of choosing such to be one's fate from the moment one commits to the intellectual life as opposed to the sensual. A circle of consequences in which the thing one aspires to be is forever affirmed by the opposition of those who aspire to something different.

These are deep waters. And the aim of this lecture, anyway, is not to establish the rules of the Jewish character. I address you as a writer, and more specifically as a Jewish writer, a Jewish novelist, a comic Jewish novelist - a doubly marginalized figure in an already marginalized culture whose taste in literature has declined to books about the Holocaust (now there's masochism!) and books about food. And marginality, the wonderful marginality of the Jews, is my subject.

Here, in the matter of our self-identity, is the choice as I see it - either we can agree with

Martin Buber, who rejects the strategies of masochism and irony, born of centuries of being slapped and not slapping back, who rejects our intellectuality, 'Out of touch with life, out of balance, inorganic', who abhorred our statelessness, no longer possessing a common language or a natural community, and who saw our only future in a spiritual leap that would unite the dualisms that had beset us for centuries, now exalted, now debased, now illustrious, now shameful, a contradiction which in another part of himself he seems to believe (as do I) is the birthplace of the eternal, or – *or* – we can wear all our dualities and contradictions with pride and be the sort of heroic Jew, let's say, that . . . Leopold Bloom is.

Forgive the going to fiction for my ideal, but I live by fiction. And forgive me going to a non-Jewish writer, but Jews don't listen to Jewish writers unless they write Holocaust or cookery books. And sometimes a non-Jewish writer, especially if he is word-crazy, God-driven, masochistic and more than a little marginalized himself, will appreciate things about us that we don't.

I'm assuming you know James Joyce's *Ulysses*, but in case it's grown dim in the memory, I will remind you of those bits of it which are relevant to my argument. The hero of *Ulysses*, the modern-day wanderer whose tribulations last a mere twenty-four hours – the somewhat wasted twenty-four hours between leaving his wife's bed-warmed rump and returning to it – is the Jew, Leopold Bloom. A commercial salesman. At one time in his life a commercial salesman for *blotting* paper – for *absorbent* materials – I ask you to keep that in your mind!

Much of the pleasure of *Ulysses*, for me, comes simply from watching Joyce getting it right – Jewish comedy of the kind we know how to enjoy in Leo Rosten or Joseph Heller. Bloom in the brothel scene, for example, trying to steer an unsteady Stephen Daedalus away from harm: 'Come home. You'll get into trouble.' Schmoozing the watch:

> Thank you very much, gentlemen, thank you. We don't want any scandal, you understand.
> Father is a well known, highly respected citizen. just a little wild oats, you understand.

The incorrigible respectability of the conspicuousness-fearing Jew, 'actuated by motives of inherent delicacy, inasmuch as he always believed in minding his own business'. 'Mistake,' as Bloom reminds himself, after a moment of relishing the memory of a revenge – 'Mistake to hit back.'

Except that, as a Jew, argument is his greatest passion. An irony and a complication which Joyce relishes, dumping Bloom in the very lair of his religious enemies and all but in the jaws of the enemy's hungry bloody gentile dog, and there showing how impossible he finds it to resist a little mental showing off.

> That can be explained by science, says Bloom. It's only a natural phenomenon, don't you see, because on account of the . . .
> The distinguished scientist Herr Professor Luitpold Blumenduft tendered medical evidence to the effect that the instantaneous fracture of the cervical vertebrae and consequent scission of the spinal cord would, according to the best approved traditions of medical science, be calculated to inevitably produce in the human subject a violent ganglionic stimulus of the nerve centres, causing the pores of the *corpora cavernosa* to rapidly dilate [ultimately resulting] in a morbid upwards and outwards philoprogenitive erection . . .

My son the doctor. My son the phallic pedant. Bloom with his argol bargol, not just pedantic but punctilious; not just punctilious but long-winded; not just long-winded but dialectical – 'but don't you see? . . . but on the other hand?' Arguing, arguing, arguing . . .

After which, because the gentile dog is now salivating, it's ben Bloom Elijah and off in a fiery chariot. A *messiah ex machina*, courtesy of the author. But who will rescue Bloom next time? 'When you go out you never know what dangers,' Bloom muses, after Gerty MacDowell has left him with a wet shirt.

It's hereabouts that he famously confuses the talismanic properties of *tephilin* with those of the *mezuzah*:

> And the tephilin no this they call it poor papa's father had on his door to touch. That brought us out of the land of Egypt and into the house of bondage.

Thus mangling the facts no less than the artefacts, since Egypt *was* the house of bondage. This confusion is often adduced as proof that Bloom is not much of a Jew (taking him to be a real man), or not much of a portrayal of a Jew (taking him to be a faulty would-be of Joyce's imagination).

'Well, the rabbis might not say that Bloom was a Jew,' David Ben-Gurion is reported to have told Gerschom Sholem, 'but *I* do.' And I do too. Bloom's mangling and misremembering are deliberate, an act of accuracy in themselves. In Bloom's languid, associative post-Gerty musings, the dim memory of what it is like to bind the forearm and the forehead with the leather straps of the *tephilin* – a ritual which strikes me still, on the few occasions when I submit to its performance, as peculiarly sadomasochistic – recalls to his mind, simultaneously, the bondage of the body which the Jews have suffered since the Lord (whose name is commemorated in every *mezuzah)* brought them out of Egypt, *and* the bondage of the heart which he, as excessive conniver in his wife's infidelities, and as reader of Leopold von Sacher Masoch, is only too willing to suffer whenever the opportunity presents itself.

If that simultaneity of association binds what is Jewish in Bloom with what is masochistic, if it gives the masochism a peculiarly Jewish cast, that suits my argument fine. The reference to the works of Leopold von Sacher Masoch at this point in the novel isn't accidental. Hold in your mind the fact that Leopold von Sacher Masoch wrote not only *Venus in Furs* but *Tales of the Ghetto,* and that Leopold Bloom glances at that second title on the porno counter, saying 'That I had' before pushing it aside.

A vocabulary of voluptuous detumescence, not a million miles from the vocabulary of Jewish anti-Jewishness, embraces Bloom in his urban travels. Soft about his day he goes, limp-languid, gentle, overpowered, cowed, solitary, mutable, abnegated, yielding, with reason jealous, beyond reason in love with his jealousy, a man – a real man, in Joyce's teasing terms – 'strong to the verge of weakness'.

In his biography of Joyce, Richard Ellman – a Jew, of course – unites Joyce and Bloom in a 'philosophy of passivity in act, energy in thought, and tenacity in conviction', noting further Joyce's preference for inactive men over swimmers, shot-putters and adulterers. 'We spend most of the book inside Bloom's consciousness,' he writes, 'and never enter Boylan's, as if coarseness had no consciousness.'

Where did we last hear the Jew described as glorying at once in his own submissiveness and intellectualism, while enjoying superiority to the mere sensualism of his neighbour? If coarseness has no consciousness, then it can no more be at the centre of a novel than a religion.

Standing beside her at the pork butcher's counter, where he is able to survey her 'vigorous hips', and to remember her (or to imagine he remembers her) 'whacking a carpet on a clothesline', Bloom plans pursuit of a girl carrying prime sausages:

> To catch up and walk behind her . . . behind her moving hams. Pleasant to see first thing in the morning. Hurry up, damn it. Make hay while the sun shines. She stood outside the

shop in sunlight and sauntered lazily to the right. He sighed down his nose: they never understand. Soda chapped hands. Crusted toenails too . . . The sting of disregard glowed to weak pleasure within his breast. For another: a constable off duty cuddled her in Eccles Lane . . .

'For another' - as if he is about to embark on a list of stings of disregard, or as if the sting from one woman will always bring to mind a sting from a second, all masochists being, in the nature of things, serial masochists. Stream of consciousness they used to call it, but in truth, in Bloom's case, it is sting or prick of consciousness; one piquant reminiscence of disregard prompting another.

Interesting that so early in Bloom's Odyssey of shames, the sting is felt in a Jewish context. While standing waiting to buy meat, thinking about the vigorous-hipped girl with the strong pair of arms - 'She does it whack, by George' - Bloom takes up a page about a model farm in Palestine on the lakeshore of Tiberias. A Moses Montefiore venture. Zionism in the pork butcher's. Alive, the question of what as a Jew you may eat and what you may not. What Bloom follows out onto the street are the whacking girl's *hams* - her *trayf*, forbidden thighs. She is non-kosher food; the sting she administers by not noticing him at all is full of gentile poisons. Sweet, those, to any self-disrespecting, horn-mad Jew, of the sort Weizmann and Buber would like to see an end. Disregarded, Bloom walks back home, 'reading gravely' the prospectus for the model farm on the shores of Lake Tiberias:

> A barren land, bare waste. Vulcanic lake, the dead sea; no fish, weedless, sunk deep in the earth. No wind would lift those waves, grey metal, poisonous foggy waters. Brimstone they called it raining down: the cities of the plain: Sodom, Gomorrah, Edom. All dead names. A dead sea in a dead land, grey and old. Old now. It bore the oldest, the first race. A bent hag crossed from Cassidy's clutching a naggin bottle by the neck. The oldest people. Wandered far away over all the earth, captivity to captivity multiplying, dying, being born everywhere.

A touch pre-Raphaelite that may be, and a touch pre-Israel, but no Jew can be unfamiliar with the desolation evoked, or with its transference from place to person, the shouldering of a sort of blame - sins of the fathers, decrepitude of the fathers, sins of decrepitude - for a history that's gone on too long and still persists. Bloom's temporary solution is to seek that seemingly most un-Jewish of all sensations - the most prohibited and the most impossible - forgetfulness: 'To smell the gentle smoke of tea, fume of the pan, sizzling butter. Be near her ample bedwarmed flesh. Yes, yes.'

Yes, yes. Worth remembering that Bloom gets in with his affirmation before Molly gets in with hers.

What will soon be sizzling in the pan, meat bought from the wrong butcher and cooked in butter, proves the measure of the apostasy. The maiden of the ample bedwarmed flesh is from among the Midianites, else she would keep a kosher kitchen. You want to know why Jewish men who would be free of the bondage of the phylactery must sometime marry out? It's all here in *Ulysses*.

I think it was a bold stroke of Joyce's to begin Bloom's day not just with Palestine and pork - that's easy - but with the concentric circles of Jewish memory and Jewish forgetfulness, of mortification and indulgence, of displacement and adjustment, of submission of the will and tyrannical application of it. In his relations with his wife, most of them conducted away from her and in his head, Leopold Bloom repeats in miniature the relations Jews enjoy with God. She is his scourge and his pleasure. She is largely unavailable to him. Most of the time she is upstairs and unanswering. Her unresponsiveness is the proof of something undeserving, and her infidelities are the proof of something unworthy, in himself. He is therefore, metaphysically speaking, always at the centre of any drama between them. What she does, she does because of him. If we Jews could persuade God to be catechized, as Bloom has been able to catechize Molly – 'who is in your mind now tell me who are you thinking of who is it tell me his name who . . .' – we would consider our masochistic religious devotions to be consummated at last . . .

It is well known, because he in detail told a friend, that Joyce spent one whole day working out the perfect order for the following fifteen words – 'Perfume of embraces all him assailed . . . With hungered flesh obscurely, he mutely craved to adore.'

I'm not surprised their ordering preoccupied him to the degree it did, because for all their promise of infinite rearrangement, their ultimate seduction lies in their perpetual reiteration and re-enactment, shuffle them how you may, of that obsessional self-abnegation which is Bloom's negative driving force, his strength to the verge of weakness. Every verb, every adverb, every adjective and every noun is in the yielding-to-victimization business. Bloom's yielding, but also the novel's. All that Joyce did for the modern novel, *and* for the modern hero, is encapsulated here. 'All' being the operative word. 'Perfume of embraces *all* him assailed' – the degree of Bloom's submission being the degree of the novel's own openness to everything, not an assured mastery of experience but an absorption – the blotting paper salesman – in it.

To the practical man of action, the idle, yielding, over-responsiveness of a man like Bloom will seem, if not disreputable, useless. But in art, *uselessness* has been an important concept this last hundred years. And few dramatic examples of uselessness in action have been more perversely energizing and positive than that of the uxorious Jew Bloom, apparently useless to his Jewishness, apparently useless to his *uxor*, beginning his day tasting 'a fine tang of faintly scented urine' and ending it – his face in his wife's behind – 'with obscure prolonged provocative melonsmellonous osculation'.

If the Jew has become the idealized figure of the modern novel, the perfect fictional recipient of every cruelty, every hardship, every bewilderment, and every pleasure, Leopold Bloom, waiting to be assailed – waiting to be *all* assailed – helps us to understand why.

In 1919, while Joyce was finishing work on *Ulysses*, the sociologist Thorstein Veblen brought out an essay entitled *The Intellectual Pre-eminence of Jews in Modern Europe*. In this, Veblen argued that Jews did their best work in the gentile world, where they never felt entirely at home, because while the gentiles revelled in tranquility and peace of mind, the intellectually gifted Jew enjoyed 'immunity from the inhibitions of quietism'.

Immunity from the inhibitions of quietism. A permanent struggle, a permanent argument, a permanent witticism, the conditions – provided, of course, we survive – for permanent achievement. Veblen was talking of men of science. I have been talking of characters in fiction. But I'm prepared to risk a generality from the particular. What if our genius is our history, what if the distortions of the shtetl and the ghetto and the margins *are* our nature now? I doubt that Israel is going to make a new Jew of us. And I doubt we cut any prettier a picture than we ever did, garnering knighthoods from the non-Jewish world and imagining we pass unnoticed. What's wrong with a future of exceptionable receptiveness, a future full of that intellectual turbulence which is both the penalty and the reward for enjoying immunity from the inhibitions of quietism?

If I weren't a comic English Jewish novelist much given to argumentativeness and irony, I'd call that prospect *glorious*.

Spring 2001

DELMORE SCHWARTZ AND ME
A Literary Rediscovery
Linda Grant

In 1937 the teenage Irving Howe sat down to read the first edition of *Partisan Review*, which was to become the house magazine of the anti-Stalinist American Left, its journal of culture and politics. Howe was impatient and hungry for polemic, but he noticed that the editors had put at the top of their table of contents a short story, 'In Dreams Begin Responsibilities', by a 23-year-old called Delmore Schwartz. So, dutifully, he read it.

'We were stunned,' Howe recalled in his Foreword to *In Dreams Begin Responsibilities and other stories* (New York; New Directions, 1978):

> Many people I know have remembered the story long after forgetting everything else in the first issue . . . We heard a voice that seemed our own, though it had never really existed until Schwartz invented it: a voice at home with the speech of people not quite at home with English speech.

In Chicago the young Saul Bellow also read the story. Its first audience was a generation of writers-to-be, the children of Jewish immigrants, the first to go to college and hence through the door into Western culture.

I read it last August, over sixty years after it was first published. The name Delmore Schwartz created a slight stirring in the mind. He was a 1930s poet. Yes. Was he black? No, it was merely the name that misled. I came to Schwartz because I discovered in the entry for Bellow in the on-line *Encyclopaedia Britannica* that the Humboldt (a Bellevue mental case) of Bellow's novel *Humboldt's Gift* (1975) was based on the author's friendship with Schwartz. I had spent the whole summer reading Bellow, devouring *Humboldt's Gift* beside the pool at a Mallorcan villa, grey, cold Chicago more real than the olive trees, the hot blue air, the smell of sun block. I was looking back to the high days of Modernism before irony and camp and knowingness created a distance between the writer and the subject. I was looking for ways of writing about the present tense and about personal life, at how Bellow and Roth and Malamud had made Jewishness an aspect of modern consciousness in a country where (unlike Britain) to be a Jew was to make your contribution to the national identity in the very process of its formation.

I had just finished writing one novel set in the strange interstices between the end of the war and the beginning of the 1950s and had already published another depicting the same period. In a book about my mother, I had excavated the mythologies of Jewish family life, so now I had a hunger for the present tense and was trying to figure out how to portray it. It wasn't Will Self or Martin Amis that I wanted to read. My urge was to return to the high masters of Modernism, and preferably the Jewish Modernists who would understand better than anyone else what it was like to be thrust head first into the twentieth century with its skyscrapers, ice makers, automobiles and movie studios, after centuries of vegetable life in the shtetls. In one of Schwartz's stories, 'America! America!' he wrote of his parents' generation drinking in the marvels of the new world:

> When the toilet bowl flushed like Niagara, when a suburban homeowner killed his wife and children, and when a Jew was made a member of President Theodore Roosevelt's cabinet, the excited exclamation was:
> 'America! America!

America indeed. Schwartz's father had immigrated to the New World from Romania, made a fortune in real estate and lost every penny in the 1929 crash, from rags to riches to rags in half a lifetime.

'In Dreams Begin Responsibilities' hit me like a blunt instrument to the head. Schwartz had written it over the Fourth of July weekend when he was twenty-one. I saw him sitting at a cheap wooden table in the days before the biro was invented. In the story a young man goes into a movie theatre. He takes his seat and what unfolds before him is the courtship of his parents on Coney Island on Independence Day, 1909. He sees on the screen his father walk through the quiet streets of Brooklyn, past trees, lawns and houses, jingling his change in his pockets, 'thinking of the witty things he will say'. He presses the bell on the house of the woman he is to marry; the family is still at dinner and the woman who will soon be the narrator's aunt answers the door, napkin in hand. The narrator's uncle, aged twelve, runs through the house. Upstairs, an older uncle studies for his final examination at City College, 'having been dead of rapid pneumonia for the last twenty-one years'. Past and present exist simultaneously.

The young courting couple leave the house and take a streetcar. The narrator's future father tells his future mother how much money he had made in the past week, 'exaggerating an amount which need not have been exaggerated'. At several points the film breaks down and sometimes returns to replay a portion that has already been shown, sometimes skipping ahead, and now the narrator's mother and father are alighting at the last stop, Coney Island. The narrator sees the boardwalk, an American flag, 'pulsing in an intermittent wind from the sea', hears a peanut whistle and sees his father going to buy a bag of nuts from the vendor. The narrator sees 'the fatal, merciless, passionate ocean' and bursts out weeping. Unable to control his tears he gets up and goes to the men's room.

When he returns to his seat, several hours seem to have passed and his parents-to-be are now riding on a merry-go-round. Dusk is falling and they look for a place to have dinner, his father suggesting they should go to the best restaurant on the boardwalk. Inside there is a string trio playing and the father orders the meal 'with a fine confidence'. He speaks of his business and of how much money there is to be made these days; he says that he is twenty-nine years old and it is time to settle down to calm domesticity. His mother bursts into tears and accepts the proposal of marriage and it is then that the narrator rises from his seat in the movie theatre and cries: 'Don't do it. It's not too late to change your minds, both of you. Nothing good will come of it, only remorse, hatred, scandal and two children whose characters are monstrous.' The whole audience turns to look at him and the usher appears flashing his torch. The old lady next to him warns him to calm down. 'Be quiet. You'll be put out and you paid thirty-five cents to come in.'

Through half-closed eyes the narrator watches the rest of the movie: his future parents having their picture taken in a photographer's booth, already quarrelling; their visit to a fortune teller. Now the narrator feels as if 'I were walking a tight-rope a hundred feet over a circus-audience and suddenly the rope is showing signs of breaking'. He begins shouting and again the usher comes hurrying down the aisle. Again the old lady next to him pleads with him to keep quiet, the whole audience is staring. 'Don't you know that you can't do whatever you want to do?' the usher demands. 'You will be sorry if you do not do what you should do, you can't carry on like this, it is not right, you will find that out soon enough, everything you do matters too much.' And, dragged into the cold light of the lobby of the movie theatre, the narrator wakes up on his twenty-first birthday, 'the window shining with its lip of snow, and the morning already begun'.

Whenever I have recounted the events of the story to those who haven't read it, the narrator's outburst always raises a laugh. For all that we cannot imagine our parents un-married to each other and ourselves never born, neither can we resist the idea that, with the benefit of hindsight, it was a mistake. We, the children, know better than the parents. I never take them further, to the story's ending, the narrator's ejection from the theatre, the intimations that something is not right with his state of mind, the waking on a cold December morning on the day he becomes officially an adult, the world getting on without him. To the young Irving Howe, reading the story in 1937, the moment in the theatre was also the natural high point, the narrative centre. 'The hopelessness, and as it seemed then, the rightness of the son's lament,' he wrote, 'appealed to my deepest feelings as another son slipping into estrangements . . . the cry against the mistakes of the past.'

To Howe, Schwartz's story (and others would follow on similar lines) was about the conflict between immigrant Jewish families and their intellectual children. But coming to it again a decade after Schwartz's death he saw that the usher's remonstrance was correct: whatever our sympathy with the narrator's outburst, 'it is not so much a protest against mistakes as a protest against life itself, inconceivable without mistakes'. For me, however, reading the story was like listening to the voice of the young Judy Garland singing 'Somewhere over the Rainbow' - unbearably poignant when one speeds ahead in one's mind to the singer in bloated, alcoholic middle age. Everything Schwartz did mattered too much to him. Things mattering, the least postmodern idea of all, was what undid him.

Within a year or two of the publication of 'In Dreams Begin Responsibilities', Schwartz was America's hottest young writer, moodily photographed by *Vogue,* invited to all the best parties, awarded with a teaching job at Harvard. He was working on a long poem, *Genesis,* which in his own mind would rank alongside *The Wasteland*. He saw himself as among the two or three greatest poets of the twentieth century, with Yeats, Eliot and Pound as the other contenders. Saul Bellow opens *Humboldt's Gift* with these words about Humboldt/Schwartz:

> The book of ballads published by Von Humboldt Fleisher in the Thirties was an immediate hit. Humboldt was just what everyone had been waiting for. Out in the Midwest I had certainly been waiting eagerly, I can tell you that. An avant-garde writer, the first of a new generation, he was handsome, fair, large, serious, witty - he was learned. The guy had it all. All the papers reviewed his book. His picture appeared in *Time* without insult and in *Newsweek* with praise.

But Schwartz went mad. 'He was crazy as a bedbug,' the short-story writer Grace Paley told me last September, remembering the time when they both taught together at the University of Syracuse in the 1960s. Bellow sighted him on the street in New York a couple of months before his death and depicts the scene in *Humboldt's Gift*:

> I knew that Humboldt would soon die because I had seen him on the street two months before and he had death all over him. He didn't see me. He was grey stout sick dusty, he had bought a pretzel stick and was eating it. His lunch. Concealed by a parked car, I watched. I didn't approach him, I felt it was impossible.

By July 1966 Schwartz, the golden boy of 1930s and 1940s literary America, was dead at the age of fifty-three, having spent years in and out of mental institutions. He was also, of course, in the manner of those days, a drunk. He had a heart attack while taking out the garbage from his room at the Hotel Dixie, in Times Square. Perhaps his most enduring legacy was the influence he had on a persistently loyal student, Lou Reed, founder of the Velvet Underground, for whom he was 'a spiritual godfather'.

The long poem *Genesis* (1943), which tells the story of this family's immigration to America, mattered to Schwartz more than anything else. He vacillated between believing that 'it is so good that no one will believe that I, mere I, am author, but rather a team of inspired poets' and a terrified anticipation that it would fail; he would be like Melville, who went to the grave 'thinking that *Moby Dick* was a failure because of the 'stupid critics'. Other times he thought it might be the longest and worst poem in the English language. *Genesis* was the product of Schwartz's deepest self-absorption and a belief that his own life (he was not yet thirty when it was published) could only be expressed by epic poetry in the manner of Milton. It would last, he wrote, 'as long as the Pyramids' and 'In days to come - mark you! - this poetic style will be seen as the beginning of Post-Symbolism, as Cézanne was the beginning of Post-Impressionism.'

W. H. Auden thought otherwise in a lengthy letter advising him not to publish: 'The central fault in your poem is, in my opinion, just this false hope that if you only look up and remember enough, significance and value and belief will appear of themselves' (see James Atlas's *Delmore Schwartz: The Life of an American poet,* New York: Farrar Straus Giroux, 1977, now being reissued by Welcome Rain). In other words, as I interpret this, Auden was saying that Schwartz's life and antecedents did not yield quite the universal resonance that he had hoped for.

The reviews ranged from okay to disastrous. Dwight Macdonald called it 'unreadable, flaccid, monotonous, the whole effort pompous and verbose'. Paul Goodman described it as 'a combination of ineptitude and earnestness'. For James Atlas, 'the most salient objection that can be made to *Genesis* is that it belabours private themes which lack even the semblance of universality needed to give them dramatic interest'. The published work, Schwartz announced, was unfinished. After some two hundred pages, the hero, Hershey Green, is only seven years old. If Schwartz had gone on with it, Atlas points out, it would have become the longest poem in the English language. At the same time as this critical mauling, Schwartz's wife Gertrude (a woman who agreed to marry him after a lengthy pestering campaign during which she declared that she wasn't interested in marrying anyone) finally left him. Atlas's biography takes 248 pages to cover Schwartz's life up to the publication and aftermath of *Genesis* and only a further 131 pages to deal with the rest of it.

Shwartz has no British publisher; I don't know if he ever had one. At the beginning of his career he was taken up by James Laughlin, the heir to a Pittsburgh steel fortune who had been encouraged by Ezra Pound to start an imprint, the literary list New Directions. Later, Schwartz's paranoia would detect 'a cabal of enemies' out to destroy his work, which could only be prevented by the most strenuous sales and marketing activities on Laughlin's part. Inevitably this ended in the sense of betrayal every author feels towards his publisher, whose fault it invariably is when a book is not the critical and commercial success the author dreamed of. Yet Laughlin remained loyal to Schwartz. No one else in America published him.

I bought my first Schwartz - a paperback collection of short stories under the *In Dreams* title, first published in 1978 after *Humboldt's Gift* and Atlas's biography had temporarily revived his reputation - on the Internet, at the Amazon site. Amazon stocks a certain number of copies of this book in the UK, but the other works have to be ordered from America. Waterstones in Hampstead has a couple of titles. Borders on Oxford Street has several copies of *In Dreams* but nothing else. There are two editions of Schwartz's poetry available, plus a volume of short pieces and a volume of his verse plays. Atlas's biography, out of print for some years, is just being republished. But for the devotee there is the lure of tracking him down on an Internet site such as Bibliofind.

This (www.bibliofind.com) is a vast network of second-hand bookstores. You type a title or an author into a search engine, you specify whether or not you want a first edition, with or without dustjacket, signed by the author or spoiled by the inscription of a former owner. A list of available items pops up and the name of the store that holds it. You check a box next to the book you want and an e-mail goes out to the store. All of Schwartz, unsurprisingly, was in America. A few hours later, depending on the time difference, an e-mail from the bookstore comes back, telling you whether or not the book has been sold since it was posted on the Bibliofind site. You hand over your address and credit card details and have a discussion about forms of postage. My hunt for Schwartz led me into a lengthy series of exchanges with a poet in Sacramento whose store, which existed only on the Internet and was not a shop you could go into, specialized in the Beat Poets. I had a courteous e-mail discussion with a gentleman in Georgia. One Schwartz was purchased from an Amazon on-line auction. I was the only bidder.

I have never been much interested in first editions. I like to see a book with its back broken. I like coffee stains on its pages, the corners folded over, scribbles in the margin. I like to see a gift inscription, even better if it also bears a date. All of these catastrophes sharply reduce the value of a first edition, which ideally should be pristine, as if it has never been taken out of the bag it left the store in, and, even better, signed by the author, preferably to someone famous or connected with the author's life. American publishers now offer limited edition signed copies in special slipcases for the collector's market, the 'true' first edition, never meant to be read or opened. The publishers of *Harry Potter and the Prisoner of Azkeban* produced a small 'first edition' simultaneously with the first print run, to be sold or given to collectors.

But I am a democrat when it comes to books. I delight in the fact that a book as art is not really an object in the sense that a painting or sculpture or installation is. Whether you read a first edition or the millionth reprint, it is in all essentials the same book, the identical text. The printing press is an agent of mass production, and perhaps this is why artists can get rich and writers of literary fiction don't. There is nothing to increase in value, except perhaps the original manuscript, but even a signed first edition of Bellow's first novel, *Dangling Man,* can be obtained for only $2,500 on Bibliofind.

All summer the postman brought packages to my door from America. The books that arrived had a particular smell, sharp, sour and dusty – to do, I suppose, with the chemical processes taking place in the structure of the paper they were printed on. They smell, perhaps, as Schwartz might have done himself in the months before he died, unwashed and neglected. *Genesis* was in a browned paper wrapper with only the title on it, a piece of spare, minimalist modern design. I opened it. Inscribed on the fly-leaf was the name of its first owner, Irwin Kremer, who, the Bibliofind entry cryptically noted, was 'an American artist'. I imagine Kremer's eager anticipation. I take it from his name that he was a Jew. I think about him sitting down to read. It was the middle of the war. Was he in uniform? Was he too old to serve? Where did the book travel with him? Did he cast it aside angrily, agreeing with Goodman and MacDonald that it was a disaster? Or did he find something in it to cherish? Laughlin published 1,000 copies of *Genesis* - it has never been reprinted - and finding one of these is the only means left of reading the poem outside a library. I read it and concurred with Atlas's judgement. Imitative of Eliot and of Milton, it lacks any sense of humour about its subject. Everything in it matters too much when some of it doesn't matter at all.

Another book to arrive was the 1948 edition of *The World is a Wedding,* which contained seven of Schwartz's stories, 'New Year's Eve', 'A Bitter Farce', 'America! America!', 'The Statues', 'The Child is the Meaning of this Life', 'In Dreams Begin Responsibilities' (again) and the title story, which, along with 'In Dreams', is probably Schwartz's best known prose. It is about a group of people a few years older than Schwartz, the children of Jewish immigrants who graduated from college at the start of the Depression with grandiose dreams about their role in creating America's artistic future but found themselves jobless and poverty-stricken, forming a self-admiring bohemian clique. Part of but apart from this group is Laura, the sister of its central member, who spends much of her time shouting comments in from the kitchen in which she attends to the baser needs of the group such as eating and being cleaned up after.

Finally, I managed to buy a first edition of *In Dreams Begin Responsibilities,* the 1938 collection consisting of the title story and poems that Bellow describes, under Humboldt's authorship. Without a dust jacket its price was considerably reduced, to only $85. The second item in the book, 'Coriolanus and His Mother: The Dream of One Performance, a Narrative Poem' looks particularly forbidding.

In his lifetime, Schwartz was mainly known as a poet, though his work has gradually fallen out of the standard anthologies, replaced by more modish authors. He continued to write up to his death but in the papers that were removed from his room, nothing of value was found. I am not a great judge of poetry but I can judge prose and Schwartz's stories indicate to me that he should have become a novelist, and that in his failure to do so, he left the way clear for Bellow, a year younger than him. In *Humboldt's Gift,* the narrator, Charlie Citrine, once the young acolyte to Humboldt's celebrity, has become a success while Humboldt is a paranoid manic-depressive. We don't know what Schwartz might have done had he not gone mad. Overweening ambition, things mattering, made him choose the rarefied forms of the verse play like Eliot's *Murder in the Cathedral* and the epic poem instead of the novel, the literary form perhaps best suited to America's size and unwieldiness. Eliot and Pound, the models for what he wanted to do, lived outside America, shaped by it but immersed in European literary forms. Schwartz never left the country in his whole life. At the time of the publication of *Genesis,* Dwight Macdonald gave him wise though ignored advice: he should, he wrote, exploit his talent for 'satiric, humorous, intimate, realistic, description and commentary' instead of trying to be the Jewish T. S. Eliot.

I too find Schwartz in the stories, the boy from the newly enriched then newly impoverished Jewish middle class, the suffering heart to whom everything matters too much. Schwartz is the shadow that haunts every writer: that what we have to say will be forgotten, obliterated. That our lesser rivals will overtake us and we will fall out of favour. Schwartz struggled to know who he was and where he had come from. He read everything, particularly the sports pages. He was also a renowned and prodigious talker. He could discourse on anything. When he died, he was buried in a Jewish cemetery with a Jewish inscription on the gravestone. 'Our house wasn't Jewish in dishes or always going to shul,' a relative said. 'Jewish is heart. Delmore was Jewish.'

Heartlessness is a particularly twentieth-century phenomenon in art. We became more heartless as the century moved on. Sentimentality was sick, a cancer in a text or a piece of music. The idea is paramount, from Schoenberg's break with the deeply moving *fin de siècle* work *Verklärtesnacht* to his invention of serialism and all that follows. You couldn't accuse Eliot or Pound of having heart. In conceptual art, there is nothing but an idea (though usually an extremely small and unimportant one). With Schwartz, there were plenty of ideas, but they were always overwhelmed by how much they mattered to him. What remains, for me, are the stories of immigrants doomed to bad marriages or no marriages at all, to making money and losing it, to dead-end jobs or to a clash of uncontrollable personality which meant they never could keep one.

Delmore Schwartz took on far more than he could handle. He inflated his personal history beyond self-importance into a universal principle. Everything mattered too much to him, he never got anything into perspective. He burned out within about ten years of his blazing arrival on the American literary scene. Yet he pulls me back, over and again, into the art of living in modern times, when things mattered with an intensity we find embarrassing today, when having a heart was still an American quality and still a male one.

Winter 1999-2000

EDMOND JABÈS
A translator's tribute
Anthony Rudolf

Edmond Jabès was one of the key personalities in European literature and one of the commanding figures in European Jewish letters. He was born in Cairo on 16 April 1912, and one can reasonably say that he brought the desert with him to Paris when he had – as a Jew – to leave Egypt forever in the wake of the 1956 Suez crisis. With him were his wife Arlette and the two daughters of the marriage. Paris was the obvious and necessary place for a man in his economically difficult situation to take up residence and continue his profession of stockbroker. But, exiled from his homeland and the desert, in one sense he had come home, for he was already a *French* writer. He had often visited Paris where he knew the Surrealists well, though he kept his distance from their collective activities and identity, as he did with all groups throughout his life.

Max Jacob, whom he met in 1935, was his mentor, and his friends included Char, Blanchot (an extraordinary epistolary relationship this, they never met), Eluard and Michel Leiris. Shortly before Jabès died he dreamed he met Leiris in the Luxembourg Gardens, Leiris having died three months earlier. 'Well, Edmond, I did not expect to see you so soon.' And one of Leiris's books was the last book Jabès ever read, in the small apartment just off the ancient rue Mouffetard. As for Jacob, he had such a high regard for Jabès that, to the horror of the young poet, he destroyed an early manuscript of his, on the grounds that you smile politely at bad poets and return their unimproveable manuscripts to them – but a good poet can take shock treatment. In Cairo in 1941, Jabès organized the Italian Anti-Fascist Group. In the following year he was evacuated for nine months to Palestine by the British.

Away from the metropolis, Jabès maintained a voluminous correspondence with many writers. He wrote and he published – in France and in Egypt – several small volumes of poetry which were eventually collected in *Je bâtis ma demeure*. This huge book of lyrical and narrative poems, reissued in 1990 with a handful of later poems in Gallimard's *Poésie* series, also contains many pages of aphorisms and short prose pieces. *Je bâtis ma demeure*, whose original 1959 publication effectively coincided with the caesura in Jabès's life as a man, as a writer and as a Jew, announces and predicts aspects of the major work to come. But, in the later books, order and chaos, discipline and freedom, will be merged in a complex structure, whereas one can risk suggesting that in the work collected in *Je bâtis ma demeure*, the discipline is in the prose, the freedom in the verse, especially in the long poems of Surrealist provenance.

It was as a result of his brutal experience of exile, the millennial Jewish condition which became his key metaphor for writing, that he assumed, in the words of his friend Paul Auster, 'the burden of being Jewish'. As Jabès himself wrote, 'Judaism and writing are but the same waiting, the same hope, the same wearing out.' It is now clear that the trauma of exile deepened his existing preoccupation with exile and with writing itself to the point that these preoccupations had to be embodied in the very structure of the text, and this came to mean, ineluctably, that the unit of measure would be the *book*. Joseph Guglielmi wrote in 1975 in his afterword to the second edition of *Je bâtis ma demeure* that its 'obsessed and rebellious pages' anticipate the way his future books will serve as 'the instruments by means of which the writer, envisaging with lucidity his own loss as *subject*, nevertheless augments and regenerates the possibilities of expression and ensures, definitely, their emancipation.'

Out of his introspection and experience during the early Paris years came his masterpiece, the extraordinary and virtually unclassifiable *Le livre des questions*, seven volumes published between 1963 and 1974, and since translated into about ten languages, including English, though it is available only in the United States. Surprisingly, it was not until Jabès was well into the writing that he began to immerse himself in traditional Jewish literature, especially the aggadic and midrashic parts of the Talmud, as well as the kabbalah. Deeply involved now in Judaism, albeit a 'Judaism after God' (translate 'Judaism after Auschwitz'), he took his proud heritage as a member of the People of the Book quite literally.

Rosmarie Waldrop, Jabès's superb American translator, has summarized *The Book of Questions* as follows:

> There is a story, the separation of the young lovers Yukel and Sarah during the Nazi deportations, but it is a 'meta-story' never fully told, only commented on by imaginary rabbis, whose aphorisms and Talmudic explications concern the writing of the book and the nature of the word.

The Book of Questions is a kind of oratorio, a recitative in prose and verse, a multivalent text, a midrashic parable of the Holocaust. When Jewish discourse and rhetoric became fashionable in the 1980s in France and America, critics discovered to their astonishment that a great poet (who wrote mainly in prose) had been reinventing Jewish modes of writing for some time already. Simultaneously Jabès is a major figure in the post-Mallarméan poetics of *écriture*.

Writing in the dialectical space between urban Sephardi Judaism and the Islam of the surrounding desert, his homeland is language: an alphabet of remembrance witnessed and recited in the anguish of his gaze. God is everywhere in Jabès's work. No atheist has ever been more intoxicated by the wine of His absence, albeit in the mirror of language. And absence is the heart of *The Book of Questions*, a bypass operation on the real. Like his friend Celan, Jabès drank 'wine from two glasses'. The work of Jabès – not only *Le livre des questions,* but also the sequels *Le livre des ressemblances* and *Le livre des limites* – has been taken very seriously by theologians like Levinas and Heschel, philosophers like Derrida and Starobinski, and by Celan - about whose attitude to Jabès much could and will be written - as well as by all kinds of psychoanalysts, structuralists, deconstructionists and post-modernists. The implicit questioning of language as such positions Jabès with Celan in meeting the challenge (disguised as a prohibition) raised by Adorno, as against the way Levi and Wiesel, for example, met the challenge – their relationship with language being less problematical, more hopeful.

A work, a great work, lives or dies by the attention of the common reader, not by that of the specialist explicator. If enough common readers of discrimination tell their friends and children 'this is a book you must read', the book will survive unto the third and fourth generations and beyond. Jabès can be read as a maker of post-Holocaust *midrash* on a par with Appelfeld, Levi, Rudnicki; he can be read as a French late modernist in dialogue with the ghosts of Kafka and Mallarmé, and with the persons of Blanchot and Leiris, not to mention the many poets two generations younger than himself whom he influenced deeply and who visited him; and he can be read as one of the grand fabulists of our time, the peer of Borges and Calvino. *The Book of Questions* is one of the most beautiful, powerful and radically disturbing poetic adventures in all modern literature.

I was introduced to Jabès and his work around 1967 by Claude Royet-Journoud, a poet now in his late forties who, then, as a tireless young proselytiser for his passionate views about French poetry, presented me with books by Jabès, gave me his phone number, and instructed me to translate him, which I did. I feel a great pride in having published in various magazines what must have been the first translations of Edmond Jabès's work: prose from *The Book of Questions* translated by Rosmarie Waldrop, and early poems translated by myself. He visited England three times, participating in Poetry International in 1974 and Richard Burns' Cambridge Poetry Festival in 1979, where his counterpointed dialogue with Rosmarie Waldrop provided one of the most innovative, enjoyable and moving performances many of us had ever witnessed. During the 1974 visit he introduced his readings with a text specially composed for the occasion. It contained a passage about the early poems:

> Long walk back to the war years when these songs rose from my earliest childhood while death raged without pity. Life-saving words when everything was crumbling. Long walk, indeed, into a written past that has become my real past across intrusions of poems and aphorisms. The distance between those texts and today is filled in by *The Book of Questions*. But they bear witness to the excitement and fear of the first steps towards the unknown where there will never be any rest.

Jabès died in Paris on 2 January 1991. A man of *gravitas* but not solemnity, slow and gentle in movement, funny, charming and affectionate and certainly not averse to gossip, he lived with his wife for fifty-five years in a classically symbiotic partnership. The wider circle of friends privileged to know him lost a mentor, a father, a *senex* in Jung's sense, a wise old man. In the words of the old Hebrew prayer, *zichrono l'vraha,* may the memory of his name be for a blessing.

Look for my name in anthologies,
You will find it and you will not find it.
Look for my name in dictionaries.
You will find it and you will not find it.
Look for my name in encyclopaedias.
You will find it and you will not find it.
What does it matter? Have I ever had a name?
Therefore, when I die, do not
Look for my name in cemeteries
Or anywhere.
And stop tormenting now the one
Who cannot respond to the call.

Edmond Jabès

Translated by Anthony Rudolf.

Summer 1991

THE POLITICS OF THE IMAGINATION
A Conversation with Adrienne Rich
Rachel Spence

Adrienne Rich has been described in the *Encyclopaedia of Jewish Women in America*, as 'too richly talented to be ignored by the literary establishment . . . too politically oriented to be comfortably digested'. Her latest book of poetry, *Midnight Salvage*, of which she writes that she is trying to 'face the terrible with hope, in language as complex as necessary, as communicative as possible', is an extraordinary *fin de siècle* work, simultaneously an indictment of the dehumanizing effects of capitalist values and a lyrical tribute to human intimacies and natural beauty. Most radically, Rich asserts the power of poetry to challenge political oppression. Our conversation concentrated on these themes, but her present concerns can only be understood in the context of a life which has always been most engaged with people 'in places where life is cheap poor quick unmonumented' (to quote from the title poem of her collection *An Atlas of the Difficult World*, 1991).

Born in 1929 in Baltimore, Maryland, to a southern Protestant mother and Jewish doctor father, Rich grew up in a world where racial segregation and antisemitism went unquestioned. She was educated at home by her father, who, though fiercely authoritarian at times, encouraged her to write as well as read, making her feel from an early age that 'I was a person of the book, even though a woman.'

University at Radcliffe was followed by the publication of her first book of poetry, which critics praised as 'elegant' and 'controlled'. W H Auden notoriously admired her for writing poetry which 'respects its elders, but doesn't mumble'. By then, however, her involvement with the Black Civil Rights Movement had started to pave the way for a new, distinctly disrespectful, consciousness. Talking of that time now, she said: 'By the mid-sixties, there were movements – the Black Civil Rights movement, the anti-imperialist movement – which were challenging "the way things were", challenging many kinds of authority, and these cleared space for a woman's movement which made gender and sexuality central issues.'

In 1970, she left her husband (with whom she had had three sons) and subsequently discovered 'the suppressed lesbian I had been carrying in me'. Throughout the seventies it was as a radical feminist and lesbian poet and prose writer that she was chiefly identified. It was these writings which introduced her to a generation of women, including myself, who thrilled to her unique ability to express the ambiguities of female existence, the psychic cocktail of anger and gentleness so rarely articulated, even now, in literature.

In the long poem 'Sources' (*Your Native Land, Your Life*, 1986), Rich muses, apparently mystified, on the political evolution of Hannah Senesh, ardent Zionist and anti-Nazi activist. Yet parts of the poem are also evocative of her own experience:

> The faithful drudging child
> the child at the oak desk whose penmanship,
> hard work, style will win her prizes
> becomes the woman with a mission, not to win prizes,
> but to change the laws of history.
> How she gets this mission
> is not clear . . .

Talking to me, she made it clear her active sense of sociopolitical responsibility, whatever its original impulse, is essential to her sense of self. Interestingly, she now rejects the writer-as-missionary image. 'It always surprises me,' she says, 'when people write of my work as if I had taken up the cudgels for the "underprivileged" . . . as a kind of missionary work. I write from absolute inner necessity, responding to my location in time and place, trying to find a language equal to that.'

Grounded in the traditional poetics of those elders Auden was pleased to find that she respected – writers such as Blake, Stevens, Yeats and Eliot – Rich was always too well-schooled a poet for the anthologies entirely to reject her. (Occasionally, she rejected them, famously turning down the National Book Award in 1979 – or rather accepting it in the name of all women, and then donating the money to charity.) Even at her most radical, her acute political consciousness does not overwhelm the other, lyric, voice in her poetry. Her controversial 'Translations', for example, uses informal but intensely crafted rhythms to weave a powerful critique of heterosexual relationships:

> . . . a woman of my time
>
> obsessed
>
> with Love, our subject:
> we've trained it like ivy to our walls
> baked it like bread in our ovens
> worn it like lead on our ankles
> watched it through binoculars as if
> it were a helicopter
> bringing food to our famine
> or the satellite of a hostile power . . .

(From *Diving into the Wreck, 1973*)

The Irish poet Eavan Boland has written of Rich's poems that '[although] they describe a struggle and record a moment which was not my struggle and would never be my moment . . . these poems came to the very edge of the rooms I worked in, dreamed in, listened for a child's cry in . . .' My own experience mirrors Boland's. I first encountered the poetry of Adrienne Rich on a contemporary women's writing course at university. As a white, middle-class heterosexual woman, with few political leanings, I was startled to find that it was a radical feminist and lesbian writer whose poetry resonated with me most deeply. Since then, a volume of her poetry has been within arm's reach most nights; even through times when both feminism and literature seemed sometimes to be 'in another country', her poetry was always a source of both comfort and stimulation, even when I didn't fully grasp its meanings.

Looking back now, Rich says, rather wonderingly, 'In the early days of feminism and of gay and lesbian liberation . . . we didn't realize what a huge paradigm shift we were calling for: it wasn't just a question of foregrounding women and "women's issues", it was about the meaning of maleness and femaleness, what it means to be human finally; and it was about the distribution of power.'

Over the years, however, the voice has changed tone: the feminism is still there (her gender and sexuality merge seamlessly through the writing); there is no softening of perspective: more a broadening of perception. In 'Dreams before Waking', she writes of a city:

> where still you can believe
> it's the old neighbourhood
> even the woman who sleeps at night
> in the barred doorway – wasn't she always there?

and the man glancing, darting
for food in the supermarket trash –
when did his hunger come to this?
what made the difference?
what will make it for you?

(From *Your Native Land, Your Life*)

By the time she writes *Midnight Salvage* her tone is less meditative, angrier; the poetry resonates with the urgency of the revolutionary. At a time when few dispute the right of market forces to dictate the material conditions of our lives, Rich is quoting Marx and Engels, Che Guevara, Blake, as people who might still have relevance to 'the way things are.'

The very first poem in the book, 'The Art of Translation', uses the metaphor of a translator smuggling a foreign, revolutionary poet's work back into her own country; here poetry is presented as a political weapon, as a serious force for change:

to wing it back to my country bearing
your war-flecked protocols –

that was a mission, surely: my art's pouch
crammed with your bristling juices.

Meshing her intense political vision with measured rhythms and a language confident in its lyricism, in the title poem Rich spits out her despair at the victories of a capitalism she sees as inimical to human feeling:

Had never expected hope would form itself
Completely in my time . . .
But neither was expecting in my time
to witness this : : wasn't deep
lucid or mindful you might say enough
to look through history's bloodshot eyes
into this commerce this dreadnought wreck cut loose
from all vows, oaths patents, compacts, promises.

I asked Rich to narrate how the initial struggle against patriarchy had evolved into a less overtly gendered critique of Western capitalism. She began by explaining how, in the sixties and seventies, Western culture was more generous to radical thought: 'It was possible then to explore questions of gender and sexuality in poetry and prose, and feel resonance from other artists making similar explorations in painting, theatre and film. That's a tremendously liberating and nourishing condition in which to work.'

However, with the election of Reagan, 'anti-feminism was part of the right-wing strategy, but so was the defamation of every past social justice movement . . . the possibility of an alternative has been denied and discredited.' Her poetry emerged from the awareness that 'my inner and outer life were threatened by the politics of arrogance and cruelty . . . that sense of danger and disturbance began to enter my poetry.'

Writing the poetry that would communicate and challenge these dehumanizing forces, she found that history itself was a nourishing source of courage and inspiration; drawing not only on a broad canvas of public events, but on a rich vein of private, human experience. Thus the poems in *Midnight Salvage* often refer to past, individual narratives, lost or distorted over the decades – such as the 1920s Mexican photographer and revolutionary, Tina Modotti, whom Rich discovers 'in the rush of breath a window/of revolution allowed you'.

As an example of her historic/poetic consciousness at work, she cites 'Then or Now', a poetic sequence from *Dark Fields of the Republic* (1995), which she says 'came out of . . . trying to imagine the way fascism can work on consciousness, not trying to compare this time with 1930s Germany but to use that as a way of looking at our own time and place, our own self-deceptions. Our desire not to know what is going on.' 'Sunset, December 1993', the third poem in the sequence, tells of an artist struggling with the dilemma of using history as metaphor:

> Dangerous of course to draw
> parallels   Yet more dangerous to write
>
> as if there were a steady course, we and our poems
> protected: the individual life, protected
>
> poems, ideas, gliding
> in mid-air, innocent . . .
>
> Dangerous not to think
>
> how the earth still was   in places
> while the chimneys shuddered with the first dischargements.

Using the cruelties of Nazi Germany – and the individual human responses to them – as a lens through which to look at social and artistic responsibility for present-day injustice, 'Then and Now' resonates on many levels, including with the Jewish experience. Today, Rich believes that historical consciousness is of particular, though by no means exclusive, relevance to Jews: 'Back in the early sixties" she says, 'I wrote the poem "Readings of History" [published in *Snapshots of a Daughter in Law*, 1963] in which the lines occur:

> Split at the root, neither Gentile nor Jew
> Yankee nor Rebel, born
> In the face of two ancient cults . . .

'But the next line is: "I'm a good reader of histories." That poem is very interesting to me now, because it's asking the question, why does history matter? . . . And the poem suggests that the present seems too deranged . . . too incoherent, unless you have a sense of the past. Now that is a very Jewish perception, it seems to me.'

Asked to expand, she explains that for people who have been persecuted throughout history, engaging with the past can be rewarding both as a way of recognizing the predominant will to survive, both literally and creatively, and as a way of holding onto the essences of identity, refusing to be diminished by complete transformation or assimilation. Then she points out that this is in no way an exclusively Jewish issue: 'I don't mean to imply that Jews have a unique consciousness about history – but that for us history has been a way of surviving the often chaotic present and holding on to some longer and larger view. Kadia Molodowsky, one of the Yiddish poets I translated, writes:

Pack up my chaos with its gold-encrusted buttons
since chaos will always be in fashion . . .

'In fact, even as we've been in this conversation, three synagogues were bombed in the early hours of the morning in Sacramento.'

For Rich herself, her Jewishness has always been a site of ambivalence: her Jewish blood, which comes - ironically perhaps, in the light of Judaism's patriarchal traditions and her own feminist consciousness - through her father, must always run, not entirely smoothly, through her gender, feminism and sexuality.

She sees Jewishness as a link, a site of empathy and identification, with other marginalized groups: 'I'm an American Jew . . . I'm not a Jew from Eritrea, Lodz, Rhodes . . . India, Israel, Britain, Chile, though I know we are connected. The way I think we are connected is through a paradigm that Jews share with other dark-skinned, non-Christian peoples, including Arabs - a paradigm of the pariah - the suspected, the marginalized, the scapegoated, the dispossessed. When Jews dispossess or scapegoat others, I have to say "Yes, we Jews also do this," and I'm passionately opposed to it.'

Whether she speaks as a feminist, anti-racist or Jew - and she speaks simultaneously as all three - passion leads to activism. As the neo-conservative, sociopolitical landscape of the eighties took its toll on the women's movement, Rich felt disenchantment set in: 'the focus on women was losing its edge, becoming much more therapeutically or spirituality-oriented, more prone to female-centred fantasies, or small-business niches of feminism.' She herself has now moved away from the Western radical feminism of the seventies towards what she describes as a 'politics of location'.

This historical-materialist perspective was delineated in her 1984 essay, 'Notes Towards a Politics of Location', published in *Blood, Bread and Poetry* (1986), which she wrote following a trip to a conference in Nicaragua. Meeting women in the Sandanista movement crystallized her growing sense that it was vitally important to recognize cultural specificity if political theory was to be usefully translated into practice. She writes, quoting the novelist Christa Wolf. '*You cannot speak for me. I cannot speak for us.* Two thoughts: there is no liberation that only knows how to say "I"; there is no collective movement that speaks for each of us all the way through.'

Inevitably, her comprehension of the complexities of identity informs Rich's poetry. The last poem in *Midnight Salvage*, 'Long Conversation', sees her fuse prose and poetry - including her familiar loose metrics, traditional ballad, jazz song and extracts from *The Communist Manifesto* - into a dialogue between a galaxy of characters about the relationship between politics and art.

When I asked her why she chose to work with what I described as these 'fragmented identities', she replied: 'I don't think of the voices in my recent work as "fragmented identities", any more than I see the characters in a play or a novel as "fragmented identities". Today there's a rather banalizing tendency to read all literature as autobiographical, to discount the real work of the imagination. The literature of the restricted "I" becomes too limiting after a while, too claustrophobic.'

The last verse of 'In Those Years' highlights the danger of an ideology of selfhood:

But the great dark birds of history screamed and plunged
into our personal weather
They were headed somewhere else but their beaks and pinions drove
along the shore, through the rags of fog
where we stood, saying *I*

(From *Dark Fields of the Republic*)

In her demand that we acknowledge 'the real work of the imagination', Rich highlights one of the fundamental impulses behind her current creative focus. Always a passionate advocate of the rights of the oppressed, it could be said she is now fighting for the rights of the poetic imagination in North American society, 'because in this nation, created in the search for wealth, it eludes capitalist marketing, commoditizing, price-fixing; poetry has simply been set aside, depreciated, denied public space'. This starving of the creative impulse is every bit as serious as the state's failure to provide its people with the means to put bread on the table: 'I do not think [poetry] is more, or less, necessary than food, shelter . . . decent working conditions. It is as necessary' *(What is Found There: Notebooks on poetry and politics,* 1996).

Almost a decade ago, she gave a presentiment of that statement in the last stanza of the title poem of *An Atlas of the Difficult World,* where she addresses herself to a series of imaginary readers:

> I know you are reading this poem as you pace beside the stove
> warming milk, a crying child on your shoulder, a book in your hand
> because life is short and you too are thirsty.
> I know you are reading this poem which is not in your language
> guessing at some words while others keep you reading
> and I want to know which words they are . . .
> I know you are reading this poem because there is nothing else left to read
> there where you have landed, stripped as you are.

Commenting on this, she said, 'It is about the need for art in many kinds of lives, a desire shared with others we may never know. I see poetry as a "wick of desire", which helps keep alive in us the capacity to change, to resist, to imagine other ways of living.'

For Rich, there is no incompatibility between political thought and art; rather one is impoverished by lack of the other. Never describing herself as a Marxist – she has often indicted Marxist theorists for their failure to ground themselves in lived, human experience – she nevertheless finds Marx useful in exploring possible dynamics between a revolutionary politics and art. In *What is Found There,* she writes: 'Marx believed that "the release of . . . creativity would ensure that no revolution turned in on itself" . . . that in "revolution in permanence", "new passions and new forces" would repeatedly arise as the creative currents of each and all found voice.'

No one is more aware than Rich that the poets of communist regimes suffered appalling persecution: a physical silencing of the body far more acute than the 'deaf ears' of capitalist democracy. Nevertheless, her reclaiming of old revolutionary manifestos is part of her struggle to find ways to mediate between polarities: to create a social system which, rather than merely tolerating the artist, is grounded in a commitment to artistic freedom and actively recognizes the value of creative energy.

As she develops her ideas about the relationship between art and politics, her poetry has become more demanding (in *Dark Fields of the Republic,* she herself says to her readers, 'From you I want more than I've ever asked'). She long ago abandoned traditional, linear narrative in favour of looser rhythms, and less formal poetic structures, better able to communicate her complex sense of the politics of history and human identity.

Several of her recent critics have urged her to confine herself to poetic ambitions. Reviewing *Midnight Salvage* in the *Independent on Sunday,* Natasha Walter writes: 'What is most precious about Rich's work is not always her grand political themes, but her ability to give us . . . pieces of beauty.'

Walter has missed the point: the beauty of those pieces lies in the very fact that they are threatened, marginalized, by a culture which too often fails to value them. If Rich were to loosen her grip on her politics, her poetry would lose the taut, angry sadness which makes it sing. If Rich were not aware that 'grand political themes' must always embrace the details of private, human experience, why would she choose as the epigraph to *Midnight Salvage* these words from fellow radical poet, George Oppen? 'The issue is happiness, there is no other issue, or no issue one has a· right to think about for other people, to think about politically, but I don't know how to measure happiness.'

In the last stanza of the poem 'Camino Real', she replies to Oppen's question, finding her answer while driving to visit her son:

– Why measure? in itself it's the measure –
at the end of a day
        of great happiness if there be such a day

drawn by love's unprovable pull

I write this, sign it

    Adrienne

There are huge rewards in confronting the challenges Rich sets. Adrian Oktenberg, writing in the *Women's Review of Books,* describes her as having 'a mission to speak truth to power'. As with all serious truth-tellers, she must speak out of ambiguity and uncertainty, out of knowing that there is never one truth (though plenty of lies to be deconstructed).

When I ask her about her future work, it is of this ambiguity of intention that she speaks, stating that, although she has no 'planned trajectory', she wishes to communicate her sense that 'the relations of production will end by affecting all human relationships, the most private and intimate included'. However, she goes on to say that she also wants to give voice to 'what's humanly possible'. This last phrase confuses me, and I ask her to unpack it. Her answer encapsulates her sense of the intimate connection between public and private experience – and also provides heartening affirmation that the values of human fellowship, can, if energetically employed, mitigate social opportunism: 'Human beings aren't simply determined by the relations of production – Marx never said that. The horrible relations of production-for-profit are conditions "not of our choosing" in which we can make history. What's "humanly possible" is what we bring to that moment of decision – that we will not simply be determined by any dehumanizing process. It may seem aggrandizing to say that poetry can have a hand in this resistance, but I believe it can, in its own way and on its own terms.'

Autumn 1999

PICTURING SYLVESTER
Michael Kustow

David Sylvester turns to look at me. An ovoid head, bald, grey-bearded, something tearful about the eyes above prominent pouches; just like mine. His nose small, his lips full; just like mine. His default expression in repose, melancholic. Like mine. It's unsettling, as always, to see mirrored in the face of another the face you know from mirrors, from photographs, from inside. Twins and doubles, signs of nature teasing us with visual recalls, disturb, as if the resembler had usurped our space. But here, in the full flesh, seventy-five, fifteen years older than me, is *mon semblable, mon frère*. His head slowly continues to swivel round and he says, 'To judge by our faces, we could be brothers.'

This demands to be written in the present tense, for it is Sylvester's tense, in which for over half a century he has been writing about the actuality of paintings as they impact and implode in him in the immediate, 'convulsive' (one of his favourite words) moment:

> The contrasts between the refreshing coolness of the insets and the merciless heat of the backgrounds, between the luminous feathery rendering of an injured, fragile body and the implacable density of the wall behind, are hair-raising.

Looking Back on Francis Bacon, from which this comes, is the latest in a line of books (on Giacometti, Bacon, Moore, Magritte), journalism and catalogue essays (collected in *About Modern Art),* edited conversations with the artists he loves and respects, television films and the curating and installing of exhibitions in the art capitals of the world, which have made him the most penetrating critic and advocate of modern art in the business, certainly in Britain. But it is not primarily to take stock of his published texts and public deeds that has brought me face to face with David Sylvester across a glass-topped Le Corbusier table in his kitchen, with his bed-sheets, which are black, whirring in the spin-dryer. It is the doppelgänger effect. And with it, his Jewishness, upon which he has rarely insisted.

Two months before this kitchen encounter, I'd met him in front of a wall of still lifes by Chardin and after a long gap, since I'd moved away from the art world three decades before. Nine o'clock in the morning in the Royal Academy, quiet as a church, empty but for a handful of people, lucky to be let in early. I'd caught sight of this round figure in a baggy black tent of a suit, in aspect not unlike an Orthodox prayer-maker at the Wailing Wall, gripped in tense concentration, breathing deeply and sighing, consumed. We exchanged glances of recognition, but neither of us wanted to intrude. After ten minutes he scuttled over, beckoned, pointed at a small Chardin of raspberries, a pewter bowl, a very dead hare: 'There's such mortality in these pictures.' Later, as we parted and agreed to meet again, he told me it would have to be after the next operation on his cancer.

Today, full-face, there's the same searchlight impact I remember receiving across the intervening weeks, years. Something baleful, louring, a fury close to ignition. 'You have always given me the impression of a thunderstorm about to break,' I say. 'Do you have rows with people?'

DS: 'Did you ever see a book, before your time called *The Lonely Ones,* by a *New Yorker* cartoonist, William Steig? All sorts of obsessional characters, with a drawing style to match each of them. There was one very good drawing: "I do not forget to be angry." My wife said that was me, and it's true. There are a great number of people with whom I'm not on speaking terms.

'I do have rows and bust-ups, and they're almost invariably on intellectual matters. Norman Rosenthal [Exhibitions Secretary of the Royal Academy] is one of the people with whom I have intellectual rows. There was the business of the American exhibition at the Royal Academy. I was asked to be a member of the selection panel. Norman had made a very sensible decision for a survey show of this kind, which was to take a crucial period in each artist's career, and represent that. For Arshile Gorky, that presented a problem. I saw one of two versions of the great portrait of the artist with his mother at the big Gorky exhibition at the Whitechapel and I said to Norman, "This work has to be included in the show. You want to represent Gorky by the work of his last three or four years, but you can't leave this out, it's an absolutely key work in American painting, please go back to Whitechapel and look at it again," which he didn't bother to do. And I resigned from the committee.

'Then, when the exhibition happened, he'd got a mixture of Barnett Newman and Mark Rothko, cheek by jowl in an octagonal room. Personally, I don't think Newman and Rothko hang well together. And then the hanging was monstrously crowded, it was horrible. And I looked at it, and I'm not kidding, I was almost sick. And . . .'

The silences between sentences get longer, pause stretching into emotion-laden silence as in Pinter (born, like Sylvester, in Hackney).

DS: '. . . And I went out of the room and Norman was talking to a couple of people, and I did something I should not have done. I went up to him, and said, in front of the two strangers, "You should not be allowed within a thousand miles of a painting." He followed me into another room and spat in my face. That was reported in some of the press reports as my having spat in his face, which is not my style.'

This story provides another echo, this time of my own disproportionate behaviour, and I tell him how I shouted at an acquaintance in the lobby of the Old Vic after the first night of a new play which had turned me over and left him tepid. It's the same excitement, I say, the same cup-runneth-over feeling, and the indignation when it's not shared. I tell him that on my way here, after a week reading and re-reading most of what he's written about art, I came up with a word for him, for his voice: *ardour*. He's immoderately pleased.

DS: 'Ardour's a good word, a beautiful word, because it's always been said of me, since I was twenty, "Oh you have to forgive him, because he has enthusiasm." So I've always hated the word enthusiasm – although Blake uses it as a term of approval. Ardour and anger go together. I'd like to think I had ardour.'

> Fluidity of vision is reconciled with a crystalline clarity of structure. A precise tentativeness in recording facts is warmed by an intoxicating breath of the sublime. Michaelangelo's belief that the sculptor brings to light a form buried in the marble he is carving becomes a metaphor for the act of drawing, even to the contrasts between totally polished parts and parts that are still emerging from the block. The air is alive, like the air in Giacometti's room when he lay on his bed and watched the dance of a pendant thread of particles of dust. Solid bodies of an uncanny lightness are locked into a space charged with a buoyant, exhilarated, numinous energy and filled and filled by light.

This description of Giacometti's late drawings has an ardour made all the more piercing by a tendency philosophically to map his sensations and feelings, even as they are seized, and semantically to position the images he sees. Unlike most philosophers, Sylvester lets the voice of the body speak. Like Hamlet – and he has just seen a production of the play, which he denies is a tragedy – he feels both along the paths of his mind and upon his nerve ends. No wonder he has for years been captivated by Bacon's lifelong search to get the paint to 'register on the nervous system'.

I think of another quotation from *Hamlet* when I consider David Sylvester's wayward and precocious beginnings, his casting around for a *métier*. It's Polonius' advice to his son: 'By indirections find directions out.'

MK: 'You were the son of antique dealer parents of Russian and Polish ancestry. The business was good, but it had its ups and downs. You were kicked out of University College School at fifteen. What for?'

DS: 'Mostly for not going. I spent most of my time in the cinema . . . After school, I studied music, both jazz and classical. Trumpet for jazz, and singing. I was earning a living by buying and selling gold objects. I made more real money than I've ever made since.'

He started painting. He wrote an art review on spec for *Tribune,* and it was published in November 1942, two months after his eighteenth birthday, and he gave up painting because he knew he would never be good enough.

MK: 'The picture I get is of your search for somewhere to plant this ardour, this burning bush inside, an angry determination not to be trapped into the wrong path – or to do anything you couldn't be best at.'

DS: You know, it's an amazing thing you've said. It's taken me until I was seventy-five, and you came to see me, to see a connection that I've never seen before. I was expecting when I was at prep school to be first in the class. If I wasn't this was shocking. And I actually remember the only time when I wasn't. I was eight or nine, and two boys, one was called Shaerf and the other Krapp, like the Gloucestershire batsman, though he was spelt with a C, they came first and second. In the eyes of my parents it was an aberration that I wasn't first. And I've suddenly realized that all this business of painting and philosophy, and music – because I wanted to be a jazz musician – I never wanted to do anything that I wasn't best at. And I've never connected it until this *minute* with that parental thing.

'I was turned down from the Army because of my health.' Long pause. 'Duodenal ulcer. I taught at prep school instead of doing military service. I studied art history at this time, and was reading philosophy and psychology. When the war ended, I decided I would like to go up to Trinity College, Cambridge, to read Moral Sciences, philosophy and psychology. I did well enough in the scholarship exam to be offered a place, in 1946. If I was good enough at a time of *intense* competition for these places, I must have been of some use at philosophy. Wittgenstein was teaching there at the time, and I was constantly reading Wittgenstein's *Tractatus.*

'At this time of my life, my heroes were Wittgenstein and Freud – not a juxtaposition Wittgenstein would have approved of – and Leavis and Eliot. Above all, T. S. Eliot – he influenced my prose style and my tendency towards Christianity. Among the poetry that I've chosen for my funeral is a piece of Eliot. A few years ago, I said, 'I can't have this fucking antisemite at my funeral.' But in the end I couldn't resist it. It's the final section of "Little Gidding." I didn't take up the place at Cambridge. I thought, I'm not going to get a First, so what career should I choose? I had a friend, John Symonds – he deflowered my sister – and he was married to Renata, a graphologist. So I gave her a sample of my handwriting and asked her whether I should write about art or do philosophy. She said I had an unusual combination of qualities in my writing, and I should choose art, which influenced my decision.

'So it's all about not being good enough – as a painter, as a philosopher, as a composer of classical music, as a jazz musician; I played piano and, for jazz, trumpet, and I once sang with a black band in a Paris nightclub . . . I wanted to write, did write poetry, but everyone writes poetry at eighteen. I was even tempted by the stage – my sister Jackie was an actress, my great-aunt played Medea in Yiddish, my great-uncle did *Hamlet* in Yiddish, in London and New York. But I didn't have real talent for the stage. In all cases, I just wasn't good enough at all.

'I did the right thing by going for art. A year or two later, I realized that it didn't just involve writing. It also involved the thing I do best, which is installation. It happens that I have the two talents which both have to do with a professional life in art. I write well about aesthetic experience

- quite well about sport, and about films too. That's why Stanley Kubrick hired me, as "Special Publicity Writer" on *Lolita*. And I've got a very good eye for selecting good art. I've got by far the best record in England for picking the winners. Art was the best choice because it continues to obsess me, and I do have a better understanding of it than most people. I have a compulsion to make lists, which is a traditional critic's thing that goes right back to Pliny. With my best friend Norman Rose, I made many lists of our favourite jazz people, an order of merit. I worshipped Leavis, the way he would argue for the greatness of Keats and the horribleness of Shelley. I had his compulsion to evaluate and re-evaluate. I was a natural critic.'

I picture Sylvester, eighteen in 1942, turned down by the Army for ill-health, mooning Hamlet-like around a wartime city, honing his mind on poetry and philosophy, not malingering but coming to the boil in his own way. An out-of-step solitary. A purposeful drifter.

MK: 'Many Jewish names have floated in and out of our conversation: your Yiddish actor ancestors, Clement Greenberg, the Shearf and Krapp - they sound like characters from Beckett or early Pinter - who beat you to top of the class.

'In your writing, one thing I admire is the tussle between the voice you grant to the body – "bodyspeech" - and your mind's delineation in language. And my hunch is that this fruitful tension comes from the Old Testament struggle between appetite, hunger and law, interdiction.'

DS: 'Almost all the best writers on art have been Jews. Bernard Berenson, Clement Greenberg, Leo Steinberg, who's one of my heroes among living writers. Gombrich. Lawrence Gowing - did you know he was Jewish, or partly Jewish? It may be because of some special relationship between the body and the intellect, you may be right.'

MK: 'But what distinguishes you from Berenson - like you, a great connoisseur - is your commitment to the modern.'

DS: 'But don't forget that Berenson was one of the first to realize the greatness of Matisse. In the 1890s, he talked about Cézanne in the same breath as Michelangelo. But he wanted to be a goy, that was the trouble.

'Another thing that strikes me is that in England, and of my generation, many of the best artists are Jewish: Lucian Freud, the Cohen brothers, Frank Auerbach, Leon Kossoff, Anthony Caro.'

MK: 'Tell me about your own Jewishness - how you acknowledge it, or don't acknowledge it, how it might relate to your obsessiveness, your ardour, your heat.'

DS: 'My father was a *frum* Jew, and also a prominent Zionist. But as my mother said, "Your father's tragedy is that he's an antisemite; the only real friends he has are goyim." I think what happened to my father was this: he grew up with a lot of brothers and then he went into the army, and there he met goyim, and saw that they didn't have the "horrible flaws" of the Jews. He hated the ostentatiousness of Jews. We had a very good rabbi at Cricklewood synagogue, and half his sermons were against ostentation - fur coats and diamonds in the forecourt, which he said was very bad taste in those times. The one thing I liked about Jews was their passion for playing cards.'

MK: 'Do you have any picture of Jewishness earlier than your parents?'

DS: 'I hated the obsession with Judaism of my paternal grandfather. My maternal grandfather, on the contrary, was only interested in seducing the maids and going to the races. I wasn't drawn to the Jewish religion, didn't like the services . . .'

MK: 'Wait a minute. My hunch is, and it comes out of this sense of some affinity I feel for you, that this ardour, this fervour of yours is connected, not with the synagogue, but - when I think about the Old Testament, its intensity and ruggedness, that throws up the image of some kind of burning bush I imagine inside you, when I think about Bomberg and how he taps into that, to me, it's deeply Jewish. If I said to you, set aside the social realization of Jewishness or its institutional religion, do you not feel that - as a myth, if you like – it's nonetheless stirring?'

DS: 'No, I hate it, I hate Yahweh.'

He repeats this twice, defiantly, firmly escorting my suggestion out of our talk.

DS: 'My first contact with Christianity was simply reading the New Testament. The Sermon on the Mount was an unbelievable corrective. One of the first things that struck me was "turning the other cheek". Another thing was "committing adultery in your heart". It seemed to me from an early age that the Jewish religion was much too concerned with external forms, all this mad thing about kashrut and so on, where Christianity was more concerned with motivation. I very nearly became a Catholic when I was eighteen or nineteen; I was under instruction, my father discovered I was going to become a Catholic, and chucked me out of home at half an hour's notice with half a crown in my pocket. I slept in a Catholic doss-house.

'I preferred the Catholic liturgy. I couldn't stand the way people in shul talked all the time, I hated the unruliness of Jews. And then there was all that showy praying, that exaggeration. In Church, at High Mass, people concentrated on the service. The thing had a quality of reverence.'

MK: 'People talked in synagogue partly because many of them didn't understand the Hebrew.'

DS: 'Good point. But aesthetically, Christianity, especially in the form of Roman Catholicism, is the superior religion. In my generation, a lot of people were attracted to Buddhism, but Roman Catholicism is psychologically much more subtle. It seems to me a very beautiful structure, and a wonderful and tragic vision of life, with a more penetrating view of sin.'

MK: 'Do you think of yourself as sinful?'

An immense pause, as if he's treading on perilous ground.

DS: 'Well, I'll tell you a good Jewish story. Mr Cohen went to heaven. Saint Peter said, "One of your privileges, Mr Cohen, is that you can meet any historical person you like." Mr Cohen says, "Well, I would like to meet the venerable rabbi Ya'acov ben Eleazar, who practised in Cracow in the 1870s." Saint Peter says, "Well, if you go along that corridor, stop at the fourth door on the left, knock and go in, you'll find him." So Mr Cohen did this, and he opened the door, and he found the rabbi in bed with a beautiful young blonde. He said to the rabbi, "I take it that this is your reward for virtue." "No," said the rabbi, "it's her punishment for vice."'

MK: 'That seems to me a very subtle view of sin.'

DS: 'Yes. I do think that in certain respects, and especially about sex, the Jews are very sophisticated. But there are other areas, like pride, which really matters more, where I think the Catholics are much more subtle.'

MK: 'Is pride one of your sins? I don't think of you as a humble person - except before a great work of art.'

DS: 'I think God manifests himself in human affairs in response to one thing, which is hubris. What God can't take is when men see themselves as God. I wish I had more pride. I think I'm too vain, and not proud enough.

'I hate God for the story of the sacrifice of Isaac. I think it was a very sadistic thing to ask. It set a pattern. I think Jewish parents have blackmailed their children the way Yahweh blackmailed Abraham: "If you love me, you'll do this."'

MK: 'Do you do that to your children?'

DS: 'I'm afraid I sometimes do. I said to my daughter in New York, I want you to cross the picket lines at the Museum of Modern Art, because I can't get to see that exhibition.'

MK: 'Why did you never take the final step of becoming a Catholic?'

DS: 'I never had any problems with miracles, the Virgin Birth didn't worry me at all. Assuming God existed, the whole thing made sense. The problem was that God doesn't exist, and I wish he did. There were two reasons at the time, in 1944. The Catholic attitude to birth control I couldn't accept. The thought of an unwanted child is the worst of human calamities, and the Church encourages the birth of millions of them. The other thing was the experience of reading Jung's *Psychological Types*. I saw there that one's intellectual attitudes are determined by temperament. If that's so, then truth is relative. But the Catholic Church is committed to absolute truth. So that was impossible.'

MK: 'What about "No graven image"? Did that bother you?'

DS: 'I never thought about it much. Later I did, when I came to Newman and Rothko. Since Soutine most of the greatest Jewish artists have been abstract artists. I want to say something about Jewish presence, but before that I want to say that – unlike my father – I'm a pro-Semite. There are one or two truly horrible people I know, deeply corrupt, disgusting characters. Sarah Whitfield, with whom I lived for nearly twenty years, said, 'When they're Jewish, you always find excuses for them, you know they're absolute monsters, yet somehow you manage to forgive them'. It may be because I feel sorry for them for being Jews. But when I think about certain of my close Jewish friends, like Charles Saatchi and Leslie Waddington, one of the reasons I'm fond of them is their specifically Jewish qualities, it's part of my affection for them that they have those qualities. My friendship with Richard Serra, who on current form is one of the most important artists alive, has to do with this. He's the product of a Spanish father and a Jewish mother. Part of Richard's poignancy for me is his being half-Jewish. It's so much part of his greatness that he's got this Jewish mother who comes through as the feminine side of him, and in contrast this very macho Spanish thing.

'When you meet a Jew, it's like meeting someone who went to the same school, someone who's been through the same mill. Think of Philip Roth. One's slightly annoyed with Philip Roth for letting the goyim know too much . . .'

MK: 'Family secrets.'

DS: 'It also makes it complicated sleeping with Jewish girls. I've always felt it was incestuous. What if I'd have pleased my parents by marrying a Jewess? What would it have been like? I've never had a long affair with a Jewish woman.

'But I was very disturbed and resentful about Adrian Stokes, who as a writer on art is probably my greatest hero. I used to talk to Adrian about 'the horrors of being Jewish'. But he never admitted to me that his mother was Jewish. And I've never forgiven him for not owning up.'

The telephone rings, and David Sylvester says he can't talk now, he's on the rack, he's being interviewed. Before we start again, he says, "That is the best-bred woman in England." I wait for him to say the double-barrelled name of some scion of high English breeding. Not at all. 'Her paternal great-grandfather was Sigmund Freud, and her maternal grandfather was Jacob Epstein.' With one teasing throwaway, he deflates but does not dissipate his early battles of belief and the impassioned spiritual, moral and aesthetic values with which he still wrestles, like Epstein's massive Jacob cleaving to the giant Angel. I am moved by the intensity of his voice – almost like a cry of ecstasy, or the call of a troubled child for a peaceful haven – as he describes the Christian sacraments, the objectivity of confession, the durability of the Church 'for all its flaws.'

But I'm also aware of some difference between our generations, that fifteen-year difference. I can't sense the politics in David Sylvester's discourse – and that was certainly the division between him and the Marxist John Berger (who wrote off Bacon and at first Giacometti), when they fought out the art territory in weekly journalism in the 1960s. For Sylvester, the aesthetic is the commanding domain. But his aesthetic is not precious or selfish; it opens onto the world because it is rigorous, penetrating, never complacent, corporeal.

He wants to amplify what he said about the sacraments.

DS: 'In the Jewish religion there's great emphasis on the rabbi, the individual teacher. What I like about the Catholic Church is that a man who's in a state of mortal sin can nonetheless, by virtue of his office, by virtue of the apostolic succession, turn the wafer and the wine into the body of Christ. It's that objectivity of the sacraments, the fact that they transcend the individual, that I find very beautiful. The individual doesn't matter. It's like art. It doesn't matter what kind of sinner the artist is.

'I did work out why, apart from two good essays, on Goya and Constable, I haven't been able to write about artists of the past. I think if there's a method in my work, it is to work out the relationship between the artist's conscious and unconscious intentions. I've been able to study enough about Goya and Constable to know about their conscious intentions, but I don't know enough about the thought of sixteenth-century Europe to be able to deal with Michelangelo in that way. I don't think I'm a good historian by nature, I'm not good at projecting myself into the past. I think I have a better understanding of how people think in my own time. Of how they think since the invention of the flushing lavatory. Though I have a great love for Dante. I really do want to believe that those bastards who got away with it here will go through eternal damnation. I like that thought.'

A big chesty guffaw from a man who is furious that life, his life, is so short. He tells me more about what he's chosen for his memorial service: Ecclesiastes ('up to the bit where God appears') and a poem about cricket at Lords.

When I tell him one of the things I like about his writing is the way it cross-cuts, re-starts, lays blocks of distinct material side by side, he says, 'Setting things against each other counters a tendency to make things run too smoothly and create artificial links, chains that shouldn't be chains.' One of the ways he stays modern is by embracing discontinuity, in the structure and gear-changes of his pieces, in the orchestration of text and illustration in his books – the new Bacon monograph almost has a visual choreography. The same principle of contrast and brokenness makes him witty, yoking disparate things together, which Doctor Johnson called the hallmark of a metaphor: it takes a prodigiously witty and mischievous mind to compare the music of John Cage (who once wrote a piece called 4'33" where the player was instructed to provide that much silence and nothing more) with the elements of Morris dancing. He knows how to tease.

He's given Bacon and Giacometti, artists who trap appearances, what Plutarch gave the rulers of Rome: instructive parallel lives. As we finish talking about them, he murmurs, like a muted confession of passion, 'But the artist of the latter twentieth century who moves me most is Barnett Newman. I'm moved more by his work than almost any art there's ever been.'

Behind my head in this kitchen hangs a Newman lithograph, *Untitled, 1961,* given to him by the artist's widow. When Sylvester was asked six years ago to write about a contemporary work that had special significance for him he wrote a thousand-word piece about it (collected in *About Modern Art),* as severe as a raked Kyoto Zen garden:

> The work I've chosen to write about is a piece I managed to live with without seeing anything special about it, and this despite the fact that it's by a painter whose art I normally respond to so immediately that when I'm in museums I use it like a drug . . . Twenty years passed before I began to see it. This happened when I finally started responding to the richness of the black, its simultaneous flatness and depth, hardness and softness. Black was a sacred colour for the Abstract Expressionists, it was their lapis lazuli . . .

And in the remaining five paragraphs he moves from asking why, in the face of such a piece, painters have ever 'bothered to put in all those arms and legs and heads', insists 'I'm no Modernist by persuasion: Michelangelo and Poussin are my cup of tea', sees in the print the essence of Bonnard juxtaposed with the essence of Matisse, the exemplification of 'less is more', and in a series of spidery questions impersonates what Newman's process of making might have been.

This, like so much else of David Sylvester's writing, makes me feel his prose as a stretched membrane, holding in a mass of molten material, and supporting sudden, final, devastating, simply passionate effusions. This Newman piece ends in monosyllabic majesty: 'What I know is that when I stand and look at it the whole of art is there.'

Unlike Bacon and Giacometti, Newman was an abstract artist. Unlike them, he was a Jew, and in a 1986 piece (also reprinted in *About Modern Art*) Sylvester rescues him from New York Jewish critics who tried to recruit him to the lineage of kabbalistic mysticism and returns him to the sublime, primal creative act of Genesis: 'His imagery does not give us the *landscape* of the book of *Genesis* (as Rothko's does); his art does give us the primal *command* of the book of *Genesis*: 'Let there be light; and there was light.''

He plucks forth the word 'zip' to describe the rending vertical line that divides the colour-fields of Newman's later pictures, and gives the word an atavistic power. 'Newman's zip can seem to go clean through us. In French a zip is *une fermeture éclair,* a lightning fastener. The zip in Newman's paintings is a bolt of lightning, with the speed and violence of a *revelation* of light.' Firing on all cylinders, Sylvester moves to his conclusive praise of Newman's art: 'that intense awareness of our own bodies and where they are which he induces through confronting us with perpendicular forms as unspecific and as resonant as the columns of a Doric temple'.

In the end, after the peopled spaces of Bacon's and Giacometti's art, Sylvester returns to Newman's naked art, made in the knowledge of the Testament prohibition of 'the graven image,' which does not imitate the appearances of God's world, though it may undertake an even more heaven-challenging task: to recreate in art God's origination of the world. (It's typical that, having re-rooted Newman in Genesis, Sylvester immediately reconnects his 'searing white zip' with 'the veil of the temple rent in twain from the top to the bottom', which Matthew describes in his Gospel. No simple return of the prodigal son to the Jewish fold here.)

From the crown of his moon-faced head to the equator of his girth and his feet projecting like enlarged Bacon extremities, Sylvester is a palpable presence in any space. He would have become a museum curator if he could, 'because that would have allowed me to handle works of art'. This dimension of Sylvester in space is finally what touches me most. From the casting-around of his beginnings, looking for a place to dock but rejecting any harbour that would have become a betrayal, to the acute sense of position, scale, shape and identity that he gets from Barnett Newman canvases or Richard Serra minimalist sculpture, to his self-description as 'a passable writer, but a very good installer of art', David Sylvester persistently gets a grip on space and his place and identity in the physical and the metaphysical world.

'Navigation' is a word which has been co-opted by software programmers for journeys into synthetic cyberspace. But Sylvester is a master-steersman, and his journeys through what matters to him so much and so violently give us heart and help us navigate. And perhaps there's another quest, which came through our conversation so fiercely: a quest for redemption, through art's unending process of creation, destruction and recreation, of breaking and remaking, which he describes in his elected artists. It's not surprising that he quotes the famous story about Matisse and therapy through painting. Matisse was traveling with his friend Francis Carco, who went down with flu. Before going out for the day, Matisse took several of his paintings and hung them in his friend's hotel room. It's not recorded whether they speeded Carco's recovery. But the belief is all.

Autumn 2000

5

LITERATURE

Josef Herman *The Fiddler* (1940-43) ink on paper

BACK FROM THE DRAFT BOARD
Sholom Aleichem

'Where I am coming from?' a tall, lanky, bearded man, with a plush hat accosts me. He had just finished praying and was putting away the folded prayer shawl and his phylacteries.

Where I am coming from? Alas and alack! I am coming from the draft board, am I. This fellow who is stretched out on the bench is actually a son of mine. I am just coming from Yehupetz with him. We went over to some lawyers to get some advice and at the same time visited some professors to see what *they* would say. Some draft was wished on me! Presented ourselves four times, and the end is not yet. And just think of it, an only son; that is, unique in the family, a true first-born, pure and simple. Why do you look at me? Do I annoy you? You may just listen won't you.

The history of the tale is a matter like this: I myself am a Mezeretcher, from Mezeretch. A native – that is I was born, so to speak, in Mazepevkeh; I was registered, that is recorded in the books of Vorotilivkeh; that is, at one time I used to live, not to think of it today, in Vorotilivkeh, I used to, but now I'm living in Mezeretch.

Who am I, and what my name is I believe should not much matter to you, but my son's name I must tell you, indeed, because it has to do with this matter, and very much so. His name is Itsik, or Abraham Isaac in Hebrew, but his pet name is Alter. That's how she named him, my wife, bless her, because he is a delicate boy, an only child, unique in the family. Of course we had, besides him, another boy, younger by a year and a half – may he live longer. He was called Izik, that was his name. And so the misfortune had to happen.

I was then, not to think of it today, living in Vorotilivkeh, was I; that is, I was a Vorotilivker. Well, the child Izik, that is, takes the notion to creep up just under the samovar and pours out on himself the boiling water, may it not happen to you, and scalds himself (a longer life to him) to death. From then on, this one Itsik, Abraham Isaac, that is, remained an only child, and she, my wife, bless her, coddled him and gave him the name of Alter.

And now you'll of course exclaim: 'My goodness! An only son, unique in the family! What has he to do with the draft, I'd like to know?' Well, there you are. That's exactly what burns me up. Why, you might think that he was, God forbid, a healthy fellow, as a child might happen to be that is reared in luxury. Then you are mistaken. You wouldn't give two copecks for him. He's a sight, an invalid! As to being an invalid, he's really not ailing, thank the Lord, but certainly he is not well.

It's a pity, he's asleep, and I don't want to wake him. Wait till he gets up and you'll see the frame of a man; skin and bones, tall and narrow, a small face like a fig, the fig of Rabbi Tzodik; and some build, I tell you, thin as a rail, the spit image of her, my wife, bless her. She too is tall and slim, that is, I mean delicate. Now, I ask you, should I be having on my mind a draft, when he's thin and lanky, and absolutely useless, and has an 'examtion' on top of everything.

Well, came the 'xamination,' then whose 'examtion,' and what's 'examtion'? 'Examtion,' my eye, as they say. What's the story? The story is a simple story. The other child, the one who scalded himself to death with the samovar, may it not happen to you, was forgotten to be struck out from the register book. So naturally I hurried away to the crown rabbi, the dope, with a howl: 'You robber, you cutthroat, what did I do to you, that you didn't take my Izik out of the register book? Why didn't you?'

'And who was Izik?' he asks me – such a dope!

'My goodness,' I say, 'you don't know Izik? Izik, the boy who overturned the samovar?'

' What samovar?' he asks nonchalantly.

Well, what do you know? I say, 'That's a nice how-do-you-do! Maybe you're a stranger,' I say, 'You've got a mighty fine head on you,' says I. ' It would be mighty nice to crack nuts on it. Why, who doesn't remember the story of my Izik who scalded himself with the samovar? I don't understand,' says I, 'what sort of a rabbi you are in our town. If you don't analyse any laws for us – for this we have a real rabbi, long may he live – then surely it would only be no more than right,' says I, ' if you attended to the dead – attended; or else, what do we need you for, with your meat-tax?'

And after all this, what do you suppose? For nothing I insulted this elegant rabbi, because the story of the samovar didn't happen here in Mezeretch, but when we were living, not to think of it today, in Vorotilivkeh. Can you beat that? I clean went and forgot all about it – did I.

To make a long story short – what's the use of bothering you with histories, and tales and stories? – before I had a chance to get my bearings in the red tape of this document and that document, my Abraham Isaac, that is Itsik, who is now called Alter, went and lost his whole examtion. No more examtion! No examtion? Pretty tough, I'll say. We raise a howl, some howl: 'Is it possible? One and only son, unique in the family, a real, honest-to-goodness first-born, and no examtion!' But you might as well cry in the wilderness. Well it looks like we're licked!

But God after all is good to us. And what do you suppose? Just think of it. Maybe my Alter, I mean Itsik, doesn't up and draw the biggest number, 699. The whole board room was agog. The chief himself slapped him on the back:

'Bravo, smart fellow!'

The whole town was envious. Number six hundred and ninety-nine! What luck – *Mazel tov! Mazel tov! Mazel tov* to you!' You would think I had just won the grand lottery – the two hundred grand! But you know our *Yiddelech* . . . When the 'physkel' came, the rejections came thick. Everyone all of a sudden became a miserable wretched cripple – each with his own failing. This one suddenly began to hop on one foot; another's eyesight grew bad, and still another developed a whistle in the ear – he developed. And a fifth managed to get himself a running sore that spread nicely on his head – excuse me for mentioning it - like a beautiful ornament.

To make a long story short, no use filling you with all sorts of stories and things. They reached my son's number 699, and my Itsik, that is poor Alter had to appear in person at the 'physkel,' and our home was full of wailing. Wailing isn't the word for it. It was a wild howling. My wife, bless her, hits the ceiling. My daughter-in-law swoons away. My God! Is that possible? An only son, unique in the family, a real honest-to-goodness first-born, and not that much of an examtion. And he, my son, that is, doesn't seem to mind it, as if he's out of it. 'What will happen to all Israel,' he says, 'will happen to Mr Israel'. That's how he puts it, sort of wisecracking, but you can imagine that inside he is shivering in his boots.

But then God is certainly good to us. The doctor begins to examine my Itsik, that is, Alter, measure him from top to bottom, tap him, size him up and bother him, one way and another; and what for? He's no good, the guy; that is, in general, he is good but he's no good for the army. His chest measurement is hardly more than a yard around. Well, again there was rejoicing and happiness. 'Good luck!' 'Good luck!' 'Good luck to you, too.' The family got together, whisky was served and we drank to each other's health. Thank the Lord: got rid of the draft.

But then our *Yiddelech,* again. Perhaps you think there wasn't some heel who made it his business to inform the central office that I used 'grease.' Well, don't fret. Before two month were up, I received a paper where Itsik, that is of course Alter, is invited to be so kind and present himself again, this time, at the State board office for inspection, so to speak. How do you like that, eh? A nice picnic.

My wife, bless her, hits the ceiling, and the daughter-in-law just faints.

Well, what's the use of talking? Stringing out long stories? When you're called to the State house you can't be a hog and refuse. Reaching the big city, I naturally began to scurry about here and there, a good word, this and that. But you might as well cry: 'I'm King Solomon.' All you have to do is to tell someone the story. 'An only child, unique in the family, a real, honest-to-goodness, first-born and an invalid, at that' – and you are greeted with the noisiest guffaw. And as to my son, a corpse looks much better. Not because of the draft, at least that's what he says. He doesn't give a hoot about the draft, if it's destined that he should serve. What he can't stand is our troubles, that is, he can't bear to see the pain of the women. That's what he can't. You know how it is: a central draft board. You never can tell. Anything might happen. It's only lucky, as you say; nothing but a lottery.

But the Almighty is good to us after all. My Itsik, that is Alter, was ushered into the State board room, and again they began all over again from scratch. They xamined him lengthwise and broadwise. Again they felt and patted and sized him up and bothered him here and there. But what's the good? The son of a gun is no good, that is he's good all right, but not for the army.

True, one of them tried to go against, and said 'Fit,' but the doctor made it short, 'Unfit.' One said, 'fit,' the other said ' Unfit.' ' Fit.' ' Unfit.' And so it went, until the governor personally took the trouble and left his seat and sized him up, saying, 'Absolutely not fit,' that means he's good for a scarecrow. Of course, I immediately sent a wire, naturally disguised, which read: ' *Mazel tov*, the goods definitely cancelled.'

Now I must turn back to the time I was still living in Vorotilivkeh, may it not happen to you, and my Itsik. Alter, that is, was still a baby, was he. Well, it so happened that there was a census in town. They went from house to house and registered each and every one, young and old – the name, the age, and how many children, boys and girls, and what they are called. When the turn came to my Itsik, my wife, bless her, says 'Alter.' So the fellow thinks, 'Alter, well I should worry ' and so he wrote 'Alter.'

Well, what do you suppose. A year after the other draft trouble, I get a new message. My son Alter is wanted to present himself kindly at the board in Vorotilivkeh. Can you beat that? Of all the dumb and crazy things! There you are! A toast to Mr. Alter.

To make it short – why bother you with long drawn-out stories – my Itsik, that is, Alter, is called to appear at the board, all over again. My wife, bless her, is just hitting the ceiling. My daughter-in-law faints away. My God, have you ever heard the like of it in all the world, corner to corner, that an only son, unique in the family, a real honest-to-goodness, first-born, should appear three times for the draft. But you might as well talk Greek, or Chinese for that matter. What am I to do?

Well, I hurried away to the community house, made a scene, and after much trouble got the Jews to make out an 'affidavid' that they know positively that Itsik is the same as Abraham Isaac, and Abraham Isaac is really Alter and that Alter and Itsik and Abraham Isaac are all one and the same person.

With the paper in my hand, I drove to Vorotilivkeh.

Arrived in Vorotilivkeh, I was hailed: ' Look who's here!' 'My, what a stranger!' 'How is Reb Yossef?' ' What are you doing here?'

Maybe, I'll tell them, what? Why should I? The less they know, I thought, the better.

'Oh, nothing. I have to see the poritz, the big shot.'

'About what?'

'About chicken-feed. You see, I bought some millet, and gave a deposit, and now, no millet and no deposit. Gone,' says I, 'the cow with the cord.' And immediately I start out for the draft board office.

As soon as I get to the office, do I, I meet up with one of those real clerks and show him the paper. He only takes one look and he falls into a rage – the clerk, that is – and flings the paper right into my face with such fury – may God take pity.

'*Stupaite kchortu* – go to the deuce with all your names and Jewish tricks. You want to get out of the draft,' he cries, 'you Jew-swindlers, so you turn Abraham Isaac into Itsik and Itsik into Alter – oh no, that kind of monkey business won't do here.'

'Aha! Monkey business,' say I to myself, 'in that case, he must be thinking of a "tip,"' and I take out a coin, and say to him on the quiet, as I present it to him, 'With my humble compliments, your honour.' As if stung, he yells out, 'Bribes!' Other clerks gathered, and what do you suppose? I was shown the door, was I. What a misfortune! My luck to come upon an empty-hander.

Of course, you might well imagine that among Jews you are never lost. I did find someone to act as a go-between . . . It was of as much use as a blood transfusion to a corpse – and, as it rested, I was supposed to have another son by the name of Alter, which Alter was invited to present himself personally before the draft board in Vorotilivkeh. A nice how-do-you-do!

If I survived the year, I must be of an iron constitution – although if you want to look at it the other way, am I not a fool to worry? What if there are ten draft board examinations, so long as I know that he's no good, the son of a gun. Well. I wouldn't say exactly that he's no good, but for the army he's no good, especially when he was turned down two times, was he. But then again, when you come to think of it, who knows? A strange town, a draft board of 'empty-handers' – who knows what may happen? But God the Almighty was good to us again. My Alter, Itsik, that is, again drew a number, again presented himself for the 'physkel,' and God worked a miracle. The draft board of Vorotilivkeh too decided 'not fit', and gave him a white card. So now with God's help we have two white cards.

Returning home, we were as gay as a lark, walking on air. We threw a party, invited nearly all the town and made merry, danced till the wee hours. What care I about anyone, and who can compare with me? A real king!

And now, we must get back to Izik, bless his soul, who scalded himself with the samovar, as a child, may his brother's years be longer. Just wait and you'll hear something interesting, you'll hear. Just imagine. Was I to be a prophet and foresee that the elegant rabbi of Vorotilivkeh, the crown rabbi, I mean, would forget to take his name out of the records in the city hall, and that I'd be credited with having another son: Izik, who must present himself before the draft board this year?

What a bombshell! What a 'catasrofy!'

What Izik? Which Izik? When Izik has long been in the other world? Thus I plead and take counsel with our rabbi.

'What's to be done? What?' Well, it's not so good,' he replies. Why isn't it good?' I ask.

'Why? Because Itsik and Izik are one and the same name.'

'Tell me,' I say, ' if you're so smart, how Itsik and Izik is one name?'

'Because,' says he, 'Itsik is Yitzchok, and Yitzchok is Isak, and Isak is Isaac and Isaac is Izik.'

'Whew, what a brain-twister!'

Well, to make a long story short, no use going into matters and details. My Izik is wanted. I am ordered without fail to present him before the draft board. At home the wailing began anew. Talk about wailing, like the destruction of the Temple. Firstly, my wife, bless her, reminded herself of the dead boy – revived her old wound.

'Why should he not be alive today and be drafted instead of rotting in the ground? And secondly maybe, it's just as the crown rabbi says: Itsik is Yitzchok, and Yitzchok is Isak, and Isak is Isaac, and Isaac is Izik - and that's no joke.'

That's what she, my wife, bless her, says, and just hits the ceiling, and my daughter-in-law naturally passes out.

Well, I got going and drove up to Yehupetz to consult a good lawyer, and at the same time took along my son, so I could consult a professor so he could tell me if he's fit or not, although I know mighty well that he's no good the son of a gun; that is, he's good, all right, but not for a soldier. And then, I thought, when I find out what the lawyer will tell me, and what the professor will tell me. I'll be able to get some rest, and be done with the draft.

The first lawyer I went to happened to be a real blockhead, even though he had a large forehead and a bald pate, as smooth as a billiard ball. He couldn't understand for the life of him, which was Alter, and which was Itsik, and who was Abraham Isaac and who was Izik. Of course I repeat and keep repeating that Alter and Itsik and Abraham Isaac are all one and the same person, and Izik is the one who overturned the samovar while I was still a Vorotilivker, that is while I lived in Vorotilivker . . . And I am beginning to guess that I am through, when he questions me all over again. 'Allow me, just one moment, which was the oldest, Itsik, Alter, or Abraham Isaac?'

'There you are!' I blurt out. 'Haven't I told you umpteen times, haven't I, that Itsik and Abraham Isaac and Alter are all one and the same person, that is, his real name is Itsik, or better, Abraham Isaac, but he's called - his mother pet-named him so - "Alter", and 'Izik' - I tell him, 'is the one who overturned the samovar while I was a Vorotilivker, that is, when I was living in Vorotilivkeh.'

'In that case,' he asks, 'when was it that Abraham Alter, I mean, Isaac Itsik, presented himself before the draft board?'

'What is he jabbering! What a mix-up,' I say. You've got the wires twisted. I've never yet in all my life,' I say, ' come across a Jew to have such a goyish head on him. Haven't I told you that Isaac and Abraham Isaac and Itsik and Izik, and Alter are all one and the same person - one and the same, the very same!'

'See here,' he says, 'what are you shouting about? Stop your shouting.' What do you know? You might think that it was my fault.

In brief, I slammed the door and went to another lawyer. This time I struck a real Talmud brain, but a little too much of a smarty. He rubbed his forehead and studied aloud, turned and twisted and worried the laws, inferred that fundamentally speaking, according to the law, the Mezeretch board had no right to register him, but seeing that this board did register him, the other board was obliged to strike him out, that is 'aliminate ' him, and then there is a law, he said. That if the board included him and the other board did not take his name out, then they must write him out, that is 'aggsamt' him, and then there is a 'statue' that if the other board refuses to take his name out, that is 'aliminate' him . . . well, this law and that law and the other law, this 'statue' and that 'statue' . . . He just made my head dizzy with laws and 'statues,' just dizzy; and I had to go to a third one now.

This time I struck a brand new *schlemiel*, a very young lawyer, just out of the shell, that is just graduated law, and a very cordial fellow with a voice like a bell, a ringing bell.

It looked to me like he was still practising to plead, was he, because one could see that he liked to hear himself talk; he just swelled with pleasure. And so he waxed eloquent, delivered a whole speech in my favour, so that I had to interrupt him, saying, 'Excellent,' I said, 'you're absolutely right, but what's the good of your "lamenting" me. You better advise me what to do,' I said, 'in case, God forbid, he's called again.'

Well, to make it short, why bother you with all sorts of stories? I finally got to the right sort, the real A1 lawyer, one who, mind you, is a lawyer of the old school, who understands a thing or two.

I related the whole story from A to Z, while he sat the whole time with his eyes closed and listened.

After I finished, he says to me, 'Are you all through? No more? Why, you just return home. It doesn't amount to a pinch of snuff. You'll not have to pay more than three hundred roubles fine.'

'What, is that all?' I say, 'If I only knew that the matter ends in three hundred roubles. What I fear is about my son, I fear.'

'What son?' he asks.

'What do you mean, "what son"?' My son Alter Itsik that is.'

'How does that affect Itsik?'

'What do you mean, "how does it affect"? Suppose they, God forbid, drag him out again, suppose.'

'But you say he has a white card.'

'Why, he has two white cards.'

'Well then, what more do you want?'

'So far as I am concerned, I want nothing. What I am afraid of is that now that they're looking for Izik, and as Izik doesn't exist, and as Alter, Itsik, that is, is registered as Abraham Isaac, and Isaac – so says our dope of a crown rabbi, is Isak, and Isak is Isaac, and Isaac is Izik – well they might, God forbid, take my Itsik, or Abraham Isaac, that is Alter, for the dead Izik?'

' Well, then,' he says, ' all the better. If Itsik is Izik, you'll save the fine too. Didn't you say he had a white card?'

'Two white cards,' I reply, 'but the two white cards were given to Itsik, not to Izik'.

'Didn't you just tell me that Itsik was Izik?'

'Whoever told you that Itsik is Izik ?'

'Why, just a moment ago, you said that Itsik was the same as Izik!'

'I? How could I tell you such a thing when Itsik is no other than Alter, and Izik is the boy who overturned the samovar while I was a Vorotilivker, that is, lived in Vorotilivkeh . . .

Getting into a purple rage he cries out. '*Stupaite vi nadoiedliveh yevrei!*'

Just think of it: I, a pest. I should be called a pest. I . . .

Translated by A. A. Roback. Summer 1959

JEWISH WOMAN
Gertrud Kolmar

I am a stranger.

Since no one dares approach me
I would be girded with towers
That wear their steep and stone-grey caps
Aloft in clouds.

The brazen key you will not find
That locks the musty stair. It spirals skyward
As a serpent lifts its scaly head
Into the light.

Oh these walls decay like cliffs
That streams have washed a thousand years;
And birds with raw and wrinkled craws
Lie burrowed deep in caves.

Inside the halls of sifting sand
Crouch lizards hiding speckled breasts –
An expedition would mount
Into my ancient land.

Perhaps somewhere I can unearth
The buried Ur of the Chaldeans,
The idol Dagon, Hebrew tents,
Or the horn of Jericho.

What once blew down the haughty walls
Now lies in twisted ruin underground;
And yet I once drew breath
To sound its note.

Inside chests choked with dust
Lie dead the noble robes,
The dying gleam of pigeons' wings,
And the torpor of Behemoth.

Amazed, I clothe myself. For I am small
And far from ages glorious and strong.
Yet all about me stare expanses shining:
Shelter for my soul.

Now I seem strange, no longer know myself
For I was there before great Rome and Carthage were,
Because in me the altar fires ignite
Of Deborah and her tribe.

And from the hidden golden bowl
A painful glistening runs into my blood,
And then a song rings out a name
That suits me once again.
The heavens call with coloured signs.
Your face is closed:
And those who steal around me with the desert fox
Will never see it.

Enormous, crumbling columns of wind,
As green as nephrite, red as coral,
Blow across the towers. God lets them fall in ruin,
And yet they stand for ages more.

Spring/Summer 1976

THREE POEMS
Selma Meerbaum-Eisinger

I am the rain

I am the rain, and like the rain
I walk barefoot from land to land.
The wind strokes playfully my hair
with its slender, brownish hand.

My frock as thin as spider-web
is grayer than the grayest woe.
I am alone. But now and then
I play around with a sick doe.

And in my hands I hold a string
on which, close-linked like pearls,
are all the tears which ever were
wept by lonely, pale-faced girls.

I took them all away with me,
from slender girls late at night,
when, wide-awake and longingly,
they waited in the dimming light.

I am the rain, and like the rain
I walk bare-foot from land to land.
The wind strokes playfully my hair
with its slender, brownish hand.

(8 March 1941)

Late afternoon

Long shadows fall on the white-shining road
and the sun sends down its last departing rays.
The thin twitter of a bird is as if, by its noise,
it wants something to steal from the stillness around.
People, ten paces away, look as if they had come
from another planet, different from our own.
And it is almost as if you wished to curse
the fading leaves which, by their rustling, disperse
the last rays the sun sends up from below.
One would wish to hear only the violets grow.

(16 April1940)

Evening

Like a line of dark-blue silence
lies the wide horizon, softly seamed with red.
The branches of the tree sway quietly as if dancing.
The light is soft and blue and dreamy as in a fairytale.
The sky is still alight, the stars are hidden still.
The air is cool and tender like a woman's hand.
Sweet melodies from a distant land
carry music of a magic song, unknown.

(12 July 1941)

Translated from the German by Jacob Sonntag. Spring 1977

THE ANNIVERSARY
Alexander Baron

The Velodrome d'Hiver is a stadium on the left of the River Seine, in Paris. One day, in July 1952, I went there, to a meeting. On the same day in July ten years before, the Germans had begun their mass deportations of Jews from Paris. Thousands of people had been herded in the stadium, loaded into transports and taken away to the ovens. Today was a commemoration.

The city was radiant with sunshine but there was no sunlight in the street. The walls on each side were high; and the railway bridge across the Seine was overhead, shutting out half the sky. Pillars and girders, shadows, litter underfoot: it was a dank, cold, graveyard street.

Groups of people stood about beneath the wall of the stadium, in the roadway, among the ugly girders. A wooden platform rose unregarded in their midst. There could not have been more than a thousand present. There was no tension in the air, no atmosphere of sorrow, of reverence, no memory-laden silence, no anger. There were only the groups, and the people wandering from group to group, and the taxis pulling up, and smiles, and shrill greetings, and laughter and handshakes; the same swirl and chatter that one sees outside a synagogue before a wedding. Here and there a lonely face, a woman's with hollow, waxen cheeks, or that of a skullcapped, bearded old man, with distant eyes, bore the marks of grief. No other face was conscious of the occasion. The shabbily dressed, the lonely, were few. There were paunches and rings and gold teeth, and good clothes and loud voices everywhere.

The speeches began. The groups closed in to form a crowd, but within the crowd there was the same hum and chatter as before. Voices rose. Bursts of laughter sounded. On the platform speakers bobbed up and down, scarcely noticed. Rabbi So-and-So. The Secretary of This. The Chairman of That. The Fraternal Delegate from Somewhere. Their bray of oratory was a background to the crowd's chatter, a rise and fall of sound that had no meaning. People grew tired of standing, changed from one foot to another, sighed with impatience. Some pushed their way out of the crowd to rest on the seats under the bridge. The speakers gabbled on. A woman got out of a taxi. She was a tall woman, with the heavy arrogance of cheek and lip and nostril of those who have no foundation for self-respect except money. She came into the crowd. She wore too much make-up. She was too well dressed. She stood near me, her expression cruel and haughty, her carriage erect, her hands folded upon the top of her umbrella as if she were at a race meeting.

The speakers were getting up and down. After each finished, there was a mutter and a conferring beneath the platform. An inner belt of the crowd, those who could hear the speakers, stood with their faces uplifted, staring at the empty structure. At the back of the crowd the shuffling and the strolling and the talking went on. Around me the conversations mingled. '. . . taking a villa at Antibes . . .' '. . . seven hundred thousand francs, she paid for it . . .' 'Cabinet-making? It's a dying trade. Gets worse every season . . .'' . . . my oldest boy married their daughter last May . . .'' . . . that servant-girl drives me mad. But what can you expect of a *Normande?* . . .' They were all safely insulated within the present; a blessed, a necessary protection; the past, their own past, become remote beyond remembering, a dream, inconceivable. The story of torment and death was no more than an unheeded rise and fall of voices from the platform.

There was a woman on the platform; small, middle-aged, with large, liquid eyes. She looked around at the crowd. Her voice was low and husky. A man in front of me cocked his head on one side. He was trying to listen. Someone else said, 'Shush!' It was her fright that attracted people's attention; her eyes, like those of the child which appeals for a hearing, her voice, nervous and

R. B. Kitaj *Drancy* (1984-1986) pastel and charcoal on paper / *Summer 1989*

hesitant. People were looking up at her, curious, quiet. A voice behind me: 'Who is she?' Another voice: 'No one. A survivor.' Another voice: 'Hush!' I could hear her now.

'. . . what was the worst thing inside the stadium, was that they separated the children from their mothers. I can remember as if it was yesterday. A fine day. The sky a pale blue. The sun shining. The faded grass in the middle of the stadium. It did not seem real. Everything that happened to us seemed to be happening in the middle of a holiday. On one side, in the stands, there were the mothers. And on the other side, in the stands, there were the children. The mothers cried for the children and the children cried for their mothers, and the guards kept them apart.'

The woman was looking up, as if she could see the past in the sky. The crowd was in a reverie.

'. . . Among the children it was chaos. There were little ones wandering about, four and five years old. They were lost. They did not know where they were. They did not know what was happening to them. They did not know why they could not go to their mothers, or who the big, rough men were who pushed them back. They could not blow their own noses. They wet themselves. They were hungry. They were thirsty. They cried. They became frightened, and they sat down on the grass and shrieked. They had all come with little bags and bundles and suitcases, and the guards had made them leave these things in heaps, and when they had to go and find their own they were bewildered, so bewildered, poor little things. We women, from the other side of the stadium, could see them wandering among the heaps of baggage, frightened, piteous, not able to find their own bundles.

'And the older ones, the girls of ten and eleven and twelve, began to take charge of them. They took the little ones under their care, so motherly, so proud of themselves, and they soothed them, and they found their bundles for them, and they told them they were going on holiday, to a nice place, and they must behave themselves, and they would soon be with their mothers again.

'And soon we saw them, the twelve-year-olds, leading the little ones away, in their innocent procession, like children going to school. The women wept and shrieked and threw themselves like wild beasts at the guards, and the guards beat them back. And over there, on the side of the stadium we saw our children, our treasures, our hearts' blood toddling away to the trains, to *those places,* and they carried their little suitcases so solemnly, and some of them turned round to wave goodbye to their mummies . . .'

A shriek pierced the quiet. It did not sound a human cry. No human emotions were articulate in it. It was as intense and piercing as the shriek of an express train's whistle. Hundreds of heads turned. The shriek sounded again and again. It was the woman who was too well dressed. She stood on the edge of the crowd. Her body kept its haughty pose. She still leaned forward upon her umbrella. But her head was flung back, her eyes glared like those of a maddened horse, her mouth was wide open, and the shrieks burst from her, the rapid, deafening, cloud-piercing shrieks, again and again, punctuated by quick, hoarse inhalations.

Two men took her by the elbows and led her to a seat under the bridge. Her shrieking grew weaker, and she interrupted it, from time to time, with a babble of heartbroken words. The woman on the platform was speaking again. But the shrieks had broken the protecting shell of present time. The crowd was stirring like a disturbed herd. I heard men around me muttering brokenly. A woman began to moan, '*Ai, ai, ai!*' in a lost voice, and other women wept, and soon, throughout the crowd, women were rocking themselves with their fists clenched at their breasts, and uttering that low, continuous ululation of grief, that incredulous, despairing, '*Ai, ai, ai, ai!*' which is the distilled essence of woman's sorrow, of Jewish sorrow. The whole appearance of these women was changed. Their proud carriage, their fine clothes, their trinkets, had been the way in which they flaunted their victorious fight back to life. Now they huddled, grotesque, pathetic, rocking themselves, moaning, their expensive hats awry, tears scrawling down through their make-up, the smart lines of their Parisian clothes disarranged, swaying, weeping, nodding to themselves before their Wailing Wall.

The tall woman had calmed down. She was whimpering quietly. They were putting her into a taxi. But her shrieks still lingered in the ears. They were the kind of sound that would always linger, lifelong scars of sound in the memory, that for us who had heard them, would become the difference between us and our neighbours; that would return, whenever we were lifted up by our own happiness, to chill the heart; that would sound in our minds when we saw the sunshine in a blue sky, or when we saw joyous and innocent children at play, a sound which, when the calm voice of the BBC announcer fills the room, 'Mr Eden said . . . Monsieur Bidault declared . . . Doctor Adenauer gave an assurance. . .' rings again in the memory, the dreadful, driven shriek of human loss, of loss that can never be made good.

Winter 1953

IN A COLD SEASON
Michael Hamburger

I

Words cannot reach him in his prison of words
Whose words killed men because those men were words
Women and children who to him were numbers
And still are numbers though reiterated
Launched into air to circle out of hearing
And drop unseen, their metal shells not broken.
Words cannot reach him though I spend more words
On words reporting words reiterated
When in his cage of words he answered words
That told how with his words he murdered men
Women and children who were words and numbers
And he remembered or could not remember
The words and numbers they reiterated
To trap in words the man who killed with words.
Words cannot reach the children, women, men
Who were not words or numbers till they died
Because ice-packed in terror shrunk minds clung
To numbers words that did not sob or whimper
As children do when packed in trucks to die
That did not die two deaths as mothers do
Who see their children packed in trucks to die.

II

Yet, Muse of the IN-trays, OUT-trays,
Shall he be left uncelebrated
For lack of resonant numbers calculated
To denote your hero, and our abstract age?
Rather in the appropriate vocabulary
Let a memorandum now be drawn up -
Carbon copies to all whom it may concern -
A monument in kind, a testimonial
To be filed for further reference
And to circulate as required.
Adolf Eichmann, civil servant (retired):
A mild man, meticulous in his ways,
As distinctly averse to violence
As to all other irregularities
Perpetrated in his presence,
Rudeness of speech or deportment,
Infringements of etiquette
Or downright incompetence, the gravest offence;
With a head for figures, a stable family life,
No abnormalities.
Never lost his temper on duty
Even with subordinates, even with elements earmarked
For liquidation;
Never once guilty of exceeding his authority
But careful always to confine his ambitions
Within the limits laid down for personnel of his grade.
Never, of course, a maker of policy,
But in its implementation at office level,
Down to the detailed directive, completely reliable;
Never, perhaps, indispensable,
Yet difficult to replace
Once he had mastered the formalities
Of his particular department
And familiarized himself with his responsibilities
As a specialist in the organization
Of the transport and disposal of human material -
In short, an exemplary career.

III

Words words his words - and half his truth perhaps
If blinking, numb in moonlight and astray
A man can map the landmarks trace the shapes
That may be mountains icebergs or his tears

And he whose only zeal was to convert
Real women children men to words and numbers
Added to be subtracted leaving nothing
But aggregates and multiples of nothing
Can know what made him adept in not knowing
Feel what it was he could not would not feel –
And caged in words between their death his death
No place no time for memory to unfreeze
The single face that would belie his words
The single cry that proved his numbers wrong.

Probing his words with their words my words fail.
Cold cold with words I cannot break the shell
And almost dare not lest his whole truth be
To have no core but unreality.

IV

I heard no cry, nor saw her dying face,
Have never known the place, the day,
Whether by bullet, gas or deprivation
They finished her off who was old and ill enough
To die before long in her own good time,
Only that when they came to march her out of her human world,
Creaking leather couch, mementoes, widow's urn,
They made her write a postcard to her son in England,
'Am going on a journey'; and that all those years
She had refused to travel even to save her life.
Too little I know of her life, her death,
Forget my last visit to her at the age of nine.
The goodbye like any other that was the last,
Only recall that she, mother of five, grandmother,
Freely could share with a child all her little realm;
Recall her lapdog who trembled and snapped up cheese –
Did they kill her lapdog also, or drive him away? –
And the bigger dog before that, a French bulldog, stuffed
To keep her company still after his early death.
Three goldfishes I recall, one with a hump on his back
That lived for years though daily she brushed her fishes
Under the kitchen tap to keep them healthy and clean;
And how she conspired with us children,
Bribed us with sweets if we promised not to tell
Our father that she, who was diabetic,
Kept a pillbox of sweets in her handbag
To eat like a child in secret
When neither could guess that sweets would not cause her death.

A wireless set with earphones was part of the magic
She commanded and freely dispensed,
Being childlike herself and guileless and wise . . .
Too little I know of her wisdom, her life,
Only that, guileless, she died deprived
Of her lapdog even, stuffed bulldog and pillbox of sweets.

V

And yet and yet I would not have him die
Caged in his words their words - one deadly word
Setting the seal on unreality
Adding one number to the millions dead
Subtracting nothing from death dividing nothing
Silencing him who murdered words with words
Not one shell broken, not one word made flesh.
Nor in my hatred would imprison him
Who never free in fear and hatred served
Another's hatred which again was fear
So little life in him he dared not pity
Or if he pitied dared not act on pity;
But show him pity now for pity's sake
And for their sake who died for lack of pity;
Break from the husk at last one naked grain
That still may grow where the massed carrion lay
Bones piled on bones their only mourners bones
The inconceivable aggregate of the dead
Beyond all powers to mourn or to avenge;
See man in him spare woman child in him
Though in the end he neither saw nor spared –
Peel off the husk for once and heed the grain,
Plant it though he sowed nothing poisoned growth;
Dare break one word and word may yet be whole.

Summer 1966

THE MAN WHO WOULD NEVER WRITE LIKE BALZAC

Arnold Wesker

The young man, who was thirty and turning prematurely bald, now knew that he would never be a writer like Balzac, Eliot or Dostoevsky. That's what he'd wanted, thought could happen and imagined long days and nights in his drifting fantasies actually happening. But now he understood, as his mother, sister, cousins, friends and employers had warned, the signs always having been there, his stories beside *Les Contes Drolatiques*, his novel beside *Middlemarch*, notes from his underground alongside those of Dostoevsky – never! He would never be a writer like them.

The final realisation came as he stared at a sentence in the Eliot masterpiece: *'The Vicar's frankness seemed not of the repulsive sort that comes from an uneasy consciousness seeking to forestall the judgement of others . . .'* He gasped. Not that it was the most extraordinary observation about human behaviour he'd ever read *'. . .an uneasy consciousness seeking to forestall the judgement of others . . .'* but the inevitable arrangement of the words, the desire to say something sweet about a character and doing so by pointing firmly yet sadly to the flaw in others, the sheer confidence of its gentle tone, its truth – why! he could relate it to himself! All these elements in the sentence seemed to crown fifteen years of reading that had grown from excitement with other men's works into a suspicion of his own. It was a shattering discovery. As can be imagined.

For what were its implications? What truth about himself was now revealed to him? He didn't really understand life, that! That was what his discovery meant. Those breathtaking perceptions about human motivation? The glowing metaphoric descriptions of character? He had produced none of them.

'I'm a fool, an idiot,' he complained to his father. 'I can't look at events and pair them off and extract their significance and link them and see cause and effect. A blind man! What else can it mean? A blind man!'

His father listened, kindly, as they walked home from work. Both were silversmiths, a dying craft, and both had the look of gloom and neglect belonging to men who pursue a love in its last gasps.

'That's what's done it,' said the son, 'this trade, this, this worn out, outdated, over-mechanized profession. We break our fingers and hearts turning silver by hand while the bright boys, the young layabouts, make shit by machine. And what's the result? No time, no energy, no love left for anything. Who can be a writer in conditions like that, I ask you?'

'Patience,' said his father, 'patience. You had two plays on the radio, a story in the *Evening News*, you did a couple of reviews for the *Hackney Gazette*, patience.' 'Patience, patience, patience! My plays were half hour nothings at lunchtime, my story was a bigger nothing about something that happened at work, and who reads the *Hackney Gazette*? You want me to feel proud of that? Fifteen years of writing! Fifteen!'

'Shaw started writing plays at forty.'

'Shaw was Shaw! Stop telling me about Shaw all the time.'

But few discoveries are ever final on first unearthing, especially one as distressing as that made by Constantine Lander, the young man's name. We delay facing such truths, find what excuses we can to forget them; and we're given straws, inevitably, or we make them, to clutch at and help us evade those truths. A straw was what Constantine found on arriving home to their Council flat in Hackney, in the shape of a letter from a little magazine called *People's Poems*. It read:

'Dear Mr. Lander, your poem "The March of Dust" reached us after redirection, we've changed address. But can we say at once we think it's splendid, just what we look for. Hackney is a borough rich in people's struggles, and poems of people are what we print. More power to your elbow.'

The note slightly dampened his pleasure at acceptance. He read it, perplexed, aloud to his parents.

'Rich in people's struggles? What are they talking about? My poem's not about that. I'm a socialist, maybe, a humanitarian, if you like, but I didn't write a poem about people's struggles.' He'd written, in fact, five verses with eight lines in each about the dust that had gathered on their silver work which fewer and fewer people could afford or cared to buy. He had felt deeply though not originally. The poem had competence but monotony.

'He's complaining!' said Mr Lander senior. 'What matters if they understand or they don't understand? They were touched. For the wrong reasons or not the wrong reasons they were touched! Who ever understands what the artist really means?'

It was true. Constantine relented. Wasn't it another acceptance? Perhaps it always starts slowly. His elation grew. At first he was sheepish and modest, then boisterous and backslapping, then jubilant. His first instinct was to write. It suddenly seemed a power was in him that could help him wield those heavy, daunting weapons: the blank, white page and the black-inked pen. He went to his study at once, reached for both, and with a thrilling smile on his lips began a sentence: *'Lester Conrad confronted his father with piety and pain and said, "You know what, dad, I'll never be a Balzac or an Eliot or a Dostoevsky!"'* It was to be a first novel, autobiographical.

But the sentence failed to please him. He was about to cross it out and start another when he cautioned himself. 'Uhuh! Careful Connie my boy. Let the thought settle. Don't rush. You have time. All the time in the world. Force your idea into shape at an ill-judged moment and it's lost. Forever.' In which spirit he screwed up the white sheet, threw it into the basket and, still jubilant, decided instead to telephone through the news of the published poem to his girlfriend, a rather lachrymose Jewish girl whose plain looks limited her choice of possible husbands but whose main attraction for Constantine was her enthusiasm for the arts which she expressed with a coy bewilderment that he mistook for perceptive awe. She was impressed and succumbed to an unscheduled date for a meal in a Chinese restaurant where he met her with flowers.

Even his mother, as he was changing, seemed to be affected.

'All right, so he may be a writer, one day' she conceded, but being too sober to leave it at that added the warning: 'Only I'm telling you, even I know, one poem doesn't make a harvest.'

'She means one poem doesn't make a poet,' said her husband.

'I mean one poem doesn't make a harvest,' she insisted.

'She means one swallow doesn't make a spring,' said her son.

'It's summer,' corrected the father.

'It's a harvest,' said the mother. And they spent the next half hour untangling *that* confusion which of course led to others and a quarrel about what an unhappy life the husband had given the wife.

February, a hovering bleak and yellow month with no claim to either winter or spring, was coming to its end. A straw can't keep an honest man afloat. Constantine, in his euphoria, had forgotten what ends-of-months brought. On the first of each of them he sent out his literary work to half a dozen different magazines and kept a special book in which was noted what went where, and when and how much postage cost, so that in this way he never sent the same work twice to a magazine nor nagged the editor too frequently. One gloomy and foggy evening, huddling into his large ex-army coat from a February damp, he arrived home to a rejection slip. Depression began. Two nights later, the weather as bleak, he came home to three more rejection slips. The next night saw another and four days later, the last.

That evening seemed one in which surely he must finally face the truth about his meagre talent. He imprisoned his father in his little room and read aloud to him the quotation from *Middlemarch*, another from Balzac and another from Dostoevsky.

'So! Aren't I right? People! How have I been looking at people? If I can't write like Dostoevsky it means I don't understand People. How can a man live like that? How have I managed to live like that till now? All these years? What sort of relationships have I imagined I've been having with men? Mistakes! Everything I've done, all my opinions, all my decisions, all my loves – mistakes!' It was a time of great anxiety for him as it is for all of us when we discover that we will never write like Balzac, Eliot or Dostoevsky; or compose like Vivaldi, Bach or Mahler; or write poetry like Shakespeare, Milton, Blake or the beautiful boys Shelley, Keats and Dylan Thomas. Sad times. Full of despair and melancholy. A man needs great comfort and consolation then.

But do we ever know what to say? 'There, there, you may not be Balzac but you're like – like – like a primitive Jack London.' Or, 'You may not be a second Dostoevsky but you're a first Lander.' Lander! Constantine Lander! Perhaps it's little wonder he was tempted to believe himself destined for high literary achievements with a name like that. Not that his mother hadn't warned about it:

'He'll be a God-knows-who-to-think-he-is mess' she complained at the insistence of his father to so name him. But Constantine's father, the cause of his and – according to Mrs Lander – much other trouble in the family, had declared:

'A man ought to have a distinctive name, something he can stand up in!'

'Boots!' she hurled back, 'give him boots to stand up in. But a name covers him all his life. You know what they'll call him at school?' she continued, 'Connie! Connie and I won't be responsible. Give him the name of Martin. He'll be a silversmith, like you, it's a good name.'

She lost. It was surprising and, we'd better add, unusual. It may never have prevented trouble from eventually happening among them but she rarely lost the battles with her husband. And that he did always lose to her never failed to amaze him.

'Men,' Mr Lander would say to his son with whom he had a gorgeously rich and relaxed relationship, 'men for some strange reason forever feel guilty. Why? Did they commit some monstrously evil crime or something? Carry it with them right over the centuries? From male gene to male gene? A mystery! Except to a woman. *She* seems to know about it! Instinctively! A man can walk through the door, innocent! completely! of everything! Eager even to embrace his wife, and yet if the mood takes her – say she's especially irritated on that day for not being a rich lady or something – so she can give him a look, such a look, out of nowhere, out of the bottom of her five-thousand-year old soul, dragging up what Cain did, and Attila and Genghis Khan and Neville Chamberlain all in one hateful moment.'

Mr Lander may never have become used to it but – and this touches the seed of our story – he'd found the way to live with it: either by going out to friends or filling their little council flat with them. And they discussed. Wives, wars, life, literature – their topics were abundant. And it was this inheritance from that multitude of evenings, in the flat filled full of friends, which became Constantine's target for the pained arrows of his frustration. For what was balm to the troubled father led, curiously and with sad irony, to a troubled son, a once-loving-son who remembered those evenings he loved, where stories were told, art was debated and every possible theme argued over again and again.

Mr Lander, to whom each fresh example of feminine resentment was a source of renewed bewilderment, used these gatherings to continue his ruminations upon wives and the female temperament. Pretending to talk to his son alone he'd affect, nevertheless, the public tone for the benefit of his friends and, with obvious relish locked in his complaints, he'd rhetorize:

'I'm not saying men are all lovely but, I don't know, men forgive each other more readily. Your mother, hard-working, devoted, one-hundred-per-cent-dependable, can forgive no-one anything – not God for the world, not her parents for making her a woman, not me for being a man, not even herself for putting up with everything. Have you noticed? You come in and say what a lovely day it is outside and she's got so much into the habit of expecting catastrophe that she clicks her tongue and says, "I knew it'd be". "But Selma," I say, "a lovely day, I said lovely day". "Don't talk to me about lovely days", she says, "have I got pleasures? Blessings? A new gas stove?" No logic. No concentration. You'd think she's a fool the way she talks, your mother, but she's no fool. She has only one fault. Me! I'm the crack in her make-up. She doesn't like me. It's no joke living with a woman who doesn't want you near her and holds you responsible for war, famine and pestilence.'

His friends listened – he was something of a prize for them – while he pretended he didn't know they were listening. And he spoke with a luminous energy, which never failed to hold the attention of his son for whom it seemed that to be able to talk like his father was to be in command of great powers. And in that, *that* concept, in the marshalling of words – lay power. In that fragile concept was the root of Constantine's problems, as we'll see.

'Mistakes' he was saying to his father, 'everything I've done, all my opinions, all my decisions, all my loves – mistakes! I mean' he moaned while, grief being one thing and order another, he still placed his rejection slips in the neatly-kept file, and filled in his little book of literary loss and achievement, 'why did you call me Constantine in the first place?' His unsuspecting father, not realizing the depth of his son's angst, answered with blithe humour:

'Funny thing you should ask, I was thinking about it only the other day and I couldn't remember. Perhaps I was just fed up with David and Geoffrey and Ruth.'

'Ruth? You were going to call me Ruth for God's sake?'

'Don't get upset. We thought you were a girl.'

'What would you have called me had I been a girl?'

'Alexandria.'

'God in heaven, pop. They'd have called me Alec at school. A boy's name. I was called Connie as a boy and as a girl I'd have been called Alec. You were determined to make a mess of me.'

'Constantine the Great I was thinking of.'

'And Alexandria the Great also I suppose. Why did you think I was a girl anyway? You couldn't tell?'

'I could tell, but I wasn't there. When I rang through to the hospital the nurse said you were a girl and by the time I'd phoned round the family and said we had an Alexandria they rang back and said they had made a mistake you were a Constantine.'   'How could they make such a mistake? Maybe I'm mixed up and I'm not yours.' 'Idiot!' said his father, 'you look like me don't you?'

'No I don't!' said his son. 'Look at us. Your hair is reddish brown, mine's jet blackish. You've got large pop eyes, I've got narrow Mongol eyes. You've got a fine Roman nose, mine's hooked. You're small and fat, I'm tall and lean. Where's the resemblance?'

'You're tall because you had milk and I didn't.'

'I'm not yours at all. Ruth! Christ!'

'I said I *didn't* want to call you Ruth.' His father was becoming fed up with years and years of discussing this wretched name. 'Why you asking me about names, now, when it's thirty years old?'

'For Christ's sake dad! Because I never *will* be a writer like Balzac, Eliot or Dostoevsky, that's why!' His son's voice cracked and suddenly became shrill. He seemed about to weep. What was this? From one moment of high laughter to one where – could it be – that behind the cracked voice was a broken heart? 'Never, never!' said the cracked voice, 'not if I live to be a hundred and fifty I'll never write like any of them.' His father could see absolutely no connection between the fact of his distressed son's name and the distressing fact of his son's small talent. 'You led me to expect too much from myself, that's the connection,' his son, with unworthy self-pity cried out. 'No one should have to live with a name like that.'

'That's a very serious accusation' his father replied, 'very serious. And if that's what I've done then I've got a lot to answer for and it makes me very sad. But is it the name? Honestly? You certain of it?'

'No, it's not the name', said Constantine, who was essentially a sensible and honest man, too honest, in fact, as we know. 'Of course it's not the name. But the name is a symbol, it's not an accident, it's a symbol! Of the flat, the whole inflated atmosphere of this flat, filled with people, always filled with people, cronies, talking about great writers, as though they were old and wise friends whom it had been your blessed fortune to know. 'Scholem Asch!' you'd say, 'now there's a writer'. And then one of your old cronies with leather patches in his elbows, what's his name?'

'Pavel Slansky'.

'Slansky, that's him, Slansky would say, 'Poh! Asch! a provincial! I'll give you one Kafka for all of Asch's work'.

'What did Slansky know about literature!' said his father, suddenly flooded with delicious memories of literary squabbles.

'And then you'd all set-to and pull the masterpieces to master-pieces, reading selections, from here from there, great diamonds of prose and revelation, and the room would throb and glow AND I GREW UP IN ALL THAT BRILLIANCE!'

So that was it. The quarrels from which the father ran away, led to soirées that frustrated the son. Mr Lander was astounded. Words, which should have been uttered in a state of exultant gratitude, emerged from his beloved offspring in a state of harrowing desolation. And it was not over, this lamentation, this recitation of regrets, this perverse accusation of death through literacy.

'What other world could there be? What other blessings, honours? "To command words!" how you'd say it, in such reverential tones. "To command words! Ah! There!" And you'd sit thinking about it, lost in wonder, and my young eyes with their young, vulnerable heart would look at your faces, radiant! incredulous! deep in contemplation of all that words had ever communicated from one great man to many men, and I would sit, shivering, thrilled. "He that is without sin among you let him cast the first stone."'

' "Let him *first* cast the stone"', his father corrected, and added, 'what a concept!' 'There you go!' Constantine raged on. '"What a concept!" That's what you always said, muttering among yourselves, smug that you knew *their* literature as well as your own.' The son mocked on. ' "What a concept! What a paralysing, breathtaking idea! And look how a mere twelve words have cocooned the idea!"'.

'Thirteen,' corrected the father.

'Thirteen, then.'

'And not cocooned. I never used that word. Slansky used it. He liked it – "cocooned!"' His father spat it out as though he were back in the old days proudly pitting his vivid feeling for words against those of his friends. 'Since when do words cocoon an idea? They *contain* ideas maybe, contain. But that would have been too simple for Slansky. He always went in for fancy sounds instead of crisp meanings. Not me. Me, I liked honest words. Words *contain* ideas, words *convey* ideas, words *carry* ideas, but . . .' 'Words! Words! Words!' His son wrenched back the drift of his complaints. 'Did you have any idea what effect words had on me? Did you ever stop to think what the effect was on a young boy to hear read out, in heart-breaking tones, that description of the last moments of a man who thought he was going to be executed?'

'A Constance Garnett translation from the Russian', his father said, as though still engaged in a different conversation: 'Dostoevsky? A genius!'

But his son, in relentless mood, refused to let go. He moved sharply around his little room in their council flat, picking up stray books, placing them back in their meticulously arranged alphabetical order, and stormed on: 'How you curled that description lovingly round your lips. "Genius. A real genius. Now there was a genius," you'd say. It was like giving me a fever. I couldn't sleep after those sessions. I'd lie in bed imagining myself sitting at a desk, scribbling away at great speed, tossing page after page across the room, indifferent to order, abandoned to a frenzy of inspiration, and I'd see groups of people, like your old cronies, even you, sitting and reading *my* chapters from *my* books with *my* name on them in those same heartbreaking tones, and sighing as though there was absolutely nothing else of such importance in the whole world and saying about *me* "now *there* was a man who could write."' Constantine was in a fever about his fever. 'My one and only image of approval, a sitting group of old Jews, nodding, eyes on fire, lost in thought, smacking their lips as though literature were food.' He stopped his wild moving and abandoned himself to the visual picture he'd created of his own impossible future, while his father, watching him carefully, like a victim uncertain which way the predatory animal will next spring, waited until the future's impossibility sank pitilessly into his son who then cried out: 'Look what you gave me! The sight of mountains I couldn't climb! Multicoloured horizons I could never reach! A passion, a love, a - a - ,' here he was lost for the third word, ' - never to be fulfilled, consummated.'

His father's astonished and very unhappy concern took a brief and traitorous break at that moment to consider that perhaps with such a purple use of language it was inevitable his son, his poor, intelligent, good-natured, witty, not-bad-looking-and-unmarried son would never be a writer. And then he said it, by way of helpless consolation, and wanting to bite his tongue even as he was saying it, he said:

'But perhaps you are a kind of primitive Jack London.' He could not have offered anything more profoundly depressing. Not that Jack London wasn't a good writer, he was, but he was himself primitive. To tell his son he might be a primitive primitive! What's that for paternal consolation - especially to a son for whom there was no consolation.

'But I don't want to be a primitive Jack London, dad,' he cried, 'I want to be a Balzac or an Eliot or a Dostoevsky! '

'Well you're not a Balzac or an Eliot or a Dostoevsky!' his father cried back, 'so pull your socks together and grow up and make peace with yourself and enjoy life a little. You're thirty and you're not married and you haven't been farther than Paris and who knows what'll happen?'

Not even Mr Lander could see the complete logic of what he'd said but he felt it was absolutely imperative to shout back something at his fast fading son. No matter what, but something, and shouted. It seemed right but it failed. His son wept. It was an embarrassing sight, a thirty-year-old son weeping, and tears from so deep down. Not mere face-tricklers but great, heavy, helpless tears drawn up from such a depth of unhappiness that Mr Lander felt his son to be a stranger, since surely no one living in his house, for all its hard times and the relentless fears for the future which his ill-lucked wife took from room to room with her, and the faults of neglect which all parents, even the wisest, are guilty of at some point along the line - despite all this - nothing had happened to cause a son of his to erupt from a bottomless misery such as these uncontrollable tears now revealed. Surely? Was he a monster, this father? Had he beaten, denied, bullied, blackmailed? Joy! He'd only ever given joy and shown tolerance, and shared loves, and indulged.

But these were real tears. With such private pain convulsing Constantine, Mr Lander tenderly felt it more delicate to leave the stricken man alone with his awful discovery. So he went from his son's room, a bit of a sanctuary actually, where he often came for a chat and to compare notes on a day's work or an evening's reading, he went from it creeping away as though from a sleeping, ailing child, saying, 'I'll be downstairs if you want me.'

Constantine Lander, who'd never wept before, continued weeping a long time. But as he wept he moved around his room as though forcing himself to conduct a normal life while this temporary aberration passed through him. He tidied papers fruitlessly in that way surely all great writers tidied fruitlessly - not that he had as many papers as they, still, it kept him busy, sustained the illusion of literary activity. And then he picked up a silver candlestick that he'd made in the style of art-nouveau for his girlfriend, and began to polish it ready for a surprise presentation, his tears lessening but his chest heaving, still. It helped him not. On the contrary, the action, as though given a special clarity by his tears, sharply focused a new perspective on both art-nouveau and his girlfriend: he cared little for the coy, sentimentally lush tempers and lines of either.

Then, just when he thought the weeping was done, he came across his file of printed rejection slips and began to weep afresh, feeling ashamed but feeling perhaps he ought to feel such shame since you never knew when it would come in handy - a thought that brought him to an abrupt halt. What a callous thought, he thought. Have you no respect for your own tears but that you must see them as a possible object for a future passage of prose?

At once he grabbed for some paper and his pen. A new, strange and - could it be? - *ecstatic* feeling overcame him; a delicious, cleansed emotion; release, like the sudden flooding of a landscape with sharp light after the horrendous storm had passed. He was convinced that now, at this very moment, he was possessed of his first ever and real fever of creativity. And it would all make sense, a wonderful poetic sense: that on the very day when he'd finally confronted himself, confessed, owned up with such simple honesty that he was not, emphatically not, a literary genius, he'd become one. It happened like that, he thought. Fate. Its strange tricks. Like people winning the football pools in the very week they'd lost their copy coupon, or hadn't bothered, out of a sense of futility, to check. One was always reading about such things in the biographies of the great artists - how their talents were stumbled upon by accident or had been reached through devious, unrelated ways, or been practiced in the first instance for the wrong reasons: as a joke, to please someone else, for a competition, to replace a sick friend. And there it was! The discovery! The thrilling revelation of one's own abundance of jewels and juices. *Abundance of jewels and juices,* he wrote the words down on a piece of scrap paper specially set aside for just such jewels and juices. And then he began: *Conrad Lester confronted his father in despair and said: 'Oh, father, I know it, now, I'll never be a Balzac or an Eliot or a Dostoevsky.* It was to be a novel of discovery.

Then he stopped, sucked his pen, glanced at his list of jewels and juices to see how soon and which of them he could use in this, his first ever and real fever of creativity, then muttered to himself: '*Conrad Lester*? What's that for a name?' and scratched it out, then the *oh*, then the names *Balzac, Eliot and Dostoevsky* replacing them with *Austen, Stendhal and Tolstoy*, which he also crossed out deciding to write a longer list from which he'd later choose the three most stunning names - *Chaucer, Dickens, Defoe, Mann, Hardy, Lawrence, Chekhov, James, Turgenev, Goethe, Kafka, Moore, Meredith, Hemingway, Gogol, Joyce, Fitzgerald, Babel, Woolf, Proust* - until the long list with its weight of genius brought him to a halt, and his heart into a very weary, empty state. He crossed out everything, screwed up the first sheet of his first ever and real fever, and confronted a new and blank page. *Leonard Constantine faced his father in despair and cried* - he wrote. But that page too, after protracted, careful contemplation, he screwed up, putting some of his first real fever into the effort of throwing the paper ball across the room. And there it was again. The blank page, a third one. *Leonard Lester* . . . he wrote. And at that name, too, he looked for a long time, but now with no feeling whatsoever for it, or his story, or his fever, which blessedly had passed, until even that small beginning he scratched out.

A writer, he thought, mustering what he secretly knew to be dead ashes of consolation, a really great writer must not be afraid to change or edit his ideas. And he sat, oh, one full hour staring at that third blank sheet – or almost blank sheet for it did have a scratching on it – and drew much comfort from its expanse of white, a thrill even, which all great writers will tell you of – though some find confrontation with such blankness the most terrifying moment in their work: upon such endless white must be written – Literature.

Spring/Summer 1975

OPERATION
Al Alvarez

The town froze, close as a fist.
Winter was setting about us.
Like birds the bare trees shivered,
Birds without leaves or nests
As the fog took over.

My words were all gone, my tongue sour
We sat in the car like the dead
Awaiting the dead. Your hair
Wept round your face like a willow
Unstirring. Your eyes were dry.

Unbodied, like smoke in the crowd,
You vanished. Later came violence.
Not that you felt it or cared,
Swaddled in drugs, apart
In some fractured, offensive dream,
While a bog-Irish nurse mopped up.

'Leave me. I'm bleeding. There's blood
Still. But he didn't hurt me.'
Pale as the dead. As the dead
Fragile. Vague as the city
Now the fog chokes down again.
A life was pitched out like garbage.

'I'm bleeding. A boy, they said.'
My blood stings like a river
Lurching over the falls.
My hands are bloody. My mind
Is rinsed with it. Blood fails me.
You lie like the dead, still bleeding,
While his fingers, unformed, unerring,
Hold us and pick us to pieces.

Summer 1966

TEACHING NOGA THE HEBREW ALPHABET
Anne Atik

Her wide eyes move, fix.
Her small lips venture.
She's at the letter kaf, its khaf,
final khaf, like hope,
eleventh of a sacred script.
Looks up to see if it's correct, and smiles.
She says the letter twists like comet tails.
Her nine-year-old tongue English moulded
in names for dolls, her bed, a dove,
glides into the fitting angle.
Her red mouth bites into consonants
in 'kabed', the root for honour;
thy father and thy mother. God knows,
the remorse they bite me with for mine,
as for her faith in our unerring power.

From kaf she steps to lamed.
Chanting it, her cheek rounds out
like the mini-globe beside her.
Twelfth past the aleph and the beth,
past the beginning to a world
accustomed to as being there before her.
The letter reins in formlessness.
She now has less than half to go
before she reads a simple Hebrew line.
The words for apple, garden, waters, dove.
Before she reads of heaven and earth,
of the spirit that hovers.
No gong resounds, and yet,
though I've uttered no warning

Child, look where you're going,
she stops, dips, goes on with careful tread.
As though initiated.
As though aware that at the end
the primal words await her: Ani
Thou shalt   Thou shalt not

Summer 1989

SHALOM BOMB
Bernard Kops

I want a bomb, my own private bomb, my shalom bomb.
I'll test it in the morning, when my son awakes,
hot and stretching, smelling beautiful from sleep. Boom! Boom!

Come my son dance naked in the room.
I'll test it on the landing and wake my neighbours,
the masons and the whores and the students who live downstairs.

Oh I must have a bomb and I'll throw open windows and
count down as I whizz around the living room,
on his bike with him flying angels on my shoulder,
and my wife dancing in her dressing gown.

I want a happy family bomb, a do-it-yourself bomb.
I'll climb on the roof and ignite it there about noon.
My improved design will gong the world and we'll all eat lunch.

My pretty little bomb will play a daytime lullaby and
thank you bomb for now my son falls fast asleep.
My love come close, close the curtains, my lovely bomb, my darling,
my naughty bomb. Burst around us, burst between us, burst within
us. Light up the universe, then linger, linger
while the drone of the world recedes.

I want to explode the breasts of my wife. Ping! Ping!
In the afternoon and wake everyone,
to explode over playgrounds and parks, just as children
come from schools. I want a laughter bomb,
filled with sherbet fountains, liquorice allsorts, chocolate kisses,
candy floss,
tinsel and streamers, balloons and fireworks, lucky bags,
bubbles and masks and false noses.
I want my bomb to sprinkle the earth with roses.
I want the streets of the world to be filled with crammed, jammed
kids, screaming with laughter, pointing their hands with wonder,

at my lemonade ice-cream lightning and mouth organ thunder,
I want a one-man-band bomb. My own bomb.

My live long and die happy bomb, my die peacefully of old age bomb,
in our own beds bomb.
My Om Mane Padme Aum bomb, my Tiddley Om Pom bomb,
my goodnight bomb, my sleeptight bomb,
my see you in the morning bomb
I want my bomb, my own private bomb, my Shalom Bomb.

Summer 1966

NEW YEAR
Elaine Feinstein

Blue velvet, white satin, bone horn: once again
We are summoned today to consider mistakes and failures
into the shabby synagogue on Thompson's Lane.
Shopkeepers, scholars, children and middle-aged strangers
are gathering to mumble the ancient prayers,

because this is Rosh Hashonah, the New Year,
we have all come in out of the Cambridge streets
to look around and recognize the faces
of friends we almost think of as relations
and lost relations who never lived anywhere near.

How are we Jewish, and what brings us together
in this most puritan of protestant centres?
Are the others talking to God, or do they remember
filial duties, or are they puzzled
themselves at the nature of being displaced?

I sit and think of the love between brothers,
my sons, who never took to festivals
happily seated round a family table;
I remember their laughter rising up to my bedroom,
late at night, playing music and cards together.

And as I look back on too many surprises
and face up to next year's uncertainties,
somehow I find it easier and easier
to pray. And this September, hope at least for
perfumes rising from a scrubby hedge
if not from flowering Birds of Paradise.

Autumn 1986

A LIFE
Sacha Rabinovitch (1910-96)
Gabriel Josipovici

Nowadays one can get from Nice to La Bourboule and Le Mont-Dore in half a day. It took us eighteen hours. Amazingly, the train was not stopped. No Germans boarded it and asked to see our papers. Slowly it passed through the southern regions of France, out of the jaws of death and into the relative security of the Massif Central.

It was dark by the time it reached Lyon, and it stayed in the station for a long time. I remember waking and asking where we were. Lyon, came the reply. I thought of lions and shuddered. I am sure I had no idea what was going on, but the fear of those around me must have seeped through to me, and even today any journey by public transport requires a bit of an effort.

La Bourboule. The train stopped. The others helped Sacha with her luggage and handed me out to her. Then the train moved on, leaving her alone, heavily pregnant, with a two-year old child and her few possessions on the empty platform.

La Bourboule is situated in a narrow valley some 1,000 metres up in the Massif Central, the great chain of volcanic mountains that rises up to the north-west of Lyon. When I visited it with Sacha in September 1967, in an attempt to exorcize for her the memory of those war years, it had reverted to its old functions: long lines of French schoolchildren, scarves drawn up over their mouths and noses, wound their way from the baths to the drinking fountains, from the fountains to the pensions, for the mineral springs are what makes this the foremost children's spa in France. In 1943, of course, there were no such lines, though here, in contrast to the rest of France, the pattern of rural life went on much as it had always done. This was the great advantage to the refugee. It was off the beaten track, so the Gestapo and the French *milice* were unlikely to visit, except occasionally in search of the *maquis* who hid in the wooded hills all around; and, since this was farming country, food was more plentiful than in the barren south. It would still be expensive on the black market – Sacha was to exchange a dictionary for a pat of butter in the latter stages of the war – but at least it was available.

The first thing Sacha did was go and see the mayor. She had decided that it was too risky to hide under false identities, that I was too young to be able to remember who I was supposed to be, and that the best thing was to tell the truth and throw herself on the mercy of the authorities. The mayor was sympathetic and promised to do whatever he could, and issued her with the residence permits. When, a little later, she went back to ask him for a permit for Jean, who was coming to be with her at the birth, he granted that too without demur. Yet at the end of the war, when the reprisals against perceived collaborators took place, he was one of the first to be taken out and shot. Often they only used it as an excuse to settle old scores, Sacha told me. It sickened her almost more than the German atrocities and confirmed her in her feeling that she never wanted to live in France again.

Armed with her residence permit she found rooms with a dour French family, the Redons. At least, she thought, I would be able to play with their children during her confinement.

This was the only episode in her life that Sacha was reluctant to talk even to me about. I knew only that a little girl had been born who died shortly after. At Sacha's own death I realized with a shock that I did not even know my sister's name.

Once again my aunt Chickie obliged: 'You asked me about your baby sister. I think I know most of the little there is to know about her – she only lived for about ten days, you know – she couldn't have left much mark on you, she must have seemed like some sort of illness Sacha had and then recovered from. But she left a sort of double-edged mark on Sacha. Partly remorse because she had almost starved herself to feed you and knew that must have debilitated the baby – and partly relief because of a dream she'd had when she was only about twelve, that she was grown up and had a child of her own, a little boy, and they were in the garden, he was playing, with a hoop I think, and came running up to her – and fell dead at her feet. And ever since she'd had you she'd dreaded that that dream was a premonition like so many others she'd had and that something would happen to you. So when Elizabeth died she felt this doom had been hers (though she was the wrong sex, but with premonitions such details don't matter) and that you would survive.

'She wrote one of her best poems about that little girl – I only remember one line:

> petite fille de dix jours,
> petite morte pour toujours.

'The baby was born the day after she got to La Bourboule.'

As often with Chickie, her memory is not wholly accurate. For after I got her letter I found a poem, in English this time, among Sacha's papers, which makes it clear that the line should have read: 'Petite fille de douze jours'. Its last lines too are characteristic of the Sacha I knew – 'Idiot, I think' – even at such a moment it is the nurse's false show of emotion which arouses her anger:

A Small Death

That wartime winter in France.
The bare quite comfortless room.
And the dying twelve-day-old
held in cold hands, my daughter.

I am acquainted with death
from my childhood, but as loss
not physical fact. I have
never seen anyone die.

And now I am mainly afraid
as, in the crook of my arm,
I clasp her close to impart
what heat my body exudes

until the death rattle stops.
then: 'Prenez-la. Elle est morte.'
And the nurse, with feigned feeling:
'Oh non, non! Ma pauvre dame!'

Idiot, I think. We both know
this is what we expected
since dawn when she vomited
blood and the doctor mumbled:

'Il n'y a plus rien à faire.'

After Sacha's death Rosalind Belben said to me: 'She once told me that when the little girl died she only went on living because of you. If you had not been there to be looked after she would have killed herself.'

Alone, without friends, in an alien country, in the middle of a war, and not just any war but one in which the side that for a long time seemed likely to win was determined to rid the earth of people like her, and then to lose one's newborn child – no wonder she would not talk about it. No wonder she said, when asked why she didn't write her memoirs: 'It would bring back too much that was painful.'

But that she did not give up, that she transformed herself slowly and painfully into the person she became, the person who made so many people feel that life was a wonderful adventure, every moment of which must be lived, gives me the strength, now that she is no longer there, to keep going in my turn. I try to imagine those first months in La Bourboule and think: if she could get through that and become the person I came to know, then surely I should have no difficulty surviving her death.

There are two photos in her album which need to be looked at particularly closely. They show Sacha standing up against a tree, looking past the camera in one, in profile in the other. Her long dark hair is swept back, revealing her broad forehead, and falls thickly about her neck. She is wearing a dark pullover and the strip of a bag cuts into her right shoulder and passes just to the left of her right breast. At first sight these are just another set of photographs of a beautiful woman. But look a little more closely and you see in her eyes and in the set of her mouth that something has happened. These are photos of a survivor, of someone who is keeping going because that is what has to be done, but for whom all hope has been extinguished.

I don't know who took these photos or when exactly, but there they are on the page in the album devoted to La Bourboule. There is one more of her, with me in a pushchair, but she is too far away for her expression to be visible. The other photos – there are not many – are devoted to me: with the Redon children; alone, in white shorts and a dark shirt, standing in a park; smiling and holding a piece of paper in my hand; in a large wicker armchair with a little girl, on a balcony, with the sunlight falling across us as, totally absorbed, we bend over a book.

I don't know how long after the death of the little girl Jean stayed in La Bourboule. Not very long, I think. But my only two memories of him date from that time. Neither may be wholly accurate. In one he stands over my bed and says goodbye – or perhaps he does not say anything, I only have the sense that he is leaving. The other is more detailed. I am out for a walk with him and Sacha. We are strolling along a grassy path through a park. We come to a pair of large wrought-iron gates. He puts his hands round two of the vertical bars and pushes. Nothing happens. We'll have to climb over, he says. This is exciting. A chance to show what I'm made of. I haul myself up and jump down on the other side. I turn and see him pushing open the gate and laughing as he and Sacha pass through. In my anger I bend down and pull up a clump of grass. A blade of grass cuts my fingers.

Most days Sacha would take her rucksack and we would set out for the farm. The farmer had six children, the third exactly my age, so that he and his wife were only too pleased to exchange the clothes I had grown out of for provisions to supplement the meagre rations.

In the hotel room to which we had moved Sacha sewed and cut, so that what clothes she couldn't exchange she enlarged. She cut the letters of the alphabet out of wood and taught me to read. She carved strange figures on the tops of the stout sticks we had picked up on our walks. She read to me from the few books that were available and told me stories from the Bible: how Moses outwitted Pharaoh; how David escaped Saul; how Jesus died.

We moved again. In the new hotel, Sacha explained to me,

'Nous aurons deux chambres communicantes.'

'Qu'est-ce-q'une icante, Maman?'

She was perpetually hungry. Perpetually having to decide which her body and mind needed more: food or cigarettes. With cigarettes you could at least join up the butts of four or five and make an extra one. Almost as bad as the shortage of food and cigarettes was the shortage of books. There was one local bookstore, which had transformed itself into a lending library, but all they had was Balzac, so she read the *Comédie Humaine* from end to end. She had never liked Balzac and came to dislike him more and more as she worked her way through his grim novels in the course of those interminable months in that dark narrow valley.

She made friends in the hotel: 'There were some interesting people, washed up there by the war. There was one young woman I was particularly fond of. She was of Russian origin, had been abandoned by her lover. She tried to kill herself several times. Eventually, she succeeded.

'One of the *maquisards* had a bad tooth. The *maquis* came into town, commandeered the local dentist and his chair. They let the dentist go when he had dealt with the tooth, but kept the chair. After that when one went to the dentist's an assistant tilted the upright chair back and one prayed he wouldn't grow tired or the chair break just as the dentist was at work in one's mouth.'

On some days, if the snow was firm, we would walk the five kilometres up the mountain to the Mont-Dore, the adult spa, and back. It was at La Bourboule that Sacha and I got into the habit of our long walks together, which we never abandoned till, in her eighty-third year, what she had always dreaded came to pass and, emerging from a series of minor illnesses, she found she could no longer walk without pain.

'Once we were out for a walk and you suddenly darted away up the side of a hill to where a large goat was tethered. Talk to it before you touch it, I called out. "What shall I say?" you asked. "Introduce yourself. Gabriel David Josipovici, garçon." That was because, with your long fair curls, in Nice you had often been mistaken for a little girl.

'Once we were on the way to the Mont-Dore in deep snow and I was walking on ahead. Suddenly I realized you were no longer at my side. I turned round and you'd vanished. Then I caught sight of your cap bobbing up above the snow. You had stepped off the path and into a deep ditch.'

And then there was the radio. In the hotel people gathered closely round to listen clandestinely to Churchill and de Gaulle broadcasting from London. That mysterious country which in a sense she had been so familiar with as a child but had never got closer to than Berck-Plage, was once more playing a key role in her life. Because of England, because of Churchill, we were alive; perhaps because of them we would survive. The war was far from over, terrible things were going on, not only far away in Eastern Europe but right there in France, yet the tide seemed, to those who huddled round the set, to be definitely turning. The unthinkable was happening: Hitler and his armies were being pushed back on all fronts. Now it seemed just a matter of time before the Allies landed and France was liberated. But when would the day come?

It came on 6 June 1944. After months of rumours and counter-rumours the Allies finally landed in Normandy. On 25 August Paris was liberated. Three weeks later the Americans reached the German border. Meanwhile, on 15 August, a Franco-American force started to make its way up the Rhone valley. Allied flags were raised in La Bourboule, then quickly taken down again when it was rumoured that a fleeing German division was going to pass through. But the rumours proved unfounded and up went the flags again. By the end of 1944 the war in Europe was effectively over.

On 7 May 1945 the Germans surrendered unconditionally. In La Bourboule as in the rest of

France the victory celebrations were long and elaborate. There were greasy poles up which men had to climb to reach packets of food tied at the top, but even those who almost got there seemed to start sliding down just as they were reaching for their reward. When the champagne corks popped I hid under the table in fear. Is that sound, I wonder, mixed up in my mind with the sound of gunfire as the reprisals took place and the mayor of La Bourboule, along with so many others, was shot?

With communication with the outside world once more re-established Sacha wrote to Chickie: 'Gabriel is, I think, turning out to be a success. The only success in my life.' Chickie for her part got some money out to Sacha, enough for boat tickets back to Egypt. In late September we finally left La Bourboule for Marseille. The first boat on which Sacha was able to find berths was an English troop-ship, the *Arundel Castle*, due to sail from Toulon the following week. The only hotel she could afford had bugs in the beds and was so squalid we spent the days walking around the town, peering into the shops and restaurants. I remember an enormous fish, elaborately dressed, in the window of one restaurant, but nothing of what we actually ate. One day Sacha took me out to see the golden statue of the Virgin in the hills high above the city. It was, in a sense, the first of the many sight-seeing expeditions we would undertake together. Finally, into a British vehicle and the bumpy ride to Toulon.

The cabin had four bunks. The other two passengers, we were told, would be boarding at Malta. I tried each of the top bunks in turn before settling down for the night.

Sacha and I were already in bed when the boat docked at Malta. Two uniformed WAFs entered the cabin, turned on the lights, and began to dispose of their belongings. 'Look at these people!' one said to the other. 'Sleeping in all the beds and leaving their dirty handkerchiefs under the pillows. ' 'I'm sorry,' said Sacha from her bed. 'It's my son. He was so excited when we first got on board.'

Embarrassed, the WAFs retreated to the bar.

Every day at sea there was safety drill. The boat might hit a mine at any time and everyone had to be prepared to take to the lifeboats at a moment's notice.

I found a few other children on board and we played hide-and-seek. That I spoke only French and they only English did not seem to be a barrier.

On the evening of 7 October 1945, as the ship was preparing to dock at Port Said the following day, the WAFs saw Sacha putting out the few presents she had bought in Marseille by my bunk as I lay sleeping. 'Is it a birthday?' they asked, still anxious to make up for their gaffe on the first evening. 'Yes,' Sacha said. 'He'll be five tomorrow.'

After rummaging in their bags the two ladies produced some bars of chocolate and laid them alongside the other presents. Not only that. They spread the news, and the following day there were dozens of bars tied to various parts of the deck and we children were let loose to try and find them and climb up to get them. So, as the boat docked in the harbour at Port Said, the war ended for me with the sheer excitement of searching and climbing and then eating this unimaginably sweet, this delicious new food.

Faut pas en manger trop, tu te sentiras mal.

Oui, Maman.

Voilà. Nous sommes arrivés.

C'est ça l'Egypte?

Oui, Gabriel. C'est ça.

Winter 1998-9

THE BLOOD OF THE LAMB
Bernice Rubens

When you see a woman in her forties, who, since you have known her, has always worn jeans, sandals, and sweaters, the dampers that soft-pedal the passing of the years, when you see that same woman wearing a fur coat, you know that her mother has died.

So you compose your face as you see her coming towards you, ruling out anticipation, preparing for surprise, and you wait for her to inform you.

'Hullo, Rose. How are you?'

'Not so good. My mother died last week.'

'Oh, I'm sorry.' Now take your eyes off the coat that screams inheritance, but where can you look that isn't suddenly Persian Lamb? Even Rose's hair has caught its black curly texture.

'Hence the coat.' Rose is saying in apology.

'It's nice,' you say, the hypocrite you are. What's nice about Persian Lamb? A bequest fur, exclusively. Who in their right mind would buy it pristine off the ewe? A hand-me-down, rifled from a moth-balled wardrobe before the grass has time to grow. Then you notice the diamond ear-rings and your eye goes naturally to the fingers, and sure enough, the matching rings are there too. Poor Rose. She tucks in her ears and her hands, but only into the collar and muff of the lamb. 'Come back for a coffee,' she says, and you know that her familiar bedsitter, lined with books and records, now blushes for the invasion of alien silver and linen.

'The place is in a bit of a mess.' Rose is saying, her key in the door. Rose's place was always in a mess, but she'd never apologized for it. You didn't apologize for books strewn on the floor, records out of their sleeves, and a desk cluttered with ash, paper and files. It was your own mess, and you had made it and it spoke of the work and the living of which you were not ashamed. But the mess that Rose was apologizing for was none of her making. It spoke not one syllable of her way of life. It was another's intrusion, another's chaos.

There was hardly room to open the door, and you had to go in singly, picking your way over chests of linen, cabinets of silver, the cluttered savings of another's mistaken priorities. 'What can I do with it all,' Rose is saying, but not asking, because you know that she is just stating a problem that she dares not solve. And you, being logical, sensible, and momentarily insensitive, say, 'Sell it,' and you look at her face and you see a friendship dying. You cover up, make the coffee, threading your way through the effects to the kitchen.

'She had a miserable life,' Rose is saying, huddled in her mother's lamb. 'Wouldn't spend a penny on herself. Saved, invested. Here it all is. And she did it for me. She was a good mother.' This last in almost a whisper, with too little confidence in its truth to spread it abroad.

'You were a good daughter,' you say, because it seems a natural corollary. Though you knew bloody well that Mrs Feigal was a rotten mother, that nothing Rose ever said or did was quite good enough, that everything merited her constant disapproval. That she had driven her own long-suffering husband to an early grave with her interminable expectations, and that for the length of her bitter widowhood, she had kept Rose by her, in the same bedroom even, and in at ten every night or she would want to know why, and who is this new feller of yours, what's his *geschäft*, and you haven't got a better dress, and must you always be with the glasses? Until Rose was pushing thirty, and looking around. and hearing the dull thunder of the years nudging her limbs, in one wild moment of sanity, she stuffed some carrier-bags, and without blessing, left her mother's house. That had been ten years ago. Ten years since her mother had threatened a heart-attack. Ten years since that heart-attack had refused to oblige, till in the end, it was bitterness and a consuming rage that carried her off, the old lady had simply died of anger. And still, from her seething grave, she refused to let Rose go, hanging on by the not-so-thin thread of Persian Lamb, shrouding her with the best linen and the blackmail of EPNS. Well, it takes two to tango, you tell yourself, but that only obtains when both partners are alive. Rose should have stopped dancing while her mother's stubborn heart still beat. What point now in such advice, when the rhythm had so taken you over that a partner was redundant.

You pour the coffee, and wish to God Rose would take off the coat, but she wraps it round her as if it gives her some sick comfort. 'Why don't you take it off?' you practically shout at her. 'And diamond ear-rings look silly during the day.' You throw away what's left of your poor discretion, because you don't want to see your friend chain herself to what now can only be the future.

She fingers the fur, as if to annoy you. 'I wish your mother the best of health, but one day, you may be in the same position as I.'

And that's precisely why you're shouting at her, because you too fear the lamb, and may your dear mother live for ever but there's no harm in a dress rehearsal if the authentic set is handed to you on a plate. Different location, it's true, but the dialogue's the same. You make a mental note to ring your mother that evening, after six o'clock, the cheap-rate time, not for your own thrift, but for hers, who would take offence at anyone's extravagance on her behalf.

'What can I do?' Rose is still saying.

'You can do one of two things,' you say, and hope that when your time comes, please God, not too soon, she, Rose, will be the sensible one. 'You can keep it, or you can sell it. If you keep it, you'll have to find a bigger flat to accommodate it all. And a posher place it'll have to be to live up to it. Or you sell it, and you use the money for the things you've always wanted. Travel, for instance.'

Rose shudders at your insulting logic. 'She never travelled,' she is saying. 'Southend, maybe. once or twice in her life. She was saving it for me.' Then you lose your cool, and you say, knowing that Rose is the end of the line, and now too unnaturally old to prolong it, you say, 'And who are you saving it for?' But all that succeeds in doing is to remind her of the barrenness of her own life, and the tears begin to flow. You get up to comfort her, climbing over the linen chest between you. And you slip, and the coffee upsets, and runs over the chest, seeping through the cracks on to the virgin linen inside. Rose leaps up like a panther and tears the chest open, winces at the trickle of coffee that slithers over the embroidered sheets and tablecloths, a gentle waterfall with the destructive force of a Niagara. 'Look what you've done,' she whimpers, crouching like a skinflint over his pile. And you look at her and marvel at how quickly the rot can set in.

'I'll go,' you say, doing yourself more of a favour than her, for you want to get out of there, back to your furless, linenless dwelling, and you pray to God that whatever the price, your own mother will live for ever.

You're back in your own bed-sitter, and you're dialling furiously, - to hell with the cheap rate - and your heart is beating while she doesn't answer, and you pray she is there and well, and when at last you hear her martyred and long-suffering 'Hullo,' you are not surprised at the overwhelming love that invades you.

'Momma?'

'Oh my God, what's the matter?'

'Nothing Momma, nothing at all. Just phoning to say hello.'

'At this time of day? So much money you have?' And at the sound of her familiar disapproval, you feel at peace and back in battle, and you thank God that she lives to irritate you so.

'I just felt like talking to you.'

'I thought a husband at least you've found.' she is saying. 'Only for such a reason should you behave like a Rothschild.'

'But how are you?' you insist.

'I'm not complaining,' she is saying, complaining all the time, 'though if I saw you settled down in my lifetime, believe you me, I shouldn't have such aggravation.'

'How's your back?' you say, easing her into specifics.

'Not so good, but I'm not complaining,' and you know she's not complaining because in the middle of the day, at twenty pence a minute, it's cheaper to be well and without detail.

'You should go on a holiday,' you say. 'Go to America to see the family.'

'Holidays,' she sneers, 'who can afford holidays.' and you can see the solid Georgian silver shrieking behind her in the cabinet, and you know it could take her round the world a dozen times.

'You still going to Paris?' she asks joylessly.

'I have to go to a teachers' conference,' you say, not daring to suggest for one moment that you might be going for pleasure.

'All right, so when you come back, perhaps I'll go to America,' she says, as if one of you has to stay at home to look after England.

'Look after yourself, Momma,' you say.

'Who else should look after me?' But you pass that one over, and tell her you'll ring her later in the week, and she tells you to do it after six o'clock, for nothing is that important, living or dying, that cannot wait to be told till the cut-price hour.

'I love you Momma,' you hear yourself saying, and you hear her silence and know she is smiling.

'You're a good daughter to me.'

'And you're a good mother,' you mouth, and as you put the phone down, you pray to God, that whatever the price, your mother's senility, her irritations, her possessiveness, her stubbornness, her pride, whatever it costs, please God, do what You will with me, but save me from the Lamb.

You let a few days pass before you call on Rose again, and when you do, it takes her some time to open the door. Through the glass pane you can see her fumblings, and you hear the cries of locks and chains. There was a time, you remember, when Rose's door was always open, and casual coffee drinkers dropped in and out. Now the hassle of opening up the place as if it were some museum precluded the casual visitor, and even you begin to doubt whether you will call again. She opens the door gingerly, and asks you inside, warning your hands off the wires that lead down from the door and touch off the burglar alarm. You feel suddenly as if you've come to the wrong place, and when you enter the living-room, you look for traces of your friend. Where are the records and the books, even the desk and the papers that throbbed through the years of Rose. Quiet now, the pulse gone from the room, stilled by the bird's eye maple table, and its linen cloth, numbed by the cabinet of silver, wholly anaesthetized by inheritance.

'Where are your books?' you say.

'I sold them.'

'Where do you work. Where's the desk?'

'Given it up,' she says. 'I have enough to live on, thanks to my dear mother, God rest her soul.'

What's this? you ask yourself. This 'dear mother' bit, this 'God rest her soul?' Where did she pick up this middle-aged obsequious phraseology, she, who only a while ago was in monosyllabic and fearless jeans? And you have to face the truth, that when Rose's mother died, it was Rose, who, by her own and helpless choice, was buried.

'Shall I make coffee?' you say, more for old times' sake.

But no. Sit down. Rose will make it, like any good hostess, but now it takes hours to prepare, with respect to the Crown Derby and the sideplates, and embroidered serviettes for God's sake, and Rose with her manicured little finger curled round the bone-china handle. And you long to go back to your Woolworth mugs, and the freedom of your comparative poverty.

'How is your mother?' Rose is saying, and you know that her question has nothing to do with concern.

'Immortal,' you say, viciously.

You get up to go, but she presses you to another cake, and suddenly you can't bear the lace doily and the silver cake fork, and all the monogrammed paraphernalia that has nothing to do with your old and loved friend, and you scream to yourself, 'I'm not an orphan yet. I cannot live like this.'

Rose sees you out coldly, with much locking of doors behind, and you know that she resents you because you are still a daughter, that you still live, and that she but survives.

Small comfort in that, for you know too, and with an absolute and trembling certainty, that sooner or later, when the lamb comes to colonize you, Rose will be your friend again.

21st Anniversary anthology, 1974

KADDISH
Tony Dinner

Break the stone over the threshold,
Let the wind in.
The wind has come down from the Mountain.
The wind has gushed out of the wound in the hills,
And wound you in.
There you lie, in a spathe of white cotton,
Stiller than a stone.
God announces His Presence in a whirlwind,
Shifting landscapes in a sudden sleight-of-hand.
The hot wind has poured dust into your throat,
Gathered up your wings and stilled your beating heart.
Come in under the shadow of My wings, saith the Lord,
And I will wash away the tears from off all faces.
Break the stone and let the spirit crumble into dust.

Come home, Dad. Come on. Get up now.
The game's over. Don't stretch it out.
Why are you being like this? Dad!
I've never had to say this to you before.
People are beginning to stare. You're being rude.
It's not funny. Please come home. Please, Dad.
We'll all be waiting for you. You'll see.
This would all be so much easier to bear
If you were here. O, come on, Dad. Come home.
The gesture is too frail; the word too weak.

The wind goes round, and round, and round.
They pour your body in the hole like sand.
We're dumb, and dumb, and dumb.

May Peace be in your bones
And in the hollows of your skull.
We shall take pleasure
From your stones, and love your dust.

A white bird flies in a white sky, silently.

Out of the black hole in the ground, God spoke to me and said:
I have My Otherness. I cannot comfort you.

Autumn 1986

IN THE MONTH OF TAMMUZ
Gabriel Levin

In memoriam Gabriel Preil

I

I can only guess the gist
of Ibn Gabirol's words
locking the rhyme-bearing verse
into place. For my soul

is dismayed and sorely afraid,
reads Zangwill's version (1923),
lifting the phrase
out of Ezekiel's shipwreck,

though even there the Hebrew
might depict a squall at sea,
or else hair standing on end.

– Anyhow, I'm tempted to speak
of the precise arrangement of vowels,
how measure was plainly thought

to keep the poem from corrupting
in the mouth of the reciter,

and leave it at that.

II

All those little notes and queries to yourself
rousing you from Oblomov's sleep.

A flourish of your pen,
and Hebrew enveloped you in a fine cloud

extending reticent tendrils of rain.

Tu Fu dreaming of Li Po
might have been dreaming of you, old friend,

as moonlight drenched your room
'to the roof-beams', and you lingered there

on the terrace, before turning in.

Winter 1996-7

'YES, MADAM'
Wanda Barford

'Fetch your blanket',
she said to the houseboy,
'and sleep in the kitchen
till the boss comes home.'
'Yes, madam,' he replied.

The Mau-mau
was spoken of at bridge and tea parties.
Father would be late back
from his Masonic lodge.

Uneasy, she asked the boy:
'if your brothers
in the Freedom Movement
told you to kill me,
you wouldn't do it, would you?'

'Yes, madam,' he replied.

Spring 1998

6

ISRAEL

Advertisement for Barclays Bank / *Summer 1956*

RELIGIOUS QUARTER
A.C. Jacobs

Grandfather, today I walked in Mea Shearim
And it was a little like it must have been
In Vilna seventy years ago.
                              Small boys
Walked between their dangling curls
With already the strange sensuality of Talmud
Scholars. Merchants, in fur hats, relaxed
In the slow pace of their closed, coinless
Sabbath; matrons went with their love blown
Away into a nagging over-all warfare
And young girls were concealing their sex
In a terrible kind of shapelessness.
                              And all this
Under the hot sky of Jerusalem.

It was a little, grandfather, of the sea
Of the past, out of which you sailed
To leave me in the north,
                              Whose speech
I take to tame, oh, centuries of such
Isolated quarters striving in my blood.

Spring 1968

THE LAST ROMANTICS
T. R. Fyvel

The memories of a stay in a kibbutz are apt to linger. Mine do so across nearly fifty years. In its early history, in my father's day, Zionism had been a romantic affair, and I felt that I caught a last glimpse of this romanticism in Palestine in the Emek, the broad Vale of Jezreel, in 1935 and 1936. This was during stays at the Hashomer Hatzair's star kibbutz of Mishmar Haemek, beautifully situated on a spur of the mountains of Ephraim on the southern side of the Emek, near Megiddo.

This was a time when we were all still young, including the members of Mishmar Haemek and the whole Kibbutz movement. The one hundred and twenty members of the kibbutz were nearly all in their very early thirties, half of them young parents. I had come from Cambridge University and knew what elitism meant, and I could see at once that the intelligent and bright looking men and women of Mishmar Haemek were a very elitist group of young Jews. They generally derived from well-to-do, assimilated bourgeois Jewish families in Warsaw and other large cities in Poland. It was mostly as boys and girls in the lycée in the stormy years after the First World War, when the winds of every left-wing opinion swept through their ranks, that they had as the original generation joined the Hashomer Hatzair movement which aimed at the left-wing settlement of young Jews in Palestine. To their often distraught bourgeois parents, this must have seemed like taking part in a Zionist variant of revolutionary Communism. I was told that when the group, mostly still adolescents under age, left for Palestine in 1921, some anxious parents even tried to get the Polish guards to hold them back.

By the time I came, the members had themselves developed what seemed a stable family and working life. Back in fading memory now were their first intoxicating years in a primitive Palestine, when they danced the Hora every night and sang '*Emek, Emek, avodah*' ('Valley, valley of work'), before wandering off in pairs into the darkness. By now they were mostly young married couples – secularly married – and firmly settled for seven years in their beautiful, relatively affluent (for the time) showpiece kibbutz, whose land and initial capital had been provided for them by Zionist institutions. However, one thing I found odd was that officially the settlers still announced themselves as convinced Marxists, sometimes talking as if they regarded themselves as the much misunderstood sector of an international revolutionary working class movement, linked to a Soviet Union temporarily estranged from them, an alienation they tried to explain away as a misunderstanding. Coming as I did from a very different British background, this leftism which seemed to me purely theoretical, mystified me. I could well understand the passionate Zionist feelings of the members, their sense of Jewish nationhood. I could make sense of the elitism which made them keep Mishmar Haemek and other Hashomer Hatzair kibbutzim small and exclusive in their membership. But their theories of pro-Soviet Zionist-Marxism seemed to me so out of place in a British colonial Palestine that I thought of them just as a rather engaging trait of these young kibbutz socialists, which one need not take too seriously, for all that they themselves appeared to do so.

My sponsor in the kibbutz was Mietek (Mordecai) Bentov, an amiable if solemn ideologist who was to become a minister in the first government of the State of Israel. At that earlier time, in the thirties, he bore responsibility within the Hashomer Hatzair movement for relations with Jews in 'the Anglo-Saxon countries', a task in which he thought I could be of help. He had tried, so far without success, to convert me to his Zionist-Marxist outlook, but politics apart, as far as the life of this elitist kibbutz was concerned, I had little difficulty in surrendering myself to its seductive rhythms.

In my memory, the sheer beauty of the surroundings of Mishmar Haemek is closely bound up with the attraction of its daily life. Dramatically situated on the foothills of the mountains of Ephraim, the kibbutz at evening enjoyed a cool sea-breeze even in the broiling summer. If most of the membership still lived austerely in wooden huts, the attractive architecture of the children's house and the school hinted at more affluent times to come. From above one overlooked the broad Vale of Jezreel, whose large wheat fields and distant Jewish settlements shimmered in pastel colours in the midday heat, with the small Arab town of Nazareth lying like a brown smudge upon the high hills opposite and the peak of Mount Hermon, snowcapped for most of the year, floating on the horizon like a Japanese water-colour. Then, towards evening, the dusty pastel browns and greens of the Valley faded to deep blue and then black, and in the clear night air the lights of Arab Nazareth opposite, miles away, shone so steadily they seemed almost next door.

Like most of the Vale of Jezreel, the area had been stony and marshy ground when the kibbutz had arrived seven years before. In 1935, on the flat plain below, the kibbutz cultivated some 3,000 dunam of rich fields of wheat, barley and corn, worked with the most modern devices of the day – tractors, combines, bale compressors and machine ploughs. On the slope above the settlement, suitable for dry farming, there was a splendid orchard of a hundred dunam and next to it a vineyard of equal size. Above that was a Jewish National Fund forest of 1,000 dunam of pine trees worked by the kibbutz.

From up there I found myself often looking at the Arab village on the next spur – which had one bent tree. In the distance one could see the small figures of its inhabitants. The Arab village had not been harmed by the kibbutz; on the contrary, it had benefited from the swamp clearance and from a little emulation. But it was kept out of mind – it was just part of the landscape.

The work in the orchard, in which in an amateurish way I accompanied a friendly mentor, was concerned with defence against parasites and the rows of plum, pear, apricot, apple and other fruit trees looked admirably cared for. After a few days it was quite evident to me why Mishmar Haemek was destined for the outstanding economic success it and other kibbutzim were eventually to achieve. The settlers were a selected group of young people, highly motivated to the collective success of their work. They had the political and financial support of the Zionist Organisation, while an urban market for their produce was springing up at their door. The growing of fruit in Jewish Palestine was by 1935 making swift progress. Jewish settlers, who had studied in France, Italy and California, were growing fruit with familiar world names – Satsuma, Formosa, Burbank, Ogen, Santa Rosa. They were continuously grafting, watching and tabulating the results and had already succeeded in producing magnificently large and marketable fruit. This was certainly the case in Mishmar Haemek, where my mentor, as we walked between the rows of scented trees, explained how part of the orchard was used for experimental research to discover the deciduous fruit trees most suitable for Palestine.

I was also quickly aware of another fact. While those who could not take the discipline of the kibbutz had dropped out, the members who remained seemed what would today be called 'high' – in the sense of feeling inspired by this discipline in their lives and work. One has to remember the world situation in that ominous time. Over in Europe, catastrophe threatened as Hitler advanced on his deadly antisemitic rampage. Against this threat, the members set their romantic vision of the importance of a Jewish Palestine and of Jewish agriculture and a Jewish kibbutz socialism as transforming the Jewish character. In this context, every moment of kibbutz work and life had a special significance.

In a curious way, I found that for me the days of the elitist kibbutz had a cumulatively dreamlike quality. At five on a warm summer morning, a penetrating gong rung by one of the armed night watchmen always on patrol sets the kibbutz astir, young men and women in rough working clothes, dim-eyed with sleep, drift into the communal dining hall for a sip of tea and a quick glance at the work schedule and then proceed to their allotted tasks in the fields, the workshops, the laundry, the children's house, in a silence redolent of a determination to face another day.

At eight o'clock, when breakfast is served in a crowded dining hall, the silence is magically dispelled by the loud voices of the members as they sit at packed tables covered with breadcrumbs and glasses of tea, with eggs, olives and tomatoes and the general smell of food. After eight o'clock, the workers return to the fields for the longest and hottest spell of work (from the distant grain fields one could not return before midday: I can still recall the welcome metallic taste of swigs from the cooled water bottle).

The midday meal consists of another half hour of crowded eating and talk, talk, talk in the dining hall. For the next hour, the kibbutz appears heavily asleep. All is silent, all I can hear is the sound of slowly moving cattle, the breath of the wind, and the tap-tap of motor pumps at work. At two o'clock the gong awakens the kibbutz for the afternoon spell of work; as a rule, a breeze now begins to bring relief from the heat. Towards six, the working spell is over for the majority, but the second part of the kibbutz day is only beginning.

The cool of the evening brings the children's hour. On the central lawn, the young kibbutz parents gather to relax and to play with their children, who have a look of clean-limbed outdoor youngsters, unselfconscious in true kibbutz style. I am told that because of the perpetual burden of discipline in kibbutz life, the escape for an hour into the carefree intimacy of family life with children is particularly treasured and that bonds between the generations are close and tender - I can well believe this.

In the evening the members are free to pursue their own occupations, but at least half are busily engaged on various work and social committees. Later, between nine and ten, the gong is often rung for the full assembly of all the members of Mishmar Haemek. The members seem short on sleep, but I found these nightly assemblies fascinating. The questions discussed could range from the problems of the work roster, the building of a new cowshed or defects in the machine repair shop to the building of world socialism. I noticed that whenever economic problems or defects were being discussed, the earnest kibbutz secretary, a humorously regarded character, would talk of a *matzav catastrophi*, a catastrophic situation . . . I also noted that although by day the working members might move in heavy silence like peasants, these nightly debates in the crowded dining hall, especially when local or world politics were touched upon, could become a very Jewish occasion. Emotions flared, partisanship could seem fierce as point after point was exhaustively gone over.

I also noticed another thing. The members of the kibbutz were 'high' in that group decisions to take action were never taken by a majority vote. Final unanimity was required and it was nearly always achieved. It was achieved romantically, in a Zionist way, I thought. In the early days of the Zionist Movement, when Chaim Weizmann, Martin Buber and my father worked together as young men at the turn of the century, Zionism had been very much a movement for young romantics. The young settlers at Mishmar Haemek could seem another such romantic Zionist generation, the last, perhaps, when one thought of Hitler in Europe and the ambivalent British colonial policies in Palestine and the to me puzzling extreme left-wing political views one could hear voiced in the kibbutz.

I thought I could understand why. No doubt it was better to sit on the lawn at Mishmar Haemek in the cool of the evening with one's children than to live as an insecure Jew in the Warsaw of their parents or to stand in a crowded Tel Aviv bus, but the members had not come to Palestine just to live in escapist socialist islands, and subsidized islands at that. They were too intelligent for such a course. For them, beyond its own restricted life, the kibbutz had to have a political purpose, an all-Jewish purpose, and with it an international political purpose.

That was a first point. The second point was that these young men and women had joined the Hashomer Hatzair as enthusiastic teenagers during the great Bolshevik revolutionary era when their own heads were full of youthful revolutionary ideas; and, although they had turned their backs squarely on official Communism and came to Palestine as convinced Zionists, they had for their political self-esteem to tell themselves that they were still revolutionaries. This desire, it seemed to me, found expression in these hot nightly debates in which the members found refuge from the realities of British-ruled Palestine in the dreams of a revolutionary Jewish-Arab Eretz Israel.

Within this dream, the present day was a mere small-scale starting point. Palestine and adjacent empty areas were a place where eventually eight or ten or twelve million Jews would be settled. Within this place, the kibbutzim were not just socialist islands but socialist strongholds to prepare for the eventual socialist Eretz Israel to come. From this thought all other views were derived. The bourgeois Jews of the West might be reactionary, but in so far as they supported Zionism financially they were helping to finance kibbutzim and so they were *objectively* helping socialism along. Arab hostility? A minor local problem. There was an answer here, too. Of course, as their immigration progressed, the educated Jewish workers would have to organize their Arab fellow-workers. But one could not start this task with ignorant fellaheen, who were so deplorably without class-consciousness in obeying their nationalist Arab landlords.

No, the start of Jewish-Arab cooperation would take place as between the Jewish workers and the newly educated Arab working class which would spring up in the towns alongside Jewish mass immigration. These Arabs would no longer let their reactionary local leaders, the rich effendis and big landowners, sway them towards sterile anti-Zionism and away from their class interests as Arab workers in a Jewish socialist state in which they, too, would have their proper role. In fact, all such problems could be solved within the wider context of Jewish colonization in Palestine, which nothing must be allowed to interrupt.

The argument could become tortuous. Britain was a reactionary capitalist and imperialist power hostile to the Soviet Union and so ought to be opposed by the members – in fact, from a few members I heard some pretty benighted views in favour of Stalin's despotism. But however autocratic British Mandatory rule in Palestine was, it prevented the Arab majority from stopping Jewish immigration and for this reason the British Mandate had to be supported: it was *objectively* progressive in providing for the emergence of a progressive Jewish working class, which would provide for that of its Arab counterpart.

I thought it all rationalization, but another point occurred to me. Hashomer Hatzair theories were really like a new Jewish secular religion. To settle in Mishmar Haemek, the members had walked out on a home background where orthodox Jewish religion explained and justified every corner of Jewish life, or almost everything. As the original Hashomer Hatzair generation, the settlers had really come to Palestine with a complete substitute religion in their Marxist-Zionism, which equally had an answer to every political question in tidying up the world.

I had elsewhere talked with Western fellow-travellers of Stalin and I supposed that the pretended Marxist stance of the settlers did no harm – except in terms of the basic Jewish-Arab conflict in Palestine. At that time, in 1935, the number of Jews seeking refuge in Palestine from the Nazi threat in Europe was rising steadily, in spite of obvious British manoeuvres to reduce the flow. The big Arab landowners were continuing to sell land to the Jews at high profits, while inciting their fellaheen tenants to acts of violence against the Jews and the British – violence which in the following year was to erupt into the countrywide series of Arab strikes and shooting known as the Troubles. I was also aware that at Mishmar Haemek a detachment of the *Hagana*, the Jewish defence force, was each night on patrol at the barbed wire defences of the settlement. Given all the circumstances, given Hitler, perhaps there was no alternative. Still, I felt that in this context the settlers' notion of letting Jewish-Arab cooperation await the emergence of a class conscious Arab proletariat – this notion seemed to me a total evasion of realities. Perhaps those Jewish leaders in Palestine who thought that conflict with the Arabs was inevitable but that the need to save Jews from Hitler overrode everything else – perhaps they were more honest. Yet I asked myself: if the members of Mishmar Haemek wanted at all costs to see themselves as idealists, was their Marxist evasion of ugly realities not forced on them? I wavered in my views.

During the next year, 1936, I again visited Mishmar Haemek, this time while a conference of delegates from all the Hashomer Hatzair kibbutzim was in progress. I watched some of the meetings. I thought that in their Zionist as opposed to their Marxist role, in dealing with technical, educational and social problems, the delegates were most businesslike and efficient, but when it came to politics it was all very different. There was my friend Mietek Bentov talking about advances of the movement in 'the Anglo-Saxon countries': what I thought he had in mind were grants from affluent Jewish supporters. Then there was the movement's leading political 'theoretician,' Meir Ya'ari, whom I watched in a detached way. He was a short, dark man with a fierce expression, who walked up and down in the kibbutz with his hands behind his back and seemed to fight against any attempt to dilute the purity of the movement's left-wing line. News had come from Moscow of Stalin's mock trials of his old Bolshevik comrades, who had of course all confessed to heinous crimes. While Ya'ari did not believe in the complete guilt of the accused, he was rigidly opposed to the idea that the Hashomer Hatzair should align itself with 'the capitalist critics of Stalin'. Ah, me!

Also present was another leader, Ya'akov Chazan; he was a large man with features I found fascinating; they were so Slav, so un-Jewish, that he could have stepped straight out of an early Soviet film . . . He was reputedly a political moderate, though not on this occasion. At Westminster, the idea of a partition of Palestine had been mentioned, and in a discussion one member asked: 'When an ordinary man, neither a Jew nor an Arab, reads that Jews and Arabs are continuously fighting for Palestine, wouldn't he also think it the fairest way to divide the country?' From Chazan there at once came an answer I remember. 'Division of Palestine? It's only a British imperialistic trick to destroy Zionism. Ask the least educated Arab sheikh, and he would laugh at the idea that the British had offered a people of sixteen million a territory fifty miles square in which to settle!'

A state fifty miles square for the sixteen million Jews in the world – that would indeed be absurd. Only what had this to do with a solution to the immediate conflict going on in Palestine between half a million Jews and a million Arabs, with two full divisions of British troops leaning towards the Arab side in ineffectively trying to keep order?

One evening shortly before my departure I went walking with S., who could be described as the cultural editor of the movement, and who was an interesting writer and charming companion. We walked past the laden fruit trees in the orchard and up into the scented pine forest above the settlement and returned to sit on the central lawn. I gazed at the view of the darkening hills around Nazareth and the fading outline of Mount Hermon and I watched the young parents around me with their children who seemed so enviably free from care.

I mentioned this feeling to S., who said he sometimes had an idea that in each generation, a group of young people were selected by history for a special task. He said: 'In our own time, after the war, it was young Jews from Europe like ourselves who were chosen to shape their lives on behalf of an ideal – we should be conscious of our great fortune.'

It seemed a possible idea. I looked across in the evening light at the Arab village next door, that wretched village with only one bent tree, and said: 'Really, why don't you start with Jewish-Arab co-operation now? You have such a magnificent large orchard here – why don't you go across and help these Arabs to plant a small orchard?'

S. smiled at the naivety of the idea. One could not cooperate with illiterate fellaheen who were incited by their effendis to hate Jews; one had to wait for an Arab proletariat to develop side by side with a Jewish working class, etc.

For once I was impatient. Why could S. not say what must be on his mind? 'You must be thinking day and night about your Hashomer Hatzair fellow groups still left behind in Poland waiting for immigration to Palestine – waiting desperately, I imagine, faced with the Nazi threat. You can't be diverted into consolidating those Arabs next door, because your whole priority is for the Jewish National Fund to purchase more Arab land on which to settle some of those Hashomer Hatzair groups in Poland in accord with British immigration regulations. I can perfectly well understand this!'

S., that sensitive kibbutz scholar who thought himself one of a fortunate generation, smiled and was unmoved. It was of course true that the movement was straining every nerve to bring further Hashomer Hatzair training groups from the diaspora to Palestine. But only future Jewish mass immigration could lay a basis for cooperation with Arab peasants and workers.

It was the official line of the movement, but I did not argue. I was after all about to depart on the road that led me first to a stay in Tel Aviv and then back to London . . . It seemed to me that evening that if my Zionist friends at Mishmar Haemek who were so successful in their elitist kibbutz life consoled themselves by building up Marxist left-wing theories about themselves, well, they were the last Zionist romantics. Let them keep their illusions. They would do so anyway.

Shortly after my return to Tel Aviv, the Spanish civil war broke out, an overture to the greater war to come. In Palestine, the anti-Zionist and anti-British Arab incidents flared into sporadic, nationwide violence – 'the Troubles.' During these, Mishmar Haemek was besieged by Arab bands led by a Syrian guerilla, Fawzi Kawkaji. For a day or so I was afraid for my friends, but needlessly. The attack on the kibbutz was successfully beaten off.

As time passed, I was never in doubt that my friends at Mishmar Haemek would turn it into the prosperous, model kibbutz it would become, with an almost Californian look and every possible gadget, unrecognizable from the cluster of wooden huts I remembered from 1935. As for the political philosophy of the Hashomer Hatzair movement, later absorbed into the left-wing Mapam party of Israel, I also did not doubt that it would consistently add a liberal and humane minority element to the Israeli political spectrum, all the way to Mapam's outright opposition to Begin and Sharon. Only I never felt that Mapam as a party would play any special role in the resolution of the Arab-Jewish conflict. Whether as Hashomer Hatzair or as Mapam, the movement never had any special links with the Arabs, no more than other Israeli bodies, if no less. In their dream of a Marxist-Zionist-Arab future in a socialist Palestine, the members of Mishmar Haemek in their beauty spot had simply been the last romantics of a Zionist era which, with the establishment of the State of Israel has undergone considerable changes.

Autumn/Winter 1983

THE KEY TO JUDAH'S CAMP
Shopping and Orientalism
Zvi Jagendorf

Say *shook* or *shuq*, *suk* or *souq*; it sounds like the same thing in an untrained throat. This is one of those pairs of words that makes the connection between Hebrew and Arabic seem obvious, even natural, which may be an illusion but makes sense when it comes to markets. Along with harems, Turkish baths and camel trains, they are an icon of the Middle Eastern spectacle of commerce and indolence sanctified by travel writers, guidebooks and Orientalist painting for centuries.

Walk through many towns in the Mediterranean basin and you will sooner or later find yourself in a crowded street shaded from the sun with dark shops narrow in front but tunnelling backward mysteriously into low buildings. The shops are set apart according to goods and services offered: the pillow stuffers and the copper merchants, the butchers and the bakers, the spice merchants and the cloth sellers. Some of the great and ancient markets of Egypt, Turkey and Syria are entirely covered, set in a network of quite impressive buildings so that the street life takes place inside. But the more humble sort are out in the open, part of the town in a place where they have always been, where produce could arrive with ease and where the buyers and sellers could meet conveniently. If they haven't always been there, they may have been put there by some decree of a sultan, a commissioner or a mayor and his town council. More likely, they just happened – and, though inconvenient now because of traffic and overcrowding, they won't go away.

Mahane Yehudah or Judah's Camp has been the main food market of Jerusalem outside the Turkish walls for almost a hundred years. It is not a venerable market like the great markets of the Arab world or its sister market in the Old City. It is a messy chaotic market born of the move of Jews from the Old City to modern Jerusalem and the subsequent development of the city and the growth of its population. It is almost a hundred years old but it may be more defined by the digestion, disappearance and quick change of tradition rather than the slow, cumulative, shaping effect of customs and practices which created the great markets of the medieval world. Although it has been there for almost a century it is a market of newcomers, of musclers-in, setters-up of new *bastas* (stalls), as *Gruzinim* (Georgians) replace *Iraqim*, *Kurdim* infiltrate the *Parsim*, and the old Jerusalem Sephardim retreat all along the line together with the tinkers, repairers of water tanks, replacers of rain gutters, grinders of knives and personal picklers of olives who belonged to the old nineteenth-century economy.

The name Mahane Yehudah sounds better in Hebrew than its translation into English. The English has a fractious, belligerent air about it. If you belong to Judah's camp, you'd better keep away from Jacob's turf. But the Hebrew is softer. It's the place where Judah dwells, where he pitches his tents, where his women cook and his children play in the dust. Given luck, he'll stay there for a while.

The market is essentially two parallel streets and a network of interlinking alleyways set close to the middle of downtown Jerusalem. Its hinterland is the spread of courtyard dwellings, low stone houses around a spacious, handsomely paved central yard with a cistern, which marked the communal and defensive pattern of Jewish life outside the Old City around the turn of the century. During the day the heady bouquet of colour, smell, noise and heat, and the pressure of crowded arms, hips, shoulders and elbows, makes you oblivious to the actual look of the market street. You are too busy trying to stay afloat in the swell. But at night, when only the rancid smell of rotting fruit is there to lead you through the empty streets, you find yourself looking about you at what might have been a proletarian quarter in Beirut or Alexandria fifty years ago.

Low, domed houses from the time of the Turks nestle against tall, monumentally seedy apartment buildings from the thirties which in turn overshadow more recent jerry-built instant slums. Every possible material seems to have been employed to keep these buildings upright. Corrugated iron sheets complement walls, concrete blocks prop up balconies, doubtful scaffolding invites you into a doorway. Balconies punctuate the built-up space like erratically assembled birdcages. They are everywhere and carry inexplicable and chaotic burdens. Iron wash-basins, broken chairs, canisters of cooking gas, empty drums of olives, kitchen sinks, unhinged window shutters. All this wealth of poor junk seems to proclaim a hope of future use - or at least a sale. But there are few people around, few geranium pots, no children and the facades of the buildings at night are dark and quiet.

The neighbourhood, which was at the heart of Jerusalem Sephardi working-class life, started seriously losing its original population about twenty years ago. The *Alliance Israélite* school has long gone and with it the Parisian message of enlightened French culture with a ballast of Hebraism for the poor Jews of North Africa and the Levant. The intricate web of family and tribal loyalties, affinities of origin and language which spilled into the music and ritual arrangements of prayer and the smells and spices of the kitchen - all these and other features which sustained the character of the area for three generations have become folklore or anthropology. If they exist at all it is not here in those streets by the market.

Yet the intimate, gaudily decorated prayer houses with their brightly coloured neon lights and crowded columns of memorial inscriptions have mostly survived and bear the names of the communities that built them, Aleppo, Yoannina, Bursa, Saloniki, Kurdim, Parsim. Like the courtyards nearby, the seats in the prayer rooms are also arranged around the central *bimah* platform, which gives them the intimacy of a coffee house or even a billiard room. Unlike the synagogues of the East End of London or the Lower East Side of Manhattan, they haven't been abandoned but have mostly lost their tribal particularity. The people who collect there to pray now haven't grown up together or quarrelled with each other in generation-long family feuds nurtured by too much familiarity and too little space. The market itself has changed languages and sounds as its population has changed over the years. Twenty years ago, one could still hear an exemplary Levantine conversation between two elderly gentlemen, quite formally dressed in spite of the heat and threading through the market in the way of Sephardi husbands who did the shopping while their wives ruled the kitchen:

> *Marhaba, Adon Yosef, Com esta? Barukh Hashem*: Greetings (Arabic), Mr Yosef, How are you? (Ladino) Blessed be the Lord (Hebrew).

Seven words, three languages, speaking of the stability of the Ottoman system, which let the tribes and religions of the Levant arrange their lives and commerce close enough to each other to be jealous rivals but familiar enough with each other to be tolerant and, at a pinch, sympathetic; all under the greedy eye of the corrupt rulers. Today, however much one learns about the dark side of life under the declining Ottoman empire, it seems like paradise.

If Monsieur Adam and Madame Eve spoke Hebrew, Arabic and Ladino (and probably French and Turkish too) in some Ottoman garden, their successors in the market today speak a chaotic and erratic mix of languages and dialects which attest to no order but that of Babel. Yet there is much linguistic energy here and, as a seed bed of a materialist poetics of Hebrew, the market has indeed been a major source of vitality. First the rhythmic chanting of the vendors, like street cries everywhere, creates patterns of sound and an imagistic rhetoric of its own. So cucumbers are *dagim dagim* (fish because they are small and thin and bend), kohlrabi rhymes with 'rabi' [rabbi], so it can be 'as good as words from the mouth of Rabi', all sweet fruits can be called *sukkar*, all white slices (radish, turnip) are *sheleg* (snow), melons attract attention for a season with the name of a local footballer hero *milon-Malmilian*. Plums are pushed as glamour girls, *Santa Rosa tafsa posa* (Santa Rosa, what a poser).

The Bible too has an important place in this Babel. Since many of the vendors know the liturgy and biblical passages by heart, it comes naturally into play in the buying and selling process. 'Let the children of Israel come and eat' ('*Bnei Yisrael yavo'oo ve'yochloo*') is heard from the direction of turnips and carrots. It is a fake quotation but not improbable and an acceptable summing up of the market's *raison d'être*.

A young elegantly bearded seller of bread fresh from the oven makes a more daring and original liturgical move. He is behind his pile of round flat bread besieged by a mob of over-keen customers clamouring for food. They are sweating, struggling, pushing their money at him, demanding his attention, desperate to be heard and served. In other words, a typical scrum.

He covers them with a look of noble pity and with the magic of words transforms them into a band of angels. '*Koolam ahuvim*,' he says '*koolam berurim*' (All are beloved, all pure). He is quoting the prayer in which the ministering spirits in orderly ranks (beloved and pure) open their mouths to praise God. He is telling the crowd they will all get their turn. He is also telling them they are more than an undisciplined mob and should show a little dignity. He is not being sarcastic and his words are far from empty. They imagine a different order of things, obscured for a while by the sweaty crowd, but timeless and graceful like the words of the prayer book.

Lately the Hebraic energy and allusive speech of the market has been changed by demography. The Arab boys from the Old City who work there now don't play with Hebrew words nor quote the Jews' liturgy. For them the language of their employers is simply a function of work. The Georgians go in for global sporting metaphors. Excellent peaches are *Ayropa Ayropa*, meaning Europe or high-quality football on TV. Primitive Russian has come into play as the women from Kiev and Sverdlovsk have to be encouraged to buy in fragments of a language they can recognize.

Though the ethnic mix may change, the level of secrecy connected to the ethnic practices of cooking remains high and unfathomable. You may point at a strangely shaped long green leaf which might be a form of spinach, only to be told that people of 'your kind' don't know how to cook this and you wouldn't like it. So forget about buying it. A young Georgian stall holder tells you that the little brown truffle-like balls brought in by Bedouin from the south are 'manna from the Torah'. Some herbs are Moroccan, some are Kurdish, even Indian. None are Viennese or Anglo-American. Some do for the stomach, some for the head, some for the fragrance of the departing Sabbath. All have different names depending on who you are and where your parents come from.

The tribes of the market may have changed as the Sephardic culture of the Levant has surrendered to the amorphous pressure of immigration but the politics of the market have been constant for generations. It was always the centre of passionate rightwing nationalistic politics: underground groups before 1948, Begin, Sharon, Bibi Netanyahu, even Kahane commanded support here. The Jerusalem proletariat saw socialism as a Polish/Russian import like herring, foreign to the local palate. They also quickly tumbled to the cluelessness of the modernizers from Minsk and Pinsk who treated the Sephardim as children who might one day grow up given a properly godless education. Even today Labour Party leaders photograph badly in the market. They look like squires dropping in on peasants. They wouldn't know how to cook that green leaf. Even their cooks wouldn't know. Would Bibi know? Unlikely, but he is 'one of us' because he is not 'one of them'. He has been pressed to the warm bosom of the market by virtue of being a scapegrace and an apparent risk-taker who likes to talk the language of power. Politics here is inherited, like loyalty to the Betar football team and to a ceremonial Judaism. Politics is also explosive, as the market has been a regular target for terror bombings in which people are maimed and die, balconies collapse and shops are shredded to bits. A routine walk through the market is therefore accompanied in one's mind by the repressed rehearsal of this often-photographed scene like a dull, buried headache. In this rehearsal the most shocking moment is the silence after the explosion when the gap between brute force and human reaction represents the mortal vulnerability of each and every one of us all the time and any place - and in this place more than most. After such explosions the market empties out but only for a few days. In due time Nissim the fishmonger comes back without one arm and there's a large picture of a wonder-working sage surrounded by amulets on the shop's rebuilt wall over the gasping carp. His 'women' collect around him like the chorus in a tragedy. They keen a while but they soon go back to vying with each other for his professional attention. The market is like the cruel and fecund sea, and Nissim, his women and all the rest of us are like the fisher folk who submit to its law for good or bad. We are drawn to it for our livelihood or for our food, but we are also drawn to its unpredictable pleasures and dangers.

The movements of Gideon the herbman are dangerous in the manner of circus performers and knife throwers. He stands on a platform above ranks of green fragrant herbs, mint, parsley, dill, sage, coriander, basil. Hidden away are more expensive items for a yuppier clientele, asparagus, rugola, six shapes and colours of lettuce leaves, broccoli. Gideon is a manic dervish whirling over a green treasure. His heavy shoulders and stocky neck anchor a pair of wildly zigzagging arms which fly out in all directions to scoop up one bunch after another either from the pile or from a customer's fist. His face is dark, unshaven and jowly, his eyes sharp in their concentration on adding up. He moves with exaggerated energy and frightening zeal like a starving man pouncing on his first meal. You must feed his hunger by choosing herbs, quickly, unhesitatingly and vocally. You must also gesture broadly and wave your parsley or the zealous scooper will pass you by and you will have failed to feed one of his many arms.

Success in buying parsley from Gideon could be taken as a test of manhood, even if the crowd around him is mostly women, because the market offers you an exercise in expressions of manhood. Not just in the obvious way of sending you into battle for tomatoes but in provoking thought about the love-hate relationship one has as a European with the Orient.

The market is seductive and displays its colours, smells and temptations in a brazenly feminine way. Everything is to be seen and fingered, pressed, tasted, taken or rejected. Even though the stallholders are almost entirely male, they are the guardians and profiteers of a copiousness which is female because it is nourishing and passed like daughters from hand to hand. This partly explains their anger and jealousy when you reject their peach for another elsewhere. They didn't just lose a sale, they have a dishonoured female relative on their hands and you are the betrayer of trust. No matter that the peach is sickly and green, hard and suspiciously wrinkled, you have violated the fake bond of trust set up by the seller whose honour demands he not be suspected of selling less than perfect fruit.

The exoticism of the market and of the ways of its people sets a temptation and a trap for the unwary beholder. It seems instinctive, direct, natural, in its way even innocent once you have made allowances for the necessary deviousness which is the ground of everything. It is so exotic you reach automatically for your camera, forgetting you live here too. The temptation is to call the ways of this culture childlike, irrational and unsophisticated, like its politics, whereas it is old and hoary with traditions, riddled with suspicions and prejudices, full of competing cultures and practices founded on the incoherently pooled experiences of places - as different and as far apart as Bokhara and Fez and Izmir and Beer Sheba.

The difficult thing is to accept the market as part of *you*, not a spectacle to watch with amusement and curiosity but a facet of your society and a factor in your welfare. The mob that surges out of this street shouting 'Death to the Arabs!' following the aftershock of a terrorist explosion is not cut from an old newsreel of riots in Baghdad. You cannot just watch it, you must take responsibility for it and address the politics which would channel such fear and anger into a disastrous style of government and a demoralizing practice of public behaviour.

One should face the uncomfortable truth: we will never be rid of our Orientalism. It is too seductive a drug, a habit we need to feed by touching fruit. We would hate the market to turn into a mall full of perfectly unreal refrigerated fruit that never rots or spills its juices in front of strangers. We wouldn't stand for white-coated vegetable consultants who smile, talk in measured tones and are permanently sweat-free. We could not be men in such an unsexed environment, where the only elbows, hips and rumps you made contact with were your own. Neither are we really ready to face the market for what it is in many ways, ugly, messy, violent, hysterical. We dive into the crowd buffeted between our narcotic fantasy and the swirling human current. We have moments of total clarity and moments of near black-out. Mostly we are somewhere in between, clutching our flimsy guide and anchor, our rationally organized shopping list which runs the whole gamut of the alphabet, beginning with A for Avocado and ending with Z for Zucchini. It is still in English; it will probably remain so. And that is entirely appropriate, for in the Babel of Judah's Camp to gesticulate, speak and think in one and the same language would mark you as odd, dull or - even worse - a tourist.

KAPPARAH, OR THE LAST CHORALE*
(Mahane Yehudah market, Jerusalem)
Claude Vigée

Before the high priest, black-hatted and armed
with a broad knife to sacrifice the fowls,
in one voice all our generations sing
beautiful lovesongs in this ancient abattoir.

Trembling bouquet of feathers, you cackle too loud –
the cry from your innocent heart pours forth in vain:
under the sharpened blade a stream of blood
looks like dying embers in your downy neck.

As soon as the lightning has flashed in their plumage
a long silence chokes
the crazy laugh of cocks, their throats now cut.

*Kapparah *is the expiatory sacrificial rite observed on the eve of Yom Kippur (CV)*

Translated by Anthony Rudolf. Winter 2000–2001

HOME, IMAGINATION AND MALICE
Ronit Matalon

I have a brother who likes to buy cars which stand on building blocks. He is crazy about old American cars, and whenever he hears of one he runs to see it. On a Saturday afternoon the delegation gathers: my brother; our brother-in-law; the two little girls; my mother, who gives the cheque for the down payment; Menashe, the melancholy mechanic; and myself. We all crowd into the ancient Chevrolet, which is already past its prime, and drive to the field, between rocks and thorns.

At the edge of the field the car rests on four blocks, turned at a slight diagonal. It's blue and spacious, its shiny sharp wings protruding, its windows wide open. The owner awaits us, not impatiently. He has time, he explains, to wait for the right person to arrive. Not anyone, someone who knows what's what.

We circle the car for long moments, our feet sinking into the ground. Mother blinks with her weak eyes, watching my brother, waiting for him to tell us what we should think. Menashe the mechanic crawls under the car. Two ravens leap on the American's smooth roof, go in, land on the white leather seats, out of which white cotton spills, over-flowing like foam. An ant stings me, locating itself between my sandal-strap and my ankle. It's not a car, I say loudly, it's a chicken-coop.

My brother lifts his eyes. I never forget his gaze: astonished, full of hatred and insult. You, he says, have no imagination, no imagination whatsoever.

I was twelve, and my brother – twenty-six. When I dreamt of the future I saw no pages of writing.

I saw shiny American cars, not in the field, but where they belong, by the cool entrances to official residences and hotels. I wanted to be a diplomat, one who passes by, comes and goes, her robe fluttering, not belonging to anyone and anything. I scornfully cast aside reality, which insulted my imagination. My brother was insulted on behalf of his imagination of reality. That's how the world is, full of people insulted and insulting.

With the years, I think, my poetic conception and my brother's drew closer. Both of us are similarly preoccupied with the issue of imagination. Fewer diplomatic clouds and hems of robes, more secondhand cars on building blocks.

My brother doesn't read what I write. He lacks a lot that would be needed: reading habits, patience, time. One of his eyes is blind, the other barely functions. His daughters tell him a little about what I write, and he is always astonished. His surprise combines pleasure and disappointment: Why do you write of what there is, why don't you invent?

I invent, I protest, I definitely invent.

Not like this, he says dismissively. Some writers really invent adventures, straight from their heads! You know what stories there are? You both laugh and cry when you read them. But you don't read, I argue.

I live from rumours, he says, sinking into the sofa in front of a National Geographic programme. In front of the peaceful antelopes we shift to other matters. He tells me of something that happened at work. A few weeks ago he renovated a private home, and they asked him to paint the brick wall surrounding it. He sprayed it, to speed the work up. He sprayed and sprayed, apparently not seeing too well, and all the cars parked by the road were also sprayed with paint. Car owners started coming out of the houses and out of the stores, pulling their hair. What a mess, what a mess - he tells me, his eyes glittering. Everyone pulls me towards his car, 'Clean here' and 'Clean there.' I ran around for two hours with the rag and the bucket.

You should have seen it! he says, most delighted. I can imagine it, I say in a sour tone. A calculator starts working inside my head: lost time, wasted money, lawsuits - another job amounting to nothing, or almost nothing. What do you think about? He scolds me. You see everything in black, everything. That's imagination too, to see in black, don't you think? I shoot back.

It's not imagination, it's just malice.

I ask myself whether he is right. I know at some point he is right, but at what point is it?

★

I have no such theological thoughts when I write. I barely have any thoughts. I attempt to cling to my mission, which will lead me on to my next mission. In my novel *Sarah, Sarah* - published in English as *Bliss* (Metropolitan Books, 2003) - the mission was clinging to malice. It's not that the people were malicious, their existence was malicious. To strain one's imagination towards a malicious existence is not a pleasant mission. At times you ask yourself - as my brother asked me - whether you are not contaminated by malice yourself. Your imagination of malice can soar high, become hyperbolic. That's not up my alley. Hyperbole for me is a failure of imagination, as a woman who dresses up and all you see is - money, money, money.

Here is another version of imagination moving towards malice: saying all the time what should not be. But what should be? I don't always know, surely not ahead of time. The 'yes' emerges, if it emerges, after a long list of negations, of options not chosen. My brother is shocked: If you were a judge everyone would go to the electric chair, he says.

Not everyone, two or three would be spared, my sister-in-law intervenes. Her name is Sarah.

What, you wrote a book about Sarah; my brother is amazed. How much could you write about her?

It's not this Sarah, it's another Sarah, I say. Only the same name, not the same person.

So who is that Sarah? He watches me with suspicion with his one, almost healthy eye.

With the years the difference between our conceptions becomes more concrete. He may say – indeed, he does say: 'What a beauty this car will turn out to be.' I can barely say 'car'.

It's not that you cannot – you do not want to, my brother says.

It's true. Time, the years, the lines that combine or don't combine, teach me humility, make me respect those obscure negativistic impasses of the writing hand. Like a mule stuck without apparent reason in the middle of the path, not responding to being whipped by its owner. There is a reason; the obstacle, the limitation, is the reason. The limitation of language, the limitation of the other, in whose territory imagination functions, announces its presence. This is the imagination which interests me in what I read and what I write, which limits me and is limited by me: imagination relating to the Other, imagination relating to language.

Imagination relating to the other, imagination relating to language, these are not only literary categories. They are also cultural, political and social phenomena. To imagine the Other, who is 'not me', is the essence of my political being. Imagining the Other is not a simple action. To allow it, you are required to move sideways a little, to withdraw. To seclude yourself from your community, your tribe, your family. To abandon second-hand cars on blocks, and, above all – to withdraw from yourself – to become 'not me'. To imagine the Other, an act of internal migration is needed. Migration from all that's familiar, from all that's usual, from the colour of your own eyes.

I believe that any act of writing, if it's honest and not false, involves such an act of inner migration. To write about my brother, to view my brother, I must withdraw from my brother, migrate from my brother, distance myself from my actual dialogue with my brother. I sit at my writing table with my back turned away from the world, from my brother. The writing situation necessitates turning my back to the world, precisely in order to deal with the world. The cold of turning my back, and the warmth of facing and watching, are intermingled and mutually dependent. The writer is always an immigrant who performs an act of betrayal towards his own world. He is not an informer, but treason towards his world is necessary to be loyal to his world.

What I just said, which is seemingly contradictory, is the essence of translation, of transformation from language to language, from culture to culture: the translator must 'betray' the literal meaning of the sentence, distort it in a way, to be loyal to its significance in its new language.

It is not by chance that I dwell here on family, politics, immigration, writing, translation. These topics have occupied me ever since I reached adulthood, both as a writer and as the daughter of an immigrant family which never succeeded in annihilating its immigrant essence.

What is common to all these themes, I think, is being between two – or more – worlds, two languages, two cultures, when identity is not derived from one place but rather from numerous places, which may compete with each other, and may complement each other.

The core of my interest in migration – both as a metaphoric existential state and as a concrete reality – is the question: to what extent must the immigrant annihilate parts of himself in order to enliven other parts? Is annihilation necessary? What are the reciprocal relations between the immigrant's divided identity, and the society, culture and language which he enters? And, more specifically: how does the experience of the Israeli place, of the Hebrew language, colour the Jewish experience of migration? How do they observe one another, what do they learn from each other?

I thought of all this complexity, quite intensely, over a year ago, when I called Bordeaux, France, to tell my uncle Bernard and my aunt Céline of the death of my father.

Uncle Bernard lifted the receiver. Felix died, I said. Bernard was silent for a long moment. Then he asked: Where? It was a bit strange as a first question: 'where', rather than 'when'.

In the nursing home where he stayed for the last month, I replied.

He was silent again, clearing his throat. The whole Mediterranean stretched out between us, between the two ends of the telephone line. You know, Ronit, he finally said: Your aunt Céline and I spoke about it the other day. We said that when we die, we would like to die together in an aeroplane, in mid-air. That's the place where we spent most time in our lives, the aeroplane. That's the right place for us.

I shiver when I quote Bernard's words, spoken before this metaphor became monstrously real. I must leap beyond a deep abyss of meanings, of horrors and fears, to reconnect to that evening, to that phone conversation, in which we reminisced about my father, another immigrant. Uncle Bernard, and Aunt Céline who joined in from another room, recollected stories from the past, and I listened.

'The past' which they discussed was very close and very remote at one and the same time. It zeroed in on the moment of death, on the fact of death. Listening to them, and in the following weeks, I thought that the question of 'the right place', as Bernard formulated it, does not evaporate at all in front of death. On the contrary, wondering about the right place to live, and about the right place to die, are of equal intensity. The place where you die is a definition of identity which radiates backwards, shedding light on one's lifetime identity. Death may indicate rupture, immigration, shift, lack of belonging, whether it occurs on a transatlantic flight as Bernard wishes, or in a kibbutz nursing home as my father did not wish at all.

What was, then, the 'right place' for my father, mother, Uncle Bernard and Aunt Céline, their brothers, sisters and cousins – Rosette, Eduard. Isaac, Edith or Albert – who left Cairo in the early 1950s and immigrated to France, Italy, Australia, the United States, Colombia and Israel? Was there a right place? How does the 'right place' perception define their immigrant identity, how could it be solved – if it could be solved at all? I would like to adopt here Uncle Bernard's choice: the aeroplane – movement from one spot to another as 'the right place'. The place which is not an actual location, but rather a means of transport for one's identity – in which the only permanent component is mobility.

I grew up in a family in which people moved all the time: from one country to another, from one city to another, from one apartment to another, between rooms, between languages, between family conditions. Everything, all the time, was in the middle of some process. If they did not actually change their apartment, city or country, they spoke about it incessantly. If they did not speak about it, they actualized it within the house – by tearing down walls, building corridors, throwing out furniture, turning the house upside-down at least once a year, no matter in what season. This mobility, constantly kicking life in the behind, did not require – so it seemed – any effort or mental mobilization. To the contrary, being fixed in one's place appeared to be an unbearable effort.

Here is a typical childhood scene: Mother and her brother Robert, an employee of Israel's electric company, sit at 11 am in my mother's small kitchen, sipping coffee. Uncle Robert takes a break from reading electric meters at this hour, and he often drops in for a late breakfast. They chat about this and that. Suddenly my mother stares with dreary eyes at the wall in front of her, separating the kitchen from the bedroom. What do you say, Robert, shall we take this wall down, open some space up here? she asks with yearning. Great idea, Uncle Robert answers without even looking. Within minutes she gathers the needed equipment: hammers, drills, saws and a particularly noisy tool with a name I love: Congo. Uncle Robert rolls up his sleeves and starts destroying the wall. In an hour there is no wall. Mother, all beaming, collects the debris. Robert goes back to work, to read a few more meters.

My brother and I never knew what house we'd meet when we came back from school or work: rooms and furniture kept switching, as in a game of musical chairs. One night is particularly memorable. My father, who used to disappear from home for months due to his political and other projects, suddenly returned from one such lengthy disappearance. He came in at 2 am, entering the total darkness on tiptoe, hoping not to wake us up. He intended to lie down on the sofa in the living room, and take a nap till morning. We woke up to a horrible noise. Where the sofa used to be there was now a heavy glass buffet, and next to it a dining table. Father hit his head against one of the glass shelves, falling on to the floor between the table and the chairs. It was indeed mother's little revenge, but it was not personal at all.

Alongside all this, or maybe afterwards, my brother developed through the years his fantasy of his dream home. In his dream home, he said, the furniture would be screwed to the floor, glued to it with cement. What had been is what will be. Mother stared at him with total incredulity. It's not a home that you want, she said, it's a cemetery. There, indeed, only the worms move around.

I often ask myself – what was all this internal running about, this passion for motion, which moulded my parents and their generation? What belonged to personal temperament, what to the mental state of immigration? Is this differentiation needed or interesting, and for whom?

Not for my parents and their peers, that so-called 'Levantine' generation. They apparently paid no attention to such differentiations or to the lack of them, not because their concept of the world was more limited than ours, but because the cultural air which they breathed did not carry the familiar virus of blurred brutality which characterizes the Israeli – and maybe also the American? – melting-pot society.

Blurred brutality in the relations between cultures, races, genders, nationalities, creates a great need constantly to differentiate. Differentiation, outlining boundaries between one phenomenon and another, between one group and another, is in such a milieu no longer an intellectual luxury of pampered individuals, but a way for a particular group to survive within the totality, within the state. This process of defining and differentiating oneself is the answer to the blurred and blurring brutality of the melting pot, an answer which may in turn lead to a different brutality which is not blurred at all, but rather crystal-clear and sharp. This is a contradiction within which we all live – in Israel in particular: unveiling violent blurring is at times a violent act in itself, or at least an act with violent consequences.

Re-reading what I have written so far, I notice that I used the words 'brutal' and 'violent' seven times in the last paragraph. This is not so surprising in view of where I live, particularly now, when our senses are all alert to differentiate various kinds and levels of brutality, rather than comparing brutality to its absence.

In our present bloodbath, in this vicious circle of blood feud and vendetta, between the Israeli immigrant society and the Palestinian refugee society, extreme brutality is omnipresent. But the horror should not silence the attempt to speak, to understand, to be. There is considerable affinity between the formation of the Israeli immigrant society on the basis of profound denial of its own refugee roots, and its attitude towards the other's refugee identity The Israeli sabra ethos demanded and still demands many costly sacrifices, and erasing the Jewish immigrant identity was one of them.

This was the ethos, this was the society, which my parents and their peers met in the early 1950s. It was an interesting encounter, but not a fruitful one. It was interesting because it juxtaposed one pattern of immigrant society – multicultural colonial Cairo, of the 1920s and 1930s, where my parents' generation had been formed – with the contrasting pattern of the Zionist Israeli melting pot. These people, who were pejoratively called 'Levantine' in Israel, evolved in the cultural crossroads of East and West. Communities of Greek, Italian, Russian, Copt, Lebanese and French immigrants, only a minority of whom were born in Cairo, lived side by side, within the Muslim society of pre-Nasserist Egypt. This Levantine generation was impregnated by a multiplicity of cultures. It had no mother tongue: they went to French schools, their parents spoke Greek or Italian, they had English or Swiss nannies, they spoke Arabic in the street. Their religious identity, just like their national identity, was the result of cross-breeding, with a multitude of imaginary options. When they said 'Allah' it wasn't clear if this Allah was Jewish, Christian or Muslim; and, what's more important, it really made no difference to them.

They did not become immigrants. They had been immigrants from way back, in the sense that the concept of immigration, and immigrant existence, embraces the perception of identity as multicultural.

One of the most precious possessions carried by this Levantine generation was the awareness of cultural relativity, not as a declared ideology, but as something organically embedded in their nature, just like eye colour or speech tone. This awareness that identity is never total, that it depends on its context, that it always interacts with its milieu, that it changes or at least carries the potential for malleability – this awareness contrasted, even contradicted, the Zionist ethos of one, new, well-rooted national identity.

Nothing in their colonial immigrant society, in their multilingual and multi-ethnic background, prepared them for their encounter with the Israeli immigrant society, where the rules of the game were utterly different: not one culture next to another culture, not one culture impregnating another culture, but rather one culture replacing other cultures, and a monolithic statehood attempting to dominate and control any colourful multiplicity.

I should mention that only a handful of this Levantine generation came to Israel. Most immigrated to other places, where the rays of the sun – as well as of national ideologies – are not as fierce.

Those who found their way to Israel, even those who were Zionist and belonged to the Hashomer Hatzair movement, like my uncles Robert and Nisso, attempted to adapt as much as they could – and as much as the new society let them – but they actually moved aside a bit, so as not to disturb, 'not to be stuck in someone's throat', as my mother used to say.

If what I say here implies some sentimental yearning for that utopian world from which my parents came, I must refute this impression right away. Colonial Cairo was far from any utopian vision, certainly for the Muslims to whom it belonged. What bothers me, or more accurately saddens me, is the feeling of waste, regarding a missed opportunity in the Israeli immigrant society, a social and cultural proposition which remained elbow-less and mute.

This expression, 'the Israeli immigrant society', is far from being natural and self-evident in the context of Israeli culture. Not long ago, maybe till the last decade, the mere usage of the word immigrant rather than the Zionist term was a demonstrative, almost subversive act of some individuals on the political margins. The moment when 'immigration' replaced 'aliyah' in Israeli cultural discourse – and replaced it quite massively – is an important moment.

We are not dealing with minute semantic details, but with two worlds of observation and contemplation. The words 'aliyah' (ascent) and 'oleh' (the ascending one) are prime examples of what I called the blurred brutality of the Israeli melting pot. They convey massive denial of the immigrant condition. The Zionist project unavoidably invented many ceremonies of cleansing. Saying 'oleh' instead of 'immigrant' is one such cleansing ceremony. When one says 'oleh' instead of 'immigrant', one is undoing the inherent misery involved in the immigrant condition. At the same time, it is implied that this condition – aliyah – is but a stage on the ladder towards becoming something else, someone else: an absolute native. *Aliyah* is a childhood disease which will pass, giving way to something healthier and new; immigration, by contrast, is a chronic condition, a wound that has not healed and cannot heal.

Let me stretch a little further this medical metaphor, which – as a hypochondriac – I came to like a lot. The most widespread representation of the immigration experience in Hebrew literature tends to emphasize the first version: immigration as a childhood disease, as a temporary phase on the road leading elsewhere. I will use as an example one of the best Hebrew texts describing immigration: Yehoshua Knaz's short story 'Henryk's secret' (from the collection entitled *A Musical Moment*).

The story describes a friendship between two children, one born in Israel, the other an immigrant from Eastern Europe, during the years of the British Mandate. The author describes with irony the well-rooted local boy, who examines his dissimilar neighbour and his 'strange' family with contempt, suspicion and anxiety. The author is critical, as we often say, of the Israeli sabra's haughtiness towards the immigrant. But is this the whole story? No, it isn't. Fundamentally, this isn't a social-realist story about Israelis and immigrants, but rather an exploration of the Israeli protagonist's capacity to observe the other, and of the price of such observation.

Knaz appears to say in 'Henryk's secret' that when you allow the other to invade you, when observing the other allows otherness in, a price will be exacted. The price, for Knaz, is disintegration. Disintegration of older ways of observing, of routines of feeling and thinking, in a certain sense of one's personality. Disintegration for Knaz is equated with growing up.

Knaz presents to us a subtle, complex paradigm, in which the other – the immigrant – plays a role for the well-rooted Israeli. The immigrant, in a somewhat vulgar formulation, represents the darker region of what is well-rooted, its shadow. Who tells the immigrant's story? Who has the language? The possessor of language in Knaz's story – and in many other texts – is the home-owner, the well-rooted Israeli. He can convey the immigrant's story in Hebrew because the immigrant's own language is suspended, he is caught in a twilight zone between two languages, the old one and the new one. He has a mother-tongue, but it was suspended by immigration. Whoever does not possess a language cannot tell his or her story. This person will always need someone else – the possessor of a language – to speak about him.

The possessor of the language, the home-owner, is primarily the Zionist context which turns immigration into a transient trauma, which transforms the immigrant into an *oleh*.

What can be done about this? How can immigration be narrated from within its own experience? How can language be transformed, from a patronizing monologue of the host into a curious friendly dialogue among equals? And how can the immigrant's story be liberated from the parameters of 'what was done to me, what was taken from me', namely from the dependence of the minority's self-definition upon the majority's definition of that minority? How can the minority – the immigrant group – define its own identity from the inside, in its own voice?

I believe these questions were on my mind, even if in a vague and unformulated form, when I wrote *The One Facing Us* (Henry Holt, 1999), a novel dealing – among other themes – with Israeli and Jewish immigrants. To speak of immigration from within the immigrant experience I needed to do two things: to break the 'one and only' language (Hebrew), and to break the 'one and only' place – Israel. Once the monolithic dominance – both of the language the protagonists speak, and of the place where they choose to live – was smashed, I felt I liberated them from a suffocating compulsion, which I – as a writer – could impose upon them. Once the compulsion of place was lifted, they could all move freely, not only in sorrow, sometimes happily too. There is no single place, roaming between locations is allowed – Uncle Bernard's aeroplane.

My family biography, I must say, allowed me to observe both versions of immigration, the stable chronic version and the transient traumatic version. I chose to focus on the former not only because it is more colourful, exotic or dramatic, but particularly because through it the 'there' of immigration made it easier for me to examine the 'here' of Israeli culture. The long-term penetration of a foreign language, of an alien culture, allows me better to hear Hebrew, and Israeli culture. The universal dimension of immigration, its universal validity, allow a mobile perspective, an identity which embraces its own potential malleability.

I admit that my words may convey a sort of idealization of immigration as an existential condition. Some idealization may appear here - or at least enchantment with the old idea of the Jew as citizen of the world, the ultimate immigrant, who not only takes a plane but becomes an aeroplane, carrying from place to place impressions, mother-tongues, father-tongues, ideas, colours, faces, constantly intermingling them all. Such enchantment must be related to my vantage point as an Israeli, more or less well-rooted myself. Immigration, whether understood as transient or as chronic, almost always represents a break, a wound. Not belonging is a wound. Belonging, though, may be a wound as well. This is apparently where I stand, alongside many Israelis: observing the wound of immigrant non-belonging, out of the wound of Israeli belonging.

These wounds are not similar. They should not be confused, should not be lied about. Similarly, the fact that I am a daughter of immigrants and not an immigrant myself should not be blurred. This means that I act out of an experience of place, out of possessing the Hebrew language; if not a home-owner, I am at least a partner in its ownership. In this partial ownership of place and language the territory of literature evolves, the capacity to narrate emerges. Literature - particularly prose - requires a home, a national home as well.

Home, the experience of location and language, may allow us to challenge the single place, and challenge Hebrew as the single language of the immigrant society. At home, walls and corridors can be torn down and rebuilt, second-hand cars resting on building blocks can be purchased, because these second-hand cars on blocks convey tremendous hope for the future, lively imagination of a future. Home allows this imagination, makes this hope viable.

The heart of the matter, I think, is not the need for a home or the capacity and yearning to make a home, but what kind of home it is. One home I know pretty well; its vision is a fortified fortress, or a devastating museum of the history of the illusion of power. This home is horribly costly. I prefer, like my mother or my Aunt Céline and my Uncle Bernard, a home which is a process, an object living in time, listening to time, arguing with time, submitting to time.

This process-home has a price too. Being always within the process may make one confused as to one's location. 'What does it mean, where I am from?' Aunt Céline may get annoyed. 'Wherever Bernard and I go, in any home we visit, the first thing we say is: *Nous sommes de Gauche*. So it will be clear: We are from the Left.'

Summer 2002

THE EL-AL PRAWN
Clive Sinclair

I first sighted the thing in 1991, the year Zbigniew Herbert won the Jerusalem Prize. I was on flight LY315 out of Ben Gurion, returning from the book fair. We were flying over Greece or maybe what was once Yugoslavia, at a height of 39,000 feet, and were dealing with the usual dilemma: beef or chicken? The hors d'oeuvre, however, was mandatory. It came in a plastic container with a transparent lid – rather like a specimen box – and my neighbour (obviously less hellenized than I) was regarding it with appropriate caution. Was it a crooked digit, beckoning him to apostasy? It was as large as an index finger, aggressively pink and curved like a comma. The sort of thing you try not to look at in public urinals. Whatever it was, it certainly did not look kosher.

'Don't worry,' said the air hostess reassuringly, 'it's only a replica made from fish.' My neighbour was not convinced; he prodded the ersatz crustacean with his plastic fork, but did not taste of the forbidden food. I had no such qualms. The El-Al prawn had the springy texture and sweetish taste of the real thing, but left a slightly polluted after-taste, nothing like the sharp, salt-waterish side-effect of a well-bred shellfish. Even so, it wasn't a bad simulacrum. The question was: why bother to make a counterfeit prawn in the first place?

Those were the days of Yitzhak the Flinty – who was succeeded by Yitzhak the Martyr, Shimon the Unelectable and Bibi the Schmoozer – when the land of Israel was afflicted with a strange mood, a mixture of shame and self-righteousness, best exemplified by the following construction: 'We have animosity towards the Palestinians, but only because of what they are making us do to them.' Put another way: Our boys may look like standard issue thugs when they break the bones of our enemies but, rest assured, they take no pleasure in their work. Or: They may look like goyim, but they are not. In short, the El-Al prawn was the culinary equivalent of a border guard thumping a Palestinian; it looked unappetizing but was acceptable in the eyes of God. There were other reasons for the prawn's existence. In the days of Yitzhak the Flinty, the gentile world was regarded as essentially hostile and antisemitic, but was also full of desirable goods and lifestyles: fast cars, mobile phones, fancy restaurants. The false prawn was born to feed the appetites of these pseudo-sophisticates, the symbol of a generation that had lost its self-respect and doubted its unique identity. It could even be argued that the El-Al prawn was, *pace* the stewardess, not really kosher since its very presence dared the consumer to try the original.

As it happens I have never seen a prawn manqué in all its naked shame since that flight. It would be pleasant to conclude that its absence marked a return of self-confidence, and a greater sense of security, but the fact is that the supermarkets of Israel are now stocked with a breaded variety – like, for example, Shrimp Style with Sesame Coating. No preservative, low cholesterol, guaranteed kosher by the rabbinate of Nahariya. Its chief ingredient is *dag zahavon alaska*. So if you fancy processed Alaskan goldfish, mixed with water, soya protein, potato starch, corn starch, sugar, sorbitol, vegetable stabilizer, vegetable oil, flavourings, salt, monosodium glutamate and natural colouring, you too can mimic the habitués of Fisherman's Wharf without risking the eternal barbecue. The titbit goes well with the likes of sweet and sour sauce, and thousand island dressing. In fact I can picture the ideal consumer. I can even picture how he acquired the taste in the first place. I see an air hostess – let's call her Sara – approach a porky Lothario – lets call him Bibi – with the aforementioned delicacy, saying 'Eat'. I see him smacking his chops.

Autumn 1997

ISRAEL AT FIFTY
David Grossman

When I was a baby, in the Jerusalem of the early 1950s, my mother would push me in my carriage through the streets of our neighbourhood. The neighbours would greet her happily and bend over to take a look at me, spit *tfu!* and exclaim, in Yiddish, 'How ugly!' Surviving photographs show that I was actually quite a pretty baby, but that was the custom, especially among those who had come from Eastern Europe – to insult the baby so as to ward off the evil eye. When I grew up and saw the same ceremony re-enacted, I was able to take a good look at the women's faces. I suddenly realized they were not trying to protect the baby from some vague, hypothetical evil eye, but from something very concrete, something they carried around with them in those gazes that had already seen so much, knowing that nothing could be more terrible than what they had already seen.

Israel was founded on a great insult, an insult to a people rejected and sentenced, in the eyes of the nations among whom it lived, to be a horrifying symbol of the foreign and the cursed. This insult is still etched in the individual and collective memory, in the form of endless wounds and small, heart-breaking humiliations. Some time ago I participated in an encounter between Israeli army officers and Holocaust survivors. Two brothers, now in their sixties sat on the stage. As children they had lived in the city of Vilna, at the time of the Nazi invasion. One day, while they were playing soccer with their Christian friends, the Nazis began rounding up Jews. They were kidnapped from the playing field and put onto a train that took them to a death camp. The tracks ran by the field where they had been playing. Through the cracks in the sides of the car, they could see their friends continuing the game

The two brothers told their story in very quiet voices, and the officers began crying like children.

Some of them ran out of the room. I especially remember one of them, little more than a boy, with a wiry body and curly hair. I cannot forget the way he kept banging his forehead, over and over again, on the barrel of his M-16.

Almost all Israelis have gashes like that in their memory. If a child is not born with one, the educational system carves one out. There are family sagas that hand them down from generation to generation. There are Jewish holidays and days of observance – so many of them – to remind each and every Israeli. Here are holidays to remind us of the miracle that saved us when the Greeks or the Persians wished to destroy us; a holiday to remind us of our flight from slavery in Egypt; a fast in memory of the destruction of the Temple; Holocaust Day . . .

Israel, which brought itself forth out of sorrow, and hoped for tranquility, lives in unending sorrow. For fifty years we have lived immersed in violence, in wars, in mourning, in terrorism and murder. More than twenty thousand Israelis have been killed in hostile attacks during the country's half-century of existence. On average, since the founding of the State, one person has been killed each day, one family destroyed. Thousands of sites all over the country remain open sores because of a battle or terrorist incident that occurred there. There are fully 900 (!) memorials to the war dead in this small country (one memorial, on average, for every seventeen dead soldiers; in Europe, the ratio is one memorial for every 10,000 dead). There is no week in the Israeli calendar without a memorial day for some sort of traumatic event – a date connected to a war, a terrorist attack or a military operation; there are even days with two scars. Someone walking through downtown Tel Aviv can, in the space of five minutes, set out from Dizengoff Street (where a suicide bomber murdered thirteen people two years ago [1996]), glance apprehensively at the number 5 bus (on which another suicide bomber killed twenty-nine civilians four years ago [1994]) and try to regain composure at the Appropo cafe where, just a year ago [1997], yet another suicide bomber killed three women; none of us can easily forget the television images of one blood-spattered, newly-orphaned baby. Even the names of the streets cast a melancholy air over such a walk - in almost any Israeli city you can stroll from a street named after the refugees who drowned when the boats bringing them from Europe sank, to a street named after the martyrs of the Holocaust or the Jewish freedom fighters hung by the British. When my daughter went with her kindergarten on their first field trip, they went to Rabin's grave and the adjacent military cemetery.

Life is full of the dead. Five boys who went to school with me were killed in wars, and many more remain injured. Not one of Israel's five decades has been without a major war. Every new-born Israeli baby receives from the government a special gift - a kind of scaled-down cradle to protect it from poison gas and germ warfare.

Yet it is the country's vitality and appetite for life that first strikes visitors to Israel. Energies pent-up during generations of repression seem to be breaking out on all sides and demanding expression (for those who can afford it) in an indulgent, consumerist, ostentatious life style. There is a craving to travel the world - there were three million departures by Israelis to other countries in 1997, almost one for every second member of the population. People are having lots of babies, too - 24 births per 1,000 inhabitants in 1996, as compared with only about 14 in the United States and Europe. There is a huge nation-wide building explosion.

Other things cannot be quantified but colour life here, and can hardly be left unmentioned. Israel is a very emotional country; Israelis are, generally, direct, open and warm, extreme in their passions, anxieties, sensitivities, manner of speaking and body language. They are also extreme in the volatility of their moods, in their periodic swings between euphoria, elation and arrogance, on the one hand, and depression, defeatism and despair.

They are even intimate with total strangers. One morning I got on a bus and sat down next to a fleshy older man with a red face. He gave me a doubtful look, as if considering whether I was reliable enough to hear what he had to say. Then he sidled up next to me and gave a quiet sigh: 'Nobody knows what the other guy keeps inside.' Even before I had a chance to ask what he meant, the man raised a huge brown envelope, drew out an X-ray and held it up to the light. 'That's me,' he said with unrestrained pride. I took a careful look, but wasn't able to identify him from the picture. 'Those are my kidneys,' he explained, 'they're always making sand and stones.' He raised the X-ray higher so that other people could enjoy it, and explained his entire inner world to a crowd that had gathered around. For a moment I was able to view the colourful crowds of Jaffa Street, Jerusalem's main thoroughfare, through the internal organs. There were school kids with earrings, a squad of soldiers gathered around two blonde tourists, Hassidim in long black coats, a pro-Israeli Japanese sect processing in lemon yellow, two policemen frisking an Arab, three-year-old kids from a nearby *cheder* running and shouting; all that swarming noisiness through a single pair of kidneys!

It is hard to admit on such a festive day, but the feeling pervading Israel is one of discomfort, of despair, of having missed something. This unfairly ignores the huge achievements the country can take credit for during its fifty-year existence - the absorption of mass immigration, the greening of the desert, the building up of its defence force, the recreation of Hebrew culture, advances in science and technology. And, despite everything, Israel is a democratic country even though most of its citizens came from countries without a democratic tradition.

Yet Israelis cannot be happy on this anniversary. Perhaps it is no coincidence that the commission appointed to plan the celebrations has resigned on three separate occasions. The mood in the country today recalls a family in crisis. Perhaps this is because, deep in their hearts, Israelis sense that for more than thirty years, since the Six Day War, they have been caught up in a profound historical error, one that has wound itself inextricably around them. It could be that the violence I described is beginning to invade our internal tissues, turning even brother into enemy. Or maybe it is the inevitable disillusion of those who experienced a great miracle that, as the years go by, has disintegrated into a human reality full of contradictions and bruises?

The Israelis direct their disillusion in all directions – at the world which, according to a popular song, is 'entirely against us' – at the international press, which always seems hostile; at the United States and Europe, which 'dare' to propose peace initiatives; at the Arab countries and the Palestinians. But above all they direct it at themselves, and sometimes it seems as if hardly anywhere is as hostile to the Jews as Israel.

'Together in pride, together in hope,' proclaims the official 'anthem' of the fiftieth anniversary festivities. But in recent years Israel has seen the gradual emergence of 'ghettoes' entirely alienated from one another, and from the state and its institutions. Immigrants from the former Soviet Union, who now comprise more than a fifth of the country's population, have created their own socio-cultural enclave which shows few signs of blending with an existing culture disdained for its 'shallowness'. To be fair, native Israelis are equally wary about getting close to the new immigrants. Oriental Jews, whose roots lie in the Muslim world, have for most of the country's history felt discriminated against socially, economically and culturally, and have not been full members of the leadership and elite. Today they are demanding compensation, rejecting those aspects of national life that seem to express the Ashkenazi or Western character of the state. Tens of thousands of Ethiopian immigrants feel that they are treated like pariahs or foreigners; the ultra-orthodox Jews do not recognize the state and Zionism at all; the million Palestinian citizens of Israel – another fifth of the population – do not identify with its national, mostly Jewish, goals. They are also compelled to finance, through their taxes, an Israeli army that holds sway over their brothers in the occupied territories. Some 200,000 foreign workers live in abominable conditions in poor neighbourhoods on the margins of the big cities, serving as Israel's 'hewers of wood and drawers of water'. They have replaced the Palestinian workers, who in turn replaced the Jews in manual labour, agriculture and industry.

The kibbutzim, too – once the country's glory, the most salient symbol of the Jews' return to their land, their earth and a normal existence have in recent years undergone a process of de-legitimization and decline. First they were depicted, by right-wingers, as a symbol of the arrogance of the Western Ashkenazi Jews; religious leaders denounced them as 'not Jewish enough'. Then they became entangled in financial adventurism. Like other Israelis during the hyperinflationary spiral of Menachem Begin's first government, many kibbutzim were tempted by dreams of quick profits and soon began to teeter on the brink of bankruptcy and collapse. Today most are deep in debt, the younger generation is leaving, and the older generation feels as if the kibbutz ideal is melting away before its eyes.

An evil wind is blowing through the country. Instead of trying to act together to save what we have, enjoying the benefits and cross-pollination of a richly varied population, different groups are declaring war on each other. Each side is exaggerating, for use against the others, its most extreme and overwrought tendencies. Religious Jews are becoming more fanatical, messianic and nationalistic; secular Jews are detaching themselves in disgust from everything that seems 'Jewish', and so losing an important part of their identity.

We have lost the sense of 'togetherness' that beat in people's hearts in the country's early days.

Different populations are generally unable to read the behavioural codes of each other. The army, once a melting pot and a young person's entry ticket into Israeli society, no longer plays this role. Today it is not uncommon, as it was in the past, to hear young people declaring they will do anything they can to avoid military service. It is good that the army is losing its centrality and power, but nothing is ready to replace it as a force for social cohesion.

It seems ever clearer that Israel has still not truly internalized a sense of common interest beyond the immediate need for security. Perhaps even the idea of the state has not been sufficiently internalized. This may require generations of democratic life, and a level of political maturity, even political education, that Israel has not yet achieved. To an outside observer it sometimes seems that if Israelis still relate to their government as if it were a foreign occupier, as if they were a minority – a minority disliked by the authorities – in their own country. At demonstrations of the ultra-Orthodox, West Bank settlers or extreme right-wingers, representatives of the law are often jeered at as 'Nazis!' Almost everywhere you turn you sense a deep scorn for the Knesset and government ministers. Religious and right-wing groups, which have been gathering strength, have recently begun to present a serious threat to the rule of law. They speak openly of their desire to replace democracy with a regime governed by religious law. Supreme Court judges and many other public figures now go about surrounded by bodyguards. That is an unprecedented sight in Israel, a country well-known – until the murder of Yitzhak Rabin, whose policies were not accepted by part of the public – for its leaders' easy connection with the people and the informality of its manners.

Sometimes, in the spring or autumn, when the weather is less harsh, one's soul longs to go out into the land itself. To the land before it was covered with a thick, suffocating layer of current events and symbols and memories of heroism or catastrophe. Sometimes there is a moment of grace, the thick cloud of clichés hugging the ground clears and the land itself appears. The margins of the desert are covering themselves with the fresh green growth of spring, a wave of yellow blooms is now, in March and April, flowing from one end of the country to the other – acacia trees and clover and carpets of mustard flowers. The ever-green Mount Carmel. The Galilee, with its erotic play of mountains and valleys, and the placid, meditative eye of Lake Kinneret open in its heart.

Sometimes, precisely in those places that are most dense with meaning, an Israeli like me feels a need to get off the main road and find a path that appears on no map, a path that has no identity other than the view. The view is generally bald and miserly. There are no thick forests, no broad lakes, no rushing rivers. There is just one little Lake Kinneret, whose water level every Israel child monitors anxiously for fear of drought, and a few woods planted by the Jewish National Fund, in an effort to create, as if by magic, an illusion of green Europe in the midst of the Orient. And there is only one river, the narrow Jordan, which must astound all the Christian pilgrims who have exalted it in their dreams.

But you can always find hidden places where you see no other human being, and no place of human habitation, neither Jewish nor Arab, neither religious nor secular, not Jerusalem, not a settlement and not a refugee camp. There you can wander a bit under the intensely blue sky, between the olive trees (that have, heaven help us, already become a Palestinian national symbol), the lumpy boulders and the yellowing stalks of grass.

I remember a moment like that, at the height of a year's odyssey that I undertook among Israel's Palestinian citizens and Jews. As I was being scarred, over and over again, by the lines of tension between populations with only citizenship in common, alien to each other in every other way, I fled for a brief moment to the land itself. I had a physical need to touch the thing itself, the way it was before it was expropriated and nationalized by politics. I lay down on a big rock that was warm from an entire day's sun, and with great pleasure I began to peel away all the names and designations and titles – Israel, Palestine, Zion, the Jewish State, the Promised Land, the Holy Land, the Zionist Entity . . . and, for a moment, I had it again, my land and country, with the deep fissures in its skin, with its harsh, troubled beauty. A land, as the poet Chernikovsky wrote, 'whose every inch of ground is to be softened, and every boulder'; to which the Palestinian Salem Jubran responded: 'As a mother loves her crippled child, so I will love you, my homeland.'

I write all this as a person who considers himself lucky to live in Israel. Not because I think it is paradise or utopia, but because Israel is the only place where Jews can live with all the essential elements of the history, culture and thought of every generation of Jews that has preceded them, and can build on them to create a new and modern reality. It is also the only place where Jews can realize the values and ideals crystallized in their culture, and can formulate them in Hebrew, the language in which their identity was forged over many generations, the language which preserves all the codes of the past and yet renews itself every day.

Living in Israel, for me, is still a spiritual adventure. It may be exhausting and frustrating, but how could I do without it? Sometimes I remind myself that my everyday life would have been an object of intense hope and longing for eighty generations of Jews who lived before me. My children play and love and fight in a language that no one spoke for two thousand years, but for them it is full of life and taken for granted. Were Abraham the patriarch (four thousand years old) to sit down for supper at my house, he would understand the greater part of the Hebrew of my five-year-old daughter. What a wonder that is!

The world certainly has more comfortable and less dangerous places. Europe and the United States offer a higher standard of living, more varied cultures, stirring scenery, tranquility. But if a Jew wants, for the first time in 2,000 years, daily to be part of the place and the society in which he or she lives, to feel all the pain, and joy, of belonging – in other words, if a Jew wants to feel truly at home, not living by the grace of others, not an outsider . . .

Not an outsider. That is what it all comes down to. To belong. A partner with equal rights and obligations. A native and organic part of this great body. What sweetness surges through me just from writing those words! What bitterness floods the heart at the thought that many Israelis have recently felt like aliens in their homeland, alien to its behaviour, its character, the plans it has chosen to put into practice.

It hurts me that I cannot fully celebrate this anniversary. I write out of deep concern. Questions, both general and deeply personal, remain unanswered. How long will we be the prisoners of our fears? Will my son, when he goes into the army two years from now, also have to fight the children of my Palestinian friends, in the streets of Hebron? To what purpose do we subordinate such a huge part of our strength, money and creativity to the army, if we are unable to use our military power to promote political concessions and bring about fundamental change in the region? Has power come to be an end in itself, and have we forgotten that it should only be a means of protecting life? Or perhaps we have forgotten, because of the unbearable lightness of death that surrounds us, what the word 'life' really means? That living isn't just surviving from one catastrophe to the next, or being saved by the skin of our teeth from another calamity. Living does not mean just defending our borders, as Israel does with great effectiveness, but doing something about what is going on within those borders. It means improving the quality of life and relations between people; promoting mutual respect, civic freedom, the rights of minorities, democracy. If we don't pursue all these ideals, we will end up like suits of armour that no longer have knights inside them.

At the age of fifty, my mother likes to sigh, everybody gets the face they deserve. If I were given the hard task of choosing a single image from fifty years that contains the very essence of Israel's 'face', I would choose the moment no Israeli can forget – 4 November 1995. Yitzhak Rabin stood on a platform facing hundreds of thousands singing 'The Song for Peace'. I saw him from just a few metres away and, for me, that is Israel's face. Not only because his career summed up all the most important stages of Israeli history – from the legendary Kadouri agricultural school, through the Palmach, the convoys to besieged Jerusalem, the Six Day War, Entebbe, and then to the signing of peace treaties with the Palestinians and Jordanians – as if he contained a genetic blueprint for 'Israeliness' within him. But also because in his face, the face of the handsome golden boy, the face of the mythical Sabra, we saw something of which we had no 'historical experience' – how a Sabra matured and grew old, and how the ideal and the miracle which he represented developed over time. We saw him as an idealistic young man, tempted by money and involved in dubious political intrigues; and we saw how, in a process that held us all in awe, he returned and renewed himself, changed his views and overcame the attitudes to life that wars had etched into him with blood. There, that Saturday night, when we stood and sang that song with him, and enveloped him in love, because we felt that he was bringing us life, that was the moment that exemplified both the strengths and weaknesses of Israel and of Judaism, once and for all – the vitality and the courage to rise above our anxieties and to be renewed again and again. But the dark forces of extremism within us were lying in wait for him in the dark. And they had a pistol.

A moment (never-seen-on-television) from the Arab-Israeli confict

In 1982 the Lebanon War broke out. I was a young reservist, and was called up and sent up north. It was a month after the birth of my eldest son, and the last place on earth I wanted to be was in that village north of Lake Kar'oun, facing Syrian tanks.

One day I stood there on guard, leaning against the wall of our improvised headquarters, dressed in a badly fitting uniform, rifle in hand. A tall woman of noble bearing approached from the end of the street, dragging along a small screaming child. She came up to me and addressed me directly: 'Do you see Hassan here?' she asked me. 'He's a bad boy! Doesn't do as his mother says!'

I could not fathom what she wanted from me, and I was afraid that this was a typical Lebanese trap, an especially detestable one. And it turned out I was right. 'Now, I want you to tell him,' the woman said loudly, 'what you do in Palestine to boys like him.'

I was absolutely baffled, and speechless. 'You take them from home,' she explained to me emphatically, talking adult-to-adult above the child's head, 'and you put them in little tiny rooms, with no food and no water. . .'

She continued in great detail, and the boy fell silent, gazing at me in trepidation. The woman did not even wait for a reply. She turned around and left.

Translated from the Hebrew by Haim Watzman. Spring 1998

Anna Sherbany The People's Memorial to Yitzhak Rabin – Kikar Malchai Yisrael, Tel Aviv, 1996
Black & white photographic print / *Summer 1999*

THE HOPE
Karen Alkalay-Gut

On the night Rabin died I dreamt I wandered the streets,
homeless and lonely in a crowd of confusion, ricocheting
off relatives and friends barely regarded, while dogs of peace
ran with panthers and tigers all loose and all free.

No-one was working – everyone
out on the streets or in groups
sleeping in different houses, using
interchangeably each others' phones –
connecting with wrong numbers
saying a few impotent words,
disconnecting indifferently.

Unseasonable cold penetrated my clothes,
and uncoated I sought shelter
in cloaks of the dead,
but found myself in other byways
before I could wrap myself in them.

The river was solid and the earth
liquid under our feet – the worst
walked on water while the best
fell in the treacherous sands.

Nothing held the dream together
and everything could fall apart
at any random moment.

Winter 1995

A SENSE OF PLACE
David Herman

In his memoir, *Out of Place*, Edward Said describes how he returned home after having been expelled from his school in Cairo. He was, he writes, 'speechless and disoriented'. 'Without my saying a word,' he goes on, his father took me into their room for a preliminary whipping with his riding crop.' This isn't the only time in Said's memoir that he describes himself as inarticulate or reduced to silence. It's an image that comes up again and again.

This image of a timid, tongue-tied child is striking, in dramatic contrast with Said's reputation today as a fluent lecturer and broadcaster, and a world-famous spokesman for the Palestinian movement. He has taught at Columbia University for almost forty years and he has given interviews and prestigious lectures around the world.

He is a prolific writer, author of almost twenty books and collections of essays, and editor of several more. He writes regularly on music for the *Nation*, on politics for *Al Ahram*, a weekly based in Cairo, and on political and cultural issues for major newspapers and small magazines on both sides of the Atlantic.

Said has now brought out a memoir, a collection of interviews published since the 1970s, another of articles and essays published since the sixties, and an anthology of essays and extracts from his books. Though he is best known as a literary critic and political commentator, he has an enormous range and these books include essays on subjects from the pianist Glenn Gould to 1930s Tarzan films, from Jane Austen to *The Battle of Algiers*, from Egyptian belly dancers to Wagner. Edward Said has, in short, found his voice.

But, and this takes us back to the silent schoolboy in Cairo, what does this mean? How do we find a voice? What stops us from speaking? What do we need to have to be able to speak or to have a voice?

In much of his work, especially since *Orientalism* (1978), Said writes about this as a political question. Who has the power to speak? What happens to people, especially colonial people, nonwhite subjects in the great European empires and people today in post-colonial societies, if they do not have that power? What does it mean to live surrounded by television and film images and newspaper headlines that are about you, but which are made by others, in the great centres of global economic and political power? This relationship between knowledge and power is at the heart of much of Said's work.

But Said has also always been interested in the question of how an individual writer or thinker finds a voice. How does he (and most of Said's subjects are men) find a place in his culture, a tradition, a set of ideas which are his and which allow him, fully, to express himself. And what are the obstacles which prevent him from finding that voice?

In Said's own career, these questions loom large. Should he write about Palestine and his experience of dispossession and exile? How should he write about it? As a literary critic, how much could he write about Palestine and politics? Could he write about literature and politics in the same books? How? Taken together, these books allow us, perhaps properly for the first time, to see how Said found his voice and what gives it lasting interest. Throughout his work there is a constant awareness of how difficult it is for an intellectual or writer to find a voice or a place in his culture. First, there is the problem of isolation, of being an outsider. Many of the writers who most interest him are essentially lonely figures: Gramsci in prison, Conrad, Lukacs, Adorno and Auerbach in exile, political intellectuals like Chomsky in America with no larger movement to sustain them.

The loneliness of a political prisoner like Gramsci or an exile like Adorno is obvious enough. But many of the other thinkers who most interest him, like Vico, Foucault, Swift or Orwell, were isolated in a different sense. They are outsiders, eccentrics. This word 'eccentric' comes up again and again in Said's writings. Every key figure or work for Said is referred to, sooner or later, as 'eccentric', by which he means not quirky or strange; but somehow away from the centre. Not just geographically, though for Auerbach in exile in Istanbul or for Vico in eighteenth century Naples, outside the French mainstream of Enlightenment thought, or for Conrad coming from Poland, the fact that they were on the margins of Europe was clearly important.

But by 'eccentric,' Said means being outside the centres of power and authority in your culture and having a voice, a way of writing or thinking, which is different from the dominant norms. Hence Said's long-time interest in exiles and refugees, certainly: Auerbach, Adorno, Conrad. But also Foucault and Genet, both homosexuals; Swift in Ireland; Orwell, who can never make up his mind whether he's an outsider or an insider; Lukacs and Adorno, Marxist Jews in central Europe. The writers and thinkers who have mattered most to Said over the years have all been eccentric, outside the centre of their culture, and this is clearly how he sees himself and the role of the intellectual.

It is no surprise, then, that Said wrote his PhD on Conrad. 'Over the years,' he writes in *Reflections on Exile*, 'I have found myself writing about Conrad like a *cantus firmus*, a steady groundbass to much that I have experienced.' Conrad has been an enduring presence for Said, through much of his work. Like Conrad, he grew up under imperial occupation. Both left home during their adolescence and ended in a culture in which they felt neither at ease nor at home. Both came from the margins: Conrad from late nineteenth-century Poland, Said from the mid-twentieth-century Middle East, both areas of turbulence and instability. And both came to the centre: Conrad to imperial London, and Said to America's top universities during the second half of the 'American Century'.

Writing on Conrad allowed Said to find a way of talking about experiences close to his heart: displacement, expatriation, being in another country and speaking and writing in another language. It also established Said as a literary critic, with a particular interest in modernism and the novel.

Having written his PhD on Conrad, Said moved to Columbia University and the first essays in *Reflections on Exile* find him writing in the mid- and late- 1960s for small literary journals (*Kenyon Review, Hudson Review, Partisan Review*). He is already immersed in French structuralism (there are informed references to Barthes, Lévi-Strauss, Jakobson and Saussure), French existentialism (especially Sartre and Merleau-Ponty) and modern Continental thought in general (Nietzsche and the young Lukacs, Husserl and the Geneva School). This was unusual for an American literary critic in the sixties and stood him in good stead when European literary theory and philosophy swept American literature departments in the seventies and eighties.

What is just as striking is what is *not* there in his writing. There are *no* references to the Six Day War, to politics in the Middle East or indeed to the upheavals of 1968 in the US. His political awakening came after 1967 and deepened in the seventies. There is a feeling about this early writing that he hasn't found a voice or a place of his own. As he wrote about T. E. Lawrence in 1970–71, 'the great question is, *what was he about*' (Said's emphasis).

Looking back now, he describes his situation as 'schizophrenic'. He refers to 'leading two quite separate lives'. 'I had been two people.' On the one hand, he was a young literary critic and scholar, interested in European literature and philosophy. On the other hand, he was a Palestinian, who had spent the first sixteen years of his life in the Middle East, and whose family still lived there. He was betwixt-and-between and couldn't find a way of writing about the two parts of his life together. Perhaps he couldn't find a way of integrating them in his life.

Said found his voice in two ways. First, through politics, and especially Middle Eastern politics. The crucial event, he writes, looking back, was the Six Day War. 'I was no longer the same person after 1967; the shock of that war drove me back to where it had all started, the struggle over Palestine' (*Out of Place*). 'For the first time since I had left to come to the United States, I was emotionally reclaimed by the Arab world in general and by Palestine in particular' (*The Politics of Dispossession*, 1994).

Looking back now as a passionate advocate of the Palestinian cause for thirty years, 1967 must loom large. It was less obvious, at the time. His published writings in 1967 consist of a review of Frank Kermode's *The Sense of an Ending*, essays on Merleau-Ponty, Strauss and Vico, a review of John Middleton Murry's book on Swift and a piece for *Partisan Review*, on the critics, R. P. Blackmuir, Georges Poulet and E. D. Hirsch. In 1968 and 1969 he is still writing on Conrad, the philosopher Cioran, Auerbach and again Swift, and there is a piece in *Salmagundi* called 'Beginnings.'

In other words, Said's interest in politics really takes off later than 1967. He spends a crucial year in Beirut (1972-3), immersing himself in Arabic philology and literature. In 1973 comes the Yom Kippur War. In the same year he writes his first political piece for *The New York Times*.

But it wasn't just a question of finding a political voice. It was a question of finding a different voice as a literary critic, of bringing together politics and culture in the same books. This required a different voice as a literary and cultural critic from the early essays in the 1960s.

Taking Isaiah Berlin's famous distinction between the hedgehog and the fox, Edward Said is a hedgehog. For all his many interests, he knows one big thing: that books and ideas – in short, knowledge – are rooted in history, society and the relations of power that exist in every society. What has interested him, in particular, have been the relations of power that existed in colonial and now post-colonial societies.

These ideas come largely from his encounters with an unlikely group of thinkers and writers. First with Vico, the eighteenth-century Italian historical thinker, who is an enormous presence in Said's first major work, *Beginnings* (1975), and with the French historian and philosopher, Michel Foucault. It was Foucault's thinking about knowledge and power which so influenced Said's best-known work, *Orientalism* (1978). Said took Foucault's ideas and used them to re-think Orientalism – western ways of thinking about and depicting the Middle East – and showed how such apparently innocent works as travel literature, novels and paintings could be part of larger power relations between colonial powers and their subjects.

The third decisive encounter was with western Marxism, in particular Gramsci, Lukacs, Adorno and the British Marxists, Raymond Williams, E. P. Thompson and John Berger. He got many things from these writers, too many to summarize here, but some are quite surprising. Gramsci gave him a new language for thinking further about power and culture, but also an emphasis on resistance and contest that he found missing in the more pessimistic vision of Foucault (and which some, including now Said himself, found missing in *Orientalism*). Gramsci also fired Said's interest in space and geography, which runs through all these books. Said increasingly thinks of the world in terms of how places and peoples which seem far apart are connected in interesting and important ways. Not only through the history of colonialism, of course, but through the histories of exile and migration, and in the ways people imagine and represent far-away places. The key essay here is Said's controversial chapter in *Culture and Imperialism* on Jane Austen's *Mansfield Park* (republished now in *The Edward Said Reader*), where he tries to make connections between Austen's English world and the slave trade in Antigua.

Together these writers also inoculated Said against the excesses of North American literary theory in the eighties and nineties. Said was one of the first American critics to immerse himself in French literary theory and *Beginnings* established him as one of the key voices of the Theory revolution. But Said became increasingly impatient with its Eurocentrism, its faddishness and jargon. Its interest in textuality and literariness seemed to him to be too limited, leaving out too many questions about the relations between texts and the world.

Finally, these writers confirmed for Said the importance of experience. Experience has always mattered to Said, by which he means what actually happened to real people in history and society, an unfashionable interest during the seventies and eighties when Theory and Formalism swept literature departments. When critics were saying there is nothing beyond the text, Said was trying to make connections between books, ideas and personal and collective experience.

This interest drew him first to existentialism and phenomenology in the early sixties, and on the first pages of *Reflections on Exile* we find references to 'lived . . . life', 'concrete situations' and human experience'. He quotes Merleau-Ponty: 'the world is not what I think, but what I live through'.

Experience is also crucial to Said's thinking about exile, his own and that of others. Exile and migration are important subjects for Said and, in the title essay of *Reflections on Exile*, it is clear that he is talking about very real experiences when he writes of exile's 'essential sadness' and 'the crippling sorrow of estrangement'. His own memoir, *Out of Place*, is about his experience as a Palestinian schoolboy who feels that he never quite belongs either in colonial Cairo or in Cold War America. Nothing seems to fit. He always feels out of place and has no language to make sense of his 'unsettled sense of many identities'.

What is interesting here is not the continuity from the 1960s to now, but the break. There is an interesting move from the language of French phenomenology to the way he describes his experience of exile. And what I think made this move possible, what made it possible for Said to write about colonialism and exile as experiences, was reading the writers I have mentioned.

This rediscovery of experience, he argues in the Introduction to *Reflections on Exile*, is one of the great breakthroughs in our time. After so much 'hostility to historical experience' in the twentieth century, so much emphasis on formalism and theory, from T. S. Eliot and the New Criticism to Deconstruction, now feminists, exiles, ethnic minorities and writers from the former colonies are talking again about experience in a rich and complex way.

This interest in experience has coincided with an autobiographical turn in Said's writing. He starts to write about his childhood and background. Before he had written about the Orient from afar, through the eyes of a critic reading the European Orientalists. But increasingly, through the late eighties and nineties, Egypt and Palestine become landscapes that he belongs to. In essays like 'Cairo Recalled' (1987), 'Homage to a Belly-Dancer' (1990) and 'Cairo and Alexandria' (1990), and in his books *After the Last Sky* (1986) and *Out of Place* (1999), we feel that he is writing about places he knows.

At about the same time, and here is the particular importance of Adorno, he starts to write for the first time about his love for the piano and for classical music. He starts an occasional music column for the *Nation* in the late eighties, writes increasingly about the Canadian pianist, Glenn Gould, and gives the Wellek Library Lectures that are later published as *Musical Elaborations* (1991). Musical terms, especially 'counterpoint', move into his critical writing.

The final crucial influence was his reading of the great writers of anticolonialist resistance. In the mid-1980s he broadens out from the Middle East, the focus of *Orientalism* and much of his earlier political writing, to include Asia, Africa, South America and the Caribbean. He writes more about writers like C. L. R. James, Tagore, Césaire and, above all, Fanon. At the same time, he became interested in post-colonial literature, writers like Rushdie, Marquez, Walcott, Achebe and Mahfouz. And he immersed himself in the post-colonialist theory that took off in the eighties, with critics like Henry Louis Gates, Gayatri Spivak and the Subaltern Studies Group. He broadens out from the Middle East, the focus of *Orientalism* and much of his earlier political writing, to include Asia, Africa, South America and the West Indies. He tries to bring together these voices and his personal canon of European thinkers, using the insights of one to enrich the other.

The voice that emerges from these encounters, and from these four books, is in many ways decent and humane. Said has always opposed religious fundamentalism and secularism is a key term for him. He unequivocally supported Salman Rushdie against the *fatwa*. He opposes nationalism and nativism. He is a cosmopolitan, and the Introduction to *Reflections on Exile* is a passionate statement of his creed: of the virtues of seeing the world as irreducibly mixed, heterogenous and contradictory. He writes of a new decentered or multiply-centered world, a world no longer sealed within watertight compartments of art or culture or society, but mixed, mixed up, varied, complicated by the new difficult mobility of migrations, the new independent states, the newly emergent and burgeoning cultures.

Massive migrations have changed our world:

The greatest single fact of the past three decades has been, I believe, the vast human migration attendant upon war, colonialism and decolonisation, economic and political revolution, and . . . famine, ethnic cleansing and great power machinations.

In such a world, how can there be purity? Ethnic or racial purity is not only impossible, it is wrong. This is why he has so opposed western stereotypes of the Arab or the Palestinian, whether in nineteenth-century Orientalist texts or today's news bulletins. For Said, there is no such thing as 'the West' or 'Islam', no image or set of theories which will define 'the Arab' or 'the Jew'.

Said himself eludes categorization. He is hard to pin down or define. He is not simply a literary critic. Although he started out writing on Conrad and literature, there are surprisingly few pieces of conventional literary criticism in these books. He rarely writes about one work or one author. Nor is he simply a literary critic who writes on politics. His interests are wider, his range is greater.

In many senses he is a radical writer, an oppositional intellectual. But even here he can't be so easily labelled. On literature and art he can be surprisingly conservative. It is a word that comes up often in interviews. In literature, he says, 'some works are greater than others. A Dickens novel is better than a Harold Robbins novel' (*Power, Politics, and Culture*). He has no time for debunking the canon or sneering talk of Dead White European Males.

Just as in literature he returns again and again to European writers like Swift and Conrad, so in music the composers that engage him are

the great Austro-Germanic symphonic tradition that begins with Haydn, goes through Mozart, Beethoven, Schumann, Brahms, I suppose Wagner . . . Mahler, Bruckner, Schoenberg . . . and then what? Nothing. It ends (*Power, Politics, and Culture*).

And it is not just when talking about art that he sounds conservative. He sees the role of the intellectual in surprisingly traditional terms. His 1993 Reith Lectures, published as *Representations of the Intellectual*, make it clear that he belongs to the twentieth-century tradition of the oppositional, committed intellectual which runs from Zola to Sartre and Russell and then on to postwar figures like Raymond Williams, Fanon and Chomsky.

The intellectual, Said argues, must be on the other side of power: 'I've always said that the role of the intellectual is to be oppositional,' he says in one interview: 'There has to be identification not with the secretary of state or the leading philosopher of the time but with matters involving justice, principle, truth, conviction' (*Politics and Culture*).

Perhaps more than anything else, this is what set Said apart from the vast majority of literary and cultural critics in America. It wasn't just that these critics were too Eurocentric, or that their prose clunked with jargon. For Said, they left out too much of the world. By which I mean not just that they had no time for Third World voices, or that they didn't criticize Reaganism. They just weren't interested in a world he saw beyond Yale French Studies: a world of struggles against oppression and of exile, migration and dispossession.

This may not sound terribly original. But in Reaganite America, at the height of the New

Cold War, when arcane theories flourished and saw no world outside the text, Said was a rare and honourable voice. More than anything it was this that made his reputation, on both sides of the Atlantic. Anyone interested in the relations between culture and power, will have encountered Said, and that is what has made him one of the most influential and interesting intellectuals of the last twenty-five years.

Yet there is also a sense of failure in these books as well as of achievement. Besides the sheer erudition and productivity, the range of interests and the humanity of his voice, there are moments of silence and of defeat.

The first is the failure of a tradition. In *Representations of the Intellectual* he talks admiringly of the great oppositional intellectuals of the twentieth century. There is the generation formed by the First World War, the Russian Revolution and the struggle against colonialism: Lukacs and Gramsci, Russell and Tagore. Then there is a later generation, formed by the Second World War, the Cold War and the end of empire: Williams and Thompson, Sartre and Foucault, Chomsky and Said himself, born in 1935. And then? Nothing. After Said? No one.

This isn't just personal idiosyncrasy. The tradition of the engaged intellectual, who bestrides disciplines and scorns specialization as much as he opposes tyranny, looks as if it will not outlive Said.

This is part of a larger crisis of the Left since the 1970s. Said has written during a time of growing reaction and conservatism in the West. And a major part of that crisis has been the loss of hope that has followed the crisis of the Arab and Muslim world and of the post-colonial world in general. The rise of religious fundamentalism, the intolerance towards minorities, the millions dead from communal and ethnic violence, from famine and poverty, from war and terrorism. Purely in terms of numbers, this has been one of the great catastrophes in human history, much of it self-inflicted.

Through Said's writings, for over a decade, he has celebrated the rich literature of anti-colonialist resistance. But now that independence has been achieved, where is there a progressive, secular constituency, let alone a government, which is committed to his values of peace, democracy, religious tolerance and ethnic pluralism? Throughout the Middle East and the post-colonial world, such constituencies are marginal, on the defensive or under threat.

To some extent, Said acknowledges this state of affairs. 'It is a sink of corruption and mediocrity and the most appalling and murderous tyrannies,' he says of the Arab world in one interview in *Power, Politics, and Culture*. 'There are no democratic freedoms.' Elsewhere in the same interview in 1992, he says: 'The Arab world itself . . . is a catastrophe. You have regimes, all of whom, with the exception of a few, are deeply unpopular. You have the resurgence of Muslim religious political feeling. You have a significant brain drain; a lot of people are leaving. And above all, from my point of view, you have a cultural class, let's say, who are either silent or in hiding or abroad.'

Said has always deplored intolerance, nationalism and fundamentalism. And yet much of this has been in passing. And this is where the larger failure becomes a personal failure. The tyranny and violence of post-colonial societies has never been a major target for Said, compared, say, with nineteenth-century Orientalism, late-twentieth-century US imperialism or post-war Zionism. The 'other side of power' turns out to be, by and large, the other side of Western power.

That, Said (and others) would argue, is because it is the West that has the power. Look at America. Look at Israel. Who has the 'smart' bombs? Who has the gunboats and the tanks? Who has the great TV networks and the film companies? He sees Third World movements as Davids, armed only with their slings and small stones, against the Goliath of the US military-industrial complex. And this image, formed partly by his understanding of colonialism, by his experience as a Palestinian and by the Intifada, and by the formative moment of Vietnam, still dominates his worldview.

It explains, in part, the stone-throwing incident in 2000, when he was photographed throwing a stone at an (unoccupied, he claims) Israeli border post. It was attacked at the time by Said's critics as a kind of hooliganism, a shameful example for a major intellectual to set to the young. But there clearly was another kind of identification going on. At some level, it was about his identification with Palestinians and other kinds of anti-imperial resistance. When professors resort to violence, even symbolically, that is not a trivial matter.

Instead of reflecting, at length, on the historical catastrophe of post-colonialism, other modes have dominated. Self-pity (for example, the way Said describes his experience of school in Cairo). Shooting the messenger (his repeated attacks on V. S. Naipaul or a recent onslaught on Samir al-Khalil, an outspoken critic of Saddam Hussein). Idealizing Palestinians (I can only recall one reference, for example, to their support for Saddam in the Gulf War). Downplaying the threat of Palestinian revanchisme. Simply denying many of the most frightening aspects of post-war Arab life.

It is as if history froze at the death of Fanon. This is what makes his interview with Gillo Pontecorvo, the director of *Battle of Algiers*, one of the most haunting moments in Said's work. Pontecorvo made his great masterpiece about anti-colonialist revolt in the mid-1960s and Said goes to interview him twenty years later, in 1988.

Clearly, and sadly, Pontecorvo's career has come to a standstill. A once great film-maker, perhaps the greatest single cinematic voice of anti-colonialism, is finding it almost impossible to fund projects. The interview is difficult. Everywhere in Said's article the language is of defeat and silence. He talks of how Pontecorvo is 'blocked'. He asks him about post-colonialism after independence. 'I drew a blank from him.' Said goes away, defeated by this encounter. The difficulty of this interview speaks volumes about how Said has responded to what has happened in post-colonial societies over the past two generations.

Said has not been reduced, like Pontecorvo, to silence. His energy is awesome. Still the op-ed pieces and columns pour out: denouncing Arafat and Sharon, criticizing 11 September as an act of terrorism and the American media's response, trying to find a humane middle position, a third way.

But is this middle position humane or utopian? The final interview in *Power, Politics, and Culture*, originally published in *Ha'aretz Magazine* in August 2000, is an extraordinary one. In a book full of sycophantic interviews by literary academics (many of them Said's former graduate students) and Third World journalists, this is one of the few times that serious political questions about the future of Palestine and Israel are addressed.

Said's answers are full of hope. He wants Jews and Palestinians to live together in one state. They have shared a terrible history and they should somehow come together, acknowledge their shared past and past mistakes and crimes, find a way to reconciliation, and through that build together a democratic, secular, pluralist and humane future.

Who could argue with such a vision, inspired as it is by the attempt at reconciliation in post-apartheid South Africa (a significant reference: for many Mandela remains the only shining light in the post-colonial darkness)?

Except that you then read the small print, here and in other recent interviews. The future of Jerusalem?

> I am not for the repartitioning of the city. I think something should be done in an imaginative way so the city . . . can express the hopes and traditions of the three faiths: Judaism, Christianity and Islam (1992).

Should returning Palestinians be able to reclaim their homes and property? 'I think some humane and moderate solution should be found where the claims of the present and the claims of the past are addressed.' How would a Jewish minority be treated in a Jewish Palestinian state? 'A Jewish minority can survive the way other minorities in the Arab world survived.' 'The genius of Arab culture,' he says a moment later, 'was catholicity.' Later, he calls for the future of Palestine in a larger pan-Arab structure and says, 'There is every reason to go for the larger unit.'

It is an extraordinary interview. Every time he is asked about these crucial issues his answer is wishful thinking, an evasion or no answer at all. These answers do not belong to the real world of Sharon and Hamas, of Israeli settlers and suicide bombers. Of course, Said must know this. At the end of his life he is taking the long view. And in the long view, he tells his Israeli interviewer, Zionism 'won't last. Take it from me, Ari. Take my word for it. I'm older than you. It won't even be remembered.'

In the long view, Said believes, his vision will prevail. The alternative would be to believe that he'd got it wrong. That there's no constituency for his secular humanism in Palestine, or perhaps anywhere in the post-colonial world. That his great tradition of oppositional intellectuals, western Marxists and eccentrics, speaks to no one in the place that matters most to him. That the voice he's found for himself is not being heard. These books, so full of learning and interest, are tragic at the core.

Spring 2002

A TOUR TO THE HEART OF DARKNESS
Michael Kustow

In Spring 2001, I showed *The Inner Tour,* a feature-length documentary film by Israeli director Ra'anan Alexandrowicz, to an audience of (mostly) Jews. The film follows a group of Palestinians from the West Bank and Gaza on a three-day bus tour into Israel. They visit places where they or their ancestors used to live, until 1948. They talk to Israelis. They stare through the coach windows at irrigated fields and shiny tower blocks, such wealth compared to the camps and towns where they now live. These exiles live, not a continent away, but just one hour's bus-ride from their previous life.

There's a rough and tumble debate after the screening. Most people are speaking from previous agendas, few are talking about what they've just seen, which is not an atrocity or propaganda film, but a patient picture of Palestinians in exile. Next day I e-mail what is now a web-group which I've built up and called, simply, 'Jews':

> I realized last night that perhaps the most important thing is to find a way to enable *individual* Jews to 'stand up and be counted' and to 'bear witness' to the loss that has been inflicted on the Palestinians.

I am knocked sideways by an epic reply from my Israeli friend, playwright Joshua Sobol, the author of *Ghetto.*

Dear Michael,

You write 'The loss that has been inflicted on the Palestinians.'

By whom? By their leaders who pushed them to start the killings of Jews in 1929, and the killings of Jews and Arabs in 1936, which ended up with the assassination of many Palestinian intellectuals by the defeated Palestinian gangs? By their leaders who rejected the UN decision of the partition of Palestine and opened war in 1948? By their leaders who unleashed the present wave of violence some ten months ago, smashing to pieces the fragile Oslo agreement?

The loss that has been inflicted on the Palestinians by whom?

By that cynical liar Arafat, who has managed to smash to pieces the Israeli Left, which was the only political force in the world that could help his poor Palestinian people get a state of their own? Or do you still believe that any nation or group of nations besides Israel will be able to offer the Palestinians an independent state?

It was only the Israeli Left that really cared about the Palestinians, and it was that slandered and besmirched Israeli Left that lifted Arafat from the planks, restored the plucked feathers to his crown, made him *persona grata* in the White House, and managed to create a majority in Israel for a peace agreement with the Palestinians.

And it was Arafat, that pathological liar, who, like the scorpion in the fable, stung the frog that was carrying him over the water. Now he is yelling and crying for help, because he is drowning.

If you wish to play the part of a new frog – please, jump into the water, swim to him and invite that drowning scorpion to get on your back. You will certainly earn his words of flattery, as he flattered us, the Israeli Left, before he will sting you, as he did us. When you ask him why he did it, he will reply that it was all your fault, because you thought he could overcome his scorpion's nature.

There is a famous Arab saying which goes 'Better a wise enemy than a foolish friend'. Unfortunately for the Palestinians and for us Israelis, the Palestinians do not have such a wise enemy, but they have an abundance of foolish friends.

Forgive me my uncontrolled outburst, but I am sick and tired of the abuse of good will and of language in the case of the stinking Israeli/Palestinian conflict. I heard about a Palestinian professor residing in London who said that peace will prevail in the Middle East when the Israelis will exist no more. All I can say to that professor is that, following his logic, peace will exist in the Middle East when the Middle East will exist no more, because the dream of the destruction of Israel is equivalent to the dream of the destruction of the entire Middle East. One will not go without the other.

God! There is no end to it.

I am really sorry, Michael, for having unloaded upon you this belly-wind of mine. This afternoon, I was planning to go on writing my 'Israeli Tragedy', which is the play I am writing these days, but your email distracted me, leading me astray into those dead-end subterranean galleries, like the one I visited in Vilnius last week, following the footsteps of the survivors of the ghetto who took to the sewers to run away from their murderers.

All my best wishes to you,

Joshua Sobol

Dear Joshua,

I was so knocked sideways by the passion of your response that I must take a day to respond. Would you like to see a video of *The Inner Tour*, which prompted my initiative?

Michael

Dear Michael,

I simply couldn't control my fingers running on the keyboard. The situation here is quite alarming, with winds of war gathering around us. Can we still do anything to stop this useless war from breaking out? Does it still depend on us at all? One more Dolphinarium incident with a score of victims, and a full-scale onslaught on the territories will become inevitable.

Joshua

Dear Joshua,

Your first reaction was to call me naive. There have been others like it from Israeli friends who are angry with what they think is my 'position'. I sense that your 'position' and mine, as Jews of the Left, are not far apart, even if we are geographically distant – are set against each other by 'the sins of the fathers'.

You tell me that the play you are writing is called *The Tragedy of Israel*. Tragedy, however, does not arise from a competition as to who makes the greatest number of errors. Tragedy comes from blindness.

In 1947, Walter Zander, an emigré from Germany and the father of one of my friends, wrote *Is This The Way? - An Appeal To Jews*. It contains these uncomfortable words: 'Never have we admitted that our return, justified as it appears to us, inevitably requires from the Arab a *sacrifice* of the first magnitude - the sacrifice of giving up his right to rule himself.' We could not see, did not want to see, the children of Shem who are our brothers and sisters. In what looks like a lurch towards another war, I believe that British Jews, and Diaspora Jews, should not give automatic adherence to threatened Israel, and keep their mouths shut.

You and I inhabit different places, and our histories overlap but do not coincide. What is certain is that we are both surrounded by loud ignorance, sentimental myth, primitive fundamentalism, and fear which explains much but does not justify stupidity and the violence of former victims.

With much affection,

Michael

Dear Michael,

I have received the video of *The Inner Tour*. It is a very strong and sad document. It leaves you with a feeling of empathy with the suffering of the Palestinians and with their loss. I am showing it to friends, and all react in a similar way.

Today we are having a meeting between Israeli Arabs and Jews in the Arab village of Kalansuwa, not far from Tul Karem. It all started with a meeting of eight people in Tel Aviv a month ago. We were a forum of six Jewish Israeli writers and university professors, and two Israeli Arab professors meeting to work out a new covenant between Israeli Arabs and Jews.

Best wishes,

Joshua

★   ★   ★

Abu Muhammad Yihya is the oldest man in the bus in *The Inner Tour*, he must be in his seventies, and the only one wearing traditional robes and head-scarf. He comes from Jelazun refugee camp. His face is wrinkled, burnished, crone-like. He squats with his walking stick in the kibbutz museum as the guide tells their official story. His bright blue eyes sweep the space. Otherwise he is utterly immobile.

After the group visits a little mosque in Acre, he halts outside. They gather round him, for he is an elder and a Haj, he has made the pilgrimage to Mecca and his impromptu sermon in this mosque garden under the stars must be listened to.

'Dear brothers,' cries this old man, summoning all his energy, for he may never see this place again. 'Our hope comes from seeing how lovely the land is. And our pain from opening the wounds and the memories. As you know, brothers, all nations have holidays. East and West of us, from Rome to Circassia, they celebrate their feasts and sing their songs. And for us, every day is a wedding day for convoys of the dead, marching on the other side of the river. And those funerals never stop following us. Years and days pass, but for us, time stands still. How long will it be this way? I cannot say. But patience and faith have been our way. We stand steadfast, our feet embedded in our land. And from here, by the al-Jazzar mosque in Acre, we say: Let no-one doubt. We are a people that won't disappear, and won't die. We will have our celebration. With God's help, it will come soon.'

It's hard as a Jew to watch this, to hear the old man's voice lifted in affirmation, and not recall *L'Shana Ha'ba B'yerushalim*, 'Next year in Jerusalem', spoken by the same kind of old men, in the same kind of voice, through centuries and continents of Jewish exile.

★   ★   ★

Dear Michael,
The meeting in Kalansuwa was important. We all agreed that it has never been so urgent to go on with an Israeli Arab-Jewish dialogue. One of the participants said that some friends didn't show up not because of the excruciating heat, but out of despair. I reminded him of a Yiddish saying: 'Don't waste your despair, because you are going to really need it . . .'
I hope we won't.
Yours,
Joshua

Dear Joshua,
I remember your words to me in London earlier this year: 'There's going to be a lot more blood. When it's over, it won't be the peace of the powerful or of the just, but the peace of the exhausted.'
Michael

Dear Michael,
'He that rejoices at calamity shall not go unpunished' (*Proverbs*, 17, 5). I am writing these words a few hours after the latest massacre this afternoon in the heart of Jerusalem, and after watching the mob on the streets of Beirut and Ramallah rejoicing and celebrating that blood-bath, in a wild explosion of *SchadenFreude*.
I am afraid the rich English language is short of the precise equivalent for that German term for the lowest degree of moral depravity: rejoicing at the disaster of another human being. So-called religious leaders poisoning the heart and soul of their own people with lethal hatred - remember them when the time comes to ask who is responsible for the loss inflicted upon the poor Palestinian people. I look at those leaders, and I pray for their miserable people whom they lead to perdition.
When you see those masses filled with that hideous *SchadenFreude* celebrating mass-murder, you catch yourself saying: God, they remind me of those other masses who shouted and yelled their hatred in the streets of Munich and Nuremberg. Listen carefully to the voices of their leaders: are they preparing the hearts of their hordes to a genocide?
There are several degrees of preparation for genocide. The first one consists in de-legitimating a people or its state. How else can we understand that Hamas leader who invited Sharon to go back to Russia? The bomb that went off yesterday in Jerusalem, like

the one that exploded in the Dolphinarium a few weeks ago, is not just one more act of blind terrorism. No. The word GENOCIDE is written in big letters on those acts. Can't you read it?

Yesterday we held here in our house a preparatory meeting for the coming Israeli-Arab-Jewish colloquia we are organising on the Palestinian claim of the 'Right of Return'.

My best to you as ever

Joshua

Dear Joshua,

You face Hamas and Islamic Jihad; the Palestinians face Kahane-ists and settler vigilantes who froth hate-speech just as much as your crowd-goading clerics. The void we stare into is now filled with rabbis and mullahs, generals and gunmen, bomb-detonators and the fervent believers Dostoevsky called 'the possessed.' If they quote holy scripture at all, they pick the bits about righteous vengeance.

There's a void because of the absence of leaders, on either side, who can pull their peoples back from the brink - maybe the nuclear brink - from which there is no way back. Is there a Mandela in the house? The Middle East has a job vacancy.

Be as well as you can in this sanatorium world,

Michael

Autumn 2001

SHYLOCK IN THE PROMISED LAND
Shakespeare without Prejudice
Jo Glanville

Sixty years before Shakespeare wrote *The Merchant of Venice*, Suleiman the Magnificent built the walls of Jerusalem. Even as the solid blocks of stone were being laid, Suleiman's Muslim army was thundering into Europe and threatening to topple Christendom. His greatness lingers on in Shakespeare's play, and when Portia's Moroccan suitor attempts to win her heart, he clearly thinks that he can impress her with a second-hand boast about the great warrior. He brandishes his scimitar and claims that it killed a Persian who once got the better of Suleiman. The reflected glory is not, however, enough to win him his bride.

My neighbour Nisreen was studying the play at school. As she read the Moroccan's lines she could look out at Suleiman's walls, which still form a mighty girdle around what is now the Old City of Jerusalem and Nisreen's home. The controversy which periodically accompanies European productions of Shakespeare's play pales beside its potential for fomenting discord in Shylock's spiritual home. That, at least, was the opinion of the Israeli authorities. Nisreen is a Palestinian and was reading the play in English, but the Israelis had banned *The Merchant of Venice* in Arabic in the West Bank and the Gaza Strip. The miserly, vengeful and bloodthirsty Shylock, reviled by the Venetians and rejected even by his own daughter, was a fine Jewish hate-figure for the Palestinians who lived so miserably under Israeli rule. As a ghetto Diaspora Jew, he also represented everything that the Israelis had left behind in Europe.

There is no getting around the fact that Shylock is a villain. He is 'the dog Jew', 'a very Jew', 'a faithless Jew' and, as I read those lines in my flat in the Old City, their sentiment chilled my blood. I had agreed to help Nisreen with her English studies, but I was now shrinking from the task. There is nothing like antisemitism for making an assimilated Jew like me feel Jewish.

At home in London, I had the luxury of a cultural Jewish identity without being a member of the Jewish community. I could not wholeheartedly call myself Jewish since I had not been brought up in the religion and its traditions were not part of my life. My mother is Jewish solely on her father's side and I would therefore not be considered Jewish by the Orthodox in any case. But there was no room for the niceties of my Jewish identity in Jerusalem and no possibility for half-measures. Whose side was I on?

I met many Europeans who had come to Israel in aid of the Palestinian cause. They disliked the Israelis with a bitterness which I never encountered in the Palestinians themselves, who mostly displayed an astonishing generosity of spirit. When these Europeans posed the inevitable question – how could a persecuted people inflict such suffering on another? – I had a great desire to commit an act of violence. Since when, I retorted, did abuse beget anything other than abuse? But I realized that I too wanted the Israelis to be beyond reproach. I could not bear to hear them criticized and yet at the same time I was deeply critical of them myself. It's okay for Jews to tell jokes against themselves, but if anyone else tells a joke against them then it's antisemitic.

The young American Zionists were also intolerable. For them, Israel was one big summer camp. They considered the Palestinians to be the enemy and when they talked about the Israelis, they said 'we' and 'us'. The Israelis did not thank them for it.

By choosing to live in a Christian Palestinian neighbourhood while studying at the Hebrew University, I was attempting to straddle both worlds and finding the exercise more difficult than I had anticipated. It is not very comfortable sitting on the fence. Most Israelis were horrified when I told them where I lived. Was I not afraid? Was I stupid? Some nostalgically recalled the days when they spent Saturdays in the Old City and ate hummus in its restaurants. Arab East Jerusalem was the only place still humming with life on Shabbat when the western, Jewish side of the city closed down, but it had been off-limits to the Israelis since the Intifida began in the late 1980s. Some left-wing Israelis stayed away as a matter of principle, but most kept to West Jerusalem out of fear. One Israeli friend asked me to take her round the Old City and so I found myself in the curious position of being tour guide to a native.

Israelis never took me for a Jew. They considered me wholly English and I realized that they were right. I irritated them excessively with the number of times I said 'sorry' in the course of a conversation. When it came to speaking Hebrew, I realized that I had great difficulty in asking directly for what I wanted. The English language serves as a very convenient cloak for one's needs and desires, which can be dressed up in numerous 'mights' and 'maybes' to disguise the fact that one actually wants something. But in Hebrew you ask directly for what you want and there are no extra frills of language to hide the nakedness of your desires. That is why people so often consider the Israelis rude and abrupt: modern Hebrew was born in a hurry and there was no time for trimmings.

It was the autumn of 1993 and at that time there was euphoria in the streets. In the build-up to the signing of the first Oslo Accord, Palestinian children marched round the narrow alleys of the Old City at night banging empty containers – a war-like sound which simultaneously thrilled me while chilling my Jewish sensibilities. Palestinian youths zoomed around the roads of East Jerusalem, which skirted the Old City, in open trucks waving the Palestinian flag which had, until then, been illegal. When Arafat and Rabin shook hands on the lawn of the White House I watched it on television and could hear my neighbours cheering. When I asked Nisreen what she felt, she shrugged her shoulders. She was a child when the Intifada began and at seventeen she was already cynical. She expected nothing from the Israelis. It was rare in that heady atmosphere to encounter such coolness as Nisreen's. What would she make of Shylock?

I was torn. I wanted Nisreen to know that I was on her side, but I also wanted to defend Shylock. Should I start by sanctimoniously lecturing her about the bitter history of European Jews and thereby try to exonerate Shylock and the Israelis in her eyes? If she chose to identify Shylock with the Israelis, as I expected, what right did I have to preach at her?

Five Palestinian families lived in the courtyard where I shared a flat with two friends. It was on the cusp of the Jewish, Armenian and Christian quarters. The Jewish quarter had been badly bombed in 1948 and later rebuilt by the Israelis after the Six Day War. Crossing from the Muslim and Christian quarters into the Jewish quarter was a little like arriving in the land of Oz from Kansas. The dark, discoloured stone of the Palestinian streets gave way to the light, airy spaces and honey-coloured stone of the wealthy Jewish neighbourhood.

Shylock might not have attracted too much attention if he had happened to wander down these streets, there were enough people already in them in the antiquated fancy-dress of their religions and denominations for him to mingle in the crowd: Franciscan monks, Greek Orthodox priests, Hassidic Jews, Ethiopian monks, Armenian priests. Then there were the groups of Christian tourists shouldering life-size crucifixes along the Via Dolorosa as they retraced Christ's footsteps and created a traffic jam. It was a religious theme park and going about one's daily business in a place so pregnant with symbolism seemed profane. I bought my stamps from a post office which faced the citadel where Pontius Pilate condemned Jesus, and I took a shortcut home from the butcher through the courtyard of the Holy Sepulchre, built, so they say, on Calvary. I would be struck down at any moment.

There were often strikes in East Jerusalem, commemorating clashes with the Israelis or protesting against an incident in the West Bank or Gaza. The shops in the Old City would close and the market streets would empty. Only a few defiant souls would carry on doing business behind their shutters. It was difficult to know how the owners of the tourist shops made a decent living in any case. Trade had fallen drastically since the Intifada and most of the shops sold the same things: rugs, pottery and olive wood carvings.

When disaster struck the Palestinians or the Israelis - when Baruch Goldstein massacred the Palestinians in Hebron, when Israelis died in suicide bomb attacks - the depression and fear were palpable. Everyone was infected by a common sense of horror and I became desperate to escape from Jerusalem, as though from the claustrophobic embrace of a family in the grip of catastrophe. Although I acclimatized quickly to the intensity of emotion and the burden of history which charged the atmosphere of the city, whenever I left Jerusalem for any period of time, I felt a sudden, physical release of pressure from my head, as if I had come down from a great altitude.

Nisreen was very down to earth. She had her own domestic troubles. Her father was a very sick man, dying slowly after a botched operation. He once lifted up his shirt to show me his stomach. There was a crater where his belly should have been. A tough rim of skin, like hide, surrounded a circle of softer looking flesh. In desperation, he had gone to India for a kidney transplant. He was given no time to recuperate and flew straight back to Jerusalem. The wound had opened on the journey home and the doctors in Israel had not been able to repair the damage. He would become deeply depressed and lie on his bed crying, 'I want to die, I want to die.'

Once, when I was visiting, he began cursing the Jews. It was in those situations that the question of my Jewish identity plagued me and I wondered why I had been so naive as to think that I could live in a Palestinian neighbourhood. My neighbours accepted me as a foreigner. They welcomed me and my flatmates into their homes. They fed us, entertained us and made us feel as though we were part of their lives. My friend Cathy had found the flat. She spoke good Arabic and had lived in Jerusalem for several years. With her ebullient, forthright personality she was more at home there than in the quiet, English seaside town where she had grown up. She was a Christian. Palestinians were always attracted by her infectious warmth and she had many friends.

One night, soon after I had arrived in Jerusalem, a group of Cathy's friends had gathered on our balcony. Someone told an antisemitic joke. I did not say a word. Suddenly, I had become a Jewish victim, shocked and alienated from their company. My grandfather had changed his name from Goldberg to Glanville to hide his Jewish identity and here was I, hiding my Jewish identity and not daring to speak out in the country where Jews were supposed to be free. But perhaps my automatic response and inherited sense of persecution were not appropriate. For it was the Palestinians who were victims here, not me. They were the underclass. They had no reason to bear any friendship for the Israelis and if they chose to let off steam by telling crude jokes, who was I to correct them? They may have been guests in my home that night, but I was a guest in their city, just passing through their lives.

However when Nisreen's father began railing against the Jews, I told him that I came from a Jewish family. 'Ah, you Jews from over there,' he said, gesturing in a direction that I assumed to be Europe. 'You are different.' I was amused, and I confess relieved, at how swiftly he reconciled his liking for me with my Jewish origins. Some Palestinian friends had advised me never to declare that I was Jewish in Palestinian neighbourhoods; others said that I should choose my moment carefully. Whenever I did 'come out', for that is what it felt like, I was always pleasantly surprised by the response.

Once I shared a taxi to the West Bank with a Palestinian. I had been told on no account to speak Hebrew there. My command of Arabic was poor and my travelling companion spoke little English. Hebrew was the only common language and we chatted merrily for the entire journey. I had the fearful sense of breaking a taboo, but I was never able to grasp the etiquette which governed the Israeli–Palestinian divide. Perhaps there were no rules and this in itself was alarming. I often had the sense that I was walking through these two cultures blindly, endeavouring not to step on the cracks in the pavement without having any idea of where the cracks actually were.

No one surprised me and shattered my preconceptions as much as Nisreen. We spent the first few sessions on *The Merchant of Venice* unravelling Shakespeare's metaphors and deciphering the punning banter of the Venetian lads. In all my apprehension, I had completely neglected to consider that the language might pose a problem for Nisreen. Her English was good, but Shakespeare was difficult enough for British schoolchildren of her age. To my astonishment, Nisreen was wholly captivated by the poetry. She declared that she wanted to marry Shakespeare. Then she began to joke that she was Shakespeare's wife and called herself Mrs Shakespeare. 'How is your husband?' I would ask her when she arrived for a session on *The Merchant*.

'He is well,' she would reply gravely and then break into a smile. I was learning to read and write Arabic and had a children's ABC in Arabic on the wall of my room. Next to each character was a corresponding picture: a rabbit for the letter *aleph*, a duck for the letter *beyt*. Nisreen would point solemnly at each picture and I would have to name them correctly. Then we would begin reading *The Merchant*. Nisreen loved the story and became as involved with the characters as if it were a soap opera. She tutted at Bassanio's recklessness and held her breath when Portia's suitors tried the caskets.

Then, one day, we read the passage where Shylock's servant, Launcelot, curses his master and runs off to serve a Christian, Bassanio. As we read Launcelot's speech, in which he declares 'the Jew is the very devil incarnation', I inwardly cringed, fearing that Nisreen would applaud his sentiment. She looked at me and frowned, 'Shylock will kill him if he hears him!' she exclaimed, entirely rapt in the plot.

I felt ashamed of myself and I thought of the Israeli authorities who had banned the play in Arabic. All that we seemed to be able to see in the play was antisemitic feeling; all that Nisreen could see was the drama. Shakespeare and his art had triumphed over our own self-obsession. Nisreen pitied Shylock – she hated the manner in which the Christians reviled him and was horrified when they stripped him of his wealth and forced him to convert to Christianity. She responded to all the characters with equally human feeling. Shakespeare can rarely have had a better audience than Nisreen.

I gave her a book of his sonnets for her birthday. She proudly took the book to school to show her teacher and then became the most unpopular girl in the class when her teacher made all the students learn one of the sonnets by heart for homework. When I heard that the play was being performed in Tel Aviv, I wanted to take Nisreen, But it was being performed in Hebrew and she was not keen to go. So I went alone. Tel Aviv is another world. It is a modern city on the Mediterranean and Jerusalem, in comparison, is a provincial town. I had begun to dress very conservatively since living in the Old City, in an attempt to fit in with the cultural norm and, when I experienced a sense of shock at seeing the women of Tel Aviv so free and easy in their short skirts, I realized that I had not even appreciated how constricting life in Jerusalem had become. Tel Aviv was far closer to the life that I knew in London and yet it felt alien.

The Merchant of Venice was playing at the Cameri theatre, one of the best-known theatres in the country. To see Launcelot cursing Shylock in Hebrew, Bassanio and chums bantering in Hebrew and Portia's suitors wooing her in Hebrew filled me with awe. Surely this must be one of the ultimate triumphs for the Jews – to produce *The Merchant of Venice* with a Jewish cast, before a Jewish audience, in the language and nation of the Jews. However it was not enough of a triumph as far as the director was concerned. The production turned Shakespeare's play on its head.

Shylock was a sober, respectable businessman in a grey, three-piece suit, while the Christians sported velvet and hung out in a hippy den. They were a dissolute bunch of layabouts and you would not lend a fiver to a single one of them.

Worse was to follow. When Jessica eloped with Lorenzo, she appeared dressed in velvet, as if she had been brainwashed and joined a cult. She handed a suitcase full of money to Lorenzo and was then raped by his cronies while he kissed the bills of cash.

When Shylock made his famous speech – 'Hath not a Jew eyes?' – the Christians gathered round him and beat him up. At the end of the speech, as Shylock spoke of vengeance, his assailants fell to the floor.

Here, in Tel Aviv, Shylock had finally had his revenge and corrected the wrongs of centuries of persecution. The stereotype of the money-loving, rapacious, lascivious Jew had been projected on to the Christians, and Shakespeare's play had been rewritten. If it had not been for Nisreen, I might have rejoiced in the Israeli production. She had the humanity to see both sides of the story and taught me a lesson about my own prejudice.

I rang the Israeli authorities to ask them why they had banned the Arabic translation of the play in the West Bank and Gaza. The Israeli official to whom I spoke was shocked to hear that the play was banned. He had had no idea and doubted that I had been correctly informed. Perhaps, he suggested, there was a particular Arabic edition of the play with an introduction which incited violence against the Israelis. Perhaps, but I was never able to find out. These days, it is Arafat who monitors the Palestinians' reading matter and bans books in the Palestinian territories.

Autumn 1997

ANYBODY WHO KNOWS ANYTHING ABOUT WASHING SOCKS IN JERUSALEM KNOWS

Jonathan Treitel

that you wear the socks on your hands like gloves

that the water is piped from far away, it comes from the Sea of Galilee

that you rub soap in, taking care not to miss the heel

that some of the water is pumped from underground, it is from the 'water table'

that the best soap in the Holy Land is made in Nablus out of olive oil and lye, actually the olive oil is
     imported Italian, since the local olive oil is too high quality, it is reserved for salad

that nobody washes gloves by wearing them on the feet like socks

that it is not necessary to turn the socks inside-out though perhaps it helps

that it is a chore that is put off yet it will be over in a jiffy

that you squeeze the soapy water out

that you rinse the socks in pure water

that you squeeze the purer water out

that the air in Jerusalem is clearer than most and less humid, if you hang the socks at night they will dry in
     your sleep, in the morning you can put them on

that if you own two pairs and wash faithfully you are sure to have one pair clean and dry and ready

that theoretically one pair would be enough

that if you drape the socks over the radiator the room will smell of drying socks

that the rich do not wash their own socks (they hire the poor to do it) just think what they miss

that the really rich wear socks only once

that the really really rich wash their own socks, that is how they became really really rich

that cotton is comfortablest

that nylon is strongest

that if you wear the same pair two days running it is not the end of the world

that water is precious

that soapless washing is better than nothing

that lather is purely decorative, non-lathering soap is just as efficacious, lather is a myth

that if you took to going sockless in sandals you might never have to wash another sock again

that all socks are the one sock, barring details of colour and fabric and pattern, not much can be done with
     the basic sock

that the right sock is the same as the left sock though the right foot is not the same as the left foot

that come to think of it the traditional Japanese sock honours the separateness of the big toe

that at this moment in Jerusalem I am probably the only person pondering the design of the Japanese sock

that at this moment in Jerusalem thousands of people are washing their socks, yet this would be a poor basis
     for an inter-faith discussion group, a theme party, or a forum for reconciliation; there again who
     knows?

that my socks are cleaner than your socks

that your socks are cleaner than my socks

that my socks are as dirty as your socks

that after we die our socks go on growing

that we shall not come naked into heaven, we shall be wearing our socks

that our socks are part of us (who would willingly wear another's?) and when after a hundred washings they
     begin to fray and diffuse we wear them a few more times reluctant to give up what was directly
     beneath us: what we stood in when we said, 'I am standing in Jerusalem.'

Spring 2000

CONTRIBUTORS

Dannie Abse is a doctor, playwright and novelist. His latest collection of poetry is *New and Collected Poems* (2002); his most recent novel is *The Strange Case of Dr Simmonds & Dr Glas* (2002).

Sholom Aleichem (1859-1916), born in the Ukraine, was a prolific writer of stories, sketches, plays and poems in Hebrew and Russian, as well as Yiddish. He is best known for his novel *Tevye the Dairyman*. He has been translated into many languages and is probably the most popular Yiddish writer of all.

Dan Almagor has written and translated over 100 plays; his translations of Shakespeare's plays are used throughout Israel. He has taught Hebrew Literature at University College, London, and received the Israeli Theatre Academy Award for Best Translator as well as the Writers' Association's Jubilee Award for Lifetime Contribution to Israeli Culture.

Karen Alkalay-Gut was born in London, raised in the US, and moved to Israel in 1972. She is the author of several books of verse and teaches English literature at Tel Aviv University.

Al Alvarez's most recent collection of poetry is *New and Selected Poems* (2002). He is the author of an autobiography, *Where did it all go right?* (1999), as well as novels, literary criticism, anthologies and several non-fiction books, including *Poker: Bets, bluffs and bad beats* (2001).

Aharon Appelfeld was born in Czernowitz, Bukovina and arrived in Palestine in 1946. He is the author of many novels, including *Badenheim 1939* (1979) and *Katerina* (1989). He is Professor of Literature at the Ben Gurion University of the Negev in Beersheva.

Anne Atik has published several volumes of poetry, including *Drancy* with R. B. Kitaj (1989) and *How it Was* (2001). She lives in Paris.

Wanda Barford was born in Milan and brought up in South Africa. She has published three volumes of poetry.

Alexander Baron (1917-1999) was the author of a dozen novels and plays for television, in addition to successful TV adaptations of nineteenth- and twentieth-century classic novels for the BBC. *The Lowlife* (1963) was reissued in 2001 with an introduction by Iain Sinclair.

Liz Cashdan teaches creative writing at Sheffield University Institute for Life-Long Learning. Her most recent collection of poetry is *Laughing all the Way*. She is Poetry Editor of *Jewish Renaissance*.

Tony Dinner, Poetry Editor of *The Jewish Quarterly,* is a painter and poet. He is working on his forthcoming third poetry collection, *Is All*.

Vera Elyashiv was born in Kaunas, Lithuania and now lives in England. She is a journalist and freelance writer and was the first female parliamentary correspondent for the now defunct Israeli newspaper *Davar*. She is a cultural critic and correspondent for the *Kölner Stadt Anzeiger* (*Cologne City Herald*).

Ruth Fainlight has published thirteen collections of poems, the most recent being *Burning Wire* (2002). Books of her poems have appeared in French, Spanish and Portuguese translation, and she has also translated and published collections of poetry from those languages. She has published two collections of short stories and written libretti for the Royal Opera House.

Elaine Feinstein is a novelist, poet and biographer. Her most recent collection of poetry is *Gold* (2000). She has translated the poetry of Marina Tsvetayeva, and is the author of biographies of Marina Tsvetayeva, Pushkin and Ted Hughes.

Alexander Flinder (1921-2001), born in Soho, trained as an architect before becoming a marine archaeologist. He was one of the pivotal figures who brought about the raising of the *Mary Rose* in 1982. The author of *Secrets of the Bible Seas* (1985), he led many expeditions to the Mediterranean and the Red Sea to dive ancient harbours and was awarded the MBE for services to marine archaeology.

Jonathan Freedland is an award-winning journalist and writer. He is Policy Editor of the *Guardian*, a columnist for the *Jewish Chronicle* and author of *Bring Home the Revolution: the Case for a British Republic* (1998). He presents *The Long View* on BBC Radio 4.

T. R. Fyvel (1907-1985) was born in Cologne and grew up in Switzerland and England. He joined the Zionist movement in Palestine before the war took him to North Africa and Italy with the British and American forces. He worked as literary editor of *Tribune*, at the BBC, and, in his retirement, as literary editor of the *Jewish Chronicle*. His books include *The Insecure Offenders* (1961) and *George Orwell: A Personal Memoir* (1982).

Barbara Garvin is a senior lecturer in Italian at University College, London.

Jo Glanville is a producer and presenter for BBC Radio 4. She has also written for many magazines and newspapers, including the *Independent, Prospect, New Statesman*, the *Observer* and the *Times*.

Frederick Goldman lectured in Jewish history. He wrote for various newspapers including the *New York Times*.

Linda Grant is the author of three novels and a memoir, including the prize-winning *When I Lived in Modern Times* (2000), and *Still Here* (2002). She is a feature writer on the *Guardian*.

David Grossman was a correspondent for Israel radio for twenty-five years. He is the author of many highly-acclaimed works of both fiction and non-fiction, including *See Under: Love* (1986), *Sleeping on a Wire* (1992), *The Zig-Zag Kid* (1994) and *Be My Knife* (1998).

Michael Hamburger was born in Berlin and educated in England. A leading poet and critic, he is the foremost contemporary translator of German poetry. He has won many awards for his translations of writers including Baudelaire, Celan, Goethe and Rilke. His most recent collection of poetry is *Intersections: Shorter Poems 1994-2000* (2000).

David Herman is a television and radio producer and writer. He has made television programmes about Saul Bellow, Isaiah Berlin, Harold Pinter and E.P. Thompson. He is a regular contributor to *The Jewish Quarterly*.

Josef Herman (1911-2000) OBE, RA, was born in Warsaw. He settled in Glasgow in 1940 before moving to South Wales where he made his name with a series of paintings of coal miners. He was closely involved with *The Jewish Quarterly*, writing mainly about art, for over thirty years.

Edmond Jabès (1912-1991) was born in Egypt, and moved to Paris after the Suez crisis in 1956. A renowned poet of the post-war era in France, he is best known for his seven-volume prose work, *Le Livre des Questions*.

A.C. Jacobs (1937-1994) lived in Israel, Scotland, Italy, London and Spain. He published two books of his own poetry and two books of modern Hebrew poetry in translation.

Dan Jacobson was born in South Africa and has spent most of his adult life in England. He is an acclaimed novelist, essayist and university teacher and the recipient of several literary awards.

Howard Jacobson is the author of six novels, most recently *Who's Sorry Now?* (2002). He has also written works of non-fiction, including *Roots Schmoots* (1993) and *Seriously Funny: An Argument for Comedy* (1997).

Zvi Jagendorf is a Professor Emeritus of English and Theatre at the Hebrew University, Jerusalem. His novel *Wolfy and the Strudelbakers* (2001) won the Society of Authors' Sagittarius Prize.

Gabriel Josipovici was born in France and lived in Egypt from 1945 until 1956. A Professor in the Graduate School of the Humanities at the University of Sussex, he is the author of several acclaimed novels and books of literary criticism, as well as a memoir of his mother Sasha Rabinovitch, *A Life* (2001).

Ghada Karmi was born in Jerusalem and trained as a doctor of medicine at Bristol University. She established the first British-Palestinian medical charity in 1972 and was an associate Fellow at the Royal Institute of International Affairs. Her most recent book is *In Search of Fatima* (2002).

R. J. Kitaj was born in Ohio, and lived in London for over forty years before returning to the United States in 1994. He is one of the most influential painters of his generation, who draws constantly on Jewish sources for inspiration in his painting.

Bernard Kops was born in the East End of London. Since his first play, *The Hamlet of Stepney Green* (1959), he has written over forty plays for stage and radio, nine novels and seven volumes of poetry, including *Grandchildren and other poems* (2000).

Gertrude Kolmar (1894-1943) was born in Berlin, where she lived until she was arrested in 1943 and deported to a concentration camp, where she was killed. Most of her poetry was published after her death, including a volume in English translation, *Dark Soliloquies* (1975).

Lotte Kramer came to Britain from Germany on a *kindertransport* in 1939. She has exhibited her paintings widely, and published nine books of poetry.

Michael Kustow is a writer, producer and broadcaster. He has been Director of the Institute of Contemporary Arts, Associate Director of the Royal Shakespeare Company and National Theatre and Head of Arts for Channel 4 Television. His most recent book is *theatre@risk* (2000).

Joseph Leftwich (1892-1983) was born in Holland. He was a Yiddishist, poet, translator and critic; among his many books are *An Anthology of Modern Yiddish* (1974) and *Great Yiddish Writers of the Twentieth Century* (1987).

Gabriel Levin was born in France and grew up in the United States and Israel. His most recent collection of poems is *Ostraca* (1999). *Poems from the Diwan*, translations of the medieval Hebrew-Andalusian poet Yehuda Halevi, appeared in 2002. He lives in Jerusalem.

Jane Liddell-King teaches English and French literature at Cambridge University. Her first play, *Davka*, was staged in Cambridge in 2003.

Sonja Linden is a playwright and writer of short stories. She has edited a number of anthologies of plays, poetry and short fiction. Her most recent play for stage has been inspired by her work with survivors from the Rwandan genocide and is scheduled for production in June 2003 in London.

Barnet Litvinoff (1917-1996) historian and the author of many books, was the author of a biography of Chaim Weizmann (1976) and *The Burning Bush: Antisemitism and World History* (1988).

Emanuel Litvinoff made his name as a poet during World War II. His acclaimed memoir of growing up in London's East End, *Journey through a Small Planet* (1972), was reissued in 1993.

Hyam Maccoby is Research Professor at the Centre for Jewish Studies, University of Leeds. He is the author of many books including *The Philosophy Of The Talmud* (2002) and *Jesus The Pharisee* (2003). He was a member of the Editorial Board of *The Jewish Quarterly* for many years and a close friend of the founder, Jacob Sonntag and his wife Batya.

Wolf Mankowitz (1924–1998) grew up in the East End. After studying at Cambridge he became an antiques dealer before writing his first novel *Make Me an Offer* (1952). He was the author of several stage and screenplays, including *A Kid for Two Farthings*, and the screen adaptation of *The Millionairess*.

Shimon Markish, born in the Soviet Union, is an author and translator. He now lives in Geneva.

Peretz Markish (1895-1952) is considered to be one of the foremost Yiddish poets of the modern era. He was one of 24 Soviet-Yiddish writers who were executed on 12 August 1952, under Stalin's orders.

Ronit Matalon worked as a journalist covering the West Bank and Gaza during the first Intifada. Her fiction includes *The One Facing Us* (1999) and *Bliss* (2003).

Mark Mazower is an Anniversary Professor of History at Birkbeck College, London. His books include *Dark Continent: Europe's Twentieth Century* (1998) and *The Balkans* (2000).

Selma Meerbaum-Eisinger (1924-1941), a relative of Paul Celan, was deported with her family from her native Czernowitz during the Second World War to the labour camp of Michailovka, in Transnistria, where she died of typhus, aged seventeen.

Sylvia Paskin is the editor and co-editor of several anthologies including *Angels of Fire* (1986) and *When Joseph Met Molly – a reader on Yiddish Film* (1999). She is Literary Editor for David Paul Press.

Corinne Pearlman is a partner in Comic Company, producing illustrated health education resources, and is Creative Director of Myriad Editions' State of the World Atlas series. She also does comic strips, cartoons and children's book illustration.

Harold Pinter is one of the pre-eminent British playwrights of the twentieth century. Born in Hackney, he trained as an actor, and made his name as a playwright with *The Caretaker* (1959). He has written many screenplays, is an acclaimed director, and he continues to act on stage, film and radio. In 2002 the BBC broadcast a season of his works.

Frederic Raphael is renowned as a novelist and for his film and television adaptations. He has published a book of autobiographical reminiscences, *Personal Terms* (2001) and a memoir of his collaboration with Stanley Kubrick, *Eyes Wide Open* (1999).

Emanuel Ringelblum (1900-1944) was the main archivist and historian of the Warsaw Ghetto. The Ringelblum Archives contain biographical sketches of some of the leading figures of the Warsaw Ghetto. In 1944 the bunker where he was living in hiding was betrayed and he, along with around three dozen other Jews, was executed by the Gestapo.

Michael Rosen is a poet and BBC Radio broadcaster. Among his many books for children are *We're going on a Bear Hunt* (1993) and *Centrally-heated Knickers* (2000). His most recent book is *Carrying the Elephant: a Memoir of Love and Loss* (2002).

Bernice Rubens was born in Cardiff. The winner of the 1970 Booker Prize for *The Elected Member*, she is the author of several acclaimed novels, including *Nine Lives* (2002).

Anthony Rudolf writes fiction, literary criticism and art criticism. He is a translator and publisher, occasional broadcaster and journalist, and visiting lecturer in arts and humanities at London Metropolitan University.

Nelly Sachs (1891-1970) was born in Berlin. She escaped to Stockholm in 1940, and lived there for the rest of her life. She published several volumes of poetry and wrote a series of plays. In 1966 she was awarded the Nobel Prize for Literature.

Rafael F. Scharf was born in Crakow and came to England in 1939. He has written and lectured extensively about the vanished world of Polish Jewry, and is the co-founder of The Institute of Polish-Jewish Studies in Oxford. He was closely involved with *The Jewish Quarterly* from its inception and was a regular contributor for over thirty years.

Anna Sherbany is a London-based visual artist and photographer; she has exhibited internationally. In 1998–2000 she curated 'Story Time', work by Jewish and Palestinian artists from Israel/Palestine, and 'Appendix A', work by British-based artists, touring to London, Liverpool, Jerusalem and Nazareth. She lectures in Photography and Visual Language.

Clive Sinclair is a celebrated novelist and essayist, whose books include *Lady with the Laptop* (1996), *A Soap Opera from Hell* (1998) and *Meet the Wife* (2002).

Joshua Sobol is Israel's leading playwright. He has written many plays, including *Ghetto* (1984), which has been translated into over 20 languages, and has been performed and awarded prizes all over the world. He is also a theatre director and a visiting professor at universities in Israel and the United States.

Rachel Spence is a freelance journalist who is currently living in Venice. She writes for *The Independent* and *Red Pepper*.

A.N. Stencl (1897-1983) was born in Poland. He came to England from Berlin in 1936 and settled in Whitechapel, regularly publishing pamphlets of poetry and his own publication *Loshn un Lebn* ('Language and Life'). He became the mentor of many Yiddishists, who regularly joined his Saturday literary afternoons, Friends of Yiddish, in Whitechapel.

Yuri Suhl (1908-1986) was a poet, novelist and translator. His book *They Fought Back* (1976) is a definitive work on Jewish resistance in Nazi Europe.

Ron Taylor was awarded the Jewish Quarterly-Wingate Prize for 1994.

Jonathan Treitel divides his time between London and Jerusalem. He is a prize-winning poet and critic, whose work has appeared in many magazines and anthologies.

Claude Vigée was born in Strasbourg and now lives in Paris and Jerusalem. He is the senior Jewish poet writing in French today, and has published many volumes of both poetry and prose.

Arnold Wesker is the acclaimed author of forty-two plays, including *Chicken Soup with Barley*, *Roots* and *I'm Talking about Jerusalem* (*The Wesker Trilogy*, 1958-1960). He has also published collections of short stories and essays.

James E. Young is Professor of English and Judaic Studies at the University of Massachusetts, Amherst, USA. He is the author of *At Memory's Edge* (2000), *The Texture of Memory* (1993) and *Writing and Rewriting the Holocaust* (1994).

ACKNOWLEDGEMENTS

I would like to thank Matthew Reisz, the current editor of the magazine, who has been a source of valued advice and inspiration, giving generously of his time and always full of fine ideas and warm encouragement; Marion Cohen who saved me from a huge amount of stress by taking responsibility for getting the necessary permissions for the articles and pictures reprinted here; and my parents, Joe and Marilyn Lehrer, for the generosity with which they have given unstintingly of their time, and for the infinite patience they have shown their sometimes unreasonably-demanding daughter.

'The Arrival of Adam and Eve at Dover' © Dannie Abse, reprinted by kind permission of Hutchinson and the author; 'The Hope' © Karen Alkalay-Gut; 'A Complaint Against the Times' © Dan Almagor, Barbara Garvin and Dan Jacobson; 'Operation' © Al Alvarez; 'The way to myself' © Aharon Appelfeld; 'Teaching Noga the Hebrew Alphabet' © Anne Atik; London Jewish Bakers' Union Banner, reproduced by kind permission of the Jewish Museum, London; 'Yes, Madam' © Wanda Barford; 'The Anniversary' © the estate of Alexander Baron; 'The Tyre–Cairo Letters' © Liz Cashdan; 'A London Synagogue – the Feast of Tabernacles' from the *Graphic*, 2 November 1872, reproduced by kind permission of Anne Cowen; 'Kaddish' © Tony Dinner; 'A letter I wrote in 1945' © Vera Elyashiv; 'The English Country Cottage' © Ruth Fainlight, reprinted from *Burning Wire* (2002) by kind permission of Bloodaxe Books; 'New Year' © Elaine Feinstein; 'The Yom Kippur Swimming Gala' © the estate of Alexander Flinder; 'Our destiny in whose hands?' © Jonathan Freedland; 'The Last Romantics' © the estate of T. R. Fyvel, reprinted by kind permission of Mary Fyvel; Photographs by Willy Georg © Rafael F. Scharf; 'Shylock in Jerusalem' © Jo Glanville; 'The Dancing Bear' © Frederick Goldman; 'Israel at Fifty' © David Grossman and Haim Watzman; 'Delmore Schwartz and me' © Linda Grant; 'In a cold season' © Michael Hamburger, taken from *Michael Hamburger: Collected Poems 1941-1994* published by Anvil Press Poetry (1995); 'A sense of place' © David Herman; Drawings by Josef Herman, reproduced by kind permission of Mrs Nini Herman; 'Song of the Last Jewish Child', Untitled poem by Edmond Jabès © Anthony Rudolf on behalf of the estate of Edmond Jabès; 'Itzik Manger in Paradise', 'Sol' and 'Jewish Quarter' reprinted by kind permission of Menard Press and Hearing Eye on behalf of the estate of the late A.C.Jacobs.; 'Vay iz mir – Who'd be a Jewish writer?' © Howard Jacobson; 'The Key to Judah's Camp' © Zvi Jagendorf; Extract from 'A Life' © Gabriel Josipovici; 'A Palestinian in Golders Green' © Ghada Karmi; *Drancy, 1984-86* by R. B. Kitaj, from the collection of the Fondation du Judaisme Français, Paris © the artist, courtesy of Marlborough Fine Art, London; 'Jewish Woman' © the estate of Gertrude Kolmar, reprinted from *Dark Soliloquy: the Selected Poems of Gertrude Kolmar*, trans. Henry A. Smith. New York: Seabury Press, 1975; 'Shalom Bomb' © Bernard Kops; 'Jewish Cemetery in Prague' © Lotte Kramer, reprinted from *Family Arrivals* (1980) by kind permission of Rockingham Press; 'In Prague' © Lotte Kramer, reprinted from *A Lifelong House* (1983) by kind permission of Hippopotamus Press, and *Selected and New Poems, 1980-1997* (1997) by kind permission of Rockingham Press; 'Picturing Sylvester' © Michael Kustow; 'A Tour to the Heart of Darkness © Michael Kustow and Joshua Sobol; 'Rudolf Rocker, mentor of the Jewish Anarchists' © the estate of Joseph Leftwich; 'In the month of Tammuz' © Gabriel Levin, taken from *Ostraca* (1999) by Gabriel Levin published by Anvil Press Poetry; 'Standing still, still standing' © Jane Liddell-King and Sylvia Paskin; 'Genocide is a cheese sandwich' © Sonja Linden; 'Chaim Superman encounters a Jewish intellectual' © the estate of Barnet Litvinoff; 'A Jew in England' © Emanuel Litvinoff; 'The Legend of the Wandering Jew' © Hyam Maccoby; 'A handful of earth' by Wolf Mankowitz, reprinted from *The Blue Arabian Nights* (1973), by kind permission of Vallentine Mitchell & Co Ltd; 'Father, Jew, Poet' © Shimon Markish; 'A mirror on a stone' © the estate of Peretz Markish and the estate of Jacob Sonntag; 'Home, imagination and malice' © Ronit Matalon; 'Homage to Salonika, the capital of vanished worlds' © Mark Mazower; 'I am the rain', 'Afternoon', 'Evening' © estate of Selma Meerbaum-Eisinger and the estate of Jacob Sonntag; 'The non-Jewish Jewish female cartoonist and Other Confusions' © Corinne Pearlman; 'Voices in the tunnel' © Harold Pinter; 'The Curiousness of Anglo-Jews' © Frederic Raphael; 'Back from the Draft Board', translation © A.A. Roback; 'Trying to be Jewish' © Michael Rosen; 'The Blood of the Lamb' © Bernice Rubens; 'Edmond Jabès: a translator's tribute' © Anthony Rudolf; 'Chorus of the dead', Chorus of the orphans,' © Nelly Sachs, translation © the estate of Jacob Sonntag, 'Chorus of those who were saved' © Nelly Sachs, translation © Albert H. Friedlander; 'In the Warsaw Ghetto: Summer 1941' © Rafael F. Scharf; 'The People's Memorial to Yitzhak Rabin – Kikar Malchai Yisrael, Tel Aviv, 1996' © anna sherbany; 'The El-Al Prawn' © Clive Sinclair; 'A conversation with Adrienne Rich' © Rachel Spence; 'For Else Lasker Schüler', 'On my 80th Birthday' © the estate of A.N. Stencl and the estate of Jacob Sonntag; 'Fifty Jews and a dead cat' © Yuri Suhl, 'Janusz Korczak', translation © the estate of Yuri Suhl; 'The White Jews of Cochin' © Ron Taylor; 'The Golem of Golders Green', 'Anybody who knows anything about washing socks in Jerusalem' © Jonathan Treitel; *Kapparah, or the last chorale* © Anthony Rudolf and Claude Vigée; 'Time parts memory', 'The man who would never write like Balzac' © Arnold Wesker; 'Because of that War' © James E. Young.